ROYAL HISTORICAL SOCIETY
STUDIES IN HISTORY 71

VALOIS GUYENNE

VALOIS GUYENNE

A STUDY OF
POLITICS, GOVERNMENT AND
SOCIETY IN
LATE MEDIEVAL FRANCE

Robin Harris

THE ROYAL HISTORICAL SOCIETY
THE BOYDELL PRESS

First published 1994

A Royal Historical Society publication
Published by The Boydell Press
an imprint of Boydell & Brewer Ltd
PO Box 9   Woodbridge   Suffolk IP12 3DF   UK
and of Boydell & Brewer Inc.
PO Box 41026   Rochester   NY 14604–4126   USA

ISBN   0 86193 226 9

ISSN 0269–2244

British Library Cataloguing-in-Publication Data
Harris, Robin
   Valois Guyenne:Study of Politics,
   Government and Society in Late Medieval
   France. – (Royal Historical Society Studies
   in History, ISSN 0269–2244;No.71)
   I. Title II. Series
   944.025
   ISBN 0–86193–226–9

   Library of Congress Cataloging-in-Publication Data
Harris, Robin, 1952–
   Valois Guyenne : a study of politics, government, and society in
late medieval France / Robin Harris.
      p.   cm. – (Royal Historical Society studies in history ; 71)
   Includes bibliographical references and index.
   ISBN 0–86193–226–9
   1. Guyenne (France) – Politics and government. 2. France
– History – House of Valois, 1328–1589. I. Title. II. Series: Royal
Historical Society studies in history ; no. 71.
DC611.G26H37   1994
944'.7026–dc20   94–16556

The paper used in this publication meets the minimum requirements
of American National Standard for Information Sciences –
Permanence of Paper for Printed Library Materials, ANSI Z39.48–1984

Printed in Great Britain by
St Edmundsbury Press Ltd, Bury St Edmunds, Suffolk

Contents

The Society records its gratitude to the following whose generosity made possible the initiation of this series: The British Academy; The Pilgrim Trust; The Twenty-Seven Foundation; The United States Embassy's Bicentennial funds; The Wolfson Trust; several private donors.

Abbreviations

Manuscript sources

AC   Archives Communales
AD   Archives Départmentales
AM   Archives Municipales
AN   Archives Nationales (Paris)
APA   Archives Départementales des Pyrénées-Atlantiques
BL   British Library (London)
BN   Bibliothèque Nationale (Paris)

Printed sources

Where possible, references to periodicals are noted as in the *Bibliographie annuelle de l'histoire de France*.

Short titles

The following short titles have been used throughout:

Basin – Basin, T., *Histoire de Charles VII*, ed. C. Samaran [Classiques de l'Histoire de France au Moyen âge, xv, xxi], 2 vols. (Paris, 1933, 1944).

Beaucourt – Beaucourt, G. du Fresne de, *Histoire de Charles VII*, 6 vols. (Paris, 1881–1891.)

Commynes, *Mémoires*, ed. Calmette Commynes, P. de *Mémoires*, ed. J. Calmette [Classiques de l'Histoire de France au Moyen âge, iii, iv], 2 vols. (Paris, 1925.)

Comptes consulaires Montréal – *Comptes consulaires de Montréal en Condomois (1458–1498)* ed. C. Samaran and G. Loubès [Collection de Documents inédits sur l'histoire de la France, Section de philologie et d'histoire jusqu'à 1610, xiii] (Paris, 1979.)

Comptes consulaires Riscle – *Comptes consulaires de la ville de Riscle, 1441–1507*, ed. P. Parfouru and J. de Carsalade du Pont [Arch. hist. Gascogne, xii–xiii], 2 vols. (Paris and Auch, 1886, 1892.)

Dupont-Ferrier, *Gallia Regia* – Dupont-Ferrier, G., *Gallia regia, ou état des officers royaux des bailliages et des sénéchaussées de 1328 à 1515*, 7 vols. (Paris, 1942, 1965.)

Escouchy – *Chronique de Mathieu d'Escouchy*, ed. G. du Fresne de Beaucourt [Soc. de l'Histoire de France], i (Paris, 1863.)

Histoire de Bordeaux, iii – Renouard, Y., *Bordeaux sous les rois d'Angleterre* [*Histoire de Bordeaux*, iii] (Bordeaux, 1965.)

Histoire de Bordeaux, iv – Boutruche, R., *Bordeaux de 1453 à 1715* [*Histoire de Bordeaux*, iv] (Bordeaux, 1966.)

Histoire de Charles VII, ed. Godefroy – *Histoire de Charles VII, roy de France*, ed. D. Godefroy (Paris, 1661.)

Histoire de Charles VIII, ed. Godefroy – *Histoire de Charles VIII, roy dFrance*, ed. D. Godefroy (Paris, 1684.)

Jurades de Bergerac, ed. Charrier – *Les Jurades de la ville de Bergerac*, ed. G. Charrier, 2 vols. (Bergerac, 1892.)

Keen, *England* – Keen, M. H., *England in the Later Middle Ages* (London, 1973.)

Leseur, *Histoire de Gaston IV* – Leseur, G., *Histoire de Gaston IV, comte de Foix*, ed. H. Courteault [Soc. de l'Histoire de France], 2 vols. (Paris, 1893, 1907.)

Lettres de Louis XI, ed. Vaesen – *Lettres de Louis XI, roi de France*, ed. J. Vaesen [Soc. de l'Histoire de France], 10 vols. (Paris, 1883–1908.)

Lettres de Charles VIII, ed. Pélicier – *Lettres de Charles VIII, roi de France*, ed. P. Pélicier [Soc. de l'Histoire de France], 5 vols. (Paris, 1898–1905.)

Livre des bouillons, ed. Barckhausen – *Livre des bouillons*, ed. H. Barckhausen [Arch. municipales Bordeaux, i] (Bordeaux, 1867.)

Livre des coutumes, ed. Barckhausen – *Livre des coutumes*, ed. H. Barckhausen [Arch. municipales Bordeaux, v] (Bordeaux, 1890.)

Livre des privilèges, ed. Barckhausen – *Livre des privilèges*, ed. H. Barckhausen [Arch. municipales Bordeaux, ii] (Bordeaux, 1878.)

Ordonnances – *Ordonnances des rois de France de la troisième race*, ed. Bréquigny et al., xiv–xxi (Paris, 1790–1849.)

Recueil des privilèges, ed. Gouron – *Recueil des privilèges accordés à laille de Bordeaux par Charles VII et Louis XI*, ed. M. Gouron (Bordeaux, 1937.)

Registres de la Jurade – Inventaire sommaire des registres de la jurade (1520–1783) ed. D. le Vacher de Boisville et al. [Arch. municipales Bordeaux, vi–xiii], 8 vols. (Bordeaux, 1896 – 1947)

Registres gascons, ed. Ducéré – *Registres gascons*, ed. E Ducéré [Arch. municipales Bayonne], i (Bayonne, 1892.)

Vale, *English Gascony* – Vale, M.G.A., *English Gascony, 1399–1453* (London, 1970.)

Preface

This book *might* have been a continuation of Dr Malcom Vale's study of English Gascony.[1] Unfortunately, however, after the reduction of Guyenne the sources which permitted Dr Vale to examine the English administration of Gascony in the period until 1453 either become insignificant or cease. The scanty records of the French administration in the South-West are all too incomplete; though Dr John Powis has traced the early history of the Bordeaux *parlement* and its personnel.[2]

As regards society in Guyenne, the evidence that remains is often unbalanced. This is particularly true of the towns: for instance, while Bayonne, Agen, Périgueux and even such towns as Riscle or Montréal du Gers are relatively fully documented, the archives of Bordeaux (including the *registres* of the jurade) have almost entirely perished.

By contrast, a good deal of useful material exists on the great noble families: the *fonds* d'Albret, de Foix and d'Armagnac shed valuable light upon the families without whom the government or defence of Guyenne was impossible. Old, though excellent, studies have drawn upon them.[3]

Professor Robert Boutruche investigated the economic and social reconstruction during the years after the ending of hostilities.[4] As a result of other recent work, comparisons are possible with the course of economic recovery in other areas devastated by war.[5] The work of Dr Christopher Allmand on Normandy in the *après guerre* period allows some wider, tentative comparisons to be made between the way in which Guyenne and Normandy were integrated into Valois France.[6]

The principal challenge posed by the disparate sources is to paint a picture of Valois Guyenne whose broad lines are at once comprehensible but are also sufficiently nuanced to reflect change over the forty years between the duchy's reduction and Charles VII's first expedition to Italy. The first section of this

1 M.G.A. Vale, *English Gascony, 1399–1453* (London, 1970).
2 J.K. Powis, *The Magistrates of the Parlement of Bordeaux c.1500–1563* [Unpublished, Oxford D. Phil. Thesis, 1975 Bodleian shelf-mark: MS.D.Phil. c.1699.]
3 A. Luchaire, *Alain le Grand, Sire d'Albret* (Paris, 1877); H. Courteault, *Gaston IV, comte de Foix, vicomte souverain de Béarn, prince de Navarre, 1423–1472* (Toulouse, 1895); C. Samaran, *La Maison d'Armagnac au xve siècle* (Paris, 1907).
4 R. Boutruche, *Bordeaux de 1453 à 1715* [Histoire de Bordeaux, iv] (Bordeaux, 1966).
5 J. Lartigaut, *Les Campagnes du Quercy après la guerre de cent ans* [Publ. Univ. Toulouse Le-Mirail, série A, xxxix] (Toulouse, 1978); see also the various contributions to *La Reconstruction après la guerre de cent ans* [Actes du 104e congrès national des sociétés savantes, Section de philologie et d'histoire jusqu'à 1610, Bordeaux, 1979], i (Paris, 1981).
6 C.T. Allmand, 'The Aftermath of War in Fifteenth-Century France', *History*, lxi (1976), 344–57; 'Local reaction to the French Reconquest of Normandy: The Case of Rouen', *The Crown and Local Communities in England and France in the Fifteenth Century* (Gloucester, 1981), ed. J.R.L. Highfield and R. Jeffs, pp. 146–57.

book, therefore, adopts a fairly strictly chronological approach, providing a framework of political events. The rest of the book is, by contrast, deliberately analytical, seeking to describe the relations between the components of political society in the province.

I am grateful to Mr P.S. Lewis and to Dr Allmand for much guidance and wise advice. M. l'Abbé G. Loubès kindly allowed me to consult his transcription of the *comptes consulaires* of Montréal, which have since been published. I am also grateful to the staff of the Archives Nationales and Bibliothèque Nationale in Paris and of the Archives Départmentales of the Gironde, Landes, Pyrénées-Atlantiques, Dordogne, Lot-et-Garonne, Gers, Haute-Garonne and Tarn-et-Garonne.

PART ONE

INTRODUCTION

1

The Military Conquest

The fall of English Gascony to the French might have been expected some years earlier than 1451. The defence of the duchy had been bedevilled by a number of what proved insuperable problems. The first of these was the overall strategy of the Lancastrian Government.[1] Before his death, Henry V had firmly committed the English to making a reality of the Lancastrian dual monarchy. The claim to the French throne quickly became inextricably linked with the prestige and, ultimately, the survival of the English Government. The prospects for the success of the strategy of the dual monarchy were always poor. With the defection of Burgundy from the English side after the treaty of Arras in 1435 they were all but extinguished. This was not, however, immediately apparent. English armies were still capable of victories in battle. But the magnitude of the task which the Lancastrian government had set itself was beyond its resources, both military and financial. Political disunity within the Council's ranks, a disunity which was itself sharpened by military difficulties, weakened the war effort.

By contrast, by the 1440s the Valois monarchy was in a far better position to bring the war to a successful conclusion. The stature of Charles VII had steadily increased. The last major noble revolt of the reign, the 'Praguerie', had been suppressed.[2] A professional standing army had been created.[3]

The future of English Gascony was bound to be affected by the disproportion both between Lancastrian ambitions and resources and between Lancastrian and Valois power. But there were two further considerations of special relevance to the duchy's prospects. First, the best hope of securing Guyenne was bound to be an agreement, on the lines of the treaty of Brétigny, by which the English king would hold it in full sovereignty. Yet, whatever the French might have been willing to concede on this point, the English government was never prepared during the period of its greatest military strength to settle for such an objective. The symbolism of the French crown had grown too important.[4]

Second, when there was a choice between making the requisite sacrifices and effort to secure Guyenne or Normandy, it was generally to the North rather than the South-West that armies from England were sent. In 1440, the earl of

---

[1] For what follows, see M. H. Keen, *England in the Later Middle Ages* (London, 1973), pp. 380–401.
[2] M. G. A. Vale, *Charles VII* (London, 1974), p. 80.
[3] P. Contamine, *Guerre, état et société à la fin du Moyen âge* (Paris and the Hague, 1972), pp. 277–78.
[4] The feudal relationship between the Kings of England, as dukes of Guyenne, and the Kings of France had been ratified by the treaty of Paris in 1259: M. Powicke, *The Thirteenth Century* (Oxford, 1953), p. 84; Keen, *England*, p. 397.

Huntingdon was provided with a substantial expeditionary force for Guyenne. It achieved some early success. But, for domestic political reasons, it was recalled before the end of the year. Further modest reinforcements were sent to the duchy in 1442 and 1443. It was intended that the duke of Somerset would in that year conduct campaigns in order to recover areas of Guyenne which were outside the English allegiance. But, at the last minute, the army assembled for this purpose was diverted to Normandy, where it spent the summer in largely fruitless activity. After the truces negotiated at Tours were denounced by the French in the summer of 1449, no English expedition was sent to Guyenne. When, in October 1452, such a force was sent under the earl of Shrewsbury, its prospects for recovering a large part of the duchy were poor.[5]

Underlying the precedence given to Normandy over Guyenne during these years was the fact that stronger interests were involved in the defence of the former. Normandy had been the site of an extensive and well planned English settlement. By contrast, although confiscated seigneuries in Guyenne had been granted to influential Englishmen, there was no such settlement in the South-West.[6] There it was left to local interests – the English officers, the Gascon nobility and, increasingly, the towns – to resist the French. Moreover, the willingness of the Gascon nobility to defend the duchy diminished as their loyalty to the English crown was eroded. The financial exhaustion of the English régime reduced its ability to reward those who remained in its allegiance. As a result of Charles VII's expedition to Guyenne in 1442, a number of important families from Périgord and the Landes decided that their interests would be better served by transferring allegiance to the Valois.[7] It was, therefore, with the knowledge of a firm base of support from much of the Gascon nobility that Charles VII could embark on the campaign which led to the duchy's reduction.

In 1438 a French army under the command of Charles II d'Albret, though unable to break into Bordeaux itself, had sacked the *bourg* of Saint-Seurin. The soldiers of Rodrigo de Villandrando pillaged Médoc, driving the peasants to take refuge in Bordeaux. The effect was economically disastrous. Exports of wine from Bordeaux that year fell below 4,000 tons.[8]

The French campaign of 1442, already mentioned, was more serious. Its immediate purpose was to relieve Tartas, held against the English by Charles II d'Albret. Much was at stake. Had the French failed to arrive before the town yielded, the cadet line of the Albrets would have sworn allegiance to the English, taking their lands with them. The loyalty of the Armagnacs was also at issue. Negotiations were under way for the marriage of Henry VI and a daughter of the comte d'Armagnac. The comte had to be shown that the French king could not be trifled with. Not only was Tartas relieved, but French forces also took Saint-Sever and Dax. Bordeaux was once more besieged. The city's

---

5 Vale, *English Gascony*, pp. 98, 108–15, 122–30.
6 C. T. Allmand, 'The Lancastrian land settlement in Normandy 1417–1450', *Econ. Hist Review*, 2nd series, xxi (1968), 461–79.
7 Vale, *English Gascony*, pp. 206–15.
8 *Histoire de Bordeaux*, iii, pp. 506–507; M. K. James, *Studies in the Medieval Wine trade*, ed. E. M. Veale (Oxford, 1971), p. 41.

inhabitants strengthened their defences and harassed the French. Fortunately for the English, an especially harsh winter compelled the French to withdraw to Montauban,[9] and the truces negotiated at Tours in 1444 restored peace to the duchy. But the weakness of its defence had been demonstrated both to the Gascons and to the French. The years of truce which followed did see a return of prosperity to Guyenne. Above all, there was a revival of the wine trade from Bordeaux to England. But, in practice, little was done to use this breathing space to secure the duchy.[10]

The immediate cause of the end of the truces was the taking of the castle of Fougères on the Breton border by the mercenary captain, François de Suriennes, at the instigation of the English. It was in Normandy that the most immediately dramatic consequences ensued. The English there had insufficient troops both to form an army and to garrison the Norman towns; consequently, the French campaign was swiftly successful against an enemy at once ill-prepared and over-stretched.

By October 1449 Charles VII and the comte de Dunois were before Rouen. The following April an English army sent to relieve the duke of Somerset was defeated at Formigny. By August nothing was left of English Normandy.[11]

Although the main French move against Guyenne had to wait until the fall of Normandy released sufficient resources, 1449 did see the beginning of the campaigns which were to lead to the reduction of the duchy. In February of that year the comte de Foix had been appointed Charles VII's lieutenant general in Guyenne. That summer he moved his armies out of Béarn and began campaigning in Labourt, taking Mauléon and Guiche. In May 1450, Foix's Labourt campaign reached a triumphant conclusion with his entry into Orthez, where he stayed during the rest of summer.[12]

Normandy having now fallen, it was decided at a royal council held at Tours in September 1450 to proceed with Guyenne's reduction. In what remained of the campaigning season, the comte de Penthièvre was despatched into the marches of Agenais and Périgord. After heavy artillery bombardment, Bergerac fell to the French. The French army then split into two. One army remained with the comte de Penthièvre. The other, under the command of the seigneur d'Orval, approached and took Bazas without resistance. However, Orval's army was then trapped and attacked by a hastily raised force from Bordeaux and Blanquefort. The result was a bloody defeat for the Bordelais. For the Gascons, it was a gloomy indication of the likely outcome of the following year's campaigning: for the French, however, the news apparently increased the king's confidence and determination.[13]

The French armies of 1451 were placed under the overall command of the comte de Dunois. In May he laid siege to the powerful stronghold of Blaye. After a full assault, the English and Gascon forces, which had retreated to the

9 *Histoire de Bordeaux*, iii, 508–10; Samaran, *Maison d'Armagnac*, pp. 78–87; M. G. A. Vale, *Charles VII* (London, 1974), p. 86.
10 Vale, *English Gascony*, pp. 130–31.
11 Keen, *England*, pp. 402–4.
12 Leseur, *Histoire de Gaston IV*, i, 47–66, 96–104, 107 n. 1.
13 *Histoire de Charles VII*, ed. Godefroy, pp. 215–21; Escouchy, i, 322–23.

castle, yielded on generous terms. Bourg, Fronsac, Libourne, Saint-Emilion and other towns now fell in quick succession. The comte d'Armagnac took Duras, Sauveterre and Saint-Macaire and besieged Rions. French forces were also successful in the Landes. In May, Dax was besieged by two armies, one under the Albrets and the other under the comte de Foix.[14]

The fate of the duchy now essentially hinged on the resistance of Bordeaux. While Dunois advanced on the city, Jacques de Chabannes entered Entre-Deux-Mers. Bordeaux quickly concluded that there was no point in continuing the struggle and, using the captal de Buch as its emissary, the city sued for peace. Once agreement had been reached on the terms for Bordeaux's reduction, resistance effectively ended in the surrounding *pays*. Only Bayonne continued to hold out. When Dunois was satisfied that Bordeaux was secure, he marched South to lay siege to Bayonne. After just three days, the bishop of Bayonne and other dignitaries were sent to treat with the French commanders and on 21 August agreement was finally reached on terms for the town's reduction.[15] English Gascony had fallen after only four months of campaigning.

The return of the English to the Bordelais in October 1452 can, in retrospect, be seen to have had less significance than appeared the case to contemporaries. By now, the chances of resisting the overwhelming superiority of the French and restoring the duchy to English control were slim indeed. John Talbot, earl of Shrewsbury, and a force of some 5,000 were able, with the help of a conspiracy within Bordeaux, to bring the city and surrounding areas back under English control. Libourne, Castillon and other towns opened their gates to the English. Talbot had, for the moment, the advantage of surprise, since the French government had been expecting the attack to come in Normandy.[16]

Only limited action was possible by the French in 1452 to restore the position: but Charles VII at least hastened to send soldiers to the South-West under the marshal de Jalognes and the seigneur d'Orval to contain Talbot. The French government spent the winter raising men, money and provisions for the forthcoming campaign and in the spring of 1453 four French armies were sent to Guyenne. As the armies of the comtes de Foix and Clermont advanced into Bazadais, the Bordelais and Médoc, Talbot fell back before them to Bordeaux. The third French army, operating on the Dordogne, took Gensac and besieged Castillon.[17] It was at Castillon on 17 July that Talbot's army was crushingly defeated. Talbot himself was killed, the remnants of the English army fleeing in disorder.[18] Castillon itself quickly capitulated and Saint-Emilion and Libourne opened their gates to the French. The comtes de Clermont and Foix besieged and took Castlenau-de-Médoc; Saint-Macaire, Langon and other towns swiftly fell. When the castle at Cadillac was forced to yield, its Gascon captain was executed – a timely warning for others tempted to prolong resistance. With the

---

[14] Beaucourt, v, 46–7.

[15] Escouchy, i, 335–39, 361–67.

[16] M. Vale, 'The Last years of English Gascony', *Trans. Roy. Hist. Soc. 5th Series*, xix (1969), 125, 129.

[17] Beaucourt, v, 267–71.

[18] For the battle itself, see A. H. Burne, 'La Bataille de Castillon, 1453: la fin de la guerre de cent ans'; *R. Hist. Bordeaux, nouvelle série*, ii (1953), 293–305.

capitulation of Blanquefort and the flight to Bordeaux of its captain, the seigneur de Duras, the French forces were able to concentrate on the reduction of Bordeaux. The city was now, amid plague and famine, blockaded from land and sea. The siege lasted three months until, on 20 October, Bordeaux finally yielded. Only Rions and Bénauges continued to hold out for some time until they were in due course starved into submission. The second and final French conquest of Guyenne was thus complete.[19]

The terms of the second treaty for the reduction of Bordeaux were considerably harsher than those of the first imposed by the French in 1451, in spite of attempts by the townsmen to ameliorate them by bribing the French commanders.[20] In 1451 the privileges and property of nobles, churchmen and burgesses had been guaranteed by the king. A *parlement* was to be created. The conduct and pay of soldiers was to be firmly regulated. The customs of the Bordelais, Agenais and Bazadais were confirmed.[21] Other compositions with the towns of Guyenne similarly ratified property and privileges.[22]

In 1453 the king was less lenient, though there was still no intention of causing a great upheaval of tenure in the province. The cost of the campaign of 1453 had been considerable, probably over 30,000 francs[23] and the French government was apparently determined to make Bordeaux reimburse this expense. 100,000 écus, later reduced to 30,000 écus, was demanded as a fine from the burgesses. New rates of customs were imposed upon wine and other goods exported from Bordeaux. In place of a *parlement, grands jours* would be sent from Paris each year or once every two years to administer justice.[24]

Subject to heavy garrisoning and the suspicion of treachery, the wine trade in sharp decline, facing uncertainties of tenure throughout the duchy, the prospects for what had been English Gascony incorporated in Valois France must have seemed bleak indeed.

[19] Beaucourt, v, pp. 276–285.
[20] This led to a case before the Paris *parlement*. See AN X^{1A} 86, fos 310r–312v.
[21] *Ordonnances*, xiv, 139–145.
[22] *Ibid.*, pp. 149–151, 155–156, 158–161, 166–167, 176–177, 180–182. Bayonne had been forced to pay a fine of 10,000 écus d'or for its continued resistance after the fall of Bordeaux: but half of this was remitted the following year, before Talbot's arrival at Bordeaux in October; AM Bayonne, AA 7, no. 4.
[23] Vale, 'Last Years', p. 135.
[24] See p. 86.

2

French Guyenne

Guyenne was essentially a political rather than a cultural, geographical or even – for the most part – an administrative unity. The duchy of Gascony had been annexed between 1044 and 1063 by the counts of Poitou: by contrast, 'Guyenne' consisted of the counts' older domain. The *livre des coutumes* of Bordeaux noted the huge expanse of what could be claimed as Guyenne, stretching beyond the geographical limits adopted for this study into Angoumois, Quercy and Limousin. Castillon and Blaye were regarded as points on the border between Guyenne and Gascony, the latter extending South to the foothills of the Pyrenees.[1] However, though not interchangeable, the terms Guyenne and Gascony were by the mid-fifteenth century used more loosely. 'Guyenne' increasingly signified the whole of the South-West, referring at different times to a number of *pays* and sénéchaussées, while 'Gascogne' had a more localised geographical sense.[2]

A number of political circumstances gave the *pays* and sénéchaussées examined here a degree of common identity.[3] They were included within the governorship of Guyenne and, during the relevant periods, within jurisdictions of the royal and ducal *grand jours* and *parlement* of Bordeaux.[4] But the most important aspect of the common experience of the *pays* of Guyenne was of the warfare leading to the duchy's reduction in 1451.

Suspicion of the 'English' sympathies of the province and fear of an English return explain many of the policies followed by the Valois government in the years which followed. Guyenne remained a 'frontier' province.[5] It was exposed, not only to the English but also to the vicissitudes of the uneasy and often hostile relations between France, Aragon and Castille: the dynastic interests of all three of the greatest noble families in the South-West – the Foix, Albrets and Armagnacs – were involved in Spanish politics. Finally, the challenges posed to royal control by the ambitions of the French princes which led to open revolt during the *guerre du bien public*, the *guerre folle* and the war of the league of 1486 had an important impact on government in the province.

---

[1] P. Chaplais, 'Le Traité de Paris de 1259 et l'inféodation de la Gascogne allodiale', *Essays in Medieval Diplomacy and Administration* (London, 1981), p. 122.

[2] The sénéchaussée of Agenais was, for example, sometimes referred to as that of 'Agenais et Gascogne' e.g. BN, PO 948, 'de Crussol', no. 11; Dax is in 'Gascogne', PO 2252, 'Pettillot', no. 5; Libourne is 'en nostre pays de gascoigne', AC Libourne, AA 4, no. 4, fo 5v.

[3] This study focuses on the sénéchaussées of Guyenne, Bazadais, Landes, Agenais, Armagnac and Périgord. But inevitably, on occasion, it has to go wider; for example, when examining the affairs of the comté of Périgord it is necessary also to allude to those of the vicomté of Limousin, the seigneur of both being Alain d'Albret.

[4] See below pp. 85–88.

[5] See below pp. 109–32.

England, Spain and France

In England the impact of the loss of Gascony and Normandy was dramatic. Not only was the nation shocked by what was seen as a blow to England's honour; the Channel was also less safe for English shipping and those soldiers who had lost their stake in Normandy thirsted for revenge. The loss of English lands in France was an important factor in the humiliation and fall of the Lancastrian monarchy. The culpable loss of Normandy and Guyenne remained a constant theme in Yorkist propaganda. The duke of York's manifestos were still labouring the point in 1460.[6]

The loss of English Gascony was, therefore, something which neither English public opinion nor the English kings could accept. Moreover, exiles from Gascony continued to exercise influence at the English court. Pey du Tasta, dean of Saint-Seurin at Bordeaux, was a member of Henry VI's and then Edward IV's council until his death in 1467. Gascon exiles, in some cases at least, remained in favour with the king of England, receiving exemptions from customs dues, grants of money and other advantages. The urge of Gascon nobles to return with an army of invasion was probably increased by grants of lands. Gaillard de Durfort, for example, was, granted the seigneurie of Lesparre in 1472.[7] The interests and ambitions which could be satisfied by a successful military venture in South-West France remained strong long after the last English army left Gascon soil.

The political turmoil which descended upon England in the years following the loss of English Gascony precluded any immediate attempt to recover the province. Indeed, until the death of Charles VII Anglo-French diplomatic relations were free of crises which might have called for special mobilisation of Valois military resources in Guyenne. However, just a few months before Louis XI's accession, the Yorkists won the battle of Towton and Edward IV seized the English throne. Whereas Charles VII had supported the Lancastrians, the dauphin Louis had inclined to York. On becoming king, Louis XI at first temporised; but in June 1462 he signed a treaty with Margaret of Anjou and so declared himself Edwards IV's enemy. Edward responded by preparing a fleet which proceeded to descend on Brittany and then raid Poitou before returning to England.[8] Louis XI, however, seems to have expected a descent on Guyenne. Artillery was accordingly sent to the South-West, and the *ban et arrière-ban* was raised, while Blaye, Bordeaux, Dax and Bayonne were singled out for provisioning. The sire d'Albret was instructed to raise men from his own and the king's domain and the comte de Foix was ordered to persuade the king of Aragon of the advantages of loyalty to the French cause.[9] In fact, as has been noted,

6   Keen, *England*, pp. 454–55, 445–46.
7   A. Peyrègne, 'Les Emigrés gascons en Angleterre (1453–1485)', A. *Midi*, nouvelle série, lxvi (1954), 116–18.
8   J. Calmette and G. Périnelle, *Louis XI et l'Angleterre* (Paris, 1930), pp. 1–3, 11, 20–21, 26–27.
9   *Lettres de Louis XI*, ed. Vaesen, ii, no. xxvi, 37–39, nos xlvii, xlviii, 75–78; BN, ms. fr. 20, 490, fo 32r.

Louis's worst fears were not realised. In September 1463 at Saint-Omer truces were agreed and the kings of France and England undertook not to harbour each other's enemies.[10]

Before resuming the account of Anglo-French relations and their impact on Guyenne, however, it is necessary to turn aside to examine the evolution of French relations with Spain. For the purposes of this study, Franco-Spanish developments had a dual significance. First, the king of Aragon quickly became the centre of a powerful anti-French coalition of interests. Second, the proximity to Guyenne of the ensuing wars and the involvement of great noble families in their conduct and outcome had a continuing impact on the French monarchy's relationship with its subjects in South-West France.

Spanish politics offered a range of tempting opportunities for French interference: though, as the century progressed, the limits on French ability to determine events South of the border became increasingly evident. As with England, so with Spain, Louis XI quickly reversed the policies which he had pursued when dauphin. Like his predecessor, the new French king chose to support John II of Aragon in his struggle to assert control over the 'rebels' of Catalonia. John II had made his daughter and son-in-law – Gaston IV comte de Foix – his heirs. So there were domestic as well as external reasons for Louis to support John's and his son-in-law's claims.[11]

It was not, however, the course of the struggle in Catalonia itself but rather events which flowed from it which most affected the balance of international politics. For the kings of France and Aragon not only concluded a treaty of mutual assistance against England and Castille: they went on, by agreements reached at Sauveterre and Bayonne, to make a transaction about the counties of Roussillon and Cerdagne. As security against payment by John II for French military assistance against the Catalans, control over the revenues of Roussillon and Cerdagne was ceded to France.[12] Not satisfied with these terms, however, Louis XI proceeded to annex the counties and, indeed, began to support the house of Anjou in its bid for the Catalan Crown, which the Catalan leaders had offered to duke René.

In the counties themselves, resentment against French rule continued to fester. John II was thus able, with widespread support, to re-take them by force in 1473. However, in 1474–5 while he was engaged in securing the succession to Castille for Isabella, after the death of Henry IV, French armies managed once more to subdue Roussillon and Cerdagne. The counties remained French until ceded by Charles VIII by the treaty of Barcelona to clear the way for French intervention in Italy.[13]

What was of more importance, however, than the course of events in the two counties was the effect of the dispute on John II. The king of Aragon, outraged at Louis XI's perfidy, made on 20 October 1468 an alliance with England and, in the following year, another with Burgundy. He managed, against Louis

[10] Calmette and Périnelle, *Louis XI*, pp. 42–49.

[11] J. Calmette, *Louis XI, Jean II et la Révolution catalane* (Toulouse, 1903), pp. 42–57.

[12] *Ibid.*, pp. 70–71, 79–87.

[13] *Ibid.*, 166–69, 271–72, 290–91, 296–97; J. Calmette, *La Question des Pyrénées et la marche d'Espagne au moyen âge* (n.p., 1947), pp. 197–201, 216–20.

attempts to have the French king's brother, Charles of France, accepted as Isabella of Castille's future husband, to secure her betrothal to his own heir, Ferdinand of Aragon: the marriage took place on 17 October 1469. The consequences for the balance between France and Spain would, of course, be momentous.

It is against this background of diplomacy and war, the temporary advance and ultimate reversal of French policy, that one must return to French relations with England. Five years elapsed before tension between the two rose again to the level reached in 1462. English foreign policy in 1467 and 1468 was dominated by the deteriorating relations between Edward IV and the earl of Warwick, the latter favouring an alliance with France. The summer of 1467 saw the development of closer English contact with Burgundy and Brittany and the failure of an important French embassy, under the archbishop of Narbonne, to extract any concessions from the English king. In May 1468, with alliances with Burgundy and Brittany concluded, Edward's chancellor informed the English Commons that the king intended to invade France.[14]

As relations with England deteriorated and the threat of invasion grew in the autumn of 1467, the garrisons of Guyenne were reinforced. In September and October the Château du Hâ at Bordeaux received another forty soldiers. Forty also went to the Château Trompette. Twenty soldiers were sent to reinforce Dax. The captain of La Rochelle was instructed to assemble a fleet and a further fleet was prepared by the comte de Foix. Panic was evidently in the air. A letter of May 1468 records the rumour that English ships had landed at Bordeaux and that those aboard them claimed that they were the spearhead of an invasion force.[15] The French government seems to have kept Guyenne in a state of preparedness for about a year.

Whether Edward IV was serious in his stated intention of invading France is doubtful. He probably wished primarily to assist his Burgundian and Breton allies, rather than launch an invasion as he was to do in 1475.[16] The period of Edward's deposition and the brief Lancastrian restoration in the autumn of 1470 had little impact upon security problems in Guyenne. For between April 1469 and May 1472 the duchy of Guyenne was the apanage of Louis XI's brother, Charles of France.[17]

Charles of France's dissatisfaction with the duchy of Berry as his relatively modest apanage had in 1464–5 been exploited to good effect by the participants of the league of the *bien public*. With considerable reluctance, Louis XI had been forced to agree to grant him the duchy of Normandy. But disagreement between Charles and his ally and patron, the duke of Brittany, allowed the French king the excuse he wanted to send his forces to take Normandy back into royal control. Charles of France's fortunes were only restored as a result of the treaty of Péronne, forced on the king by Burgundy. Louis granted his brother Champagne and Brie in place of Normandy: but, doubtless in order to keep him well away from his former Breton and Burgundian allies, he

14 C. Ross, *Edward IV* (London, 1974), pp. 109–12.
15 BN, ms. fr. 20, 496, fo 74r; Calmette and Périnelle, *Louis XI*, pp. 96 n. 6, 101 n. 2, 106 n. 6.
16 Ross, *Edward IV*, p. 114.
17 H. Stein, *Charles de France, Frère de Louis XI* (Paris, 1919), pp. 263, 455.

subsequently induced Charles to accept Guyenne as his apanage instead.[18] The royal letters granting Guyenne were only registered on the king's orders on 10 July 1469; but Charles was acting as duke since May or June. Charles of France enjoyed control over an extended Guyenne until his death on 24 May 1472, by which time the king was already preparing an army to take back the province.[19]

Charles of France's death was singularly opportune for his brother. For in 1471 Edward IV had overcome his Lancastrian opponents in England at the decisive battles of Barnet and Tewkesbury; and from 1472 he was making plans for an invasion of France, negotiating with Brittany, Burgundy and Aragon.[20]

From the winter of 1474 English preparations for invasion were in earnest;[21] while in France equally vigorous measures were instituted. In December 1474 the governors of every province of France were ordered to review the bans et arrière-bans.[22] In Guyenne, where it was feared that the blow might fall, royal commissioners organised provisioning, and reinforcements were sent to the province's garrisons. In March 1475, in order to resist a possible English attack, the king ordered 300 lances of his ordonnances to be sent to Bayonne.[23] In August, Pierre Aubert, captain of the Château du Hâ at Bordeaux, had to appoint a deputy to go and receive the musters of 100 lances of reinforcements sent South to Guyenne under the comte de Comminges. As late as this he felt unable to go himself because of the English threat.[24] These measures of reinforcement applied to strongholds which were already well manned. Though there is no evidence to suggest that more than 100 of the 300 lances ordered to Guyenne ever actually arrived, it seems likely that there were at this time some 1000 soldiers in the province.[25]

By the end of June Louis XI was hurrying to Normandy, at last convinced that this was where the English would land.[26] Although the question of the duchy of Guyenne was a subject of negotiation between the French and English in August,[27] the treaty of Picquigny in effect suspended English territorial and dynastic claims in exchange for a substantial pension and a marriage for Edward's daughter with the dauphin of France. In January 1476 better relations were cemented by a commercial treaty.[28]

Anglo-French diplomatic relations were smooth enough for the next few years and it was only in the last year of Louis XI's reign that an English invasion of the South-West of France again appeared a possibility. In October 1482 Odet d'Aydie, comte de Comminges, ordered the publication of the renewal of the

18 Ibid., pp. 25, 52, 121, 137–40, 254–61.
19 Ibid., pp. 263–79, 443–44, 455.
20 Keen, England, pp. 475–76.
21 Ross, Edward IV, p. 218.
22 Calmette and Périnelle, Louis XI, pp. 165–66, 169.
23 BN, ms. Clairambault 236, no. 207.
24 BN, ms. Clairambault 137, no. 44.
25 See below, p. 128.
26 H. de Chabannes, Preuves pour servir à l'histoire de la maison de Chabannes, ii (Dijon, 1893), no. ccxv, 386–88.
27 Commynes, Mémoires, ed. Calmette, i, 46.
28 Ross, Edward IV, p. 233; Calmette and Périnelle, Louis XI, pp. 252–54.

Anglo-French truce at Bayonne.[29] But just two months later Edward IV responded to Louis XI's overturning of the terms of the Picquigny settlement and the ending of the pension payments agreed there with immediate preparations for war. Although Edward died in April, the threat of an English invasion continued.[30] In August 1484 the comte de Comminges ordered Antoine de Carbonnières to raise the *ban et arrière-ban* of Périgord in order to defend Guyenne.[31] The French government and the authorities in Guyenne remained convinced of the immediacy of the English threat. In November Comminges wrote to the king from Fronsac. He told him that an English fleet which had been cruising along the coast of Guyenne had left, but that another great fleet was rumoured to be on its way.[32]

There is, in fact, no reason to believe that the preparations for war made by Edward IV in his last days and the aggressive posture adopted by his successor were aimed at intervention in the South-West. Richard III was most preoccupied with the demands and threats of his Breton allies; and he was unable to intervene at the duke of Brittany's request against the French either, for he had more pressing problems at home.[33]

The death of Richard III at the battle of Bosworth and the subsequent accession to the throne of Henry VII, who had been helped in exile by the regency government of Charles VIII, introduced several years of good diplomatic relations between France and England. But by February 1489 England had once again been impelled by anxiety about French intentions in Brittany to enter an anti-French alliance.[34]

With the worsening of Anglo-French relations, rumours and anxieties about the possibility of an English attack on Guyenne began once more. In March 1489 Charles VIII wrote to Roger de Gramont, sénéchal of the Landes and captain of one of the castles at Bayonne. The king had been informed that an army of English, Spanish and other foreign soldiers had landed not far from Bayonne. The town must, therefore, be properly guarded and provisioned. Gramont was instructed to raise the *ban et arrière-ban* and put soldiers into garrison there. Corn was to be brought down by river from the hinterland of Bayonne.[35]

Tension between England and France was further heightened by the marriage of Charles VIII to Anne of Brittany on 6 December 1491, which realised Henry VII's worst fears. England's response came in October 1492 when English troops besieged Boulogne.[36] In the intervening period, however, when it was unclear where the attack would come, vigorous measures were taken to

---

[29] *Registres gascons*, ed. Ducéré, i, 133.
[30] Calmette and Périnelle, *Louis XI*, pp. 252–254; Ross, *Edward IV*, p. 415.
[31] *Jurades de Bergerac*, ed. Charrier, i, 333–35.
[32] *Registres gascons*, ed. Ducéré p. 327.
[33] S.B. Chrimes, *Henry VII* (London, 1972), pp. 19–20.
[34] *Ibid.*, pp. 33–34, 39–40, 47–49, 279, 280.
[35] *Registres gascons*, ed. Ducéré, pp. 314–315.
[36] Chrimes, *Henry VII*, pp. 281–82.

defend Guyenne from the long-expected English invasion. The towns were put on the alert. Reinforcements were sent to Bordeaux.[37]

In fact Henry VII had good reasons for not continuing with a war which had begun late in the season and peace was quickly concluded. The king of France had still more pressing reasons to want peace. In 1492 and 1493, Charles VIII signed three treaties which were to pave the way for his intervention in Italy. By the treaty of Etaples, the French agreed to pay the arrears of the pension, due to the English king as a result of agreement of Picquigny, and other sums – amounting to 750,000 écus d'or payable at the rate of 50,000 a year. By the treaty of Barcelona, Roussillon and Cerdagne were returned to Ferdinand of Aragon. By the treaty of Senlis, Artois and Franche-Comté were yielded to the archduke Philip and Maximilian. Charles VIII was now free to try to assert the Angevin claim to Naples which he had inherited.[38]

Politics, the Princes and Guyenne

It has already been noted that the fortunes of the comte de Foix were closely involved in Franco-Spanish relations. Louis XI's support for the house of Anjou in Catalonia did not prevent Gaston IV from pursuing his and his wife's rights in Navarre by force. Having remained loyal to Louis XI through both the *guerre du bien public* and the conflicts with Burgundy which led to the treaty of Péronne, the comte de Foix had, by 1469, fallen into disgrace. Against the king's orders, Gaston IV's daughter was married in that year to Jean V d'Armagnac. Gaston was also deprived of his governorship of Navarre by his father in law, John II. The position was given to Gaston's son, the prince of Viana. Louis XI forced the comte de Foix to accept this unwelcome decision. The death of the prince of Viana was soon followed by that of Gaston IV himself: in July 1472 the inheritance of the house of Foix passed to a minor.[39]

Like the Foix, its traditional rivals, the house of Armagnac also had ambitions in Spain, though they were frustrated. While Gaston IV had supported John II of Aragon against the rebels of Catalonia, Jean V d'Armagnac had supported the champion of the Catalans, John II's son, Don Carlos. Similarly, it was to Spain in 1461 that Jean V fled from Charles VII. In 1467 the comte d'Armagnac fought alongside Jean of Calabria in support of the Angevin claim to Catalonia.[40]

The third great noble family in the South-West, the Albrets, proved rather more successful in exploiting Spanish politics to its advantage. Through the marriage of Alain d'Albret's eldest son, Jean II, to the daughter of the princess of Viana, Jean II acquired the title of king of Navarre. This was undoubtedly a great *coup* for Alain, though the Albrets' ability to enjoy the Foix inheritance,

---

[37] AC Périgueux, FF 101, no. 13; AC Saint-Emilion, II 1, no. 6; BN, ms. Clairambault 238, no. 353.

[38] Y. Labande-Mailfert, *Charles VIII et son milieu* (Paris, 1975), pp. 117–33, 171–72.

[39] H. Courteault, *Gaston IV, comte de Foix, vicomte souverain de Béarn, prince de Navarre* (Toulouse, 1895), pp. 287, 324, 327, 335, 340, 354.

[40] Samaran, *Maison d'Armagnac*, pp. 113, 156–57.

after the early death Gaston IV's grandson and heir in 1483, was affected by the bitter war which had to be fought for it with the vicomte de Narbonne.[41]

The interests and ambitions of the great noble houses of the South-West not only tempted them to look to involvement in Spanish affairs. They also led to their involvement in the struggle to assert French sovereignty over Brittany and Burgundy and French royal control over the other princes of the realm. Before tracing those events, however, it is worth glancing at the feudal geography of the South-West.

The predecessors of Gaston IV had acquired for the Foix a great inheritance. They had repeatedly intervened in Spanish affairs since the fourteenth century: their vicomté of Castelbon in Catalonia was itself an important fief. The family's hereditary patrimony included Béarn (held in sovereignty), Marsan, Tursan, Gabardan, Nébouzan and, of course, the comté of Foix. Further seigneuries were acquired by Jean I, Gaston's father. From the valleys of Soule to the Western frontiers of Roussillon all the *pays* were in the control of the comte de Foix. Gaston IV bought the vicomté of Narbonne.[42] With the comte de Dunois he enjoyed temporarily – and precariously – the inheritance of his cousins, the captal de Buch and comte de Candale, while they were in exile in England.[43] It was only the untimely death of Gaston's heir, the prince of Viana, which prevented the house of Foix challenging the Albrets at the end of the century for dominance in the South-West.

It was, perhaps, the comtes d'Armagnac – at least in the years following the reduction of Guyenne, in which Jean V d'Armagnac had participated with distinction, and until the comte's flight before the royal armies in 1455 – whose territorial rights and power were most impressive. Although somewhat dispersed, and therefore vulnerable to royal armies, the comtes d'Armagnac enjoyed extensive seigneuries in Auvergne and Rouergue in the North to the so-called 'Quatre Vallées', at the foot of the Pyrenees in the South. The heart of their domains were the seigneuries clustered around the *pays* d'Armagnac itself, including Éauzan, Fezensac and Fezensaguet, Lomagne, Pardiac, Rivière and Bruilhois.[44]

Jean V's scandalous incest with his sister, Isabelle, his attempt to impose his own candidate as archbishop of Auch and his continued exercise of rights of sovereignty against the French king's instructions led to his being stripped of his lands and banished. Restored by Louis XI on his accession, Jean V was soon once more in conflict with the royal officers. Against such a background, it is not suprising to find him among the rebels in the *guerre du bien public*. Jean V extracted a heavy price for his return to the royal obedience. He received back his possessions, obtained annulment of his previous condemnations and obtained a pension of 16,000 livres.[45] Disorders in the *pays* d'Armagnac, however, continued. A large royal army was sent South against the comte d'Armagnac in

---

[41] Dom C. de Vic and Dom Vaissète, *Histoire générale de Languedoc*, viii (Toulouse, 1844), 184–85, 187–88, 207–209.

[42] Courteault, *Gaston IV*, pp. 11, 16, 130–37.

[43] See below, pp. 104–105.

[44] Samaran, *Maison d'Armagnac*, pp. 5–25.

[45] *Ibid.*, pp. 114–53.

April 1469. After appearing to submit, the comte used the opportunity provided by the intrigues of Charles of France and the duke of Brittany to seize
back his fortress of Lectoure. This time, however, the king's limited patience
was exhausted. Two more royal armies were sent and, in highly suspicious and
controversial circumstances, Jean V was killed.[46]

The house of Armagnac never recovered its influence after this disaster,
mainly because of the incompetence of Jean V's successor, his brother Charles
vicomte de Fezensaguet. Imprisoned for various crimes until Louis XI's death,
Charles was restored to the Armagnac inheritance in April 1484. But a combination of the new comte's increasingly evident insanity and the irrepressible
ambitions of Alain d'Albret, who claimed custody over Charles' affairs, ensured
that at no time until the latter's death in 1497 was the house of Armagnac in a
position again to disturb the peace of Guyenne.[47]

Between the reduction of Guyenne and the beginning of the Italian wars it
was undoubtedly the house of Albret whose position in the South-West was
most dramatically strengthened. The Albrets possessed almost all of the major
seigneuries and were dominant in the *pays* which composed the Landes.
Married by his grandfather, Charles II, to Françoise de Blois-Bretagne, Alain
thus became comte de Périgord and vicomte de Limousin, acquiring lands in
Normandy, Penthièvre and Hainaut. Within Guyenne, apart from his possessions in the Landes, he owned castles and tolls along the Garonne from
Bordeaux to Agen. He controlled parts of Bazadais, of Condomois and the
comté of Gaure.[48] For some years he ruled over the inheritance of Charles
Armagnac; and, as has been noted above, through his son's marriage he came
to control the main Pyrenean fiefs and Navarre.[49]

Against the background, outlined above, of troubled relations with England
and Aragon and from such powerful territorial bases in and outside the South-
West, it is not suprising that the Foix, Armagnacs and Albrets sought to exploit
tensions between the king and the other princes. Between the reconquest of
Guyenne in 1453 and the end of Charles VII's reign, the impact of wider
French politics on the province was limited. Neither the plotting and trial of
the duc d'Alençon nor the conflict between the king and the dauphin Louis
appears to have prompted wider dissension in Guyenne. The behaviour of Jean
V comte d'Armagnac affected his own lands and subjects, not for the most part
those of the province as a whole.

Between Louis XI's accession and the outbreak of the *guerre du bien public*,
however, the onset of political crisis involved all three of Guyenne's princely
families. In his early years Louis XI offended a range of powerful interests which
combined against him. In Brittany he had embarked upon a radical assertion of
French sovereignty, alarming the duke.[50] In Burgundy, the increase in the
influence of the comte de Charolais brought to effective power one who

46 *Ibid.*, 154–93
47 *Ibid.*, 216–301
48 A. Luchaire, *Alain le Grand, sire d'Albret* (Paris, 1877), pp. 6, 10, 14–16.
49 *Ibid.*, pp. 22–24.
50 [A. Le Moyne de La Borderie and] B. Pocquet, *Histoire de Bretagne*, iv (Rennes, 1906),
431–43.

already had plenty of reasons for hostility to Louis. The king had also stopped the duke of Bourbon's pension and thwarted his ambition to be Constable of France: Bourbon and his family joined the king's enemies. The discontent of Charles of France has already been mentioned. Above all, as Commynes notes, Louis XI had disappointed the expectations of a number of his father's most powerful servants, such as the comtes de Dunois and de Dammartin, the marshal de Lohéac, the seigneur de Bueil and many others.[51]

In early July 1465 the comte de Charolais advanced towards Paris with a large army, while, moving more slowly, an army under the dukes of Brittany and Berry marched to join him. For his part, the king had successfully acted to bring Bourbonnais back under his control, when he learned of the other forces now assembling against him. In particular, he discovered that from the South-West the sire d'Albret, the comte d'Armagnac and the duc de Nemours were march-ing North at the lead of a large if undisciplined army. The king decided to enter Paris in order to try to prevent its falling to his enemies. After the inconclusive battle of Montlhéry on 16 July 1465, and seeing Rouen and Pontoise fall to the rebels at the end of September, Louis decided to buy off his opponents one by one.[52]

The way in which Charles of France's ambitions were satisfied has already been described. So have the immediate and subsequent fortunes of the comte d'Armagnac. What the ageing sire d'Albret had demanded or expected is unclear: however, he continued to receive his pension until his death. Indeed, most of the princes received pensions, cash gifts or lands. With neither the future duke of Burgundy nor the duke of Brittany, however, was any permanent accommodation possible. The former saw restored to his inheritance the Somme towns and the towns and castellanies of Péronne, Roye and Montdi-dier. He was also given the comtés of Guines and Boulogne which were in his father's possession.[53] The duke of Brittany received little of substance, except the postponement of the ultimate clash with the king of France on those grounds of sovereignty which Louis XI had prematurely raised in his manoeuvres on the eve of the *guerre du bien public*.

By the time of the other wide-ranging princely rebellions which affected Guyenne – the *guerre folle* and the disturbances of 1486–90 – a number of important political circumstances which had affected the outcome of the *guerre du bien public* had significantly changed. On the one hand, Charles VIII's minority and the government of the Beaujeus offered an opportunity for the discontented princes again to take their discontents to arms, free of the terror inspired by Louis XI. But on the other, the fall of ducal Burgundy and the reluctance or inability of the king of England after Edward IV's death to become heavily involved in a continental war now left Brittany more exposed to France. The revolt of the French princes thus became increasingly depend-ent on Breton politics; and, for all its administrative development as a separate

---

[51] R. Vaughan, *Philip the Good, the Apogee of Burgundy* (London, 1970), p. 379; Commynes, *Mémoires*, ed. Calmette, i, 20.
[52] Vaughan, *Philip the Good*, pp. 383–85. For the movements of Albret, Armagnac and Nemours see below, p. 164.
[53] *Ibid.*, p. 390.

state aspiring to sovereignty, Brittany did not have the resources to stand alone against the Valois.[54]

It did not take long after Louis XI's death for the duc d'Orléans and the other princes to signal their intentions. Orléans' last appearance at the royal council before he took up arms was in early October 1484. Two coalitions quickly emerged. The comte de Dunois, Orléans and the duke of Brittany were joined in their endeavour allegedly to free the king from the excessive influence of his sister and brother in law, the Beaujeus, by the comte d'Angoulême, the duc d'Alençon and the king of the Romans. For her part, Anne de Beaujeu established treaties of alliance with the duc de Lorraine, the duc de Bourbon and – for the moment – the sire d'Albret.

In January 1485 Louis d'Orléans attempted unsuccessfully to invoke the authority of the Paris *parlement* against the Beaujeus' government. He and Dunois were promptly stripped of their offices and the royal army marched on Normandy, so preventing Orléans from joining forces with his Breton allies.[55] After a brief reconciliation with the government, Orléans again began to plot revolt with the duc de Bourbon. However, the fall of the strongly anti-Valois Pierre Landais, the duke of Brittany's *trésorier général* and chief minister, and the impossibility after the battle of Bosworth brought Henry VII to the English throne of expecting early assistance from England, significantly reduced the rebels' prospects of success. The duc d'Orléans was forced to yield in mid-September and had to join the royal army as it marched against his former allies, the duc de Bourbon, the comte d'Angoulême and the sire d'Albret. The *guerre folle* thus quickly ended.[56]

The duplicitous behaviour of the sire d'Albret in the disturbances has already been noted. In December 1486 Breton reaction to an over-hasty attempt by the Beaujeus to move against the duchy gave Albret and the other discontented princes a further opportunity for intervention. Nantes became the centre of princely disaffection; though strains soon began to appear between the French exiles and Breton seigneurs.[57] The government struck first at the South-West, where Albret had involved Odet d'Aydie, his family and supporters in his plans. After a quick and entirely successful campaign, Charles VIII entered Bordeaux on 9 March.[58]

Against the princes and the Bretons, the French government made good use of the disaffection of a section of the Breton nobility, who agreed at the treaty of Chateaubriant to recognise the French king as duke François II's successor under certain strictly defined conditions. In 1487 the French armies besieged Nantes; but faced with a strong reaction in Brittany against infringement of the conditions of the treaty of Chateaubriant, the French had to withdraw. By now, however, most of the Breton barons had been won over either by French

---

[54] Pocquet, *Histoire de Bretagne*, iv, 491; J. Kerhervé, *L'Etat breton aux 14e et 15e siècles. Les Ducs, l'argent et les hommes*, ii (Paris, 1987), 947–48.
[55] P. Pélicier, *Essai sur le gouvernement de la dame de Beaujeu, 1483–1491* (Paris, 1882), pp. 85–97.
[56] *Ibid.*, pp. 97–106.
[57] *Ibid.*, pp. 123–27.
[58] *Ibid.*, pp. 129; see below p. 167.

pensions or by a shrewd calculation of likely future events. The sire d'Albret, in pursuit of the hand of Anne of Brittany, continued to support the Breton cause. But the end effectively came with a crushing defeat for the Breton army at Saint-Aubin-du-Cormier in 1488.

In August the duke was forced to expel the rebel princes from his domains and to agree not to marry his daughters without the consent of the king of France. François II died on 9 September. While the French invasion proceeded, Albret continued, with the support of the marshal de Rieux, to seek marriage with Anne – a project which the latter, repelled it seems by Albret's appearance and behaviour, vigorously rejected. The Breton government promised Albret 100,000 écus d'or and for his son, Gabriel, the hand of Anne's sister. But dubious, no doubt, of the ability of the Bretons to deliver such promises and offended, perhaps, by the marriage agreed between Anne and Maximilian on 19 December 1490, Albret entered into negotiations with the French government. On terms highly favourable to himself, he proceeded to let the French army into Nantes.[59]

[59] Pocquet, *Histoire de Bretagne*, iv, 530–76. On the rewards Albret received, see below pp. 170–171.

PART TWO

INSTITUTIONS

3

Government

The Framework of Government

Perhaps the most valuable aspects of the English kings' legacy to the French government in Guyenne were administrative and institutional. The institutional framework for English Gascony had been established long before its reduction. Indeed the system had changed little since 1289. The functions of the seneschal of Gascony had been both military and judicial. He, or usually his lieutenants, held four assizes a year. In 1399 the duchy had been formally divided into four seneschalcies – those of Guyenne, the Landes, Bigorre and Agenais; the last three, however, were regarded as having sub-seneschals. Supreme control in times of war might be bestowed on specially appointed lieutenants with wide powers. With the breaking off of feudal relations with France, the supreme court of appeal for Gascony ceased to be the Paris *parlement*: appeals were heard instead by a special sovereign court or by special commissioners appointed to judge according to the law of Guyenne.[1]

This system of justice and administration was broadly retained and apparently highly valued by the French, whose attempts at reform were often made with a view to restoring arrangements thought to have obtained under the English, rather than new ways imported from Valois France. The duchy continued to be governed by sénéchaux under the authority of a governor or lieutenant-general based in Bordeaux. The office of *juge* de Gascogne, who heard appeals within the sénéchaussée of Guyenne, was not immediately abolished. The *parlement* of Bordeaux, whether consciously or not is unclear, in some sense filled the role of the English fourteenth century court of sovereignty. The financial functions of the English constable of Bordeaux continued to be performed by a French royal receiver known as the 'connétable' or 'comptable' of Bordeaux.

The dearth of evidence from surviving sources makes it far more difficult to examine the working of the French than of the English administration of Guyenne. Comparing the little information from documents relating to the province with information from elsewhere, the broad lines of the system can, however, be glimpsed. The French king's direct representative was the governor of the province, sometimes also referred to as lieutenant and captain-general or lieutenant and governor-general, although special lieutenants and captains-general were sometimes appointed to deal with some pressing crisis. The governorship of Guyenne could be held with that of Languedoc and even

[1] Vale, *English Gascony*, pp. 4–7.

Dauphiné. Its exact territorial limits do not appear to have been definitively fixed until the reign of Louis XI.[2]

In Guyenne, after the reduction of the province and until the beginning of the Italian wars, the governorship was a military and political appointment made with careful regard to the loyalties and ambitions of the nobles and other inhabitants of the province.[3] The accumulation of other positions in Guyenne could further increase a governor's influence: Odet d'Aydie, for example, combined with it the sénéchaussées of Guyenne, Bazadais and the Landes and the admiralty of Guyenne. In fact, this concentration turned out to be dangerous.[4]

Little can be learned of the governor of Guyenne's ordinary administrative functions. He was responsible for assembling the three estates and generally for supervising the security and provisioning of the province, in cooperation with royal commissioners and sénéchaux. He had a council: but its membership is obscure.[5] It was probably his political influence, which varied by appointment and by circumstances, which ultimately determined his importance.

Although this was disputed by the sénéchaux of Guyenne, who often, following English precedent, referred to themselves as 'grands sénéchaux', the appointment of the sénéchaux of the province was made by the king. The post of sénéchal of Guyenne was, however, clearly the most prestigious and important of those; it was often combined with the sénéchaussée of Bazadais. The post of sénéchal was also combined with captaincies of various strongholds, depending on the sénéchal's influence and on the prevailing military situation. Sénéchaux, like governors, might well be expected to undertake tasks for the government which kept them away from their direct responsibilities. Moreover, unlike the governor, the sénéchal also had to provide for courts to which it is likely that the majority of the important royal cases came. Consequently, the sénéchal's administrative and judicial functions usually had to be carried out by lieutenants-general or particular, the latter deputing for the former.

The principal royal officers of the sénéchaussée formed, under the sénéchal's lieutenant, a council whose existence and advice can be perceived in quittances and orders for payment of various administrative expenses. Present at it would be the royal legal and financial officers of the sénéchaussée.[6] Of the working of the lowest tier of administration – that of the royal prévôté et châtellenie – nothing of significance in Guyenne survives.[7]

There is, inevitably, a degree of artificiality in distinguishing the adminstrative from the judicial framework of Guyenne. The Bordeaux parlement, in particular, acted not only as a sovereign court but as an agent of royal authority

[2] G. Dupont-Ferrier, Les officiers royaux des bailliages et des sénéchaussées et les institutions monarchiques locales en France à la fin du Moyen âge [Bibl. Ec. Hautes Etudes, cvl] (Paris, 1902), pp. 27–31.
[3] Early in the following century, governorships began to be more honorific and even hereditary; R. Doucet, Les Institutions de la France au xvie siècle, i (Paris, 1948), pp. 229–32.
[4] See below, pp. 165–70.
[5] BN, ms. Duchesne 103, fos 78r–79v; ms. fr. 26,095, fo. 1407r.
[6] BN, PO 2900. 'Tustal', nos 2,3; PO 2843, 'du Tilh', no. 2; PO 178, 'Balsac', no. 16.
[7] On the prévôté et châtellenie, see B. Guenée, Tribunaux et gens de justice dans le bailliage de Senlis à la fin du Moyen âge (Paris, 1963), p. 72.

in other ways.[8] A similar artificiality is implied by distinguishing royal from urban government, since the king appointed from among his own most trusted officers to the mayoralties of Bordeaux and Bayonne.[9] Similarly too, the royal officers who administered the ordinary and extraordinary finances of the province acted as part of an institutional framework centred elsewhere.[10] For these reasons and because of the limited evidence of working of the processes of government in Guyenne, it is most fruitful to examine in closer detail the personnel of government. Through the careers of the king's officers – both those whose value to the government was primarily military and those with whom it was mainly administrative – the Valois government's own success can be gauged.

Military personnel under Charles VII

After the reduction of the province, the monarchy was faced by a pressing problem. On the one hand, it was intended that the terms of the settlement of claims after the Valois conquests of Guyenne should be conservative. Apart from those who had forfeited their rights through treasonable dealings, there was no mass disappropriation of lands or goods.[11] Yet, on the other hand, those who had fought in the royal armies and continued to hold the province for the king in the face of what were believed to be threats of invasion and revolt had to be rewarded.

Moreover, there was a strong argument in these years for giving key offices and commands to those who had proved themselves as royal captains. Such, for example, was the case of Boniface and Théaude de Valpergue, Italian captains who had served in the royal armies in the days of the *écorcheurs* and given good service since. Both were used by the monarchy in pacified Guyenne.[12] Boniface de Valpergue was captain of Bayonne in the late 1450s and drew a pension on the constable of Bordeaux.[13] Théaude de Valpergue seems to have made his first appearance in Guyenne when in 1454 he was commissioned to take on the powers of the *sénéchal* of Guyenne, in the absence of Olivier de Coëtivy, who was still in England.[14] Théaude took over the captaincy of Bayonne from Boniface de Valpergue from 1459, becoming at about the same time captain of Lectoure.[15]

Another former *écorcheur* whose services were similarly employed in Guyenne was Estèvenot de Talauresse. In the great reform of the *ordonnance* companies of 1445 Talauresse temporarily lost his command; but after Louis

---

8 See below, pp. 85–86.
9 *Histoire de Bordeaux*, iv, 80, 542; AM Bayonne, AA 3, fos 309r–310v.
10 See below, pp. 53, 61–62.
11 See below, pp. 100–105.
12 Contamine, *Guerre*, pp. 254 n. 98, 265 n. 149, 269 n. 161; BN, PO 2924, 'de Valpergue', nos. 10, 11.
13 BN, PO 2924, 'de Valpergue', no. 12.
14 BN, ms. fr. 6963, fo 26r.
15 BN, PO 2924, 'de Valpergue', nos. 13, 14, 16, 18, 21.

XI's accession he was once more promoted to a captaincy in the *ordonnances*. He kept this command till his death in 1477.[16] In the years after the fall of Guyenne to the French, Talauresse and his family seem to have become closely involved with the Albrets. Albret made Estèvenot baile of Montferrand and his uncle, Estève, baile of Tartas. They were referred to in 1457 as Albret's 'esquires and councillors'.[17] In November 1464 Estèvenot de Talauresse was made mayor and captain general of Bayonne, Saint-Jean-de-Luz and Capbreton, on the death of the seigneur de Sarraziet.[18] Perhaps because he was suspect through his links with the Albrets during the *guerre du bien public*, the wages of his offices were unpaid in 1466. His career in the South-West seems to have ended shortly afterwards. By 1475, two years before his death, he had been made sénéchal of Carcassonne.[19]

The longest serving former *écorcheur* captain to hold commands in Guyenne was Poton de Xaintrailles. He held the captaincy of the Château Trompette at Bordeaux till his death in 1461.[20] In 1453 Poton de Xaintrailles' services were rewarded by his appointment as marshal in place of Philippe de Culant.[21]

Two other military figures who had distinguished themselves in the royal armies played active and important parts in keeping the South-West under royal control. Both were liberally rewarded with lands as well as offices. The first is Antoine de Chabannes, comte de Dammartin. In his long career Antoine de Chabannes had the distinction of being disgraced three times yet continuing to be recognised as one of the king's most expert captains.[22] Consequently, he was a leading figure in the 1451 reduction of Guyenne, during which he took Blanquefort from the English. He was then granted it by Charles VII. The comte de Dammartin was twice at the head of royal armies taking control of the lands of the comte d' Armagnac. On both occasions he was rewarded with Armagnac lands.[23] In disgrace at the accession of Louis XI, Antoine de Chabannes' seigneurie of Blanquefort was confiscated and given to Antoine de Castelnau du Lau.[24] When in 1465 Chabannes returned to the king's service he was compensated for the loss of Blanquefort by the grant of other lands outside Guyenne.[25] It was upon the comte de Dammartin that Louis XI relied to keep watch with his army on the borders of Guyenne during its duke's last days. But the king never permitted him again to become a great seigneur in the province.[26]

The family which was most successful in using royal gratitude for military service and need for military support was that of another former *écorcheur*,

[16] Contamine, *Guerre*, pp. 404, 411.
[17] AD Gers, E 917.
[18] BN, ms. fr. 24, 058, no. 32.
[19] BN, ms. Clairambault 236, no. 237.
[20] G. Dupont-Ferrier, *Gallia regia*, iii (Paris, 1947), 459.
[21] Contamine, *Guerre*, p. 431.
[22] For an account of Antoine de Chabannes' career, see *ibid.*, pp. 413–14.
[23] H. de Chabannes, *Histoire de la maison de Chabannes*, ii (Dijon, 1894), 47–50, 134–35, 145.
[24] See below, p. 29.
[25] AN, X[1A] 8608, fos 120v–125r.
[26] Chabannes, ii, 167. However, Jacques de Chabannes was seigneur de Curton, near Libourne, which he left on his death in 1453 to his son Gilbert (*ibid.*, i, 178–79).

Olivier de Coëtivy. The Coëtivys built up a powerful position as seigneurs. Olivier de Coëtivy and his brothers, Prégent and Christophe, all served in the royal armies.[27] Prégent had been granted before his death the seigneurie of Lesparre.[28] Olivier de Coëtivy was taken prisoner by the English in 1452 and did not return to France till 1455. A ransom of 12,000 écus, silver plate and a charger was demanded for him; but Charles VII gave him the ransom of the comte de Candale, who had been captured at the battle of Castillon, in order to pay Olivier's debt. Candale's ransom was of 44,000 écus d'or, so for all the inconvenience of imprisonment Coëtivy probably lost nothing financially.[29] Since 1451, Olivier de Coëtivy had been holding the office of sénéchal of Guyenne and continued to do so till Charles VII's death.[30] Moreover, Charles VII gave Coëtivy his own daughter in marriage. Her dowry included the seigneuries of Royan and Mornac in Saintonge, confiscated from Jacques de Pons.[31] However, like many others who had enjoyed Charles VII's favour, Olivier de Coëtivy fell into disgrace on Louis XI's accession. He was stripped both of his sénéchaussée and of these lands. The latter were returned to the Pons family.[32] A long court case between the Coëtivys and the Pons ensued and eventually, in 1480, Louis XI made over the seigneurie of Rochefort in Saintonge to the former as compensation for their lossess.[33] Coëtivy's heirs held Rochefort for more than a century.[34]

The Coëtivys were the exception to the general rule that those who had served the king in the campaigns which culminated in the reduction of Guyenne did not manage to put down firm enough roots for their families to become permanently settled as members of its aristocratic society. Of course, many of the circumstances which led to this were fortuitous. No-one could guarantee that Poton de Xaintrailles would not have a male heir or that the crises of Louis XI's reign would prevent Antoine de Chabannes from securing a seigneurie in Guyenne proper. But even Estèvenot de Talauresse, a Gascon, failed to establish himself in the *pays* through the king's favour and had to look to the support of Charles II d'Albret. Those seigneuries which *were* granted and which had been confiscated from those Gascon nobles who had been 'English' were less than sure rewards, not least because of the return of confiscated seigneurs to the royal favour.[35] For many like the Valpergues the prospect of future commands and offices elsewhere in France must have seemed more tempting.

Paradoxically it was more likely to be those of less exalted status who would more easily forge links with the *pays* into which they came as soldiers and from

[27] Contamine, *Guerre*, pp. 238, 400.

[28] AN, JJ 180, no. 19.

[29] P. Marchegay, 'La Rançon d'Olivier de Coëtivy', *Bibl. Ec. Chartes*, xxxviii (1877), 6–8.

[30] On the comte de Candale's return, Coëtivy had to drop his claims to the rest of the ransom, being 18,000 écus (AN, X^{1A} 8606, fos 17–18), Dupont-Ferrier, *Gallia Regia*, iii, 437.

[31] AN, JJ 190, no. 210.

[32] AN, X^{1A} 8608, fos 160v–162r.

[33] *Ibid.*, fos 17r–18r.

[34] Marchegay, 'La Rançon', 8–9.

[35] See below, pp. 100–105.

which they might, in time, emerge as full civilians. Many soldiers farmed local tithes, invested, lent money and bought property.[36] Even some foreign soldiers bought their way into the status of minor seigneurs. In 1459, for example, a Scottish archer serving under Robin Petillot, John Bron of Coulton, paid sixty écus d'or for a half share in a seigneurie near Saint-Sever.[37] At Montflanquin in Agenais in 1473, one of the town consuls was the Scot, John Ross.[38] The career of Patrick Abercrombie was another such case. In 1449 he had been entrusted by Charles VII with the administration of the town toll. By 1467 he had become a consul of Agen.[39]

Foreign soldiers like Bron, Ross and Abercrombie were, however, never great figures in the *pays*. The only Scottish soldier to become so was Robin Petillot.[40] Like the Valpergues and like Patrick Folcart, his fellow countryman who became sénéchal of Saintonge,[41] Petillot was rewarded for his services in the royal armies by promotion to high office in the conquered province; but unlike them and most other *écorcheurs* he became a great seigneur in his own right. In 1451 he was given a pension of 500 l. t.[42] The following year he was liberally reimbursed for losses incurred on a previous campaign.[43] Charles VII made him sénéchal of the Landes and captain of Dax and Saint-Sever.[44] He also served the king in maintaining control over the Armagnac lands and became captain of Manciet and of Lectoure.[45] Petillot was granted by the king the seigneurie of Sauveterre.[46] He married the daughter of the seigneur de Gramont and may have been involved in the intricate web of conspiratorial intrigue of 1452–1454.[47] Lack of male heirs rather than any other cause ensured that the Petillots did not become a new noble family in the area.

Charles VIII's appointments, therefore, succeeded in their aim. They kept the province militarily secure. They rewarded those who had taken part in the reduction of Guyenne. Yet they did not result in those who were most powerful – and so most dangerous – forming such strong links with local interests that royal control itself was threatened.

[36] ADG, H 738, fo 99r–v; H 776, fos 3r–4v; H 1185, fo r; H 1186, fos 24v–25r; G 1161, fo 210v.
[37] AC Saint-Sever, DD 1, no. 8.
[38] AM Bordeaux, ms. 207, no. 71.
[39] AM Agen, CC 42, unnumbered, FF 218, unnumbered.
[40] Though usually referred to as 'Robin Petit-Lot', he signed 'R. Petillot' (BN, PO 2252, 'Petillot', nos. 7–10).
[41] Dupont-Ferrier, *Gallia Regia*, v, 297; Folcart continued to receive 1000 l. t. pension after the duke of Guyenne's death (BN, ms. fr. 20,497, fo 41r).
[42] BN PO 2252, 'Petillot', no. 5.
[43] *Ibid.*, no. 3.
[44] *Ibid.*, nos. 4, 7, 8,
[45] *Ibid.*, no. 9; BN, ms. fr. 25,778, fo 1905r; AD Tarn-et-Garonne, A 285, unnumbered [fo 6r].
[46] AN, JJ 198, no. 287.
[47] See below, pp. 153–56.

Military personnel under Louis XI and Charles VIII

Like his father, Louis XI was determined to ensure both that those in charge of
the province were capable of defending it and that they had every reason to be
loyal to him. Paradoxically, the continuing effectiveness of royal power
depended on political change. Where Charles VII had been able to exploit the
conditions of Guyenne's reduction to reward his servants, Louis XI had to
appoint his own creations by dispropriating others. Some of Louis's appointments came from the Dauphiné, some from elsewhere in France and some from
the service of his brother, Charles of France; but none had enjoyed significant
power or patronage in Guyenne under his father.

On Louis XI's accession be entrusted the governorship of Guyenne to Jean,
bastard of Armagnac. He also put him in charge of a range of important
fortified centres in the Bordelais and Agenais, such as La Réole, Penne,
Marmande and Puymirol.[48] In August 1461 the king granted him the comté of
Comminges and, two years later, other adjoining rights.[49] The bastard of
Armagnac was essentially a military figure. He fought in Louis's campaigns in
Roussillon and Catalonia and received other grants for his services there.[50] He
was legitimised in 1463.[51] Other important seigneuries were made over to him
at about this time, such as Langoiran and, on the death of Robin Petillot,
Sauveterre in Comminges.[52] He never seems entirely to have lost his links with
Dauphiné. In 1467–1468 his pension was being levied on revenue from taxes
raised there. When Guyenne was alienated to Charles of France he resumed his
military career and in 1470 was in command of 95 lances, and once more went
to Dauphiné as governor, not again, it would seem, to return to the South-
West.[53]

Hardly less important in these early years was Antoine de Castelnau du Lau.
On Louis XI's accession he was made sénéchal of Guyenne, Bazadais and the
Landes, captain of Monségur and Grand Butler of France.[54] In 1461 he was
granted Duras, confiscated from Gaillard de Durfort who was in exile, and in
1463 he received the seigneurie of Blanquefort which had been confiscated
from Antoine de Chabannes, who had, it will be remembered, fallen into
disgrace on the new king's accession.[55] In circumstances which remain obscure
he, too, was disgraced and his seigneuries confiscated; but he was pardoned in
1472 and immediately brought fully back onto the king's good graces.[56] In
December 1472 he was made governor of Roussillon and received a pension of

[48] BN, ms Clairambault, no. 70; PO 94, 'Armagnac, comtes de', nos. 315, 323. He was the son
of Arnaud-Guilhem de Lescun (Samaran, *Maison d'Armagnac*, p. 116, n. 1).
[49] AN, X^{1A} 8606, fos 31v–33v.
[50] *Ibid.*, fos 50v–51r.
[51] AN, JJ 199, no. 341.
[52] AN, JJ 198, nos. 47, 287.
[53] BN, PO 94, 'Armagnac, comtes de', nos. 324, 329; ms. Clairambault 235, no. 157.
[54] ADG, 3E 2517, fos 48r–49v; BN, PO 700, 'de Chasteauneuf, seigneur du Lau', no. 2.
[55] AN, X1A 8605, fos 268v–269r, 8606, fos 28v–29v.
[56] BN, ms. fr. 20,428, fo 45r.

4,000 l.t.[57] Two years later be became sénéchal of Beaucaire with a pension of 3,000 l.t. and remained in that position until at least 1483.[58]

The third powerful figure implanted in Guyenne by Louis XI in the years before the alienation of the province to Charles of France was Gaston du Lyon. By 1463 Louis XI had made him sénéchal of Saintonge, and *premier varlet tranchant*.[59] He was granted the seigneurie of Taillebourg and, when it had to be returned to Olivier de Coëtivy, was compensated with lands in Cerdagne.[60] In April 1468 he received, in addition to that of Saintonge, the sénéchaussées of Guyenne, Bazadais and the Landes, which had been taken from Antoine de Castelnau du Lau.[61] Of all the three, Gaston du Lyon was most successful both in retaining office and in using it for his own purposes. He received the profits of the *jugèrie* of Rivière, which had been taken into the king's hand,[62] a pension of 2,200 l.t.,[63] and later became sénéchal of Toulouse, a post which he held at least until 1486.[64] He was still fit enough to serve Charles VIII against the rebels at Saint-Aubin-du-Cormier.[65] Gaston du Lyon's wealth and power enabled him to strike two notably successful bargains which markedly increased his status and wealth. In November 1473 Isabelle d'Armagnac, the late Jean V's daughter, agreed to hand over to him La Barthe and make him her universal heir, in exchange for his protection and aid in fighting her lawsuits.[66] In November 1482 he married Jeanne de Lavedan, daughter of Raymond Garsie, seigneur de Lavedan. Gaston du Lyon was to buy back all the alienated rights and lands of the Lavedan inheritance and succeed to it.[67]

Charles of France's brief rule as duke of Guyenne saw the introduction into the province of men whose careers would probably not otherwise have led them to the South-West. It allowed other families from the province to attain positions which they could hardly have hoped to achieve if the structure of power and patronage which existed after Louis XI's accession had been allowed to continue. As Commynes noted, on the duke's death Louis XI made most of his late brother's servants welcome.[68] Indeed the king had allowed this to be publicly known. In June 1472 Louis promised to maintain the officers of Charles of France in the privileges and advantages they had previously enjoyed.[69]

Several officers served both Charles of France and Louis XI in a predominantly military capacity. One such was Jean de Volvire, seigneur de Ruffec. In

---

[57] BN, ms. Clairambault 150, no. 71.
[58] *Ibid.*, nos. 72–75; BN, PO 70, 'de Chasteauneuf, seigneur du Lau', nos. 7–11, 13, 30–35.
[59] ADG, 1B1, fo 57r–v.
[60] AN, P 2299, fos 480r–482v.
[61] J. de Métivier, *Chronique du parlement de Bordeaux*, ed. A. de Brezetz and J. Delpit, i (Bordeaux, 1886), 55.
[62] AD Haute-Garonne, B 3, fo 66 r.
[63] BN, ms. fr. 26,096, no. 1555.
[64] AD Gers, I 1193, no. 4; BN, ms. fr. 26,100, no. 241.
[65] *Lettres de Charles VIII*, ed. Pélicier, iii, pièce justificative vi, 383.
[66] AD Gers, I 111, no. 8.
[67] AD Gers, I 1193, no. 5.
[68] Commynes, *Mémoires*, ed. Calmette, i, 240.
[69] Stein, *Charles de France*, piéce justificative cxlvi, pp. 814–15.

1480, for example, Volvire was commissioned to a raise men-at-arms in Périgord.[70] Another was Louis Sorbier. He was Charles' captain of Domme and Bergerac and was placed by the duke in charge of fifty lances.[71] After the duke's death he retained the captaincies of Domme and Bergerac and was made sénéchal of Perigord.[72] In 1474 he was entrusted with raising soldiers in Périgord for Gaston du Lyon's army in Spain and was still holding all his offices in 1482.[73] A still longer period of ducal and royal service – till at least 1493 – was that of Jean de Rochechouart, vicomte de Bruilhois.[74]

It is, however, the career of Robert de Balsac which best illustrates the success of Louis XI in turning former officers of the duke of Guyenne into the monarchy's loyal servants. Balsac seems to have begun his long career in Charles of France's army in Normandy. On Charles's arrival as duke in Guyenne, Balsac was made ducal chamberlain, sénéchal of Agenais and captain of Puymirol.[75] On the duke's death he became a royal councillor and chamberlain and remained as royal sénéchal of Agenais.[76] The gift of the seigneurie of Clermont-Soubiran, which Balsac had received from the duke of Guyenne in 1470, was confirmed by Louis XI.[77] Balsac served as sénéchal of Agenais for altogether over thirty years, longer than any other notable officer in the province.[78] He was in receipt of a pension of 900 l.t. as sénéchal but this was augmented by other grants and by wages paid him as captain of the royal men-at-arms.[79] Moreover, he succeeded in obtaining for his son, Pierre, succession to the sénéchaussée and to the captaincy of Penne, Tournon and Castelculier – all important fortified centres in Agenais – in spite of Pierre's being a minor. Robert de Balsac would continue to hold these positions for him.[80] This is the only known example, even under Charles VIII when these practices were creeping into Guyenne, of such a concession in the province relating to an important military and administrative post.

Towards the end of his life Balsac spent more of his time outside Agenais, indeed outside France. He was one of the king's captains at the siege of Nantes in 1487.[81] He fought with the royal army at Saint-Aubin-du-Cormier.[82] In 1494 and 1495 Balsac was with Charles VIII in Italy.[83] He was made captain of Pisa, which he was told to hand back to Florence in 1494.[84] He was once more captain there in 1500 for Louis XII. While in Florence he took as his second

70 AC Périgueux, E 19, no. 1.
71 BN, PO 2717, 'Sorbier', nos. 2–4.
72 *Ibid.*, nos. 6, 7.
73 *Ibid.*, nos. 8, 10, 11.
74 BN, ms. Clairambault 192, nos. 44, 45, 47–50.
75 BN, PO 178, 'Balsac', nos. 6, 10–13; ms. fr. 26,092, fo 869r.
76 BN, PO 178, 'Balsac', nos. 15, 16, 18.
77 AN, X^{1A} 8607, fos 30v–31v.
78 *Ibid.*, fo 21r; AM Agen, CC 44, unnumbered.
79 ADG, G 84, unnumbered; AN, K 73, no. 27; BN, mss fr. 2900, fo 8r, 2908, fos 7r, 49v.
80 AM Agen, CC 45, unnumbered.
81 BN, ms. Clairambault 139, no. 35.
82 *Lettres de Charles VIII*, ed. Pélicier, iii, pièce justificative vi, 384.
83 Comte de Dienne, 'Robert de Balsac', *R. Agenais*, xxxvi (1909), 27.
84 *Lettres de Charles VIII*, ed. Pélicier, v, no. mcxxxi, 258–62.

wife the daughter of one of the gonfalonieri of the Republic. He died in 1506.[85] Robert de Balsac was one of the few ducal and royal servants without any apparent links with Guyenne – he was of a noble family from Auvergne – who managed to install themselves as great political and social figures in the *pays*.[86] Robert's brother, Ruffec, remained in the royal service while Robert himself served the duke of Guyenne, an arrangement which perhaps served as an insurance against political mishaps.[87] But, in fact, from the time of his entry into the royal service, Robert de Balsac seems to have remained entirely loyal to successive monarchs. There is no evidence of his involvement in the disaffection of the years after Louis XI's death, in spite of the undoubted influence of the house of Albret in Agenais.[88] His use to the king was probably increased by his culture and literacy, shown in the authorship of a short moral treatise.[89]

The success of Balsac's career may also owe much to an apparent determination to concentrate his offices and grants in Agenais, rather than acquire them elsewhere in Guyenne, the result of which was to ensure that his influence as sénéchal and seigneur were complementary. Yet even Balsac's prestige could not ensure that he held his seigneurie of Clermont-Soubiran without opposition. As late as 1486 he was faced by vigorous resistance from his tenants there, perhaps because Clermont-Soubiran had been acquired by confiscation from the Armagnacs.[90] In such circumstances as this it was undoubtedly expedient for a 'new' seigneur to be able to reply on the royal authority to back his claims.

Of those who joined the king after the death of Charles of France, Odet d'Aydie and his associates occupy a place apart. As Commynes records, they were able to negotiate terms with Louis XI for entry into his service which were highly advantageous.[91] Odet d'Aydie's military career was a long and distinguished one. Unlike most of the other officers recruited by Louis XI after the duke of Guyenne's death, Odet d'Aydie had already benefited substantially from royal generosity. He had been a captain in the victorious royal army at Formigny in 1450, was made bailli of Cotentin, and joined the comte de Foix's army for the conquest of Guyenne in 1451. By the time of Louis XI's accession to the throne, Odet had become seigneur of Lescun through marriage.[92] Though he had refused to continue in the royal service, in 1462 he was already considered worth offering a 6,000 l.t. pension and command of the strategically important centre of Blaye in Guyenne.[93] When Odet joined Charles of France and the duke of Brittany, he ensured that he received in 1469 a special pardon for his involvement in their intrigues.[94]

---

[85] Dienne, 'Robert de Balsac', pp. 27–29.

[86] *Ibid.*, p. 26; BN, PO 178 'Balsac', no. 16.

[87] BN, ms. Clairambault 138, nos. 121, 130.

[88] See below, pp. 188–89.

[89] R. de Balsac, *Le Chemin de l'ospital*, ed. P. Tamizey de Larroque (Montpellier, 1887), p. 20.

[90] BN, PO 178, 'Balsac', no. 20

[91] Commynes, *Mémoires*, ed. Calmette, i, 242–43.

[92] J. de Jaurgain, 'Deux comtes de Comminges béarnais au xve siècle', *B. Soc. archéol. Gers*, xvii (1916), 128–31.

[93] AD Dordogne 2E 1851/67, no. 3.

[94] AD Dordogne 2E 1851/68, no. 2.

By the time of his return to the service of Louis XI, the seigneur de Lescun's authority had grown substantially. He had been the duke's captain general in Normandy,[95] and when Charles of France received Guyenne in appanage Lescun became sénéchal of Guyenne and Bazadais, captain of Blaye and Bazas.[96] In 1472 Louis confirmed Lescun in all that he had received from the late duke of Guyenne.[97] According to Commynes, through the agency of Guillaume de Soupplainville, Odet d'Aydie demanded as the price of his support for Louis XI a 6,000 franc pension, the governorship of Guyenne, the sénéchaussées of Guyenne and Landes, the captaincy of one of the two castles of Bordeaux, the two castles of Bayonne, command of Dax and Saint-Sever, 24,000 écus in cash, the order of Saint-Michel and the comté of Comminges. Commynes maintains that all of this was granted.[98] Most of it certainly was. Indeed the sénéchaussée of Bazadais was also given,[99] as was the admiralty of Guyenne.[100] Moreover, at the end of Louis's reign the comte de Comminges was receiving 9,000 l.t. over and above the wages of his offices.[101]

After Louis XI's death, the authority of the comte of Comminges in Guyenne was still further increased.[102] He retained his old posts. In 1486, just a year before he fled with other conspirators to Brittany, he was receiving 1565 l.t. for his three sénéchaussées and a further 200 l.t. as captain of Bazas, Bourg and Blaye.[103] In 1484 he was made lieutenant-general of Guyenne with power to provide for justice, assemble the three estates, organise the duchy's defence, receive homages and investigate the misconduct of officers.[104] For the admiralty of Guyenne he was in receipt of 2,000 l.t. pension.[105] Comminges seems to have died in Brittany shortly after the agreement of January 1491, by which Albret and other rebels returned to the royal allegiance, was drawn up.[106]

Odet d'Aydie's long political and military involvement in Guyenne allowed him to acquire a powerful, if uneasy, position as one of the province's important seigneurs. His acquisition of the comté of Comminges, after the death of the bastard of Armagnac, was a measure of the extent to which the king intended that he should fill the latter's role as key political figure in Guyenne.[107] The comté, after Odet's death, reverted to the royal domain.[108] His son-in-law, the vicomte de Lautrec was, by the agreement of 1491 with the rebel princes, to be

---

95 AD Dordogne 2E 1851/67, no. 1.
96 BN, PO 155, 'd'Aydie en Béarn', no. 24.
97 Ibid., no. 26.
98 Commynes, Mémoires, ed. Calmette, i, 241–42.
99 BN, PO 155, 'd'Aydie en Béarn', no. 25.
100 BN, ms. fr. 2900, fo 8r.
101 ADG, G 139, fo 209r.
102 See below, p. 165.
103 BN, PO 155 'd'Aydie en Béarn', nos. 36, 37, 40.
104 AM Agen. AA 13, no. 10.
105 BN, ms. fr. 26,099, no. 27.
106 AD Dordogne, 2E 1851/68, no. 4.
107 C. Higounet, Le Comté de Comminges de ses origines à son annexion à la couronne, ii (Toulouse and Paris, 1949), 618–19.
108 Ibid., pp. 620–21.

compensated for the loss of this substantial part of his wife's inheritance, but it is by no means clear that he was.[109]

Comminges itself was not within Guyenne, but Odet d'Aydie received other lands which were. In 1472 Louis XI had granted him 2,000 l.t. to take from the revenues of the vicomté of Fronsac. However, since the revenues were not annually worth that amount, the king gave him 5,000 écus d'or instead and made over to him in perpetuity Fronsac itself.[110] The grant however, did not go unchallenged; it led to long legal disputes with powerful litigants.[111] Lack of male heirs prevented Odet d'Aydie from establishing his family securely in Guyenne. However, an advantageous marriage linked his daughter, Jeanne, with the vicomte de Lautrec in 1479, to whom, as her father's sole heir, she brought what, at the time of the marriage, was a rich inheritance.[112]

The ladder of opportunity which Odet d'Aydie provided was also climbed by his close associate, Guillaume de Soupplainville, and by the other members of the Aydie family. In ducal Guyenne Soupplainville had been vice-admiral, constable of Bordeaux,[113] and was in receipt of a 1,000 l.t. pension.[114] The arrangement to take Soupplainville into the king's service was a personal one entered into with Louis XI. A written undertaking was given by the king which promised Soupplainville the mayoralty of Bayonne, the *prévôté* of Dax and the seigneurie of Saint-Sever for life. He was also to receive a pension of 1,200 l.t.[115] The terms of the agreement were carried out and Soupplainville's pension was still being paid on Louis XI's death.[116] Until he was stripped of his offices for rebelling against Charles VIII, he retained these positions and when, with Albret and others, he returned to the royal service not only did he do so again on highly favourable terms[117] but he was also given the arrears of his pension.[118]

Guillaume de Soupplainville was only one of several figures associated with the swift rise of Odet d'Aydie, though he was certainly the most successful and the only one who was not a member of the Aydie family connection. Odet d'Aydie's cousins of the line of Ognoas were likewise able to gain from his position. The old seigneur d'Ognoas's younger son, Pes d'Aydie, through Odet's association with the sire d'Albret, was able to make a profitable marriage. In November 1482 he married the widow of Albret's old servant Estèvenot de Talauresse. Her brothers were the archbishop of Toulouse and the seigneur de Campet, a notable connection.[119] The seigneur d'Ognoas's elder son, Lubat, figured more prominently in Odet d'Aydie's military entourage. Lubat served as

---

[109] AD Dordogne, 2E 1851/68, no. 4 [fo 2v].

[110] AD Dordogne, 2E 1851/69, unnumbered.

[111] *Arch. hist. Gironde*, xiii (1872), no. xxx, 69–74; no. xxxiii, 85–94; APA, E 161, unnumbered.

[112] AD Dordogne, 2E 1851/8, no. 4.

[113] M. Gouron, *L'Amirauté de Guyenne* (Paris, 1938), p. 203; BN, PO 1487, 'Harpin', no. 5.

[114] BN, PO 2721, 'Soupplainville', no. 2.

[115] BN, ms. fr. 20,497, fo 39r.

[116] BN, ms. fr. 2900, fo 7v.

[117] For the terms offered to Albret and his associates, see below, pp. 170–71.

[118] BN, PO 2721, 'Soupplainville', no. 5.

[119] AD Gers, I 228, no. 7.

Odet's lieutenant in his captaincy of Bayonne under Charles of France.[120] He was subsequently one of Odet's men-at-arms[121] and, as seigneur d'Ognoas from 1472, received substantial sums from the revenues of his cousin.[122] He became bailli of Labourt and captain of Bayonne.[123] Although Lubat was sufficiently distrusted by the royal government to be warned not to stop Bayonne being handed over to the seigneur de Gramont in 1488, his family seems to have flourished.[124] His son and successor, Jean, was in 1496 made a royal *maître d'hôtel* for his services in Italy.[125]

Odet d'Aydie's two brothers, Odet and Bertrand, also shared in the honours showered on him. Of the two, Bertrand never seems to have been more than a soldier, who, towards the end of Louis XI's reign, was receiving a pension of 600 l.t.[126] Odet the Younger, often referred to by contemporaries as 'the captain', though, as his *soubriquet* suggests, he was similarly above all a soldier, was of far greater political importance. After the duke of Guyenne's death, Odet d'Aydie the younger was made, like his brother, a royal councillor and chamberlain, given a 1,200 l.t. pension and put in command of 95 lances.[127] In 1480 he was fighting in the war for possession of the Burgundian inheritance.[128] Probably in reward for his services there, he was made sénéchal of Carcassonne and retained the position after Louis XI's death.[129] After his elder brother's flight to Brittany to join the rebels, Odet d'Aydie the younger remained behind in Guyenne drawing the comte de Comminges' wages for his three sénéchaussées and plotting against the royal government.[130] On his return to the royal allegiance, the terms negotiated by Albret on his behalf secured the return of his offices and pension and further increased his power and wealth in Guyenne.[131] He went on to give Charles VIII military service in Italy.[132] The close association he had built up with the sire d'Albret was used to secure his claims to lands and seigneuries.[133] His marriage to Anne, daughter of Guy seigneur de Pons, linked him to one of the principal families of Guyenne and gave him the right of succession to a third of the Pons inheritance.[134] Like Robert de Balsac, though by a different and more dangerous route, Odet d'Aydie the younger was one of the few outsiders to implant themselves firmly in Guyenne's aristocratic society.

---

120 BN, PO 155, 'd'Aydie en Béarn', nos. 16, 17, 19.
121 BN, ms. n. a. fr. 8609, fo 17r–v.
122 AD Gers, I 228, no. 7.
123 Jaurgain, 'Deux Comtes de Comminges', 233.
124 AD Gers, I 229, no. 6.
125 *Ibid.*, no. 11.
126 BN, PO 155, 'd'Aydie en Béarn', no. 18; ms. fr. 2900 fo 14v.
127 BN, PO 155, 'd'Aydie en Béarn' nos. 27, 28, 42.
128 *Ibid.*, no. 1.
129 *Ibid.*, no. 9.
130 BN PO 155, 'd'Aydie en Béarn', no. 43. For his conspiratorial activities and rebellion see below pp. 166–67.
131 AD Dordogne, 2E 1851/68, nos. 4–5.
132 Jaurgain, 'Deux Comtes de Comminges', 239.
133 See below, pp. 189–90.
134 AD Dordogne, 2E 1851/72, no 1. This led to a protracted legal dispute with Guy de Pons for possession of Ribérac (AD Dordogne, 2E 1851/74, nos. 1, 2).

Those upon whom the king relied to control Guyenne in royal interests had, for all their differing origins, had certain common features. Both the three appointments which Louis XI made on his accession from among those who had proved their loyalty in his service in Dauphiné, and the Aydie family and connection, consisted of soldiers rather than simply administrators. Even when in office they were frequently to be found engaged in commanding the royal men-at-arms. Their function was primarily to withstand a possible English attack and to suppress any domestic upheaval. The men most likely to be entrusted with such a role were those who were not entirely ignorant of conditions in Guyenne but were not too heavily influenced by them. Jean, bastard of Armagnac, Antoine de Castelnau du Lau and Gaston du Lyon were from the South-West. But of those Gaston du Lyon was from Béarn, outside the kingdom, Antoine de Castelnau du Lau was not the principal seigneur of the Gascon noble family from which he sprang, and the bastard of Armagnac inherited no lands of note in the province. Robert de Balsac, of an undistin-guished Auvergnat noble family, though no *parvenu*, became a great figure in Agenais only through royal patronage and promotion. Like Gaston du Lyon, the Aydies were of a noble family in Béarn. The king chose men of ability whom, while loyal, he would shower with rewards – but whose disloyalties could be punished with total disgrace. So it was that, in spite of the authority they wielded, all those whom Louis XI appointed to rule the province owed almost everything to the king's continuing favour.

During Louis's lifetime the policy was remarkably successful. Its longer term results, however, were less desirable. The lack of male heirs to the Aydie brothers was a boon to the government, ensuring that their offspring would not inherit a dangerously powerful position in the province. But the principal danger to the royal authority was still that without continuing strong central control the Aydies and other royal servants would become ever more closely attached to the principal noble connection in Guyenne, that of the Albrets. This was what the minority of Charles VIII permitted to occur.[135]

Office and officers

Administrative and judicial office became steadily more important as a source of power, patronage and promotion after the recovery of Guyenne by the French monarchy. Although the framework of government which had been created under English rule broadly remained intact, the French government seized the opportunity presented by the swift campaign of conquest in 1451 to avoid continuity of administrative personnel. Indeed the only case of such continuity seems to be that of a humble clerk,[136] although it is possible that at the level of *bailie*, *prévôté* or town some minor figures continued in office. This sweeping change of personnel gave the monarchy its first (and only) chance to install its servants, largely free from local pressures and interests. Moreover, in the institution of the *parlement* of Bordeaux and the introduction of the judicial

---

[135] See pp. 165–71.
[136] Vale, *English Gascony*, p. 223 n. 3.

system of Valois France the government was presented with an important new opportunity to reward its servants with office.

Yet, as in other spheres, the years of relative stability in government after 1453 brought with them ossification. The tendency by royal government and officers to regard office as property, and indeed heritable property, grew. So did group interests among the families which came to dominate office-holding in the province; so did interests in the *pays* itself. This was not unique to Guyenne. It was happening elsewhere in France too. At Toulouse, for example, *parlementaire* families formed their own dynasties.[137] But in Guyenne the change was perhaps even more important in its consequences. For there within forty years the balance of control between the royal government and local, group interests was clearly being reversed and the attitudes of officers played a crucial part in this.

In the years following the reduction of Guyenne the monarchy was largely successful in ridding itself of obligations to promote to administrative and judicial posts those upon whom it had had to rely during the campaigns to subdue the province. For example, Pierre Boutin had been granted the *prévôté* of Bayonne for his wartime services; but in the mid-1450s he was persuaded to relinquish his claim to it in exchange for 300 écus d'or. Similarly Guillaume de Blaye was recompensed at about the same time for his loss of the *prévôté* of the Ombrière at Bordeaux.[138] The debts which the king owed to noble families which had assisted him, though liberally repaid, were not for the most part done so at the expense of appointing members of their families to administrative and judicial posts.

The monarchy drew widely from the officers of the royal administration elsewhere in France and in some cases from those of seigneurs to fill the officers now vacant in Guyenne. From Paris, Pierre Bérard, a *trésorier général* and royal councillor, was sent as *trésorier* or receiver in Agenais.[139] Maître Pierre Bragier, who had been the royal advocate of Saintonge and La Rochelle in the 1440s, became lieutenant-general of the sénéchal of Guyenne, and later a councillor and then president of the *parlement* of Bordeaux.[140] Two notable figures in the new royal administration of the province were recruited by the king from the servants of Jean de Bretagne, comte de Périgord. Maître Pierre de Pelisses was born in the vicomté of Limousin where he joined Jean de Bretagne's service, acting in 1452 as chancellor of the vicomté and a member of the comte's household. He subsequently became royal proctor general in the sénéchaussée of Périgord.[141] Hugues Bailly had similar origins. He was the son of the seigneur

---

[137] A. Viala, Le Parlement de Toulouse et l'administration royale laïque, 1420–1525 environ, i (Albi, 1953), 179–184. By contrast, it has been argued that the links between the parlementaire families of Paris established a greater esprit de corps which made the court a powerful agent of the royal will. See F. Autrand, Naissance d'un grand corps de l'état. Les gens du parlement de Paris, 1345–1454 (Paris, 1981), pp. 264–65.

[138] BN, ms. fr. 25, 712, fo 303r.

[139] BN, PO 948, 'de Crussol' no. 11.

[140] BN, PO 491, 'Bragier', nos. 2–6; ADG, G 235, no. 1.

[141] AD Dordogne, J 1384, unnumbered cahier [fo 15r]; APA, E11, unnumbered; APA E 734, unnumbered.

de La Cour in Limousin, and had joined the service of Jean de Blois-Bretagne in 1435 after spending some years studying law at the university of Poitiers. He served the comte till the latter's death in 1452, having charge of the family archives and the conduct of its law-suits.[142] He had been rewarded for this service with the town and castellany of Razac in Périgord on the occasion of his marriage with Marguerite de Lubersac the year before Jean de Bretagne's death[143] Bailly entered the royal service and was *élu* in Bas-Limousin before becoming lieutenant-general of the sénéchal of Périgord.[144] He appears to have been a powerful figure in the *pays*, worth bribing and capable of acts of brutality and even murder.[145] His seigneurie passed on his death in 1494 to his grandson and heir, Jean Bailly.[146]

The institution of the Bordeaux *parlement* in 1462 brought further recruits from the royal administration of Valois France to Guyenne, above all from the Paris *parlement*; though by now others with deeper interests in and experience of life in the province, such as Henri de Ferragnes once clerk of Bordeaux, had penetrated into the ranks of the important royal judicial officers.[147] As a centre of Valois French language, manners, legal custom and personnel the *parlement* in these early years increased the monarch's political control over affairs in Guyenne.[148] Yet for all the apparent success of the government in exerting its authority over the province, other trends at work moved in the opposite direction.

To begin with, there were the views held about office itself. It has already been observed that those appointed to office before the reduction of Guyenne had to be compensated for its loss afterwards. This continued to be the case. In 1476–1477, for example, Pierre Aubert, master of the royal household, received from the king 160 l.t. when the *prévôté* of the Ombrière was removed from him.[149] Problems also arose when the right to appoint to an office was disputed. As the years went by it was the royal rights on this score which were most likely to be eroded by such uncertainty. This was probably not the case until the death of Louis XI, who seems to have had little respect for corporate rights in matters of appointments. On his accession Louis appointed Pierre d'Acigné not only sénéchal of Périgord but also mayor of Périgueux. This drew a vigorous protest from the town. However, the king, while accepting that the office was not officially in his provision, still requested that it be given to Acigné.[150] In this case the king was apparently unsuccessful. By the end of Charles VIII's reign the position had been reversed. In 1498 a case came before the Paris

142 BN, ms. Périgord 120, 'Bailly de Razac', fo 11v; AD Dordogne, J 1385, unnumbered *cahier* [fo 19r–v].
143 BN, ms. Périgord 120, 'Bailly de Razac', fos 11v–12r.
144 AD Dordogne, 4E 123, no. 8; BN, ms. fr. 26,082, fo 627r.
145 AC Bergerac, jurade 15, 1456 [fo 16v]; AN, JJ 190, no. 28.
146 BN, ms. Périgord 120, 'Bailly de Razac', fo 13r.
147 Métivier, *Chronique*, i, 6–8.
148 J. K. Powis, *The Magistrates of the Parlement of Bordeaux c.1500–1563* [Unpublished Oxford D. Phil. Thesis, 1975; Bodleian shelf-mark; MS, D. Phil. c.1699] p. 1.
149 *Comptes du trésor 1296–1472*. ed. R. Fawtier and C. V. Langlois [*Recueil des historiens de France. Documents Financiers; ii*] (Paris, 1930) p. 178.
150 AC Périgueux, FF 185, no. 5.

parlement in which it was claimed by one of the parties that the post of lieutenant-general of the sénéchal of Guyenne was not in the appointment of the king at all but rather in that of the sénéchal. Moreover, the two parties appear to have made a transaction without reference to the king at an earlier date by which one was to enjoy the office for two years and have 200 l.t. wages, presumably in exchange for a sum of money or some other advantage.[151]

Other offices too had by the end of the period become the subject of financial transactions. In February 1492, for example, with the consent of the king and the mayor of Bordeaux, Jean de Rostaing paid 60 l.t. to Jean Jaubert for the resignation in his favour of the latter's claim to the office of man-at-arms at Bordeaux.[152] How far the venality of offices had gone it is difficult to say: concrete evidence of it in Guyenne is scarce. But perhaps financial considerations of one sort or another underlay many appointments in the province.

Two other trends in office-holding in Guyenne are more clearly discernible. First, there was that towards the multiplication of offices in response to a growing demand for royal appointments which would otherwise have been unsatisfied. The estates general of 1484 complained about the number of officers.[153] Some attempts were made to reduce their number. Louis XI abolished both the *juge-mages* and the *jugerie* de Gascogne. But in practice the temptation to increase the number of royal officers was usually irresistible. This can be seen from the increase in size of the *parlement* of Bordeaux after 1462. By 1483 the number of presidents of the parlement had increased from one to three.[154] Royal declarations in favour of administrative economy resulted in little action. The government instructed that councillors' offices be suppressed and that their resignation in favour of others of their choice be prevented in order to reduce the number of councillorships to earlier levels.[155] But by 1497 there were 100 councillors, not including the twelve seigneurs who sat as peers of France. A fourth president was now being warned that he would not be allowed to resign his office to another, because the king wanted to reduce the number of councillors.[156]

Second, there was the trend towards the treatment of office as an heritable right. Resignations in favour of members of one's own family became common among the councillors of the *parlement* during the reign of Charles VIII. Three Bordeaux councillors in 1497 were said to be serving in place of their fathers.[157] Bertrand Le Piochel had also obtained a councillorship for his son, Artus, by *survivance*, granted by special grace by Charles VIII.[158]

It was not, however, simply, or even principally, the idea of office which

151 AN, X¹ᴬ 8324, fos 419r–420r.
152 *Arch. hist. Gironde*, xiii (1871), no. xxxiv, 94–95.
153 J. Masselin, *Journal des états géneraux de France tenus à Tours en 1484 sous la régence de Charles VIII*, ed. A Bernier (Paris, 1835), p. 683.
154 Métivier, *Chronique*, i, 105–108.
155 *Ibid.*, p. 109.
156 *Ibid.*, pp. 122–25.
157 *Ibid.*, pp. 124–25.
158 *Ibid.*, p.129; ADG, 3E 86, fo 325r. For Robert de Balsac's *survivance* obtained for his son, see above, p. 31.

developed during the forty years after the fall of English Gascony to the French that served to undermine the degree of control exerted by the king over his professional servants in the province. Even more important was the web of private interests among the officers themselves which bound them and their families increasingly to the province in which they served and to the social grouping which they and their colleagues began to constitute. Those who came to the province from elsewhere in France acquired property and other connections. At the same time, families living in Guyenne provided recruits for the royal service who rose with their families to high office. Links by marriage and interests bound both to the society of Bordeaux and the seigneurial families among whom they lived.

The councillors of the Bordeaux *parlement* were well-placed to buy property in Bordeaux, and many of them did so. Raymond Guilloche, for example, had become the owner of a number of houses and other property by the time of his death in about 1487.[159] One of his houses in the parish of Saint-Pierre at Bordeaux was rented from the church of Saint-Seurin.[160] He also possessed two houses in Floirac, in Entre-Deux-Mers, and vineyards there.[161] Jean Bérard, first president of the *parlement*, purchased several adjoining houses from different individuals in the rue de Puy-Paulin and converted them into one.[162] Nor, of course, was it only councillors of the *parlement* who purchased their own houses when they came to Bordeaux. The royal proctor in the court, Pierre Baulon, in 1475 bought a house in the parish of Saint-Pierre.[163]

Other royal officers too became deeply involved in the towns to which they were posted. Agen seems to have had a tradition of absorbing outsiders easily into its affairs. Jean Dauphin's many years as royal proctor of Agenais allowed him to put down deep roots in the town.[164] He became one of the consuls of Agen; a post which he should not have held while being a royal officer.[165] In this he was, however, far from unique. Both Jean Lambard and Pierre Tort, respectively receiver and *juge-mage* of Agenais, became consuls of Agen.[166]

Still others became closely linked to noble families and connections in the province. Maitre Jacques Chaussade, councillor of the Bordeaux *parlement*, became seigneur de Calonges by marrying the daughter of Peyroton de Ganolx when Chaussade was still proctor in the court. The seigneurie was transferred to him by Ganolx – and the marriage probably also agreed – because Chaussade would be better able to defend his right to the seigneurie in law than would Ganolx, especially since it was claimed by the sire d'Albret.[167] The sire d'Albret himself required his legal advisers, and these could hardly be better chosen than from among the royal legal officers. In 1473 Etienne de Maleret, lieutenant-general

159 ADG, G 2031, unnumbered.
160 ADG, G 1161, fos 160v–161r.
161 ADG, 3E 85, fo 247v.
162 ADG, 2E 2723, unnumbered.
163 ADG, G 1161, fos 235r–236r.
164 AM Agen, BB 19, fo 6v.
165 AN, JJ 207, no. 210.
166 AM Agen, BB 7, no. 23; FF 134, unnumbered *cahier* [fo 130v].
167 ADG, G 4845, fo 11v; APA, E 93, unnumbered.

of the sénéchal of Guyenne, and Bertrand Tustal, then proctor in the sénéchaussée, were both referred to as Albret's servants.[168]

Families with interests already well-formed in the affairs of the province also
began to penetrate the ranks of the royal officers. Henri de Ferragnes, once
clerk of Bordeaux, has already been mentioned. Ferragnes became a councillor
of the *parlement* of Bordeaux, served the duke of Guyenne as councillor and
lieutenant of the sénéchal of Guyenne and became once more a councillor of
the *parlement* after its return to Bordeaux.[169] His family origins are obscure, but
by the time of his first marriage in 1465 he was already a man of property.[170] His
wealth grew by investment in property and *rentes* and probably by judicious
marriages. In 1485 Ferragnes married Madeleine de Lamothe who brought him
a dowry of 1000 livres bordelaises in *rentes* on her death and – shortly before his
own – Ferragnes arranged another profitable marriage – with Jacquette du Puy,
daughter of Hélie du Puy, seigneur de La Jarte in Périgord and a mayor of
Périgueux. Her dowry of 1000 livres bordelaises was also in part payable in
rentes.[171]

A similar career of high judicial office and involvement in the Bordelais
world of commerce and property was enjoyed by Bertrand Tustal. The Tustals of
Bordeaux may have sprung from a family of that name still influential during
the period in Sarlat.[172] Bertrand Tustal had been both lieutenant-general of the
sénéchal of Guyenne and proctor general in Périgord for the king before he
became a councillor of the Bordeaux *parlement*.[173] He was subsequently appointed one of the presidents of the *parlement*.[174] He had several houses in
Bordeaux and vineyards in Entre-Deux-Mers.[175] Bertrand Tustal's brother,
François, was a wealthy merchant of Bordeaux and one of the jurats.[176] Both
brothers were in the business of exporting wine. In 1479, for example, Bertrand
Tustal received 157 francs from a merchant of Totnes in Devon for wine he had
sold him.[177] François Tustal dealt in silk and woollen cloth and invested some
at least of his wealth in property purchased from the sire d'Albret.[178] Bertrand
Tustal was the sole heir of his brother François when the latter died in 1498 and
seems to have continued with the kind of mercantile ventures in which his late
brother had engaged.[179] He provided capital for merchants dealing in woad,
Breton and Norman cloth and silk.[180] By the time of his death in about 1508

---

168 ADG, H 240, unnumbered; APA, E 74, unnumbered.
169 Métivier, *Chronique* i, 7; BN PO 1092, 'de Fabas', no. 6; ADG, 3E 83, fos 17r–18r.
170 ADG, G 1714, unnumbered.
171 ADG, 3E 4808, fos 43r–45r, 47r–v, 146r, 270r–272v, 290r.
172 AC Périgueux, AA 13, no. 13; *Les Chroniques de Jean Tarde*, ed. G. de Gérard (Paris, 1887),
p. 196 note a.
173 *Arch. hist. Gironde*, xxvi (1888–1889), no., xxxvi, 165; ADG, H 240, no. 16; ADG 3E
6532, fo 1r–v; BN ms. fr., 25, 716, fo 9r.
174 BN, PO 2900, 'Tustal', no. 4.
175 ADG, 3E 6532, fo 1r–v; G 1256, fo 15r–v.
176 ADG, 3E 6532, fo 5r.
177 ADG, 3E 85, fo 279r.
178 ADG, 3E 6532, fos 18v, 21r; 3E 85, fo. 276v.
179 ADG, 3E 6532, fos 2v–4r.
180 *Ibid.*, fos 2v–4v.

Tustal must long have been one of the most prominent figures in Bordeaux society.[181]

Of the Bordelais families which came to play a leading role in the royal judicial and administrative service the Makanans may have been the oldest.[182] Those members of the family who remained loyal to the Valois government after the reduction of Bordeaux or who returned from exile flourished.[183] Etienne Makanan was a trusted servant of the monarchy. He became royal proctor of Guyenne, controller of the constabulary of Bordeaux, visitor of the ships arriving from England and then mayor of Bayonne.[184] When Makanan lost his post in 1492 to the seigneur de Gramont he was compensated by Charles VIII with a pension of 500 l.t. payable on the receipt of the constable of Bordeaux and a cash grant of 1,000 l.t.[185] Etienne Makanan's elder brother, Baude (or Baudinot) Makanan, married the daughter of a rich Bordeaux merchant, Thomas de Saint-Avit. She brought with her, as Saint-Avit's heiress, vineyards, mills, houses and gardens situated in and around Bordeaux, Cenon and Entre-Deux-Mers.[186]

Among the Bordeaux *parlement* councillors who invested heavily in property and *rentes* none was more prominent than Bertrand Le Piochel. Le Piochel had begun his career as clerk of the town of Libourne and then proctor of Bordeaux.[187] In 1487 he was appointed a clerical councillor of the *parlement*.[188] Le Piochel placed much of his wealth in *rentes*, purchasing them in the *graves de Bordeaux*, Saint-Medoc-en-Jalles and Entre-deux-Mers.[189] He had bought property as far away as Quercy by the time of his death.[190] He held vineyards from the hospital of Saint-André.[191] Le Poichel, like the Tustals, placed large sums with merchants, receiving a share of the profits they made. His own house was in the parish of Sainte-Eulalie; but he also bought adjoining property there too.[192] By the time of his death, shortly before February 1504, Le Piochel had probably amassed a sizeable fortune in *rentes*, merchandise and other property.[193]

Finally, in examining the penetration of members of families with strong local interests and connections into the royal official service it is worth noting that though this is most clearly demonstrated in Bordeaux, where the notarial registers provide evidence not available concerning most other areas of Guyenne, the phenomenon itself was by no means restricted to the Bordelais.

181 BN, PO 2900, 'Tustal', no. 4.
182 M. Meaudre de Lapouyade and A. Arlot de Saint-Saud, *Les Makanam, les Ayquem de Montaigne. Recherches historiques* (Bordeaux, 1943), pp. 9–12.
183 *Ibid.*, pp. 29–34, 37–47.
184 BN, PO 1810, 'Makanan', nos. 2–5.
185 BN, ms. fr. 25,717, fo 139r.
186 ADG, 3E 285, fo 74r; 3E 81, fos 1r–v, 2v, 3r–6v.
187 AC Libourne, AA 8, no. 1, fos 3r, 4r.
188 ADG, B 5, fo 118r.
189 ADG, 3E 4808, fos 102v, 115v–116r, 123r–v, 134r–v.
190 ADG, 3E 11012, fos 198v–199r.
191 ADG, 3E 4811, fo 66r–v.
192 ADG, 3E 4810, fo 84r–v.
193 ADG, 3E 11012, fo 69r–v.

In Périgord, for example, it was not only the Salignacs and Abzacs who were to provide magistrates of the Bordeaux *parlement*.[194] Etienne de La Martonie was the son of a local noble, Raymond de La Martonie, and of the daughter of the seigneur de Pompadour.[195] Etienne was appointed lieutenant-general of the sénéchal of Périgord and subsequently became a councillor of the Bordeaux *parlement*.[196] He also succeeded to the family seigneurie and continued to purchase property in the area.[197] Similarly Aymeri de Laborie was of a noble house of Sarlat.[198] He became one of the councillors of the duke of Guyenne's *grands jours*, a royal *juge-mage* of Périgord and eventually councillor in the Bordeaux *parlement*.[199]

The growth of local ties and interests among those officers who moved into Guyenne, and the penetration of local families into royal administrative and judicial office, were both cemented by marriage and by inheritance. Some of the officers and their families married into the great mercantile families of Bordeaux. The daughter of Etienne Makanan, Pérégrine, for example, married Raymond de Rostaing, bringing to this member of one of the most powerful families of Bordeaux a dowry of 600 francs bordelais.[200] Similarly two, and perhaps three, of the daughters of Bertrand Le Piochel married merchants of Bordeaux with dowries of 400 francs bordelais.[201] Others became linked by marriage to their colleagues and their families. For instance, Maître François de Proillac, himself probably son of a royal proctor of Périgord and advocate of the *parlement* of Bordeaux in 1487, married Catherine daughter of Henri de Ferragnes.[202] Bertrand Tustal married in 1484 the daughter of Maître Pierre de Pelisses who had by this time become a councillor in the *parlement*.[203] The daughter of Maître Guillaume de La Haye councillor of the Bordeaux court married François Bérard, son of the first president.[204]

Through marriages, wealth, influence and sometimes the formality of *survivances* and resignations, families which had once aspired to high office in the royal judicial and administrative service strove, often successfully, to remain there. Thus Bertrand II Tustal, who may have been Bertrand I's grandson, served as a councillor in the Bordeaux *parlement* between 1520 and 1578.[205] The La Martonies benefited from the promotion of Etienne as a councillor of the *parlement* in order to advance members of their family to be bishops of Dax, a first president of the Bordeaux *parlement* and then of that of Paris, a master of the royal household and an archdeacon of Bordeaux.[206]

---

194 See below, pp. 178, 180, 182–84.
195 BN, ms. Périgord 151, 'La Martonie', fo 2r.
196 BN, ms. n. a. fr. 23, 793, fo 79r; AN, Z^{1A} 69, fo 243r.
197 APA, E 661, fos 86r–87r.
198 BN, ms, Périgord 123, 'La Borie de Campagne', fos 1r–8r.
199 ADG, H 281, no. 1; APA, E 77, no 30.
200 ADG, 3E 4809, fos 208r–10v.
201 ADG, 3E 4808, fos 413r–14v, 476r–78r, 518r–20r.
202 BN, ms. fr. 26,082, fo 627r; ADG, 3E 4808, fo 290r–v.
203 BN, ms. fr. 25,716, fo 9r.
204 ADG, 3E 2723, unnumbered.
205 BN, PO 2900, 'Tustal', nos. 8–14.
206 BN, ms. Périgord 151, 'La Martonie', fo 2r.

Perhaps the most successful dynasty of officers of Guyenne, however, was that established by the brothers Guillaume and Jean Belcier. Guillaume became substitute of the royal proctor in Périgord.[207] Jean also became royal proctor of Périgord, and then lieutenant of the sénéchal there.[208] Guillaume's son, Jean, also followed the legal profession, becoming an advocate in the *parlement* of Bordeaux. His marriage to the daughter of Hélie du Puy seigneur de La Jarte linked his fortunes with those of a notable Périgourdin family; it also made him brother-in-law of Henri de Ferragnes.[209] Guillaume Belcier's brother, Jean, had two sons, both of whom subsequently became first presidents of the *Parlement* of Bordeaux.[210]

Officers easily became entangled in local interests not just through marriage and property but also through financial inducements. The ecclesiastical foundations of Bordeaux seem to have retained some of the king's legal officers in their interests. In February 1463, for example, a small pension of 25 sous was being paid by the chapter of Saint-Seurin to the king's advocate in the *parlement*.[211] The payment of officers' 'expenses' when they came to a town on royal business seems similarly to have served simply as a minor bribe, for expenses of officers were also paid by the royal government.[212] Presents were frequently given in kind. Wine was the most frequent gift. For example, when the president of the Bordeaux *parlement* passed through Périgueux in 1492–1493 he was given eight pints of wine.[213] At Cadillac, salmon from the Garonne were sometimes given in order to make more attractive the usual present of local wine.[214] Money and gold pieces were also often given.[215] Specially elaborate presents, such as candles and wine given to the councillors of the *parlement* by Périgueux in 1464–1465, might be used in order to gain favour in times of political tension.[216] Royal officers quickly learnt that influence should be sold dearly because the demand for its application from suitors was apparently limitless. Some, like Raymond Arnal, receiver of the *aides* of Périgord, who seems to have used some of his substantial bribes in order to expand his landed holdings around his home at Montignac, turned the use of influence on behalf of those who needed it into a fine and profitable art. For many were the individuals and communities who thought like Bergerac's jurade that someone who 'can help us when something needs to be undertaken before the king' was worthy of valuable bribes and presents.[217]

The final way in which royal officers came to establish closer links with the society of Guyenne was through promotion to benefices. Initially, of course, the

---

[207] AC Périgueux, BB 14, fo 23v.
[208] AC Périgueux, CC 88, fo 5r; FF 100, no. 1.
[209] BN, ms. Périgord 121, 'de Belcier', fo 10r; ADG, 3E 4808, fos 270r–272v.
[210] BN, ms. Périgord 121, 'de Belcier', fo 10r; APA E 657, unnumbered.
[211] ADG, G 1455, fo 64v.
[212] BN, PO 2900, 'Tustal', no. 2.
[213] AC Périgueux, CC 94, fo 15r.
[214] AC Cadillac, CC 3, fo 127v.
[215] *Comptes consulaires Montréal*, p. 92; *Comptes consulaires Riscle*, i, 76, 78.
[216] AC Périgueux, CC 88, fo 12v.
[217] AC Périgueux, CC 91, fo 23v; AC Bergerac, jurade 22, 1484–1485 [fos 22r, 27v].

acquisition of such perquisites, particularly where royal assistance was directly or indirectly invoked, might bind officers more closely to the government through gratitude: but subsequently they could become too closely involved with other interests. Because of the proximity of the Bordeaux *parlement* or *grand jours*, it was the chapter of Saint-André at Bordeaux which was most subject to requests for benefices for royal and ducal officers and their *protégés*. The canons were bombarded by a series of contradictory demands which required to be dealt with by means of the most tactful diplomacy and which were sometimes quite impossible of fulfilment. Councillors of the *parlement* were the most frequent candidates. In 1467, for example, Baudinot Makanan and Jean d'Avril, both councillors of the Bordeaux *parlement*, were elected as canons of Saint-André.[218] Another request for a canonry was made by a councillor that December.[219] Other appointments from the cathedral church of Bordeaux were sought and obtained by councillors too. For instance, the following year the councillors Jean d'Avril and Jacques Loup are referred to as the archbishop's vicars.[220] Between 1468 and 1471 the canons of Saint-André were the unfortunate subjects of a struggle for patronage from different quarters.[221] Confusion resulting from contradictory demands for benefices continued after the duke of Guyenne's death. In March 1476, for example, Louis XI ordered that Jacques de Pombilla should be received as a canon by the chapter of Saint-André after a benefice had fallen vacant.[222] Yet the following June the king demanded the previously vacant canonry for the son of a president of the Toulouse *parlement*. The chapter, which had already elected Pombilla to the benefice, faced a serious dilemma. They decided not to tell the king that the benefice was filled because this might have 'bad consequences'.[223] The demands for patronage from Bordeaux councillors continued. In 1477 Jean de Pons, a councillor of that court, was chosen as a canon.[224] Three years later the chapter had to provide a canonry for the son of the president of the Bordeaux *parlement*.[225] The church of Saint-André was, therefore, certainly providing a regular source of rewards for the royal officers. But to what extent this flow reflected the king's real intentions rather than his officers' own influence and pressure is far from clear. It is likely that at a comparatively early date, before the accession of Charles of France to the duchy, the canonical benefices of Saint-André had come to be regarded as a special perquisite of the Bordeaux *parlementaires* and their families and that they continued to be so.

By the end of Charles VIII's reign the initiative in government provided by the almost total change of administrative and judicial officers after the reduction of Guyenne was, therefore, quite rapidly being lost. The growth of officers' interests in the province undoubtedly brought with it greater political and social stability, in that it made it all the more impossible to conceive of the kind of political upheaval which would have permitted an English return. But the process also had severe drawbacks for the government. The king's servants, once they had properties and other interests in Guyenne, were less likely to

218 ADG, G 285, fos 31v, 33v.
219 *Ibid.*, fo 43v.
220 *Ibid.*, fo 47v.
221 *Ibid.*, fos 50v, 52r, 65v, 78r.

222 *Ibid.*, fo 130r.
223 *Ibid.*, fo 132v.
224 *Ibid.*, fo 140v.
225 *Ibid.*, fo 164v.

give him unconditional service. The possibility of major administrative or judicial reform, which was always unlikely, was effectively destroyed by it; for now too many had too much to lose. The links established by royal officers with members of the mercantile hierarchy of Bordeaux, with the ruling cliques of other towns and, perhaps above all – in view of the ambitions of the sire d'Albret – with the seigneurs of the province, ensured that the balance of power and wealth in society could not in future be upset by the actions of the government. Not just through policy but also through interest, government in Guyenne would henceforth be a force for conservatism.

4

The Finances of Guyenne

Insufficient evidence exists for the domain, for the yield of the customs dues or for direct taxation to permit any exact measurement of the government's success in raising money in Guyenne. But that it *was* successful is clear. Although the royal domain made a diminishing contribution to the government's finances, largely because of its alienation, the worth of the customs dues levied at Bordeaux and Bayonne grew as commerce recovered. Above all, the yield of taxation increased sharply under Louis XI and – after an interval – again under Charles VIII. Both economic revival and astute political management lay behind that.

The story is not, though, one of unalloyed royal success. The fiscal administration was unsystematic. It depended heavily on bribery and threats; and exemptions and privileges, partial or total, for various interests had to be accepted. But this was part of the price which had to be paid by a government determined to ignore or over-ride local and provincial estates in its pursuit of higher taxes without formal consent. Undoubtedly, the French government could claim by the early 1490s that it had achieved a transformation of its finances in the province and done so against remarkably little outright opposition.

Economic recovery

The success of the French government's financial policy depended heavily on Guyenne's economic revival. Both the extent of the devastation and the pace of recovery are difficult to measure. Towns, in particular, had a strong interest in exaggerating their poverty when seeking the confirmation of privileges and other advantages. On Louis XI's accession, Bayonne complained of its great desolation, the poverty of the surrounding country and the effects of plague.[1] According to the citizens of Bordeaux, their town was set in unfertile country, with poor crops insufficient to feed the *pays*. The special pleading continued. The Bordelais argued into the reign of Charles VIII that they were almost totally dependent on their vineyards, by contrast with the *haut-pays* which was 'fat and opulent', growing a variety of crops as well as producing wine. Consequently the town's exclusive privileges must be upheld.[2] At Libourne in December 1486 an elderly notary claimed that he remembered when there had been three times as many hearths there.[3] Such claims, which were frequently accompanied with dire warnings of the effect on the province's security if such

1 AN, JJ 198, nos. 419, 423.
2 AC Saint-Emilion, II 1, no. 2. fo 2r; AM Bordeaux, AA 9, AA 14.
3 AC Libourne, AA 8, no. 2, fo 29v.

vital and exposed centres fell into decay and disrepair, must be treated with caution. Although de-population and untilled land bore witness to the effects of war and although the heavy garrisoning under Charles VII brought further problems, the military reduction of the province had not itself brought great devastation.[4]

The most immediate and intractable problem for Bordeaux and other areas heavily dependent on their vineyards was the collapse of the wine trade with England. Most of the 1451 vintage was able to be exported and the trade flourished during the brief period of English rule in 1452–1453. Apart from a short period in 1455, when the king of France forbade the granting of safe-conducts to the English, exports continued, though at a much lower level than before the reduction. The most important burden was the imposition by Charles VII of a tax of 25 sous per barrel on all wines shipped from Bordeaux: this burden was considerably lightened by Louis XI, who both reduced it to 18 sous and exempted the wines of the citizens of Bordeaux from it entirely.[5] The wine trade continued, however, to be closely subject to international political tensions – nor least the alternating fortunes of the Lancastrian and Yorkist parties in England. In 1462 the trade with England ceased entirely, but began again under a régime of safe-conducts in the following year. The treaty of Picquigny marked the beginning of a serious, sustained recovery in the wine trade with England. The English could henceforth trade without safe-conducts and from 1482 they could remain and travel in and around Bordeaux freely. It was, therefore, the last quarter of the century which saw revival of the Bordeaux wine trade, though not to the level reached under English rule.[6]

The same period saw a more general restoration of Bordeaux's and probably Bayonne's commercial fortunes. English, Hanseatic, Flemish, Dutch, Spanish and Breton merchants visited both towns.[7] How much the revival of sea-born trade stimulated or just accompanied agricultural revival it is difficult to know. But a range of sources makes clear that a wider recovery was under way, at least during the last years of Louis XI's reign. With some notable exceptions, this seems to have been true of France as whole.[8] The most obvious evidence for it is provided by immigration.

Immigration flowed Westward to lands most recently affected by war. For example, immigrants from Limousin, Auvergne and Rouergue came to Quercy, while the quercinois spread West into Agenais and Périgord. In Limousin peasant families restored cultivation of untilled land.[9] In the lands of the Bordelais abbey of La Sauve-Majeure, immigrants from Périgord, Angoumois,

---

4 *Histoire de Bordeaux*, iv, 9–10.

5 *Ibid.*, p. 18; AN, JJ 198, no. 328.

6 Y. Renouard, 'Les Conséquences de la conquête de la Guienne par le roi de France pour le commerce des vins de Gascogne', A.*Midi, nouvelle série*, lxi (1948) 23–31; M. K. James, *Studies in the Medieval Wine Trade*, ed. E. M. Veale (Oxford, 1971), pp. 45–49.

7 *Histoire de Bordeaux*, iv, 21, 74–76; *Registres gascons*, ed. Ducéré, pp. 125, 137, 148, 208.

8 M. Le Mené, 'La Conjoncture économique angevine sous le règne de Louis XI', *La France de la Fin du xve siècle. Renouveau et apogée*. [Colloque international du centre national de la recherche scientifique] (Paris, 1985), pp. 51–52.

9 J. Lartigaut, *Les Campagnes du Quercy après la guerre de cent ans* (Toulouse, 1978), pp. 83–99; J. Tricard, 'Comparsonniers et Reconstruction rurale dans le sud du Limousin au xve siècle,' in

Saintonge, Poitou and Dax were offered lands to farm on attractive terms. There was also immigration into Bordeaux itself.[10]

Population growth in the South-West was not, though, just the result of immigration but also of a more general demographic revival. From towns as far away as Montréal in Condomois and Périgueux comes evidence of larger indigenous families and a diminution in the once devastating effects of recurrent plague.[11] In Périgueux there was a strong population growth from about 1480.[12]

To what extent was economic recovery the result of deliberate government policy? There is no doubt that, in constrast to the years after the reduction, Louis XI's reign saw a number of important measures favourable to commerce in the towns. Not only Bordeaux, but also Bayonne, Dax and other towns benefited from reductions in dues levied on commerce. Free fairs and markets were granted, both reflecting and seeking to stimulate economic revival.[13]

It is easy, however, to exaggerate the degree of coherence in the royal policy. Not all its aims were complementary.[14] Moreover, privileges granted to one group worked to the economic disadvantage of another, and perhaps more generally. For example, both Bordeaux and Bayonne secured the exclusion of wine – and in Bayonne's case wine and cider – not of their own production from their towns after the harvest.[15] Bayonne was to be provisioned with corn and other produce free of all dues, wherever they were collected: but this disadvantaged other towns.[16] Bordeaux and Bayonne not only benefited from reductions in royal dues under Louis XI: they were also allowed to raise dues for their own expenses.[17] In these ways, the government showed itself at least as interested in satisfying the demands of powerful and important interests as in pursuing a general policy of reducing obstacles to trade.

Yet, to what ever limited degree it encouraged economic revivial, the royal government undoubtedly benefited from it. Through the customs dues levied at Bordeaux and Bayonne and through the increase in the taxable capacity of local communities, the king had the opportunity to increase his income from the province, as long as the obstacles posed by administrative weakness, political pressure and the local and provincial estates could be overcome.

La Reconstruction après la guerre de cent ans [Actes du 104e congrès national des Sociétés savantes: Bordeaux, 1979. Section de philologie et d'histoire jusqu'à 1610] i. (Paris, 1981), 51–56.

10 *Histoire de Bordeaux*, iv, 31–36, 65.

11 M. Bordes et al., *Histoire de la Gascogne des origines à nos jours* (Roanne, n.d.), p. 115; *Comptes consulaires Montréal*, p. 52.

12 A. Higounet-Nadal, *Périgueux aux xive et xv siècles. Etude de démographie historique* (Bordeaux, 1978), pp. 132, 154–160 and chart.

13 AN, JJ 198 nos. 29, 325, 328, 343, 419, 423, JJ 210, no. 246, JJ 223, no. 7.

14 H.Dubois, 'Le Commerce de la France au temps de Louis XI' in *La France de la Fin du xve siècle*, pp. 24–29.

15 AN, JJ 198, no. 343; AM Bayonne, AA 15, fos 62v – 63r.

16 *Ibid.*, fos 37r–38r, 40r–v.

17 AN, JJ 198, nos 328, 419; AM Bayonne, CC 1, nos. 3, 16.

The domain

It was still demanded that the king should live off the ordinary revenues of his domain.[18] But by the second half of the fifteenth century this was no more realistic in Guyenne than elsewhere. Under English rule, Gascony had been worth little to the administration and only derisory sums were obtained from the ducal domain.[19] Charles VII's reduction of Guyenne brought to the government an opportunity to reverse this. However, even in these years political expediency sometimes dictated that grants of exemption from tolls and dues be made to many towns.[20] A few royal dues were abolished altogether. As a pious gesture after the fall of Bordeaux, Charles VII abolished the due called 'bourdonnage' levied on pilgrims on their way to St James of Compostella.[21] Royal piety also contributed to grants of privilege and exemption to great ecclesiastical foundations like the churches of Saint-André and Saint-Seurin at Bordeaux.[22]

The reduction of Guyenne brought an increase in royal domain revenues through confiscation, but it was difficult to keep confiscated lands in the royal hand for long. Confiscations, were reversed, like that of the Candale inheritance in 1462.[23] Yet under Charles VII there were fewer such reversals than under his successor and these were sometimes only partial. For instance, in May 1454 Bertrand de Montferrand was not granted the return of his seigneurie of Langoiran, because Charles VII intended to keep it for himself in lieu of a debt to Pierre de Montferrand, whose property was in the king's hand.[24] As a result of this policy, even towards the end of Charles VII's reign confiscated lands still made an important contribution to royal revenues. In 1459–1460 in the Landes the substantial sum of 1556 l.t. was raised from this source, 40% of that year's domain income in the sénéchaussée.[25]

More of a problem for Charles VII was the legacy of grants and promises alleged to have been made by him or by his predecessors before the conquest of Guyenne. In 1442 François de Gramont's allegiance to the Valois cause had been obtained through the grant of a generous pension. From 1451 this was assessed on the customs and dues collected at Bordeaux and Blaye. For financial and strategic reasons Gramont was later induced to exchange these rights for lands in Comminges.[26] By 1491 a further exchange had taken place and and Gramont's pension was then being paid on the customs of Bayonne.[27]

Still more delicate and politically dangerous was the question of the rights

---

[18] M. Rey, Le Domaine du roi et les finances extraordinaires sous Charles VI, 1388–1413 (Paris, 1965), p. 41.

[19] Vale, English Gascony, pp. 8–9, 203.

[20] For instance, at Bordeaux (Ordonnances, xiv, 143); at Dax (ibid., 160); and at Libourne (ibid., 161–62).

[21] BL, Add. MS 21, 411, fo 41r.

[22] Ordonnances, xv, 582–83; AD Gironde, G 338, unnumbered.

[23] See below, p. 105.

[24] Arch. hist. Gironde, xxvi (1888–1889), no. xcii, 366–68.

[25] BN, ms. fr. 11, 220, fos 51r, 54r.

[26] AN, JJ 190, no. 85.

[27] BN, ms, fr. 26, 102, fo 663r.

claimed by Charles II d'Albret. These 'rights' went back almost a century. Charles V had granted them to Arnaud-Amanieu d'Albret in 1368 in recompense for what he lost from Edward III of England when Albret appealed to the Paris *parlement* and so precipitated the re-opening of the Anglo-French struggle.[28] The Albrets, claimed Charles II, had never received the lands, revenues and pension which they were promised. The arrears of the pension alone were said to amount to the enormous sum of 520,000 francs d'or.[29] These claims were used to justify Albret's continued tenure of many royal domain rights and revenues which the royal commissioners and other royal officers wished to retrieve for the king. In October 1456 these rights consisted of no fewer than seventeen major assets – ten of them baronies – in the sénéchaussée of the Landes alone.[30] In practice, Albret had to drop his most far-reaching claims. But the king also had to accept Albret's possession of most of the disputed lands.[31] Politically such an outcome was predictable, but that did not diminish its financial implications.

In spite of such limitations upon it, Charles VII's policy towards the domain was financially successful compared with that of his successor. In 1474–1475 the constable of Bordeaux's accounts show that 'lands held in the king's hand', that is the confiscations, brought in nothing.[32] On Charles VIII's accession an estimate was drawn up of the worth of royal domain lands and rights alienated by his father. One must allow for the tendency of royal officers to maximise the king's claims. Yet even so the figure of 41,400 l.t. for alienations in Bordelais, Bazadais and the Landes is sufficiently impressive.[33]

Alienations of the domain were undertaken by Louis XI for a number of motives. By the agreement reached with Edward IV of England at Picquigny in 1475, Louis agreed to receive back the seigneur de Duras into the French obedience and granted him the royal domain lands of Blanquefort and Villandraut.[34] Other grants were pious donations. In May 1483 the king granted to his new college of the Saint-Esprit at Bayonne the revenues of the *prévôtés* of Bayonne, Dax and Saint-Sever, half of the 'great custom' of Bayonne, the royal tithes of Saint-Macaire and other sources of income.[35] He gave the seigneurie of Badefols and 4000 l.t. *rentes* to the monastery of Cadouin in Périgord, specially favoured because of its possession of the '*saint suaire*'.[36]

However, most of Louis XI's grants were motivated by the needs of domestic politics. Alain d'Albret's loyalty was secured by important gifts of lands.[37] The king's favoured servants dug their hands deep into domain revenues. On Louis XI's death, Odet d'Aydie, comte de Comminges, was enjoying the profits of the

28 E. Perroy, *La Guerre de Cent Ans* (Paris, 1945), pp. 133–35.
29 BN, mss. Doat 219, fos 113v–15r; 226, fos 253r–58v; APA, E 84 bis, no. 1, fo 16v.
30 APA, E 229, unnumbered *cahier* [fos 5r–6r].
31 APA, E 89, fo 5r.
32 BN. ms. fr. 11, 220, fo 32v.
33 BN, ms. fr. 20, 498, fos 68r–69v.
34 BL, Add. MS. 21, 411, fos 40r, 41r.
35 APA, G 84, pp. 8–11.
36 J. Maubourguet, 'Le Suaire de Cadouin', *B.Soc. hist. archéol. Périgord* (1936), 355–56.
37 BN, ms. fr. 1219, fo 344r.

royal salt *grenier* at Libourne and Etienne Makanan had the *prévôté* of La Réole. Among other sources of income, Guillaume de Soupplainville, who with the Aydie brothers had now gained virtual control of patronage and power in the South-West, had been granted all the profits of justice in the Landes, worth 700 or 800 l.t. a year.[38]

Much of the only major aquisition of domain lands through confiscation, the Armagnac inheritance, was also quickly alienated to the king's servants.[39] Even before Jean V comte d'Armagnac's death, alienations of the Armagnac domain had begun. For instance, in 1467 the duc de Bourbon was granted the revenues of the comté of Isle-Jourdain.[40] In the same year Imbert de Batarnay received the profits from the *franc-fief* and *nouvaux acquêts* dues in the lands of the late duc de Nemours and those of his cousin Jean V.[41] In February 1471 Robert de Balsac received the Armagnac seigneurie of Clermont-Soubiran, which may possibly have served as an incentive for Balsac to ensure that Jean V would not live to recover it.[42] After Jean V's death, Balsac was also given the comte's share of the seigneurie of Astaffort in Agenais.[43] With confirmation of the death of Jean V, the alienations of domain to those in positions of influence multiplied. The seigneur de Beaujeu received the comté of Armagnac, though without the title of comte.[44] Armagnac lands in Rouergue and elsewhere were alienated to Imbert de Batarnay and Balsac's brother, Ruffec.[45] The vicomte de Narbonne was granted Rivière from among the Armagnac domains and, from the inheritance of the duc de Nemours, the comté of Pardiac and the seigneurie of Monlezun.[46]

Charles of France's tenure of the duchy of Guyenne led to more alienations to those favoured by the duke. When local receivers were reluctant to hand over such important seigneuries as Duras, or the ducal *chambre des comptes* refused to ratify grants, their opposition was over-ridden.[47] On the duke's death, Louis XI appointed Pierre Morin, Charles's former *trésorier-général*, to inquire into past alienations.[48] But the political difficulties of effective resumption were considerable and probably little was achieved.

The accession of Charles VIII marked only a temporary reversal of the trend towards alienation of the domain. Resumption of all domain lands was ordered by the government on 22 September 1483 and 29 December 1484. The *chambre des comptes* was not to verify royal letters of donation submitted after the resumption of 1483.[49] But exemptions multiplied; neither resumption was

---

[38] BN, ms. fr. 20, 498, fos 68r–69v.
[39] Samaran, *Maison d'Armagnac*, pp. 223–27; BN, mss fr. 2902, fo 19r; 2905, fo 102r.
[40] BN, PO 94, 'Armagnac, comtes de', no. 316.
[41] BN, ms. fr. 2902, fo 3r.
[42] AN, X^{1A} 8607, fos 30v–31v.
[43] *Ibid.*, fos 12v–13r.
[44] BN, PO 94, 'Armagnac, comtes de', nos. 271, 317, 320.
[45] Samaran, *Maison d'Armagnac*, pp. 224–25 and notes 1–5.
[46] AN, X^{1A} 8607, fo 2v.
[47] *Arch. hist. Gironde*, xxv (1887), no. v, 15–16, 21–22.
[48] BL, Add. MS. 21, 411, fo 40r.
[49] Pélicier, *Gouvernement de la dame de Beaujeu*, p. 91 n. 3; *Lettres de Charles VIII*, ed. Pélicier, i (Paris, 1898), no. xiv, 20–21.

effective. By June 1491 important seigneuries and lands once of the royal domain in Guyenne were in the hands of powerful opponents whom it would be difficult to dislodge, such as the queen of Navarre and the comte de Candale.[50] When a survey of royal domain in Guyenne was prepared in May 1494 it may have been with a further resumption in mind.[51] But in October that year, in order to pay for his Italian venture, Charles VIII ordered his domain assets in the kingdom to be mortgaged to the extent of 120,000 écus.[52]

Alienation was not the only cause of the dwindling of royal domain revenues in Guyenne. Bad management also contributed. Overall control was vested in the *trésorerie* of Languedoïl-Guyenne.[53] In practice it was up to the local *trésoriers*, or ordinary receivers, to make most decisions. There was one for each sénéchaussée in the province except, apart from the early years, for that of Guyenne. There the constable of Bordeaux managed the ordinary revenues.[54] The Armagnac lands were also a special case when under royal control. In 1460–1461 Guy Filleul, already ordinary receiver of Agenais, was appointed as receiver general for those Armagnac lands in 'Gascogne'.[55]

Sovereign jurisdiction over disputes arising from the domain was in principle the preserve of the *cour du trésor* at Paris, though in practice no evidence of appeals from the South-West survives.[56] Royal letters, however, specified that disputes should be heard there.[57] The Bordeaux *parlement* also claimed to exercise rights of jurisdiction in matters of the domain and this conflict must have weakened the Paris court's influence.[58]

It was a frequent cry that 'reform' of the domain was needed.[59] Special commissions were issued for this purpose. Charles VII's important commission of 1455 had this among its responsibilities.[60] Such commissioners operating on a local basis remained a regular feature of life in the *pays*. For instance, an isolated domain commissioner turned up to 'reform' the domain at Montréal in 1456.[61] Other princes, like the Albrets, used similar officers.[62]

The exact purpose of such commissions varied. Sometimes they sought to bring back royal, ducal or seigneurial lands and rights into the domain; sometimes they were just a prelude to an attempt to farm out anew all *bailies, prévôtés*

[50] BN, ms. fr. 26, 102, fo 665r.

[51] BL, Add. MS. 21, 411, fos 40r–41v.

[52] BN, ms. fr. 21, 486, fos 1r–2r.

[53] G. Dupont-Ferrier, *Les Officiers royaux des bailliages et des sénéchaussées et les institutions monarchiques locales en France à la fin du Moyen âge* [Bibl. Ec. Hautes Etudes, cv] (Paris, 1902), p. 537.

[54] Dupont-Ferrier, *Gallia regia*, i, 23–24, 137–138; *ibid.*, iii, 451,518; *ibid.*, iv, 426–27.

[55] BN, PO 94, 'Armagnac, comtes de', fos 314r, 317r.

[56] G. Dupont-Ferrier, *Les Origines et le premier siècle de la cour du trésor* [Bibl. Ec. Hautes Etudes, cclxvi] (Paris, 1936), pp. 25–26, 29. The Archives nationales series would be Z^{lf}.

[57] *Arch. hist. Gironde*, xvii (1877), no. xxxi, 209–11.

[58] AD Gironde, B l, fo 13v.

[59] G. Tholin, 'Le Livre de raison de Bernard Gros, commandeur du temple de Breuil en Agenais sous Louis XI et Charles VIII', *B. hist. phil. Com. Trav. hist. sci.* (1889), 123.

[60] For other work of this commission, See below p. 80.

[61] *Comptes consulaires Montréal*, p. 77.

[62] APA, E 214, unnumbered, E 659, unnumbered.

and other offices.[63] Moreover, commissioners in the South-West on other business were expected to report to Paris, as did those of 1462, analysing the value of domain revenues for the forthcoming year.[64]

The long-term failure of such commissions can be attributed to several causes. First, attempts to take back lands and rights into the royal or ducal hand were vigorously resisted. The government's political reliance upon many of those who were the worst offenders, like the sires d'Albret and comtes de Candale, meant that major disappropriation was impracticable. The duke of Guyenne similarly tried and failed. Those occupying ducal lands and rights in Agenais alone in October 1469 included the greatest figures of the *pays*, like the seigneurs de Montpezat, Lustrac, Biron, Estissac, Albret and Caumont. With some resistance to ducal demands was judicial, with others violent.[65]

Second, ignorance was a major problem. Paradoxically, this was partially the result of an excess of information, but of information which was out of date. The constable of Bordeaux's accounts of 1474–1475 were compared with others of 1307 and perhaps earlier to find out what had been alienated.[66] Five registers of homages compiled in the 1450s, but in fact referring to the circumstances of English rule, were passed on to Etienne Makanan, when he became constable of Bordeaux in September 1475.[67]

This concentration on out of date information meant that time and energy were wasted in investigating assets which had long since become worthless or indeed ceased to exist altogether. In 1475 some royal assets, like the dovecot at Libourne, had been destroyed 'for a long time'.[68] A similar lack of realism affected the analysis of royal lands. Most 'alienated' lands had by then been held by their possessors so long that, like the Albret tenure of Puynormand, they were said to be 'by inheritance'.[69] In 1494 it had still not been grasped that the *jugerie de Gascogne* had long since become amalgamated with the séné-chaussée of Guyenne.[70] The rigidity of royal claims meant that though time might not run against the king, it did not run for him either. It seems, more-over, that when assets were isolated as being worthless, as with rents in Agenais in 1471–1472, nothing was done to improve them.[71] Very rare are cases of real capital investment in domain assets.[72]

This gloomy picture of alienated and mismanaged resources needs, however, several important qualifications. First, there is a sense in which the domain was there to be alienated, though this was not explicitly recognised. Under Charles VII, it has been argued, only about 50,000 l.t. was raised annually from the royal domain compared with 1,200,000 l.t in direct taxation.[73] The increase in

[63] AM Bordeaux, ms. 208, no. 55.
[64] BN, ms. fr. 20, 487, fo 30r.
[65] *Arch. hist. Gironde*, v. (1863), no. clviii, 344–45, 351, 354–55.
[66] BN, ms. fr. 11, 220, fo 28r.
[67] BN, ms. fr. 26, 095, fo 1456r.
[68] BN, ms. fr. 11, 220, fo 28r.
[69] *Ibid.*, fo 28r–v.
[70] BL, Add. MS. 21, 411, fo 40r.
[71] BN, ms. fr. 11, 219, fo 342r.
[72] For a rare exception in Labourt, BN, ms. fr. 26, 102, fo 592r.
[73] R. Gandilhon, *Politique économique de Louis XI* (Paris, 1941), p. 294.

taxation under Louis XI in Guyenne, as elsewhere, furthered this trend.[74] The domain was becoming less important as a source of revenue and more important as a means of rewarding those of whom the king, for pressing political reasons, had need. To that extent its function had changed.

Second, some 'alienation' was not just politically, but also financially, justifiable. Domain revenues were used as security to raise loans. For example in 1462 Louis XI granted Carolle d'Anglade the royal salt revenues of Agen and other places in Agenais for a loan of 7,000 écus d'or.[75] Revenues of this sort were also formally incorporated among the perquisites of administrative and military office and paid in lieu of or as part of wages. For instance, the seigneur de La Rochefoucauld held the *bailie* of Bergerac as an attribute of the captaincy of the town in 1468–1469.[76]

Third, though kings and dukes might irresponsibly override opposition from their own *chambre des comptes* and *trésor*, there were other diverse and important interests which were hostile to the permanent alienation of royal assets. Towns were vigorous in their demands to be regarded as inalienable parts of the royal domain and this was a privilege frequently granted to them.[77] At Bergerac in 1464 and 1466 rumours that the king had granted away the town provoked consternation.[78] Sometimes, as at Lectoure in 1486–1487, a town could prove more royalist in this regard than the royal officers.[79] Among local interests opposed to permanent alienations were also those who regularly farmed royal revenues. To judge from those who farmed tolls and other domain profits in Périgord these were often articulate people of some local importance, royal and town officers, notaries and lawyers.[80]

The most important qualification to the picture of dwindling royal ordinary revenues is the consideration that in this the king was not alone. Indeed, compared with most of his leading subjects he was better placed. Surviving evidence suggests that the ordinary revenues of towns were usually inadequate to conduct their business. At Périgueux, Bergerac, Cadillac and Montréal, for instance, *tailles* were frequently raised for the town's needs.[81]

Still more suggestive, however, is the comparison to be made with the exploitation of domain rights by the Albrets and Armagnacs. The comté of Périgord and vicomté of Limousin, which Alain d'Albret acquired through marriage, were heavily pledged and alienated. Françoise de Bretagne's guardians complained that the comté of Périgord was thus only worth 600 l.t. a year.[82] Some progress was made under Alain's control. In 1471 the comté and vicomté were said to be worth 3,300 l.t.[83] When money was available, as it was after

74 *Ibid.*, p. 295.
75 BN, ms. fr. 1219, fo 354v.
76 *Ibid.*, fo 359v.
77 For instance, see *Ordonnances*, xiv, 171–76.
78 AC Bergerac, jurade 17, 1463–1464, fo 46r.
79 *Lettres de Charles VIII*, ed. Pélicier, v, no. mlxxxviii, 204–205.
80 BN, mss fr. 26, 080, fo 6474r; 26, 088, fo 81r; 26, 092, fo 826r.
81 For instance, AC Périgueux, CC 90, fos 29r–42v; AC Bergerac, jurade 15, 1456–1457 [fos 19v–25v]; AC Cadillac, CC 3, 1463–1465, fos 55r, 61r; *Comptes consulaires Montréal*, p. 89.
82 APA, E 74, unnumbered, E 653, no. 31.
83 APA, E 650, fos 38v, 43r.

Alain d'Albret's return to the royal allegiance in 1490, domain lands were re-purchased and new land aquired.[84] But this was infrequent; and in 1495, when an investigation was made in order to estimate the worth of the Albret domain, its unhealthy state was revealed. Cash receipts from the Albret lands in 'Gascogne' (the Landes, Bazadais, Gaure and Armagnac) should have been about 15,200 l.t. a year.[85] But the revenues from Gaure and Amargnac were at best unreliable. Moreover, important sums were pledged to Albret's family and servants, while other assets were the subject of legal actions. 14% of Albret's revenues in Périgord were alienated.[86]

It was, in fact, upon grants of taxation that Albret was now increasingly relying to maintain his income. Compared with perhaps 12,200 l.t. voted to him in his 'Gascon' lands alone, Albret's ordinary revenues totalled about 13,815 l.t.[87] In other words, he was relying almost equally upon ordinary and extraordinary receipts. The balance of importance still inclined financially to ordinary revenue for the sire d'Albret, whereas for the king it had decisively shifted towards direct taxation. But for Albret too it had ceased to be possible to rely upon domain revenues to finance the role which ambition and necessity led him to play upon the political stage.

Equally instructive in a different way is the comparison of the royal domain with that of the comtes d'Armagnac. The conclusion from it is clear. When they were under royal control the Armagnac lands were better administered than when they were in the hands of the comtes themselves or other princes.

The Armagnac accounts for 1454–1455 reveal that the comte's domain was in a sorry state. The accounts themselves were incomplete. Revenues were pledged for long periods or were worthless. Dues were not being paid and other courts were unsurping comital jurisdictions.[88]

In June 1455, however, Jean V d'Armagnac fled before an invading royal army and was not restored till 11 October 1461. This led to an improvement in book-keeping methods and general administration. Totals appeared in the accounts and estimates began to be given for the value of revenues in kind. Justice became profitable.[89] In 1460–1461, before Jean V returned, the receipts of Armagnac brought in 7,186 l.t. Very few revenues were entirely alienated.[90]

Jean V's restoration meant a worsening of standards of administration. In Fezensaguet in 1462–1463 thirteen assets were worthless for unspecified reaons.[91] The receipts of Éauzan for the following year are incomplete.[92] In 1475 the expenses in the account for Cazaubon and Mauléon were improperly drawn up.[93] The same deficiencies – worthless assets and poor accounting –

---

[84] APA, E 657, unnumbered.
[85] APA, E 89, fos 6r–106r.
[86] Ibid., fos 14r–Vv, 104r, 106r, 110r, 114r.
[87] Ibid., fos 6r–106r.
[88] AD Tarn-et-Garonne, A 284 [fos 1r, 9r, 25r].
[89] AD Tarn-et-Garonne, A 285, cahier [fos 1r–12r].
[90] BN, ms. fr. 24, 057, fos 14v–16v.
[91] AD Tarn-et-Garonne, A 286, unnumbered cahier [fo 3r].
[92] AD Tarn-et-Garonne, A 280.
[93] AD Tarn-et-Garonne, A 288 [fo 14v].

were present in 1481 when Pierre de Beaujeu had control of the comté of Armagnac.[94]

In 1484 Alain d'Albret gained control of the comté. In the following year instead of detailed accounts being drawn up, the revenues were farmed out *en bloc* to a few wealthy *entrepreneurs*. Albret ruthlessly exploited what the exercise brought in to reward his allies and associates. Albret's councillors' wages were paid with the Armagnac revenues at the expense of the local officers, many of whom went without their salaries.[95] No accounts survive to show how the royal administration dealt with the problems with which Albret's removal that year must have left it. However, in 1487–1488 the Armagnac inheritance as a whole was once more making a substantial contribution to royal revenues. It brought in almost 20,000 l.t.[96]

The sparsity of royal domain accounts for the other ordinary receipts of Guyenne makes the Armagnac records invaluable. They suggest that though the shortcomings of the methods used in managing the royal domain helped render it of diminishing financial importance to the crown, the standards of administration and control applied to it were higher than those employed by the king's leading subjects.

Yet if the royal domain in Guyenne had consisted exclusively of territorial rights and revenues it would have been of little worth. But that was not the case. Under English rule the customs had proved a far more important source of revenue.[97] How the French king set about exploiting this income was, therefore, crucial to his domain finances.

Charles VII intended fully to draw upon the mercantile wealth of Bordeaux and Bayonne. He imposed heavy fines on both, though these were partly remitted.[98] As a long-term measure he revolutionised the customs collected in both cities. He ordered that at Bordeaux, in place of the old customs like the custom of Royan, those of Blaye and Mortagne, the custom of Cordouan, '*quillage*' and other dues, new ones should be imposed.[99] This was done with the consent of the estates of the Bordelais. In exchange for the king's remitting 60,000 of the 100,000 écus fine imposed on the city and promising not to raise *tailles* and other taxes there, the Bordelais agreed to the move.[100] 25 sous per ton would henceforth be levied on wine exported by burgesses and outsiders alike, while 12 d.t. per pound would be raised on other goods, with certain named exceptions.[101]

At Bayonne a due called the *cize* and another separate due on iron had been levied under English rule. These revenues had gone to the town's own funds.[102] As with Bordeaux, the king relied upon a mixture of compulsion and consent

94   AD Tarn-et-Garonne, A 289 [fos 1r–39v].
95   AD Tarn-et-Garonne, A 290, unnumbered *cahier*, pp. 9, 12–15.
96   BN, ms. Doat 225, fo 241r.
97   Vale, *English Gascony*, Table 6, p. 237.
98   *Ordonnances*, xiv, 272; AM Bayonne, AA 7, no. 4.
99   BN, mss fr. 23, 915, fos 62v, 66r; 11, 220, fo 35r.
100 BN, ms. fr. 23, 915, fo 65v.
101 *Ordonnances*, xiv, 273.
102 AM Bayonne, AA 15, fos 76r–77r; CC 1, no. 16, fo 67r–v.

to impose the new customs dues. At the request of Bayonne he agreed to abolish the *cize* and iron due, which he had taken into the royal domain, and imposed 25 s.t. per ton on wine and 12 d.t. per pound on other goods, as at Bordeaux.[103]

As with the matter of domain lands, Louis XI pursued a more liberal policy than his father. Yet as far as the customs were concerned his concessions were more apparent than real. They certainly must have appeared striking enough. The 12 d.t. due was not to be levied on burgesses of Bordeaux and that of 25 s.t, which was reduced to 18 s.t, was not to be payable on wine from their own vineyards.[104] For a brief period Bordeaux was allowed to raise half of the 12 d.t. on foreigners for its own use. Later, the ending of the need for safe-conducts for foreign vessels and the revival of trade allowed this royal concession to be withdrawn.[105] Louis XI pursued a similar policy towards Bayonne. In May 1462 the king granted Bayonne the right to levy half the 12 d.t. due for its own purposes and this was confirmed by Charles VIII.[106]

The real loss to the royal domain of such concessions was, however, much less than might be imagined. There were two reasons to this. First, royal and ducal officers continued to levy old dues which had ostensibly been abolished, even when new ones had been instituted. In 1474–1475 the ancient customs of Bordeaux, which Charles VII had ordered to cease, were still making the important contribution to the constable of Bordeaux's receipts of 5,785 l.t.[107] At Bayonne where half of the 12 d.t. due should have been going to the town, only one sixth in fact was doing so, at least in the first part of Louis XI's reign. The rest was being levied for the king. In order words, the old 4 d. *cize* due was still being raised by the royal officers.[108]

Second, the revival of trade with England increased the value of the customs of Bordeaux and Bayonne to the king during the last quarter of the fifteenth century.[109] The constable of Bordeaux's accounts only survive for 1474–1475. But the effect of the Picquigny agreement of 1475 and its commercial counterpart in January the following year is apparent from a comment at the end of the accounts. It was there remarked that the customs dues were already worth much more than in 1474–1475 at the time of the drawing up of the accounts.[110]

The 1474–1475 receipts of the constable of Bordeaux show that 14,571 l.t. was received in that year from the ordinary royal revenues in Guyenne proper and in Bazadais. Of that, the Bordeaux customs contributed 63%.[111] The evidence for the worth of the Bayonne customs is scantier. In 1491, when Roger de Gramont was receiving half of it as his pension, the 12 d.t. due at Bayonne

---

[103] AM Bayonne, AA 15, fos 76r–77v; CC 1, no. 16, fo 67r–v.
[104] BL, Add. MS. 21, 411, fo 41v; *Livre des privilèges*, ed. Barckhausen, no. i, pp. 3–11; AN, JJ 198, no. 328.
[105] BL, Add. MS. 21, 411, fo 41v; BN, ms. fr. 23, 915, fos 67r, 68r; *Livre des privilèges*, ed. Barckhausen, no. ii, pp. 16–19; *Recueil des privilèges*, ed. Gouron (Bordeaux, 1937), pp. 127–28.
[106] AM Bayonne, AA 15, fo 77r–v; CC 1, fo 67r–v.
[107] BN, ms. fr. 11, 200, fo 35r.
[108] AM Bayonne, CC 1, no. 2.
[109] See above p. 48.
[110] BN, ms. fr. 11, 200, fo 35r. The date at which the accounts were drawn up is not given.
[111] *Ibid.*, fos 27r, 34v–35r, 40r.

would have been worth 4000 l.t. a year to the king. The rest of the domain revenues in the Landes for 1459–1460, the only surviving accounts for the area, show receipts of 3,769 l.t. in cash.[112] Even allowing for an increase in the value of the Bayonne customs between 1460 and 1491, this evidence suggests that customs receipts were even more important as a proportion of the Landes ordinary revenues than for those of Guyenne proper and Bazadais.

The financial importance of the customs levied at Bordeaux and Bayonne helped to determine royal policy in Guyenne towards ordinary and extraordinary revenues. It meant that alienation of the territorial domain was even more tempting. For whereas to manage domain lands was difficult and the political advantages of alienating them to important figures were great, the customs continued to bring in their income reliably as long as trade continued to flourish. It also meant that there was no real need to impose direct taxation in the sénéchaussée of Guyenne, for the customs had all the merits of taxation without the disadvantages: that is, they increased as the overall value of taxable wealth increased, yet their collection was not subject to consent by local assemblies.

The monarchy had a further source of ordinary revenue derived from the exploitation of feudal rights. Some of these, associated with the receipt of homages, were trivial or just symbolic. A mark of silver, for instance, was paid by Gilbert de Chabannes annually, as a recognisance for the seigneurie of Curton. A pair of gloves was given annually to the king by Guillaume de Lansac for a house he held.[113]

Far from insignificant, however, was the levy of fines and compositions for *francs-fiefs* and *nouveaux acquêts*.[114] There is evidence of only three attempts to collect these dues in Guyenne during the period, in the 1460s, in 1483–1484, and in the early 1490s. As was the case with direct taxation, the monarchy ran up against claims of exemption. The sire d'Albret, as vicomte de Limousin, claimed that his subjects by ancient right need not pay the dues, though this was strongly contested by the *franc-fief* commissioners of Louis XI.[115] Even more troublesome were the exemption claims of the towns. Charles VII and Louis XI granted the inhabitants of Bordeaux the right to acquire noble fiefs without paying fines.[116] The Bordelais also claimed exemption on the grounds that their lands were held in allod, not by feudal tenure. Other less important towns like Sarlat and Agen also gained exemption.[117] Once confirmed, such grants created precedents which it would be difficult for the commissioners to overcome and which would even apply to citizens of an exempt town holding property in other sénéchaussées.[118]

---

112 BN, mss fr. 26, 102, fo 663r, 11, 220, fo 51v.

113 BN, ms. fr. 11,220, fo 27r.

114 Dupont-Ferrier, *Les Officiers royaux*, pp. 568–70.

115 APA, E 652, unnumbered *cahier* [fos 1v–2r]; Luchaire, *Alain d'Albret*, pp. 169–73.

116 *Recueil des privilèges*, pp. 90–91.

117 AC Saint-Emilion, II 9, fo 12v. For tenure '*in allodio*', see R. Boutruche, *Une Société provinciale en lutte contre le régime féodal: l'alleu en Bordelais et en Bazadais du xie au xviiie siècle* (Rodez, 1943), pp. 19–22.

118 AM Agen, AA 13, no. 2.

However, under the determined harassment of special commissioners appointed to investigate *francs-fiefs*, few such privileges were entirely secure. Detailed instructions were issued in the commissions prescribing the amount of composition to be demanded from clergy and townsmen based on the value of the property and its length of tenure. Those for Saint-Emilion of 1492 show that even *roturiers* who had been nobles for forty years since they had acquired the land in question had to pay.[119]

In the sénéchaussée of Guyenne the fact that Bordeaux was the most important party in the negotiations as to what would be paid to the commissioners made a mockery of the 'feudal' nature of the dues. In January 1484 the king ordered that the nobles of the sénéchaussée should be forced to pay their share of the 6,500 l.t. composition which had been made. Not surprisingly this was resisted and more than ten years later the sum had still not been fully paid.[120]

If a city so well-endowed with privilege as Bordeaux could be forced to pay a composition for *francs-fiefs*, other towns had good reason to be apprehensive. In July 1464, expecting the worst, the jurade of Bergerac decided to reach a quick composition with the commissioners. In pursuit of this policy they agreed to pay 500 l.t.[121] They were luckier than Périgueux. In November the commissioners demanded more than 3000 écus there.[122]

From the patchy evidence available it seems that the *franc-fief* and *nouveaux acquêts* dues provided a valuable addition to royal domain revenues. There was no temptation to alienate them. They were relatively simple and cheap to collect. Above all, unlike other domain rights, they were well fitted to supplement military and fiscal demands in royal attempts to extort money from the towns.

The landed domain was, then progressively subject to alienation, particularly under Louis XI, Charles of France and Charles VIII. Inefficient management of assets remaining to the king or duke further reduced their value. However, to some extent the function of the domain was political, not just financial, and this became more so during the period. Moreover, in spite of concessions by Louis XI and his successors, the customs dues of Bordeaux and Bayonne provided a crucial and growing addition to the duchy's ordinary revenues. This was supplemented by sums raised through the exploitation of feudal rights. Compared with those of towns and nobles, the king's domain receipts were relatively valuable and well managed.

The evidence which survives of the finances of Guyenne suggests that perhaps about 40% of total royal income in the province in any year would derive from ordinary revenues and the rest from taxation. If the contribution made by the customs of Bordeaux and Bayonne were deducted from total ordinary income, the importance of domain revenue in a year in which taxation was levied is reduced much further. That is why it was the king's ability to raise ever larger sums from direct taxation which was to prove the most important source of the government's financial strength.

---

119 AC Saint-Emilion, II 1, unnumbered.
120 *Registres de la jurade*, pp. 313–14.
121 AC Bergerac, jurade 17, 1463–1464, fos 49r–v, 55r–56r.
122 AC Périgueux, CC 88, fo 14r.

Taxation

In matters of taxation, as of domain finances, Guyenne was awkwardly dependent upon more than one authority. Between 1476 and 1479 the province was under the control of the *général* of Languedoïl.[123] However, by 1483 'Aquitaine' was a *généralité* – one of six in the kingdom – and included Guyenne, Armagnac, Foix, Agenais, Périgord, Quercy and Rouergue.[124] For most purposes over-all authority was vested in the Paris *chambre des comptes*. But in August 1456 the administration of salt dues and matters relating to their collection was stated to be the prerogative of the *chambre des comptes* of Languedoc.[125]

Some tax demands treated the whole South-West as one large unit; in 1480–1481 a levy of *taille* was imposed upon 'Gascogne'. This included Agenais, Armagnac, the comté of Comminges, Bigorre, the Landes, Condomois, Gaure and Bazadais, in fact all of South-West France, except Guyenne proper.[126] More usually demands were made upon specific *pays*.[127] The little evidence which survives shows that at different times there were specific receipts-general for Guyenne-Bazadais (under the constable of Bordeaux), for Agenais, for Condomois, and for Armagnac.[128]

The same confusion characterised the administration of fiscal justice. For Périgord, the sovereign court to which appeals concerning taxation were supposed to go was the *cour des aides* at Paris. The rest of Guyenne was probably officially attached to the *cour des aides* of Languedoc, although there is no evidence of cases from the province being heard there.[129]

Taxation was imposed and levied by *élus* in only two sénéchaussées in Guyenne. Périgord had been incorporated into the Languedoïl fiscal system from 1453, though it was first formally referred to as an *élection* in September 1483.[130] In December 1474 Louis XI appointed two *élus* for the Landes, one at Dax and one at Saint-Sever, to impose taxes and hear disputes, in place of the commissioners who previously performed these functions. This was justified on the grounds that the old system had been oppressive.[131] The receipt-general of the constable of Bordeaux remained outside the system; for it was understood from the second reduction of Bordeaux that, in principle, no tax would be

123 G. Dupont-Ferrier, *Les Elections et leur personnel [Etudes sur les institutions de la France à la fin du Moyen âge, i]* (Paris, 1930), Appendix iii, p. 265.
124 Masselin, *Journal*, pp. 68, 70.
125 AD Hérault, 1B 13, fo 56r–v.
126 AM Agen, CC 44, unnumbered *cahier*, fos 1r–4r.
127 AN, K 73, no. 52; K 74, no. 17; K 76, no. 9; AM Agen, CC 44, unnumbered, fo 1r; BN, ms. fr. 21, 425, fos 7r, 8r.
128 BN, mss fr. 11, 220, fo 40r; 23, 915, fo 79r; 24, 057, fo 12r; AN, K 74, no. 17.
129 G. Dupont-Ferrier, *Les Origines et le premier siècle de la chambre ou cour des aides [Nouvelles Etudes sur les institutions financières de la France à la fin du Moyen âge, i]* (Paris, 1933), pp. 64–65, 67.
130 J. Maubourguet, *Sarlat et Le Périgord méridional*, iii (Paris, 1930), 17 n. 80. For a similar process in Auvergne, Limousin and La Marche, see A. Thomas, *Les Etats provinciaux de la France centrale sous Charles VII*,i (Paris 1877), 165–69.
131 BN, ms. fr. 25,715, fo 222r.

levied there.[132] The other *pays* of the province were *pays à commissaires*, subject to *ad hoc* fiscal and other demands by specially appointed commissioners.[133]

In practice, however, one basic system of taxation prevailed throughout the province, outside the sénéchaussées of Guyenne and Bazadais. The men of Sarlat stated in February 1474 that in Périgord an 'equivalent' was imposed on the pays in place of *aides*.[134] This was also the case elsewhere. Neither *aides* nor *gabelle* were, in principle, collected in the province. Moreover, all distinction between the different sorts of taxation had become blurred and all, voted by assembly or imposed just by royal *fiat*, were known as *tailles* and theoretically based upon an assessment of hearths.

Who paid tax? The answer is: those who were not able to substantiate a claim to exemption. In this regard, the style and content of royal tax imposi- tions varied. Louis XI's tax demands recognised in principle no exemptions at all. In 1478, for example, a demand for 1300 l.t. with 50 l.t. *'frais'* was to be levied on everyone in Périgord, exempt and non-exempt, privileged and unpri- vileged.[135] Charles VIII's tax demands, as in 1495, specified who the 'exempt' were. Churchmen, those too old to bear arms, those already in the royal army, nobles and ordinary officers of the royal family and princes of the blood, students residing at university and beggars were the categories mentioned.[136] There is little evidence as to the success or failure or exemption claims made by those of the *plat pays*. It is clear, however, that the great nobles of the province strongly resisted the payment of taxes and royal dues by their subjects, though probably with little and decreasing success.

In May 1457 Charles VII confirmed the Albret subjects in their exemption from taxation throughout the realm. But in October 1459 the *aide* imposed in the Landes for the building of castles at Bayonne, Dax and Saint-Sever was ordered to be levied on the Albret subjects like those of the king 'without prejudice' to their privileges.[137] The lingering doubt about their position as tax payers was reflected in local assemblies. In 1463, for instance, 2550 l.t. was imposed upon 'the seigneuries and lands of Albret which are accustomed to contribute to the building [of the castles]'.[138]

Given the opportunity, nobles continued to order their subjects not to pay. The donations made to Philippe de Savoie when he became governor of Guyenne were, after his resignation, taken into the king's hand. But the sire d'Albret, the seigneur de Montferrand and the comte de Candale all forbade contributions in their lands.[139]

It is hard to be sure about the relationship between demands made on towns and those on the rest of the pays. But whenever they failed to secure exemp- tion, the towns were likely to pay a high proportion of the total sums levied.

---

132 *Ordonnances*, xiv, 273.
133 Dupont-Ferrier, *Les Elections*, Map i.
134 AD Dordogne, 4E 123, no. 3.
135 AN, K 72, no 18.
136 BN, ms. fr. 21, 425, fo 7r; AN K 73, no. 34.
137 APA, E 68, unnumbered.
138 APA, E 2191, unnumbered.
139 BN, ms. fr. 20, 497, fo 93r.

Unfortunately, the *assiettes* made within particular *pays* rarely survive.[140] Moreover, often, as with the Albret lands in 1470, the use of the castellany as the basic financial unit obscures the relation in importance of towns to *plat pays*.[141] In Guyenne proper, however, in 1483, Bordeaux bore no less than 48% of the tax levied to pay for the promotion of the former archbishop of Bordeaux, Pey Berland's, canonisation. About 40% of the rest was assessed on small towns like Saint-Emilion and Cadillac.[142] In 1489–1490 the town of Condom paid 30% of the sum levied on the *pays* de Condomois.[143] When towns in Périgord did not escape taxation, their contributions too were likely to be high. In short, if the towns' claims to exemption from royal taxation were accepted, the monarchy's revenues would be markedly reduced.

The only detailed evidence for the relations between towns, *pays* and tax commissioners in this regard comes from Périgord. Even within the sénéchaussée the arrangements varied from year to year. As a witness in 1474 pointed out, sometimes the inhabitants of the vicomté of Turenne were taxed, and sometimes not. The first two *tailles* imposed on Périgord after 1451 allowed no exemption for the privileged towns at all.[144] Sometimes, though, all of them managed to gain exemption. In March 1485, for example, not just Périgueux and Bergerac but the less important town of Domme were freed from the *taille*.[145] Yet in 1477 Bergerac, and probably even Périgueux, had to contribute to 1000 l.t. assessed on the towns of the *pays*.[146] Moreover, some towns were regarded as more 'exempt' than others. Hugues Bailly maintained that Bergerac was more privileged than Périgueux, though probably most officers, and certainly Périgueux, would not have agreed.[147]

There were three principal ways to secure exemption. The first method was to fight for it in the courts. This was expensive but it sometimes worked. In May 1496 Excideuil's exemption from *taille* was confirmed after fifteen years' litigation.[148]

The second way was through diplomacy with the rest of the *pays*. In 1470 the syndic of the three estates of Périgord opposed Charles of France's confirmation of Périgueux's exempt status.[149] Consequently the town had to persuade the leading figures and institutions represented there to overcome this. The consuls obtained, and probably – considering the fixed form which these followed – also dictated, written affidavits supporting their claim from leading clerics, nobles and even from Bergerac.[150] How much compromise and inducement lay

---

140 That for Périgord of 1484–1485 is mentioned in AC Bergerac, jurade 22, 1484–1485 [fo 28v].
141 APA, E 650, fos 27r–35r.
142 AD Gironde, G 274, fos 26r–27r.
143 AN, K 74, no. 17.
144 AD Dordogne, 4E 123, no. 3, p. 35.
145 AD Dordogne, 4E 42, no. 2.
146 AN, Z1A 31, fos 234r–36v.
147 APA, E 77, no. 3, fo 3v.
148 AD Dordogne, 4E 54, no. 4; AC Bergerac, jurade 20, 1475–1476, fo 27r–v; *Jurades de Bergerac*, ed. Charrier, ii, 12–13.
149 AC Périgueux, AA 13, no. 3.
150 *Ibid.*, nos. 1, 4, 9.

behind the exercise is unclear. However, it seems that the local nobility supported the validity of Périgueux's privileges and reckoned that to derogate from the rights of the 'principal town' of the *pays* would be to imperil those of the whole community.[151] Bergerac's diplomacy, by contast, was perhaps less successful. In December 1484 it was reported to the *jurade* that the whole *pays* was against them and had agreed that only Périgueux could be considered exempt.[152]

The third way of securing exemption was a more or less subtle form of bribery. To defend its privileged position a delegation was sent by Périgueux to Jean Bureau in 1454. A sum was raised for presents to be given to him and to the king. More gifts were sent to one of the *taille* commissioners, to persuade him to give a good report of the town's poverty to the assessors. Other presents went to Jean Bureau's son who happened to be passing. Bribes were again given to the proctor of the *cour des aides* and to an *élu* in 1467.[153]

The towns clearly placed high hopes on the intervention of royal officers in their interests. Whether they were justified is another matter. Raymond Arnal was regarded as a friend of Périgord's exempt towns, and as the local receiver he could be a useful one. In 1477–1478 – difficult years for the 'exempt' – he offered to impede attempts to make Périgueux pay *taille*. Since in his position he could not speak openly, one of his nephews was assigned the task of wielding his uncle's influence. He was well rewarded for it. But it seems to have done no good.[154]

In 1484 it was Bergerac's turn to be duped by their 'good friend' Arnal. The town soon found it had been misled and that its exemption had been overridden.[155] In 1489, when pressed for back payments of taxation, Bergerac again turned to the receiver. They agreed to pay 300 l.t. to the king and 100 l.t. 'expenses' – that is, a bribe – in exchange for a promise that the *élus* would not comprise the town in future assessments. That exercise was equally fruitless.[156]

If and when a town's 'exemption' from royal taxation was overcome, the local and royal authorities were faced with the problem of exemptions claimed by different categories of inhabitants. From the point at which a tax levy was reluctantly accepted, however, townsmen and royal officers shared an interest in seeing that such exemptions were minimised.

The first question which had to be settled was whether those who normally enjoyed exemption from taxation should retain that privilege if they were resident in the town. Bergerac's counsel before the *cour des aides* argued against this. He produced the thesis of 'necessity'. A royal tax which was imposed in spite of previous exemptions and without prejudice to privileges was, it was claimed, of a special sort, required by 'urgent necessity'. As such, nobles had to pay their share of it like anyone else.[157]

---

[151]   AC Périgueux, AA 13, no. 1.
[152]   AC Bergerac, jurade 22, 1484–1485 [fo 25r].
[153]   AC Périgueux, CC 85, fos 6v, 9r, 14r; CC 86, fo 10r; CC 90, fo 4r.
[154]   AC Périgueux, CC 91, fo 23v; AN, Z1A 31, fos 234r–36v.
[155]   AC Bergerac, jurade 22, 1484–1485 [fos 25v, 27v, 28v, 30r].
[156]   *Jurades de Bergerac*, ed. Charrier ii, 56–57.
[157]   AN, Z^{1A} 31, fo 308r.

More far-reaching were the arguments used by Sarlat to make its clerics pay *taille*. First, it was mentioned that the *'taille des aides'* was only levied in cases of urgent necessity. By that doctrine the clergy should pay tax even for their spiritualities. It was, therefore, certainly the case that they should pay for their lay property.[158] The second argument Sarlat used went to the heart of the matter, for it concerned the nature of the *taille* in Guyenne. The town maintained that it was a property tax, so that the status of persons was unimportant. The clergy, however, claimed that it was a personal tax, so their exemption should apply.[159]

This last question was unlikely to be satisfactorily resolved, for the *taille* at this level was at once a personal and a property tax. In Périgord, after a sum had been voted or imposed for the whole *pays*, its levy was left at a local level to 'collectors' and the 'principal inhabitants' of the area.[160] This meant, for the towns, their governing bodies and those they appointed to the task. A town's allotted share was negotiable both with the royal officers and with the local estates.[161] But it was in theory at this point still, as in the original royal imposition, a personal levy, calculated according to a number of hearths. For instance, in 1453–1454 a *taille* was imposed upon the town of Périgueux at a theoretical rate of 2 l.t. per hearth.[162] The tax was levied within the town, it seems, according to an assessment of wealth, but there is no evidence from the period as to how precisely that was done.[163] It seems likely, however, that it followed the method used in 1490 to levy a loan in Périgueux. This was done by local assessors appointed by the town council for each *quartier* of the town. However, the unwillingness felt by the leading townsmen to embark upon a thorough revision of the assessment led to many inaccuracies and anomalies.[164]

The two most difficult 'exempt' groups with which towns had to deal were the nobles and the clergy. Because of the uncertainty about the personal or 'real' nature of the *taille*, towns wishing to tax their noble inhabitants usually preferred to allege that they were not noble at all. Unfortunately, this was difficult and expensive to prove, especially when an unfavourable precedent had been created. In 1473 the royal *franc-fief* commissioners arrived at Bergerac and recognised the noble status of three of the town's leading citizens, Raymond and Maître Aymond de La Baume, and Mathurin de Clermont.[165] This decision gave the latter grounds to oppose the 1477 and 1478 tax assessments made on them. The case dragged on, first before the *élus*, then before the *cour des aides*. The town lost it definitively in April 1483, when the noble status of the defendants was confirmed as long as they lived nobly.[166]

158 AD Dordogne, 4E 123, no. 3, pp. 7–10.
159 *Ibid.*, pp. 8–10.
160 AN, K 73, no. 5.
161 AM Agen, CC 44, unnumbered; AC Bergerac, jurade 22, 1484–1485 [fo 25r].
162 AC Périgueux, CC 85, fo 13v.
163 AC Périgueux, CC 90, fos 29r–42r.
164 AC Périgueux, CC 93, fos 49r, 45v.
165 The La Baumes and Clermont were jurats of Bergerac (AC Bergerac, jurade 23, 1487 [fo 8r]).
166 AN, Z^{1A} 31, fos 234r–36r; Z^{1A} fos 24v–25r; AC Bergerac, jurade 21, 1481–1482 [fo 32v].

This was not an isolated incident, but rather a test case. From 1480 Bergerac had been involved in a similar dispute before the *cour*. So was Périgueux, and it lost too. The effect of the verdict against Bergerac retrospectively justified the jurade's determination to fight so hard. In 1489 there were so many people in the town refusing to pay *taille* that this produced a financial crisis.[167] At Périgueux, exemptions and non-payment of tax led to a still more serious dispute.[168] Within the *cité*, exempt nobles were the main problem. In that part of the town known as Puy-Saint-Front it was the clergy. But the town officers and other groups claimed exemption as well.[169]

In the case of the town-dwelling clergy the royal government was more prepared to give positive assistance to the towns. It intervened to make clerics contribute to the fines levied at Bayonne and Bordeaux after the reduction of Guyenne. In March 1452 the king ordered the bishop and chapter of Bayonne to pay their share.[170] In May 1455 the archbishop of Bordeaux was still protesting about the levy on clerics at Bordeaux of their share of the 30,000 écus owed to the king. By refusing to intervene on his behalf, the royal council gave tacit support to the town's inclusion of clerics in its assessment.[171] The government's support was also forthcoming when it was royal and urban *tailles* which were at stake. Montréal and Agen obtained letters forcing the clergy to pay.[172] Other exempt groups which resisted taxation included university students who could hold up proceedings and appeal to the guardians of their privileges and royal officers and their families, who could also put up vigorous opposition. Jean Belcier and his wife did so at Périgueux in 1495.[173]

That the royal government was able to increase the income which it gained from taxation in the fact of such difficulties was no small achievement. But before analysing how this was done, it is worth glancing briefly at non-royal taxation in the province.

Just as the king was not alone in enjoying 'ordinary revenues', so he was not the only one to levy taxes in Guyenne. Towns did so, though with royal permission. Local customs, like those of Sainte-Foy, prescribed that taxes were to be granted by the 'community of the town' in assembly.[174] The few attempts to impose a genuinely 'popular' administration of town finances were probably short-lived and unsuccessful.[175] At Saint-Emilion in 1496 collection of a tax was left to a popular representative. Summoned to present his accounts in September 1497 before the royal commissioner, he failed to turn up, preferring

---

[167] AN, Z^{1A} 31, fo 342r; Z^{1A} 32, fo 1r–v; Z^{1A} 69, fo 191r; AC Bergerac, jurade 23, 1489–1490 [fo 35r].

[168] See below p. 158.

[169] A. Higounet-Nadal, *Périgueux aux xve et xve siècles. Etude de démographie historique* (Bordeaux, 1978), pp. 124–32.

[170] AM Bayonne, AA 15, fo 70r–v.

[171] N. Valois, *Le Conseil du roi aux xive, xve et xvie siècles* (Paris and Mâcon, 1888), pp. 302–303.

[172] *Comptes consulaires Montréal*, p. 129; AM Agen, AA 13, no. 8.

[173] *Recueil des privilèges*, ed. Gouron, pp. 51–52; BN ms. Perigord 84, fos 40r, 41r, 44r–45r.

[174] AD Gironde, 1B 4, fo 278r–v.

[175] See below pp. 160–63.

to stay drinking, and had to be arrested.[176] Usually popular participation was combined with firm royal control where reforms had to be undertaken. At Saint-Emilion this course was adopted for the principal town accounts which were heard by a royal commissioner in the presence of representatives from each of the town's parishes.[177] The king and his officers were always ready to intervene if it was thought that town taxes were being raised without royal authority or mis-spent. At Agen it was claimed that in and before 1494 the consuls had been levying taxes upon their own authority and the royal proctor was brought in.[178]

The raising of taxes by the nobility without royal *fiat* had been proscribed by Charles VII in 1439.[179] The practice of sharing between king and prince the proceeds of taxation had also long since grown up.[180] But what the reality was in Guyenne it is hard to say. Certainly both the Albrets and the Armagnacs continued to raise taxes and grants made to them by local assembles. No trace of royal permission survives; but an argument *e silentio* on this would be dangerous. The sums raised varied from year to year. In 1470 only 156 l.t. was voted to Alain d'Albret by the comté-vicomté of Périgord-Limousin, and of this amount in some areas less than half seems actually to have been collected. It was, moreover, an insignificant sum beside the ordinary revenues of about 3,300 l.t. and the comte's royal pension of 4,700 l.t.[181] Yet in the early 1490s Albret's lands in 'Gascogne' voted him 12,200 l.t.[182]

Jean V, comte d'Armagnac, raised taxes in his territories too. In 1451 *tailles* were levied to pay for his expenses at the reduction of Bordeaux.[183] Another *taille* of three *écus* per hearth was levied for him in 1462.[184] In Fezensaguet in 1464 and 1465 200 *écus* were granted to the comte.[185] Alain d'Albret raised a tax in Armagnac when he gained control there.[186]

The only noble levy which the king seems to have suppressed altogether in Guyenne was the *commun de la paix*. This was done by Louis XI. A case came before the *cour des aides* in May 1468 in which the vicomte de Turenne's right to levy the due was contested by his subjects and by the royal proctor.[187] In 1470 the king levied it himself in Périgord.[188] It was not very valuable. In the castellany of Bourdeilles it was worth only 23 l.t. in 1471–1472.[189] At

176 AC Saint-Emilion, BB 48, fos 1r–20r.
177 AC Saint-Emilion, BB 46, pp. 1–123.
178 AM Agen, CC unnumbered *cahier* [fos 1r–2r].
179 Beaucourt, iii, 407–409.
180 E. Boutaric, *La France sous Philippe le Bel* (Paris, 1861), pp. 260–61, 263.
181 APA, E 650, fos 38v–43r.
182 See above p. 56.
183 *Comptes consulaires Riscle*, i, 46–47.
184 *Ibid.*, p. 70.
185 APA, E 247, fo 39v.
186 APA, E 89, fo 110r.
187 AN, Z¹ᴬ 27, fo 138v.
188 AD Dordogne, J 773.
189 APA, E 704, unnumbered.

Bigaroque it was said to have been suppressed altogether about this time.[190] It was financially hardly worth collecting.

It was, therefore, more by increasing his own extraordinary revenues than controlling his subjects' that the king strengthened his financial position. The irregular but substantial growth in the size of royal and ducal tax demands was a crucial element in the consolidation of Valois rule in the province.

In the years before the reduction of Guyenne in 1451 the cost of frontier defence and other military expenditure had fallen largely upon the surrounding areas – upon Saintonge, La Rochelle, Limousin, Languedoc, and then, with further progress by the French armies, upon Quercy and Agenais. After the conquest the continued cost of occupation and the building of defences was borne principally by the customs receipts at Bordeaux and the grants made by the estates of the Landes. Little evidence survives for demands in other areas for the rest of Charles VII's reign. What there is shows, however, that *tailles* were raised in Périgord to pay for the *gens de guerre*.[191]

Louis XI's reign saw an increase in taxation in the kingdom as a whole.[192] But in Guyenne, at least, it may have been the methods used to raise taxes as much as the fiscal burden itself which provoked opposition. Unlike his successor's, Louis XI's instructions for the levy of taxes were framed in uncompromising terms. In ordering the levy of 3,100 l.t. on Armagnac in July 1477 the text of the imposition noted that the *pays* was very large and so perfectly able to pay the sum. It was to be raised over two quarterly terms only, not the usual four, and to be effected notwithstanding appeals or opposition.[193] A royal demand for taxation in Périgord in May 1478 required that payment be made within only six weeks and recognised no exemptions and privileges at all.[194] Louis's demands were also unpredictable, so that it was all the more difficult for local communities to budget for them. The *taille* assessment in Périgord in 1478 was, for instance, increased by about 60% over that of the previous year.[195] In a difficult year like 1475 heavy taxation could unbalance a small town's accounts. In that year Montréal paid 266 l.t. in royal *taille*. Yet only 83 l.t. were raised from its ordinary revenues.[196]

Louis XI's last years saw a particularly sharp increase in the tax burden, principally to pay the soldiers who had replaced the *francs-archers*. Heavy sums were imposed for this *taille*: 2,200 l.t. on Armagnac in 1482 and 1275 l.t. on Agenais in 1483.[197] In the castellany of Montignac, in Périgord, taxation was nearly doubled through these and other exactions over those years. It was not until 1493 that the sums demanded there again reached the size of those of Louis XI's last years.[198]

---

[190] 'Extraits du cartulaire de Philippaire', ed. A. Vigier, B. Soc. hist. archéol. Périgord, xxxvi (1909), 100–101.
[191] APA, E 781, unnumbered *cahier* [fos 28r–81r].
[192] Gandilhon, *Politique économique de Louis XI*, pp. 294–95.
[193] AN, K 72, no. 5.
[194] *Ibid.*, no. 18.
[195] AN, Z^{1A} 31, fos 307r–308r.
[196] *Comptes consulaires Montréal*, p. 130.
[197] AN, K 72, nos. 62, 74.
[198] APA, E 781, unnumbered *cahier*, fos 11v–63v.

It was also Louis XI who seems to have introduced the device of the 'exceptional' levy or surcharge, called the *crue*, into Guyenne. Like others 'exceptional' measures it was regularised, at a lower sum, by his successor. In Louis's last year a demand for a *crue* of 2,600 l.t. was made in Périgord, twice that of a normal *taille* levy.[199] It was, significantly, the *crue* which provoked the only rebellion in the period in Guyenne which is directly attributable to royal tax demands. The *crue* of 707 l.t. levied on Agenais and Bazadais provoked a riot in the mid 1470s. Villagers of the *pays* d'Albret near Marmande gathered to the sound of the tocsin, armed themselves and resisted all attempts by the royal officers to collect the tax. The rebels even tried to force their way into Albret's castle of Casteljaloux to free one of their number.[200]

Extortion was added to the inconvenience stemming from the irregularity of such demands. Charles of France required payment from Saint-Emilion before agreeing to confirm its privileges. The sum had partly to be paid in kind because another 23 l.t. had to be raised as the town's share of what had been granted to the duke by the three estates on his accession.[201] Special grants were made, more or less unwillingly, in Armagnac and intimidation used to exact payment of them. The *pays* granted 1000 l.t. to the sénéchal of Toulouse, Gaston du Lyon, when Lectoure was taken.[202] When representatives of the local townsmen met to discuss the matter they were arrested.[203] The arrears of such grants accumulated. In August 1474 a commissioner arrived to demand sums owing to Charles of France, Jean V and the latter's widow.[204] The same methods were used, though less often, outside Armagnac. In 1468 two commissioners arrived at Condom and claimed that the *pays* had granted Philippe de Savoie 430 francs and that the king now wanted the sum for himself. All the consuls of Condomois were arrested and only after they had paid the commissioners five écus were they released.[205]

A further source of extortion was the revival by the king of archaic rights and dues to be granted to members of the royal court. In 1473–1474 a commissioner of the duc de Bourbon, calling himself the '*roi des merciers*' had to be bought off by Cadillac when he demanded payments from all the town's haberdashers.[206] Another commissioner arrived in 1484 to demand 5 sous each from the haberdashers of Bergerac. They bought him off too.[207]

Charles VIII's reign began with an important measure to relieve the tax burden on Guyenne and elsewhere. Large sums of taxation which had been imposed before his father's death were remitted. In September 1483 Périgord

---

199 AN, K 73, no. 37, K 72, no. 18. Similarly in Languedoc, where supplementary tax demands had been made since the 1440s, these substantially increased through 'crues' under Louis XI (H. Gilles, *Les Etats de Languedoc au xve siècle* (Toulouse, 1965), p. 59).

200 Comte de Dienne, 'Une Emeute en Albret sous Alain-le-Grand', *R. Agenais*, xxxi (1904), 351–54.

201 AC Saint Emilion, CC 26, fos 31r, 36r.

202 *Comptes consulaires Riscle*, i, 118.

203 *Ibid.*, pp. 133–34, 153.

204 *Ibid.*, p. 173.

205 *Comptes consulaires Montréal*, pp. 92–93.

206 AC Cadillac, CC 3, fo 102r.

207 AC Bergerac, jurade 22, 1484–1485, [fos 21v, 66r].

received a reduction in its *taille* assessment of 1700 l.t. and Rivière of 800 l.t.[208] Moreover, at the estates general held at Tours in 1483-1484 a new agreement was worked out, which was reported back in detail to Périgueux.[209] The Tours estates voted a grant of 1,200,000 l.t. for two years to be levied as *taille* and a special grant to be levied, once only, of 300,000 l.t. No sums in future were to be levied without the calling of the estates general.[210]

The resilience of the settlement was soon put to the test. The regency government had to pay for soldiers to put down rebellion and resist invasion. Contrary to the Tours undertaking, in November 1485 the government imposed 1,500,000 l.t. on the kingdom, of which Périgord was to pay 7000 l.t. and 565 l.t. for the expenses of the levy.[211] This was by far the largest sum in *taille* levied there. In 1486–1487 a *crue* of 350,000 l.t. was added to the *taille* levy in the kingdom of 1,500,00 l.t. Périgord's share increased to 8,800 l.t.[212]

A special *crue* of 1200 l.t. may have been the only levy on Périgord in 1488.[213] But with the Breton war to fight and Maxmilian of Austria to be resisted there was a further huge increase in fiscal pressure. In 1490–1491 no less than 2,300,000 l.t. was levied on the kingdom as a whole. Périgord paid 13,677 l.t. with 615 l.t. for the expense of raising that sum.[214] Between 1492 and 1495 a slight increase brought the share of the *pays* to 14,300 l.t. and 615 l.t. expenses.[215] This meant for Périgord an increase in the rate of taxation between 1485–1486 and 1494–1495 of almost 100%. The surviving evidence for Agenais shows a parallel development. In 1480 6,458 l.t. *taille* was levied. Between 1494–1495 and 1497–1498 the sum was 12,200 l.t.[216]

How was such an increase in extraordinary revenue possible? The answer is fourfold. First, it was possible because of an increase in the taxable wealth of the South-West, resulting from the economic revival which has been described above. Second, it was done by using new fiscal means. Third, the government had resort to skilful propaganda. Finally, the government was able to ignore national, provincial and local assemblies.

Of the fiscal devices, first there was the *crue*. As has been observed, this was an innovation of Louis XI. But Charles VIII's government regularised it. For the whole kingdom the sum imposed varied between 300,000 and 575,000 l.t. This last high figure was only imposed in June 1494 when Charles VIII was preparing his Italian expedition.[217] More usually the figure was 300,000 or 350,000 l.t.[218]

The king also had recourse to the expedient of claiming an advance on the

---

[208] AN, K 73, no. 5; BN, ms. fr. 25, 716, fo 3r.
[209] There is an eye-witness account in the Périgueux *livre jaune* chronicle (AC Périgueux, BB 14, fo 39v).
[210] Masselin, *Journal*, pp. 448, 450.
[211] AN, K 73, no. 34.
[212] *Ibid.*, no. 46.
[213] *Jurades de Bergerac*, ed. Charrier, ii, 32.
[214] AN, K 74, no. 21.
[215] AN, K 75, nos. 2 bis, 9.
[216] AM Agen, CC 44, unnumbered; BN, ms. fr. 21, 425, fos 7r, 8r.
[217] AM Agen, CC 44, unnumbered.
[218] AN, K 73, nos. 46, 52.

following year's tax and justifying it by his avoidance of an increase in the assessment. However, since the size of the advances themselves grew, so implicitly did the following year's levy. In 1493–1494 Agenais was assessed at 8,200 l.t. but an advance of 4,000 l.t., described as a third of the following year's levy, was raised to give a total of 12,200 l.t. Even this was too little for the king's needs and the receipt for this sum was overcharged by 1000 l.t.[219] In 1494–1495 the advance in Agenais increased 5,794 l.t., up by about 45%. The following year it was up to 6,406 l.t. another 11% increase.[220] The king's very indigence could, by this method, be used to establish his claims the next year. The method also prevented yearly negotiations with towns and other bodies holding up royal assessments, a great boon to the king's finances.

The estimated expense of levying taxation was, under Charles VIII, regularly imposed as a surcharge on the *pays*. Louis XI used the device too, but usually in times of financial stress only and then the sums were comparatively small. Périgord in 1478, for instance, had only to pay 50 l.t. for the expense of levying 1300 l.t. that year.[221] Though as a proportion of the original tax levy these sums did not increase, in cash terms they did – and very markedly. At 565 l.t. in 1485–1486 and 615 l.t. from 1490–1491 to 1494–1495, these sums made a useful addition to the royal revenue and formed a sort of surcharge, or second *crue*, in the year's income.

A further method of supplementing the royal income, apparently first used in Guyenne by Charles VIII's government, was the raising of loans. The loans were made after negotiations either with individuals or with communities. At Bordeaux, in the summer of 1491, 8,000 l.t was ordered to be borrowed by royal commissioners from individuals rich enough to lend. In the rest of the sénéchaussée of Guyenne, however, where raising personal loans would have been more difficult, one large loan was demanded from the estates, which levied it as they thought fit.[222]

The case of Périgueux may provide a typical example of the mixture of negotiation and intimidation which was used to exact loans. Commissioners arrived there in 1490–1491 and demanded a loan for the Breton war. They first addressed themselves to the mayor, consuls, nobles and other notables assembled in the consular house. They drew to the attention of those present the privileges and advantages enjoyed from the king. The mayor and his colleagues replied by pleading the town's poverty. The commissioners threatened to take the town's revenues into the king's hand and finally agreed a compromise loan of 800 l.t. to be reimbursed by the receiver of Périgord.[223] The populace was assembled and told about it. When one of its number protested he was put under arrest and later fined.[224] At this assembly it was agreed that the loan

---

[219] BN, ms. fr. 23, 915, fo 195r.

[220] *Ibid.*, fo 197r.

[221] AN, K 72, no. 18.

[222] AM Bordeaux, AA 13.

[223] AC Périgueux, CC 93, fos 49r, 49v–50r.

[224] *Ibid.*, fo 38r. An upheaval at Saint-Emilion caused by those who regarded the levy of a loan in the form of *taille* as a '*prise*, exaction and act of pillage' is mentioned in AC Saint-Emilion, BB 46, p. 113.

should be raised in the form of a *taille*. A large number of inhabitants, however, could not or would not pay.[225]

In 1492–1493 the townsmen sent a consul to obtain reimbursement of their 800 l.t. loan, but they met with delay and obstruction. Moreover, by now other commissioners were at Périgueux demanding a further loan. They settled for one which was half as large again as that of 1490–1491. They stayed in the town, running up expenses, until they were paid 600 l.t. in cash. The men of Périgueux had to send to the royal court to obtain repayment of their previous loan and spent 50 l.t. there in bribes and other expenses. Bribing their 'friend', Raymond Arnal, proved the only means of obtaining reimbursement, however. He was given 100 l.t. for himself and was advanced 400 l.t. more of the next loan. This last sum was levied as a *taille*.[226]

Loans, therefore, increased the king's extraordinary revenue in two ways. First, they were in practice levied as *tailles* by the communities from which they were demanded and so supplemented income raised from *taille* impositions. Second, repayment was so difficult and expensive to obtain that much of what was raised as 'loans' by the commissioners must have been written off as unredeemable by the king's 'creditors'.

Changes in the methods used to raise revenue do not, however, of themselves explain the success of the monarchy in doubling the rate of direct taxation. A few riots but no major rebellion in the South-West can be traced directly to the impact of taxation.[227] Yet none occurred during the period of greatest sustained fiscal pressure. Why?

Persuasion may have been part of the answer. The king took every opportunity to explain and justify his demands. The communities of the province, for their part, were all the more willingly persuaded because they felt they had much to lose. Charles VIII and Louis XII, unlike Louis XI, used their tax impositions to justify themselves. Sometimes the king emphasised the state of the royal finances. In September 1489 he was anxious that Condomois should know that not only the 'poor people' were bearing the brunt of his financial difficulties. Loans had been raised from royal officers and the rich, and a quarter of a year's pensions had been stopped.[228] In 1492 he claimed that his finances were overdrawn by 800,000 l.t.[229] Accounts of the king's political aims, necessities and achievements were also given. In 1497 the appeal was directly to patriotism. Taxes were to be raised in Agenais 'for the honour, profit and reputation of us and of the French nation'.[230] The king's problems were described in detail. In 1490 Agenais was to pay its share to resist the English and Spanish brought into the kingdom by Anne of Brittany's treachery.[231] The king's successes were also fully described. In July 1495 the king emphasised his

[225] AC Périgueux, CC 93, fos 51v, 90r–95r.
[226] AC Périgueux, CC 94, fos 20r–23v.
[227] For riots at Agen, Périgueux and Bayonne see below pp. 156–63.
[228] AN, K 74, no. 17. Officers' pensions payable at Bordeaux were, however, exempted (BN, ms. fr. 25, 716, fo 88r).
[229] BN, ms. fr. 21, 425, fo 6r.
[230] *Ibid.*, fo 8r.
[231] AM Agen, CC 44, unnumbered, fos 1r–4v.

achievements in Italy and his hopes for the future, while demanding 12,200 l.t. from Agenais.[232]

A further inducement for local taxpayers in Guyenne to co-operate was the fear that new types of taxes might be imposed upon them. This was particularly so with salt dues. In principle, the salt of Poitou and the Atlantic coast which was used in the South-West had no *gabelle* levied on it, but rather a less burdensome due called the *quart de sel*. For this reason the salt of Poitou had a tendency to oust the salt of Languedoc in regions like Auvergne and Quercy, where the two competed.[233] However, in Guyenne itself not even the *quart de sel* was traditionally payable. Instead, dues were levied at different rates at the royal salt *greniers* in the towns through which the salt passed or in which it was sold. It was claimed by a delegation from Guyenne to the royal court that these dues were worth more to the king than the *quart de sel* would have been. Important *greniers* existed at Agen, Libourne and Bergerac. Moreover, the 12 d.t. per livre due levied at Bordeaux was payable on salt.[234]

The attempt to impose *gabelle* upon Guyenne's salt was probably not seriously made, though it was provided for in an ordinance concerning the Montpellier *cour des aides* and was the subject of legal controversy in the *parlement* of Toulouse.[235] The attempt by royal commissioners to impose the *quart de sel* on the province in 1487 may, however, have been more determined. It was vigorously opposed and the estates in Guyenne met at Libourne to discuss it.[236] The demand seems to have been dropped. But it must have served to remind taxpayers in Guyenne that for them the alternative to co-operation over *taille* and loans was loss of their privileged fiscal status in other respects.

The principal problem which the monarchy had to overcome in order to raise the sums needed was the relationship between taxation and consent. In Guyenne there was a provincial assembly of estates and one for each of the sénéchaussées, except that of Bazadais. Some *pays*, like the *pays* de Condomois and the *pays* d'Armagnac, which did not precisely correspond to sénéchaussées, also had estates. Yet the *pays* de Labourt sent its representatives to the estates of the Landes, just as the bailliage of Labourt was dependent upon the sénéchaussée of the Landes.[237] The local estates existed where common feeling, common interest or administrative unity caused them to grow up.

The function of the estates was not exclusively political, and this, indeed, contributed to their vitality. They were, for example, a vehicle of favour and patronage. Bayonne's deputies who were sent to the estates at Bordeaux in September 1483, for instance, were offered the comte de Comminges' services if the town allowed him to pass 100 tons of wine through to Fuenterrabía.[238] Consequently those chosen to go on behalf of local communities had to be men of authority, particularly if it was to a national assembly. In 1468 Périgueux sent

232 BN, ms. fr. 21,425, fo 7r.
233 Gandilhon, *Politique économique de Louis XI*, pp. 307–309.
234 AC Saint-Emilion, II 1, fo 2v.
235 AD Hérault, 1B, 13, fo 56r–v; BN, ms. n. a. fr. 3567, fo 72r.
236 AC Bergerac, jurade 23, 1487 [fos 18v–19r, 20v, 24v].
237 *Registres gascons*, ed. Ducéré, i, 118, 219.
238 *Ibid.*, pp. 277–78.

three representatives to the estates general at Tours: they were selected not by the general assembly but by the governing council. Those chosen included the mayor and the town proctor.[239] The same criteria applied in the selection of noble representatives. The seigneur de Montpezat was chosen by the nobles of Agenais in 1483 to go to Tours because he was influential at court.[240]

The estates were also a focus for pride in and for the interests of the *pays*. The whole of Périgord co-operated in the tricky matter of keeping that valuable relic, the '*saint suaire*' of Cadouin, in the monastery's hands. The three estates ordered a *taille* to be raised in 1456 for expenses incurred on visits to the pope and king about it.[241] On a similar matter in June 1483 the estates of Guyenne proper met at Bordeaux. They voted 3,500 l.t. to press for Pey Berland to be canonised. The estates seem to have performed the detailed assessment themselves and it is significant of the potential vitality of the institution that after years of inactivity they were capable of doing so.[242]

Less frequently the estates took up a 'political' stance through the formulation of grievances. The estates of the Landes did so.[243] The estates of Armagnac were capable of searching criticism of the comte's standards of administration or indeed of intervening with the king on his behalf.[244] The estates of Guyenne too were vigorously critical under Charles of France.[245]

Moreover, in a special sense the very foundations of Valois political control were laid upon consent by the estates. The settlement of the province during the first and second reductions had only been concluded by reference to the estates. At a humbler level, it was, for instance, in May 1450 a meeting of the 'bailes, churchmen, gentlemen and good men' of the baronies of Gosse and Benhanx in Labourt which reached agreement with the sire d'Albret about joining the French obedience.[246] The three estates of the Bordelais had negotiated the terms of Bordeaux's submission in 1451.[247]

The shared characteristic of the local estates which survived was that they had enjoyed a more or less independent political life.[248] But it was taxation which most frequently stimulated this vital activity. The provincial estates of Guyenne assembled to resist tax demands in 1487.[249] The estates of Agenais certainly showed considerable vigour. In 1468 a petition from them obtained an inquiry into the year's *crue*, a notable achievement.[250] Indeed their

[239] AN, K 73, no. 46.
[240] Arch. hist. Gironde, xxxv (1900), no. vii, 42; Masselin, *Journal*, p. 28.
[241] *Jurades de Bergerac*, ed. Charrier, i, 238.
[242] AD Gironde, G 274, unnumbered *cahier* [fos 26r–27r].
[243] AD Landes, AA 2, no. 4.
[244] Samaran, *La Maison d'Armagnac*, pièce justificative xxv, pp. 396–97; *ibid.*, pièce justificative lix, pp. 452–54; *ibid.*, pièce justificative lx, pp. 454–55; *ibid.*, pièce justificative lxiii, pp. 458–59.
[245] Stein, *Charles de France*, pièce justificative lxxxiii, pp. 717–19.
[246] APA, E 169, unnumbered.
[247] *Ordonnances*, xiv, 140.
[248] P. S. Lewis, 'The Failure of the French Medieval Estates', in *The Recovery of France in the Fifteenth Century*, ed. P. S. Lewis (London, 1971), pp. 308–309.
[249] AC Saint-Emilion, II 1, no. 2.
[250] AM Agen, CC 43, unnumbered.

independence caused them to incur royal displeasure in May 1479. It was claimed by commissioners sent to Agen that they had of their own authority and without royal permission levied a surcharge on the ordinary *taille* of the *pays* and spent it as they saw fit. Characteristically, the estates requested a new meeting to discuss the accusation.[251] Other local estates more prudently sought permission before levying taxes. In October 1469 the three estates of Périgord were allowed to impose on the *pays* 1000 l.t. for expenses which they had incurred in dealings with Charles of France and Louis XI.[252]

The vitality of the estates varied from *pays* to *pays*. The full provincial estates of Guyenne met in 1470, probably 1483, 1487 and perhaps 1496.[253] This spasmodic existence was probably not the result of political prejudice felt by Charles VII or his successors.[254] It may, rather, have been the result of a lack of common consciousness among the *pays* of the province. Principally, however, it must be ascribed to the position of the estates of Guyenne proper. These seem to have met only once separately from the larger provincial assemblies after the province's second reduction, and that was in 1483 to compose with the *franc-fief* commissioners.[255] This was almost certainly because of the lack of direct taxation in the sénéchaussée and royal reliance upon the growing revenue from Bordeaux's customs.[256]

The estates of the Landes enjoyed a period of regular and vigorous activity under Charles VII and Louis XI.[257] This was principally the result of the fiscal needs created by the king's determination to build fortified centres there. The estates consequently met to vote men and money.[258] There is no evidence, however, of their having been called for financial purposes under Charles VIII. They met in 1490 and made a comprehensive statement of noble privileges.[259] But now that the building projects at Bayonne, Dax and Saint-Sever seem to have been completed, the king had no more use for estates which claimed that the money they voted should only be spent within the *pays*.[260] In February 1492 Charles VIII ordered the collection of a 2,000 l.t. *crue* in the Landes. It does not appear to have been the result of a grant by the estates. Moreover, it was to be spent on warfare in Normandy and Picardy so it over-rode the traditional

251 AM Agen, AA 13, no. 9.

252 BN, ms. fr. 26, 092, fo 864r.

253 Stein, *Charles de France*, pièce justicative lxxxiii, pp. 714–16; *Registres gascons*, ed. Ducéré, i, 277–78; AC Bergerac, jurade 23, 1487 [fo 24v]; AC Saint-Emilion, BB 46, p. 29.

254 L. Cadier, in *La Sénéchaussée des Landes sous Charles VII, administration royale et états provinciaux* (Paris, 1885), p. 34, mentions this.

255 *Registres de la jurade*, vi (Bordeaux, 1961), 313–14.

256 See above, pp. 57–59. J. R. Major exaggerates the vigour both of the estates of Guyenne proper and of the provincial estates in *Representative Government in Early Modern France* (Newham and London, 1980), pp. 98, 109.

257 Cadier, *Sénéchausseé des Landes*, p. 64 is wrong in stating that the estates disppeared under Louis XI; cf. APA, E 2191, unnumbered.

258 See below, pp. 111–12.

259 AM Dax, AA 2, no. 4.

260 See below, pp. 111–12.

check exercised by the estates on both grounds. In September a further sum was levied in the same way.[261]

Most evidence survives concerning the estates of Périgord. This shows that they met regularly to vote or dispute about taxation or exemption from it. Sometimes, as in 1455, they seem to have been in almost continuous session, moving from centre to centre.[262] For Louis XI's reign six meetings are known and more may have been held.[263] There is no evidence of their having met to grant tax during Charles VIII's reign.[264] Nor does anything suggest that the estates of Agenais met after Charles's accession. It seems likely, that as for the Landes, this lack of evidence of meetings of the estates after Louis XI's death, in spite of the increasing tax burden, indicates a removal of the hitherto acknowledged power of local assemblies to grant taxes. Only in Armagnac did the estates retain their vitality.[265]

The contrast between the inherent vitality of the estates in most of Guyenne and the ease with which they came to be disregarded can only be explained by reference to a number of weaknesses. First, the effect of the estates general of 1483–1484 was to sap the vigour of local assemblies in Guyenne and yet put no effective national assembly in their place. By 1486 the sums voted to the king at Tours were being regarded as 'ordinary' *taille* for which no further sanction was needed.[266] More explicit was the wording of a tax imposition on the Landes in September 1492. It was openly justified by the grant of the three estates at Tours at the beginning of the reign which avoided the need to summon local or provincial assemblies.[267]

Second, local and national assemblies which could have acted as a check on the king were plagued by residual problems. Those who attended meetings of the three estates locally, even on important occasions, could be very few. The names of and positions held by those attending the estates of Périgord in January 1477 are recorded. The greatest nobles of the *pays* did not turn up, but sent proctors instead. Some proctors came representing a number of lay and clerical seigneurs at once. The seigneur de Salignac came representing himself, the seigneur de Grignols and other nobles, the bishop of Périgueux and the abbot of Brantôme.[268] The process saved money, but it must also have meant that such assemblies were often small, informal gatherings, inspiring little awe in the *pays*.

Moreover, when dignitaries assembled personally, divisions within the ranks

261 BN, ms. fr. 25, 717, fos 122r, 134r
262 AC Périgueux, CC 86, fo 8r–v.
263 AC Périgueux, AA 13, no. 1; CC 88, fo 10v; AC Bergerac, jurade 17, 1463–1464, fo 27r; jurade 20, 1475–1476 [fo 21r]; *Jurades de Bergerac*, ed. Charrier, i, 276; Stein, *Charles de France*, pièce justificative lxxvii, pp. 709–710.
264 The Périgord estates were held in 1485 for an unspecified purpose and again in 1487 to debate the *quart de sel* (*Jurades de Bergerac*, ed. Charrier, i; 356; AC Bergerac, jurade 23, 1487 [fo 24v]).
265 *Comptes consulaires Riscle*, i, 90; ibid., ii, 345–46, 358–59, 377, 380–81, 386, 395–96, 400, 402, 406, 432, 434, 438, 449, 456, 464.
266 AN, K 73, no. 46.
267 BN, ms. fr. 25, 717, fo 134r.
268 AC Périgueux, FF 185, no. 14.

of the gathering were liable to burst forth and these reduced the authority of decisions or elections made there. The account of the election of representatives in Agenais to go to the estates of 1483–1484 at Tours reveals this. The clerical estate was divided between those supporting the abbot of Clairac and those supporting the bishop's vicar-general. The nobles were divided between supporters of the powerful seigneur de Montpezat and those who preferred the seigneur de Lustrac. The towns took sides too. The only thing upon which the third estate seemed united was its determination to pay no more than its share of the delegates' expenses. The defeated parties appealed to the *grand conseil*.[269]

Meetings of the local estates were hampered by the restrictions placed upon the powers of some of those attending. The representatives sent by Bergerac in 1487 to the estates at Périgueux were told that they could speak but make no grant.[270] Consequently, towns reserved the right to withhold consent from decisions made by the assemblies. In the summer of 1475 the estates of Périgord voted 2000 francs bordelais to the seigneur de Beaujeu. But Périgueux and Bergerac refused to be bound by the decision even though their delegates had been present.[271]

Finally, there were means other than the formal meetings of estates to effect common projects. In Condomois, common meetings between the consulates of the *pays* seem to have performed many of the functions of local estates elsewhere.[272] Such co-operation among towns would be centred upon the principal town of the *pays*. Just as Saint-Emilion looked to Bordeaux, the consulates of Condomois looked to Condom or Agen for a lead.[273] The same consultation occurred in Armagnac.[274] The estates were to that extent not indispensable. These weaknesses, combined with new fiscal developments and the use of skilful propaganda, ensured that the local and provincial estates of Guyenne were in no position effectively to resist the monarchy's demands. A major increase in taxation was the result.

269 *Arch. hist. Gironde*, xxxv (1900) no. vii, pp. 27–48; Masselin, *Journal*, p. 28.
270 AC Bergerac, jurade 23, 1487 [fo 24v].
271 *Jurades de Bergerac*, ed. Charrier, i, 293.
272 *Comptes consulaires Montréal*, p. 160.
273 *Ibid.*, p. 173.
274 *Comptes consulaires Riscle*, ii, p. 374.

5

Justice and the Courts

The French government retained most of what it had inherited from the law and customs of English Gascony. Throughout the period, legal confusion and incoherence in Guyenne abounded. Although the institution of a *parlement* at Bordeaux was an important step towards making Valois justice more effective, it did little or nothing to diminish the clashes of jurisdiction which were characteristic of justice in Guyenne; moreover, its own *ressort* was far from unquestioned.

Much of the burden of justice was borne by local courts judging according to ancient custom. Seigneurial and – to a lesser extent – ecclesiastical justice remained important. With the king's justice so notoriously slow and costly, the temptation to apply extra-judicial pressures was bound to be considerable. The system of justice was, moreover, heavily weighted against those who lacked influence, prestige and wealth. Indeed, the essentially conservative attitudes embodied in the judicial practice of Guyenne secured the great against permanent disinheritance and recognised important inequalities among litigants. Although there were some short-lived, largely unsuccessful attempts to change the system and structure of justice in Guyenne, it remains true that the Valois government failed to reform the province's law and justice because, for the most part, it did not try very hard.

Law, customs and records

By the time of the establishment of French rule in Guyenne, it had become accepted that the king, under certain conditions, could make laws binding upon the whole of his kingdom.[1] Moreover, the fifteenth-century king was, perhaps, above all seen as a judge; to do justice to his people was his highest duty.[2] But the supremacy of the king of France as law-giver had evolved along side two essentially different systems of law, which neither the growth of the king's judicial power, through his sovereign courts, nor of his executive power would have allowed him to ignore. From the eleventh century the distinction between 'pays de coutume' and 'pays de droit écrit' had grown up.[3] Customary law was no less binding or valid than written law, for both were guaranteed and

---

[1] J. Declareuil, *Histoire générale du droit français des origines à 1789* (Paris, 1925), p. 797.
[2] S.B. Chrimes, *English Constitutional Ideas in the Fifteenth Century* (Cambridge, 1935), pp. 14–20.
[3] Declareuil, *Histoire générale du droit*, p. 831.

upheld by the king, even if the contents of customary law had not originated directly from the king's will.[4]

The law which was administered in Guyenne was a frequently incoherent mixture of both customary and written law. It was influenced by the proximity of the *parlement* of Toulouse and other courts of the Toulousain which judged according to written law. But the area of the Landes, Bordelais, Bazadais, Armagnac, Condomois, Astrac and Agenais also had certain customary features in common which distinguished its judicial climate from that of Toulouse.[5] The *coutumiers* of this area reflected the impact of Anglo-Norman, Roman and still earlier 'customary' law.[6] It was according to the contents of these *coutumiers* that justice in most of the courts of Guyenne was administered. But whereas the judicial decisions in town or seigneurial courts could in most cases be taken according to the customs of the individual community or the *pays* which more or less successfully accommodated the conflicts between written and customary principles, disputes which came before the *parlement* and other royal courts were less easily resolved. Before the royal courts reference to the *dicta* of the *coutumiers* was unlikely to be sufficient to clinch a legal argument. Lawyers and litigants explored and exploited the differences of procedure which would ensue if Guyenne were subject to *droit coutumier* or to *droit écrit*. The confusion on this issue was a fertile source of legal wrangling and resentment. No ultimate solution was found, or apparently sought, to the clash of two systems of law in one province.

The arguments about the law of Guyenne were deployed before the *grands jours* of the province in 1456, when legal reforms introduced recently by Jean Bureau and other royal commissioners had drawn attention to some of the anomalies of procedure in the courts.[7] In one case, the royal proctor intervened in order to prevent the introduction of new evidence because customary law forbade it. The other party claimed, however, that written not customary law had applied in Guyenne from days of old.[8] The royal proctor before the *grands jours* firmly maintained that Guyenne was subject to customary law. The judicial commissioners' ordinances had been perfectly in accord with the procedures of a *pays de coutume*.[9] However, neither litigants themselves nor the *grands jours* were so adamant on the issue. Counsel in one case said that he did not know which sort of law applied in the *pays*, but that it was probably customary rather than written law.[10] It was also claimed before the court that if the province was not subject to written law, it was at least a mixture of customary and written law which should prevail there. In this instance the *grands jours* may have been favourably impressed by the argument. For while the court would not allow the appellant to add new material to his case (as he

---

[4] *Ibid.*, p. 871.
[5] J. Poumarède, *Recherches sur les successions dans le sud-ouest de la France au Moyen âge* [Thèse de doctorat en droit] (Toulouse, 1968), pp. 14–15.
[6] *Ibid.*, p. 74.
[7] See below, p. 80.
[8] *Arch. hist. Gironde*, ix (1867), no. i, 13.
[9] *Ibid.*, p. 56.
[10] *Ibid.*, pp. 6–7.

would have been able to do under *droit écrit*) he was to conclude according to the procedures allowed under the latter, rather than under *droit coutumier*.[11]

No official statement, issued as a royal ordinance or through the *parlement*, definitively clarified the issue of whether Guyenne was *pays de coutume* or *pays de droit écrit*. What was done, however, was to introduce specific, limited legal reforms in order to bring procedures more closely into line with those obtaining elsewhere in France. The first of these reforms, though, was ostensibly justified by reference to alleged practice in English Gascony. Claiming that the number of 'frivolous' appeals being made was holding up justice intolerably, Jean Bureau and his fellow royal commissioners of 1455 alleged that papers found in the Ombrière palace proved that under the English it had been customary to fine such appellants. They ordered that those appealing from any judge in the sénéchaussée of Guyenne must now take up that appeal within a fortnight if they lived inside Bordeaux's jurisdiction, within a month if they lived outside it. If not they would be fined by the *juge de Gascogne*. Appellants renouncing their appeals should have their renunciations noted down by the registrar and pay a smaller sum. Appellants from the sénéchal of Guyenne or from the *juge de Gascogne* to the *parlement* were given three months in which to take up their appeals. If they failed to do so, or their appeal was judged 'frivolous', they too were fined. Appeals to the *parlement* in criminal cases were not to stand in the way of arrest. Nor would such appeals prevent adjournments before the courts.[12] Although these ordinances were made specifically for the sénéchaussée of Guyenne and relations with its superior and inferior jurisdictions, the authority of the *grands jours* and the Bordeaux *parlement* encouraged, through the claims of litigants and the royal proctors, the spread throughout the province of these new '*styles*'.[13]

A second French innovation also had overtones of English, if not Gascon, practice. The Anglo-Norman procedure known as the 'assize of novel disseisin' does not appear to have been employed in Gascony, which had its own laws and customs.[14] There seems, therefore, to have been real, if doubtless exaggerated, resentment at the introduction of the similar procedure known as the 'arrêt' or 'statut de querelle de novel disseisin'. The attraction of the procedure in response to complaints in cases of 'seisin et nouvelleté' was that justice could quickly be done on the facts of whether the complainant had been disseised, something of obvious benefit in the uncertain conditions of tenure which followed Guyenne's reduction.[15]

Letters of Odet d'Aydie, sénéchal of Guyenne, granted to a cleric of Puynormand in July 1477 contain the wording of the procedure and illustrate its aims and how they would be put into effect. The emphasis is placed on the

[11] *Ibid.*, p. 64.

[12] *Livre des coutumes*, ed. Barckhausen, no. xxiii, pp. 642–49.

[13] For the full meaning of '*styles*', see Declareuil, *Histoire générale du droit*, p. 871.

[14] D. Sutherland, *The Assize of Novel Disseisin* (Oxford, 1973), pp. 9–10; Vale, *English Gascony*, p. 5.

[15] For a description of what was involved for litigants in such cases, see Guenée, *Tribunaux et gens de justice*, pp. 222–30; for variations of the procedure, see A. Viala, *Le Parlement de Toulouse et l'administration royale laïque, 1420–1525 environ*, i (Albi, 1953), 371–73.

need to give speedy and effective execution of justice. So the fact of dispossession is the only one upon which the sénéchal in the first instance is to decide. Worthy men and others are called by the sénéchal as witnesses of fact and sources of information. It was of the essence of the process that only after this – the 'first head' – had been effected, should parties then be adjourned if necessary before the nearest judge to plead on the matter of *possession réelle*.[16]

Opposition to the new *styles* introduced into Guyenne by the Valois and their commissioners and judges came both from individual litigants and from the town of Bordeaux. In 1456 the townsmen of Bordeaux complained about the commissioners' provision that notarial instruments should be sealed with the royal seal at the '*contraux*' of each sénéchaussée. They accused the sénéchal of Guyenne's court of having introduced new procedures, which were allegedly contrary to the commissioners' own ordinances. The introduction of fines for default in cases where neither party appeared before the sénéchaussée court, the townsmen of Bordeaux claimed, was also an abuse of proper legal practice. Both the opposition of Bordeaux to the new legal procedures and the king's response to it were at this stage cautious and conciliatory. Thus the commissioners' ordinances were not challenged in principle, and the king agreed for his part to refer the townmen's objections back to the commissioners for their further consideration.[17]

Three years later the tone of the complaints from Bordeaux's mayor and jurade was more strident; but the *grands jours* of 1459, briefed no doubt by the royal officers, were correspondingly less conciliatory also. This time the townsmen of Bordeaux attacked the device of *novel disseisin* directly. Its introduction, they claimed, was contrary to the king's own confirmation of the *styles* and customs of Bordeaux. The *grands jours*, however, replied that any reforms of legal procedure enacted by the sénéchal of Guyenne and his council were to stand. The sénéchal's and the *juge de Gascogne*'s right to issue '*attaches exécutoires*' – instructions adjoined to royal letters relating to their execution – to particular royal officers was similarly upheld. The *grands jours* adopted a radical approach to legal custom in the province by stating that 'unreasonable' procedures and customs had been alleged, presumably by the royal proctor or perhaps the commissioners, and that these were now to be reformed in consultation with the lawyers and wise men of the town court of Bordeaux.[18]

The status both of the commissioners' ordinances and of the procedures of *novel disseisin* were also challenged by individual litigants in the courts of the province. Sometimes it was argued that the ordinances were not retrospective, that is that they did not apply to cases begun before they were promulgated; if accepted, this argument would have postponed their effective introduction in long-standing disputes for many years. At other times they were challenged on the traditional grounds that Guyenne was only subject to written law.[19]

It was, however, local custom – administered though local courts – rather

16 ADG, H 1271, no. 8.

17 *Recueil des privilèges*, ed. Gouron, pp. 69–70.

18 *Arch. hist. Gironde*, ix (1867), no. ii; 398, 401–403. It is, however, unclear what resulted from this initiative.

19 *Arch. hist. Gironde*, ix (1867), no. i, 64.

than the law of the *parlement* which provided the standard by which most disputes were judged. Though unreasonable custom might be reformed in certain instances, the king and the *parlement* generally helped to strengthen and clarify custom rather than undermine it. The customs were both a practical and a flexible guide. Most of the customs recognised that they could not provide a definitive answer on every disputed issue and that resort should be had in some circumstances either to other, more authoritative, customs or to Roman law. According to the *livre des coutumes* of Bordeaux, for example, when the customs of Bordeaux proved insufficient, resort should be had to similar customs, then to natural reason and finally, if all else failed, to written law.[20] The customs of a small town might reasonably be expected to prove insufficiently comprehensive more frequently than those of Bordeaux. At Nérac, for instance, the customs confirmed by the sire d'Albret in 1469 stated that where Nérac's customs failed, those of Agen should be employed.[21]

Customs could be by-passed by skilful lawyers and litigants. At Bordeaux it was alleged that parties who knew perfectly well what custom required had been reaching agreements with one another on certain matters of inheritance which avoided having resort to custom at all.[22]

Customs could also be amended by the exercise of the royal authority, though this was rare. For example, murderers in the *prévôté* of Saint-Sever were enabled by the customs there to avoid capital punishment for their crime by paying a fine of 400 sous. This was amended shortly after the French reduced Guyenne in order to bring the punishment into line with that applying elsewhere in France.[23]

The fact that the provisions of custom were on occasion evaded or altered testifies to the fact that custom as a source of law was important. So do the royal confirmations of customs for different communities. Sometimes, as in 1498 for the customs of Sainte-Foy and 1499 for those of La Réole, the king made detailed references in his confirmations of customs to their contents.[24] The little evidence which survives of the proceedings of town courts shows that these judged above all with reference to the local customs. In June 1481, for example, a case before the court of the mayor of Bayonne was suspended 'in order to look at the customs'.[25]

The contents of the *coutumiers* were freely recognised and referred to by the royal courts. In a case of March 1453, before the Paris *parlement* between representatives of the branches of the family of Salignac, a disputed inheritance was divided in the *pays coutumier* according to customary provision there, and differently in the *pays de droit écrit* where the principles of Roman law relating to inheritance applied.[26] It is clear that the *parlement* of Bordeaux too recognised the binding force of custom in its judgments relating to inheritance

20 *Livre des coutumes*, ed. Barckhausen, no. iii, 176.
21 *Arch. hist. Gironde*, xxv (1887), no. cclxii, 576.
22 *Ordonnances*, xvi, 41–42.
23 AD Landes, E 57, fo 9r; AN, JJ 198, no. 246.
24 ADG, 1B 4, fo 279r; AC La Réole, AA 4, fos 4v–17r.
25 *Registres gascons*, ed. Ducéré, i, 15.
26 AN, X¹ᴬ 82, fos 119v–120r.

and contract.[27] The court defended rather than undermined the principles of customary law.[28] Even the influence of the Toulouse *parlement* was less destructive of them than has sometimes been alleged.[29]

The contents of the customs had to be widely known and able to be consulted if they were to be effective. This was often achieved just by word of mouth by the local figures known as the '*coutumiers*'. The *coutumiers* were called upon in local courts to read out, and perhaps enlarge upon, the contents of the written customs.[30] Wise and experienced lawyers and litigants could themselves, at least posthumously, be referred to as *coutumiers*, men whose opinions on such matters should be given great weight in subsequent years. At the beginning of the sixteenth century the late abbot of Verteuil and someone called Lafite were referred to in that capacity forty years on.[31] By such means custom became 'notorious' in the *pays* so that even the ageing soldier, Jean d'Abzac, seigneur de Bellegarde, who was baffled by some of the more complicated provisions of custom in matters of inheritance, could pronounce on custom in such a matter as confiscation.[32]

But the durability of customs, privileges and rights by title deed, for communities and individuals, was most reliably safe-guarded by written record. The re-writing, compilation and regulation of such records was a common feature in the years succeeding the disturbances of war time. Supervised by the royal government and the courts, the keeping of records became a major preoccupation of urban communities and noble houses, and the loss or destruction of documents became something worth taking elaborate measures to avoid. The principal result of this activity may well have been a strengthening of customary provision in the *pays* and of the rights founded upon it.

The lengthy disorders of wartime caused the loss and destruction of private and town records. The seigneur de Montpezat, for example, claimed that his family archives had been burnt.[33] At Saint-Sever in March 1461 the jurats wrote that many of the registers and papers of the town were lost when it was re-captured by Charles VII in 1434.[34] In 1463 the town of Villefranche in Périgord explained what may have been the case for may small communities. Forty-five years previously the town was destroyed by the English and had remained uninhabitable for about thirty years. Many original documents had been destroyed with the town; since then the rest had rotted or become illegible.[35]

Some towns consequently sought a blanket confirmation of privileges which could only be specified after inquests had been made; such was the case at

---

27 For example, the case of a men dying intestate: ADG, B1 fo 9r.
28 Poumarède, *Recherches sur les successions*, p. 117.
29 Viala, *Parlement de Toulouse*, i, 513.
30 BN, ms. Duchesne 31, p. 101.
31 *Ibid.*, p. 100.
32 *Ibid.*, pp. 72–73.
33 AM Agen, FF 141, unnumbered.
34 AD Landes, E 57, fo 24r.
35 *Ordonnances*, xvi, 13.

Belin, near Bordeaux.[36] As at Mimizan and Domme, when the customs were proven in detail they were transcribed and sealed under the royal seal.[37] At Villefranche it was necessary to hold inquests on the contents of copied rolls and registers.[38] Similar circumstances probably prompted the compilation of the *livre rouge* of the chapter of Auch between 1446 and 1453.[39] The *livre noir* of Dax, although all the town court's decisions there recorded, except one, are of the second half of the fourteenth century, was written some time shortly after 1468, when a final document was included.[40]

The French government was determined to ensure that its records were properly kept. The ordinances issued by the commissioners for reforming justice in Guyenne in 1455 stressed the importance of this in judicial processes.[41] The Bordeaux parlement shared this concern. In 1466 the royal proctor in the Limousin was adjourned before the sénéchaussée court for having made alterations to a sentence of the sénéchal when it was transcribed into an act. He replied that this was customary procedure among lawyers in the Limousin. It was done in the *'feuillet'* of the case and only with the registrar's permission, never in the register itself. The court was satisfied and freed him.[42] The *parlement* could give short shrift to attempts to interfere with court records. In February 1467 it rejected the request of Amadan de Marsan to have the register of his pleading before the *prévôt* of the Ombrière altered. He had to pay costs.[43]

The archives of the smallest town were one of its most treasured possessions, a guarantee of privileges and the legal arsenal for battles of litigation. Retiring town officers had to make inventories of the documents in their possession. The *trésorier* of Cadillac on 24 June 1454 handed over to his successor eleven documents. The practice was repeated in 1458, 1464, and 1487. In 1492 a specially full inventory was drawn up. The archives then contained 20 documents dating from 1280 to 1491. If the originals were lost at least the town would have its copies. In 1493 the clerk was to have them written out and sealed.[44] By regulations of 1476–1477 the consuls of Périgueux also were told to hand over all the town's papers to their successors.[45]

For the house of Albret the family archives were no less precious, and probably much fuller. To the inexperienced they must have been a bewildering array of documents. Alain d'Albret had to write to an old servant of his grandfather's to ask where various useful documents in his own archives might

36 *Ordonnances*, xv, 413.

37 Ordonnances, xvi, 630–36; AD Dordogne, 4E 42/2 [Domme, AA 3].

38 *Ordannances*, xvi, 13.

39 *Le Livre rouge du chapitre metropolitain de Sainte Marie d'Auch*, ed. J. Duffon [Arch. hist. Gascogne, 2e serie, xi], i (Paris and Auch, 1907), iv–v.

40 F. Abbadie, *Le Livre noir et les établissements de Dax* [Soc. des. Arch. hist. Gironde] (Paris, 1902), viii.

41 *Livre des Coutumes*, ed. Barckhausen, no. xxiii, pp. 650–51.

42 ADG, B 6, fo 4r–v.

43 ADG, B 6 fo 40v.

44 AC Cadillac, CC 2, fo 114r, CC 3, fos 14r, 58r–v, CC 4, fos 44r, 97v–98r, 158r.

45 AC Périgueux, BB 1, fo 5v.

be found.[46] On the death of Alain's leading courtier, Estèvenot de Talauresse, an inventory was taken of all the documents found in his house.[47]

The maintenance of legal records depended in the last resort most frequently upon the notariate. The notariate was deemed unsatisfactory by the *grands jours* in 1459, which issued ordinances to reform it. The sénéchal was to organise an inquest into its working. Notarial letters in cases of contract were to be sealed under the royal seal by its keeper.[48] The customs of local communities regulated the notariate too. At Auch and La Réole the procedure was detailed by which the papers of a dead notary were secured immediately to prevent their dispersal.[49] Similarly, Sauveterre in December 1451 obtained from Charles VIII the ordinance that records of dead notaries should not be moved from the town without permission.[50]

The law of Guyenne, therefore, remained largely unchanged – a confusing mixture of *droit coutumier* and *droit écrit*. A limited number of controversial procedural reforms were introduced. It was, though, according to the customs that most legal disputes were resolved: this the Government accepted and implicitly endorsed. The French government's main contribution to better royal and local justice was probably its insistence on better record keeping – a habit which, for reasons of self-interest, was followed by towns and nobles alike.

The courts and the quality of justice

The Valois Government adopted broadly the same attitude towards the judges and courts of Guyenne as towards the province's law and customs. The institutions of justice inherited from the English were, with few exceptions, maintained or developed. Even the most important change, the setting up of a *parlement* at Bordeaux, was not without an English precedent.[51]

At the apex of the judicial pyramid in Guyenne stood the sovereign court. For a brief period in 1451–1452 and then from 1462 onwards, with the exception of the period during which Charles of France was duke of Guyenne, this was the *parlement* of Bordeaux. As the supreme court of appeal, civil and criminal matters of all kinds could come before it. Unlike the *grands jours* of 1456 and 1459, the *parlement* could consider matters of even the greatest financial importance.[52] It enjoyed wide executive powers. It could punish officers. It could overturn contracts which it considered inequitable. It

---

[46] APA, E 84 bis, no. 4.

[47] APA, E 229, unnumbered.

[48] *Arch. hist. Gironde*, ix (1867), no. ii, 402.

[49] P. Lafforgue, *Histoire de la ville d'Auch*, ii (Auch, 1851), 7–8; AC La Réole, AA 4, fo 16v.

[50] *Arch. hist. Gironde*, x (1868), no. xciii, 194–95.

[51] G. Hubrecht, 'Jurisdictions and Competences in Guyenne after its Recovery by France', in *The Recovery of France in the Fifteenth Century*, ed. P.S. Lewis (London, 1971), pp. 83–84; [Originally appearing as 'Juridictions et compétences en Guyenne recouvrée', A. *Fac. droit Univ. Bordeaux, série juridique*, iii (1952), 63–79].

[52] *Arch. hist. Gironde*, ix (1867), no. ii, 256.

appointed guardians for minors.[53] It considered internal security in the province and pronounced sentence in cases of lèse-majesté.[54] For example, 'scandalous and seditious words' spoken by one Jean de Soupre were punished by the court in 1483.[55] All that concerned the royal authority and the king's rights was, unless evoked, the responsibility of the parlement; this could even include the royal domain. The parlement was the almost omnicompetent agent of the king in the South-West.

The authority of the parlement and of the grands jours was re-inforced by the dignity of some of the councillors. For example, the archbishop of Bordeaux until his death and then the bishop of Dax were among their number.[56] Great figures such as the comte de Clermont and the cadet d'Albret attended the opening of the grands jours.[57] As has been noted, other noble families increasingly penetrated the parlement membership.

The jurisprudence of the parlement is almost entirely obscure, because, unlike those of the grands jours of 1456 and 1459, none of the court's plaidoiries for the period have survived. The arrêts themselves are perhaps deliberately curt, not revealing the reasoning behind the court's decisions. The parlement's attitude to the justice administered in inferior courts in the province is consequently difficult to perceive. Much more clearly evidenced, however, are the problems which the parlement and grands jours faced in maintaining their jurisdiction in the face of the encroachment of other sovereign courts and the confusion which resulted from this.

As has been observed, in June 1451, at the request of the estates of the Bordelais, Charles VII promised that a sovereign court would be set up at Bordeaux, as indeed it was. But by the terms of the pardon at the second reduction of the city the parlement was not re-created, though grands jours were to be sent to Guyenne once or twice a year.[58] In fact, the grands jours only came twice before the re-creation of the Bordeaux parlement. In 1454 Charles VII stated that Guyenne should henceforth be within the jurisdiction of both the Paris and Toulouse parlements.[59] But Louis XI threw this state of affairs into chaos by ordering at his accession that the province be attached to the parlement of Toulouse.[60]

The disarray which this latter edict caused may have been one reason for the king's institution of the parlement of Bordeaux in June 1462. The principal consideration prompting this move, made at the request of the three estates of the Bordelais, was ostensibly the physical difficulties faced by those who had to go to Paris to conduct pleas. The parlement jurisdiction was ordered to be 'Gascogne', Guyenne, the Landes, Agenais, Bazadais, Périgord and Limousin.[61] None the less, subsequent royal letters reveal considerable uncertainty about the new parlement's area of jurisdiction. This allowed the parlements of Toulouse and Paris to justify their encroachments. For example, in royal letters ordering the Toulouse parlement to send back cases to Bordeaux in June 1462, Limousin

[53] ADG, B 7, fos 22v–23r.
[54] ADG, B 5, fo 12r.
[55] ADG, B 2, fo 13v.
[56] Métivier, Chronique, i, 51.
[57] Arch. hist. Gironde, ix (1867), no. i, 120.

[58] Ordonnances, xiv, 143, 272, 274.
[59] Ibid., p. 274.
[60] Ordonnances, xv, 119–20.
[61] Ibid., pp. 500–501.

was no longer mentioned as being in the latter's jurisdiction and Saintonge was included instead.[62] Further royal instructions effectively cancelling this change had to be sent in December.[63]

The population of Bordeaux, lay and clerical, continued to press for the extension of the jurisdiction of their *parlement*. In February 1463 they obtained the inclusion within it of Limousin once again and now that part of Quercy – the bailliage of Martel – which had previously been described as within the province of the Paris *parlement*.[64] Soon Saintonge and La Rochelle, Angoumois, Limousin and all of Quercy were adjoined to Bordeaux, though there was some lingering uncertainty as to Quercy's position.[65]

Neither the population nor the royal officers, however, could be relied upon to take much notice of royal orders concerning the new *parlement*'s jurisdiction. In Saintonge and Angoumois royal officers publicly ordered that appeals were to go to Bordeaux and nowhere else on pain of a fine of 100 marks of silver.[66] In Agenais, Condomois and Landes, however, it seems that the sénéchaux continued to issue letters of *pareatis*, ordering litigants to appear at Paris and Toulouse, and this had to be firmly forbidden.[67]

In July 1469 Louis XI transferred the Bordeaux *parlement* to Poitiers where it was to resolve those cases already before it.[68] At Bordeaux Charles of France, now duke of Guyenne, was allowed to install his own *grands jours*, which acted as a sovereign court for his dominions.[69] After Charles's death Louis XI lost no time in re-establishing the *parlement* at Bordeaux. He appointed as its councillors the same personnel as had been at Poitiers, with the additions of a councillor from Toulouse, of two who had been councillors at Bordeaux on the eve of the translation in 1469 and of one other magistrate. The old Bordeaux registrar was similarly re-appointed.[70] The continuity of the court, not just from 1472 but from 1469, was thus stressed.

However, the re-established court lost part of its old jurisdiction for good. La Rochelle and the bailliage of Aunis were now placed in the jurisdiction of Paris.[71] The close association of the interests of the *parlement* with those of Bordeaux led the three estates of Guyenne to seek and obtain a 'recompense' for this loss. The death of Jean V comte d'Armagnac and the confiscation of his lands had led to the creation of a new royal sénéchausée of Armagnac. This included areas that had hitherto been attached to Agenais, Condomois and the *prévôté* of Saint-Sever, all once within the Bordeaux jurisdiction. The sénéchaussée of Armagnac was now, in April 1474, removed *in toto* from the Toulouse *parlement* and adjoined to Bordeaux. In May a further 'recompense' was made to Bordeaux in the form of the confirmation of its jurisdiction over the whole of Quercy.[72]

The *grands jours* and the *parlement* were jealous of their authority. The *grands*

62 *Ibid.*, p. 502.
63 *Ibid.*, pp. 595–96.
64 Métivier, *Chronique*, i, 14–16, 85–89.
65 *Ordonnances*, xv, 608–13; xvi, 175–76.
66 *Ordonnances*, xv, 610–12.
67 *Ibid.*, pp. 613–16.

68 *Ordonnances*, xvii, 231–33.
69 Stein, *Charles de France*, pièce justificative lxxi, p. 702.
70 *Ordonnnances*, xvii, 512.
71 *Ibid.*, p. 513; Métivier, *Chronique*, i, 86.
72 Métivier, *Chronique*, i, 82–89.

jours of 1459, for example, instructed the captain of Blaye to hand over English prisoners there, no matter what instructions the sénéchal had given him.[73] The Bordeaux *parlement* when it returned from Poitiers made an exception in its decision to uphold all the judgments of the *grands jours* of Charles of France; but then that now defunct court posed no threat to its own prestige.[74]

Other courts, however did. The Toulouse *parlement* continued to hear cases from within Bordeaux's jurisdiction. In May 1477, royal letters were issued ordering an appeal from the sénéchal of Agenais to go to the *parlement* of Toulouse.[75] In December 1481, the Toulouse court confirmed the privileges of Lectoure, thus implying jurisdiction over the sénéchaussée of Armagnac.[76] In March 1492 it pronounced upon a dispute involving Vic-Fezensac within the same sénéchaussée.[77] More serious must have been *arrêts* from Toulouse concerning office-holding within the Bordeaux *parlement* jurisdiction, as in 1487 concerning the *jugerie mage* of Agenais.[78] The Toulouse court in practice seems to have continued to exercise jurisdiction in Armagnac throughout the period.[79]

A challenge which was even more difficult for the Bordeaux *parlement* to overcome was that posed by *évocation* to the *grand conseil*. This could occur if a litigant with influence at the royal court managed to obtain the relevant royal letters alleging a clash between two sovereign jurisdictions. For instance, a case between Agne de Pons and the seigneur de Bueil which had been proceeding at Bordeaux and Toulouse was evoked in July 1489.[80] In 1484 the three estates of Tours demanded that no more *évocations* be made and that evoked cases be returned to their original courts.[81] This call provided further grounds for the *parlement* to resist such letters when they were next presented.[82]

The powers and location of every court were always of concern to *pays*. This was not simply because of considerations of convenience to litigants of the area. Particularly in the case of the sovereign court, the prestige of the institution reflected on that of the town in which it was based. The needs of councillors, staff and the litigants who attended must have provided commercial opportunities too. Only in times of plague does the Bordeaux *parlement* seem to have moved around the province, and then it remained in the more important and populous towns. In this is differed from the *grands jours* of Charles of France. When the latter court was about to arrive in Saint-Emilion in 1471, the mayor and jurats of the town were instructed to prepare a room where it could sit, to find innkeepers and obtain cheap food, and all this in four days or pay a fine of 30 l.t.[83] Larger towns, however, could more easily meet such demands and competed to ensure the temporary presence of the *parlement* in their midst. Such was the case in 1463, when Bergerac asked Maître Henri de Ferragnes to use his influence in order to have the Bordeaux *parlement* come to

[73] *Arch. hist. Gironde*, ix (1867), no. ii, 384.
[74] ADG, B 5, fos 3v, 9v, 11v, 12v, 48v.
[75] AM Agen, FF 7, unnumbered.
[76] AD Haute-Garonne, B 6, fos 5r–6r.
[77] AD Haute-Garonne, B 8, fo 449r.
[78] AD Haute-Garonne, B 7, fo 301r.
[79] AD Haute-Garonne, B 9, fo 466r.

[80] *Lettres de Charles VIII*, ed. Pélicier, ii, no. ccccvii, 373–75.
[81] Masselin, *Journal*, p. 686.
[82] Powis, *Magistrates of the Parlement of Bordeaux*, p. 19.
[83] ADG, B 3, fo 21v.

Bergerac to avoid the plague.[84] In fact, however, the court went to Périgueux and stayed there all that winter.[85] Périgueux itself tried hard to have the court prolong its stay in order, as the seigneur de La Jarte was mandated to tell the king and the lieutenant general of Guyenne, to bring more people to the town, thus increasing the revenue from which their fortifications could be maintained.[86] There may in this case, though, have been political reasons for keeping the *parlement* at Périgueux too.[87]

If the justice of the Bordeaux *parlement* is obscure, even less can be known of that administered in the lower courts of Guyenne. The courts of the the sénéchaux were undoubtedly important: but none of the registers for them survives. As has been observed, the practical work in them was usually performed by the sénéchal's lieutenants.[88] However, Guyenne's position in one regard was distinctive in the special relationship existing between the jurisdiction of the sénéchal of Guyenne and the other sénéchaux of the province. This was part of the legacy of English Gascony.

The royal commissioners of 1455 instructed the sénéchal of Guyenne to hold assizes in Bordelais, Bazadais, the *prévôté* of Saint-Sever, Dax and Bayonne. The sénéchal or his lieutenant was to attend in person. It was noted that he needed a special lieutenant in the Landes. In these courts only royal and baronial cases were to be adjudicated, others being dealt with by inferior judges.[89]

These measures were perhaps too closely based upon English practice in earlier years and failed to reflect political realities. The other sénéchaux of the province were unlikely to tolerate the powers this arrangement bestowed upon the sénéchal of Guyenne, who would in effect occupy the position held by the 'great senechals' of the years of English rule. The sénéchaussée of the Landes was also arguably too important and too vulnerable to entrust merely to a lieutenant, and Agenais would need a sénéchal too. How serious an attempt was made to put the commissioners' instructions into practice is unclear. But the immediate effect was a bitter fifteen year dispute between the sénéchaux of Guyenne and the Landes.

Olivier de Coëtivy, sénéchal of Guyenne, Vidal du Palais, *juge de Gascogne*, and, royal proctor in the *juge's* court, claimed that the sénéchal of the Landes, Robin Petillot, was really a sous-sénéchal, appointed by Coëtivy, and that appeals from the Landes should go to the *juge*. They based their claim on custom and the commissioners' ordinances. Petillot, his lieutenant, Jean Lefils, and the proctor of the Landes may have felt that they enjoyed royal support for their position. They wished to address the king on the matter. Lefils claimed that the firm policies pursued by the sénéchal and himself had restored order in the Landes within eighteen months. The royal proctor in the *grands jours* may have sympathised with this viewpoint. He asked the court not to proceed with

---

[84] *Jurades de Bergerac*, ed. Charrier, i, 253.

[85] AC Périgueux, BB 14, fo 19v.

[86] AC Périgueux, CC 88, fo 10r.

[87] For the disturbances at Périgueux in 1464, see below pp. 157–60.

[88] Dupont-Ferrier, *Les Officiers royaux*, pp. 71–73, 92–96, 122–23, 139–140, 330. See above p. 24.

[89] *Livre des coutumes*, ed. Barckhausen, no. xxiii, pp. 678–79.

the case, but just to give a provisional sentence.[90] In November 1456 the Paris *parlement* ordered an inquest to be made to establish the facts of the matter.[91]

The abolition of the *jugerie* de Gascogne by Louis XI seems to have revived the whole dispute. The *jugerie* itself was probably reckoned a source of inefficient complication and expense like the *juges mages*, though, unlike them, it was never revived.[92] The royal letters which abolished it specified that all appeals from the bailli of Labourt, *prévôts* of Bayonne and Saint-Sever, the mayors there and the *prévôt* of Bazas and other inferior judges should now go before the sénéchal of Guyenne. The lieutenants of the sénéchal of the Landes at Bayonne and Saint-Sever appealed against the letters; but their appeal was found void by the Bordeaux *parlement* and they were fined in August 1467. According to Gilbert de Chabannes, Charles of France's sénéchal of Guyenne, his colleagues of the Landes and his lieutenants there still continued to hear appeals, however, and were doing so when a new injunction against them was issued in June 1470.[93]

As with the *parlement* of Bordeaux, the location of the *sièges* at which the sénéchal's lieutenants administered justice was a source of dispute and fierce lobbying. The benefits of having the court in one's town were perhaps recognised by the government. According to Lectoure, Louis XI's reason for placing the principal *siège* of Armagnac there was his concern at the town's desolation after the pillaging which followed Jean V's death. In September 1490 the townsmen had his decision confirmed for fear that without royal letters to this effect it might be moved elsewhere.[94]

In Périgord the towns of Périgueux and Bergerac engaged in a dispute with varying fortunes over the location of *sièges*. In 1467, for instance, Périgueux sent a cash present to the sénéchal's lieutenant in order to persuade him not to hold his court at Bergerac. The lieutenant and others, no doubt hoping to benefit from opportunities for bribery, had informed them of this possibility.[95] By September 1478 there was indeed a *siège* at Bergerac, for in that month Périgueux sent a messenger to tell the lieutenant there to send back to the town all the cases originating from the *bailliage* of Périgueux.[96] The quarrel was still continuing in 1485. In July of that year Bergerac sent a letter to the sénéchal of Périgord after it was learnt that the officers of Périgueux were trying to have the *siège* at Bergerac abolished.[97] The letter may have failed in its purpose, for in 1490 Bergerac was fighting a case before the sénéchaussée court at Périgueux.[98] Agenais was the scene in 1492 of a similar quarrel between towns competing for the prestige and material benefits which flowed from the location of a sénéchaussée court.[99]

At the level of the sénéchaussée, therefore, justice was probably administered much as in the years before the reduction of Guyenne. The only important judicial office which was permanently abolished was that of the *juge* de

90 *Arch. hist. Gironde*, ix (1867), no. i, 80–83.
91 AN, X[1A] 86 fos 1v–2r.
92 BN, ms. fr. 25, 714, fo 117r.
93 AC Saint-Sever, AA 1, unnumbered.
94 *Ordonnances*, xx, 250–51.
95 AC Périgueux, CC 90, fo 11v.

96 AC Périgueux, CC 91, fo 8v.
97 AC Bergerac, jurade 22 (1484–1485) [fo 75r].
98 AC Bergerac, jurade 23 (1489–1490) [fo 7r].
99 AM Agen, BB 20, unnumbered.

Gascogne. The one attempt to codify the relationship between the sénéchaus-sées was closely based upon the practice in English Gascony and its outcome is uncertain. The changes which did occur reflected the judicial *mores* of the French royal officers rather than the decisions of government, for example the greater independence claimed by the other sénéchaux from supervision by the senechal of Guyenne.[100] Yet the system and structure of the judicial adminis-tration of the province through the sénéchaux was remarkably similar forty years after the second reduction of Guyenne to that which the Valois had inherited.

In local courts – whether of towns or nobles – it is probable that proceedings were usually carried on in Gascon, thus differentiating them from hearings before the *parlement* or sénéchal. In May 1451, for example, the seigneurs de Poylehaut and de Poyanne can be found pleading in Gascon concerning a mill in the presence of the *prévôt* of Dax.[101] The 'registres gascons', which are the record of the deliberations of the proceedings before the mayor's court at Bayonne, are in that tongue.[102] The sentences of the *juge* of Marsan, one of the comte de Foix's officers, were also written in Gascon.[103]

The town courts had to deal with a very broad spectrum of disputes and issues. Most evidence survives for Bayonne. There the town court met twice a week. The lieutenant of the mayor and a *quorum* of échevins and jurats had to be present. The court registrar had also to be in attendance. The royal *prévôt* sat in on cases and matters which had some political importance.[104] The court decided on civil and criminal matters brought before it and issued ordinances on a wide range of issues concerning the town's welfare and security. Most of the cases concerned questions of debt, inheritance, and commercial disputes of various sorts, particularly dealing with wine and cider.[105] Criminal matters ranged from cases of wounding to ones of murder. Alleged infractions of the town's privileges and matters of military and political importance were also dealt with.[106] Guardians were appointed for minors.[107] The more patchy evi-dence which survives of the working of other town courts in Bordeaux and Saint-Emilion confirms the picture of the courts' business suggested by that of Bayonne.[108]

Certain crimes were reserved to the royal justice, though the interpretation of exactly which these would be might vary according to local custom. For example, at Bayonne crimes concerning public order were the preserve of the king's judges. If anyone complained either of expoliation by force of arms or of

---

100 For the position of the English Gascon sub-seneschals, see Vale, *English Gascony*, p. 6.
101 BN, ms. fr. 26,080, fo 6363r. The surviving *plaidoiries* of the *grands jours* are in French, as are the *arrêts* of the Bordeaux *parlement*. So are the notes of a pleading of the abbot of La Sauve's lawyer before the sénéchaussée court of Guyenne, ADG H 242, unnumbered.
102 *Registres gascons*, ed. Ducéré, i.
103 ADG, H 248, no. 16.
104 *Registres gascons*, ed. Ducéré, i, p. ix.
105 *Ibid.*, pp. 6, 7, 8–12, 25, 29, 30.
106 *Ibid.*, pp. 64, 75, 79, 102, 105, 119.
107 *Ibid.*, pp. 4, 23.
108 ADG, 3E 84, fos 228v–229r; AC Saint-Emilion, BB 2, pp. 5, 53, 235, 318.

riotous assemblies then the royal justice was automatically involved.[109] At Bordeaux cases involving treason, forging money or counterfeiting seals were specified as matters outside the town court's competence.[110]

There were repeated clashes of jurisdiction between town and other local courts. In some cases jurisdictions were shared by formal agreement with other parties. Most of these acts of *paréage* and similar transactions regulating shared justice pre-dated the reduction of Guyenne, though not all.[111] But in general the towns defended their rights of jurisdictions energetically against all comers. Agen seems to have pursued its jurisdictional vendettas, against churchmen, judges and seigneurs, with great resolve.[112] Bordeaux, though, was probably best placed to ensure that its rights were secure. But here too the jurade were alert to any attempts by royal judges to circumscribe the town court's jurisdiction. For example, in October 1459 the mayor and jurats of the town brought a number of complaints before the *grands jours* concerning infractions upon their jurisdiction by royal judges. They claimed that they had always wielded criminal justice in Bordeaux, except in cases reserved to the king. But the sénéchal of Guyenne had been taking cognisance of all the crimes committed by the officers and lawyers of the sénéchaussée whether they concerned burgesses or not. The *juge* de Gascogne had also allegedly been hearing property cases in Bordeaux. Bordeaux's jurisdiction in all but royal cases was confirmed; if burgesses submitted themselves to the jurisdiction of the royal seal or a royal court then the sénéchal should try the case. But the mayor's and jurats' claim to do justice on foreigners living in the town when crimes had been committed against a burgess was upheld. The royal *prévôt* of the Ombrière was recognised as the judge for foreigners in personal matters. The town's jurisdiction over royal officers, if they were burgesses, was confirmed.[113] However, this did not conclude the matter, for once again in March 1490 Bordeaux was defending the jurisdiction of the town court.[114]

In Bordeaux's case, after the town privileges had been restored, the jurisdiction of the town court was probably not fundamentally threatened.[115] The framework of Bordeaux's relationships with both royal and ecclesiastical justice had been established in the fourteenth century.[116] Under Louis XI it was able to build significantly on that foundation. The king granted the town confirmation of letters of Philippe IV which accredited Bordeaux with high, middle and low justice over the Gironde.[117] After alleging a failure on the part of the *prévôt* of

[109] AM Bayonne, AA 6, fo 30v.
[110] *Arch. hist. Gironde*, ix (1867), no. ii, 397; *Livre des coutumes*, ed. Barckhausen, no. iii, 37–38.
[111] M.A Vigié, *Histoire de la châtellenie de Belvès* (Périgueux, 1902), p. 42; AD Gers, E 163, fos 15r–v, 17r.
[112] AM Agen, FF 7, unnumbered.
[113] *Arch. hist. Gironde*, ix (1867), no. ii, 397–400; *Recueil des privilèges*, ed. Gouron, pp. 78–80.
[114] AM Bordeaux, II 17.
[115] *Ordonnances*, xiv, 271.
[116] *Livre des bouillons*, ed. Barckhausen, no. cxv, pp. 349–59, and no. cxvi, pp. 360–64.
[117] *Livre des privilèges*, ed. Barckhausen no. i, pp. 4–6.

the Ombrière, in May 1473 these powers were further extended.[118] The *prévôté* itself was at least temporarily granted to the town soon afterwards.[119]

For the nobility of the South-West, just as much as the towns, rights of jurisdiction, as symbols of autonomy and sources of profit and influence, were worth striving to maintain. The nobility of the Landes through the three estates of the sénéchaussée in 1490 demanded that their traditional rights of justice be upheld by the royal officers. The latter were not to proceed to execute their orders within private seigneuries without summoning the seigneur of the place, unless in a case of refusal to do justice. If the sénéchal and others failed to follow this procedure their acts were to be invalid. Royal officers were not to try to take cognisance of seigneurial cases in the first instance. Subjects of seigneurs should not be arrested or imprisoned by royal officers unless after a judicial hearing in the seigneurial court, again so long as the seigneur was not negligent in doing justice. The only other exception was for royal debts, when arrests by royal officers were permitted.[120]

Among the nobility of Guyenne the family of Albret stood out because of the extent of its claims to wield seigneurial justice. Like the king himself, the Albrets at least early in the period exercised the prerogative of grace. In December 1454, for example, Charles II d'Albret pardoned an inhabitant of Fargues in Condomois for a murder he had committed.[121] His grandson, Alain, claimed the right to have judges of appeals in all his lands from whom cases on appeal went direct to the *parlement*. He also seems to have desired to imitate royal justice and have his judges issue letters of *querelle de novel disseisin*.[122] The rights of the Albret judges of appeals were defended also by Alain's son, the king of Navarre.[123]

The king's officers resisted such claims; in answer to the sire d' Albret's claims that royal officers and sergeants who executed royal letters within high jurisdictions should address the seigneur's officers, the commissioners in October 1455 agreed, but only in civil not criminal matters.[124] Charles II, however, demanded that it apply in criminal matters too. The commissioners tactfully agreed – and then excepted cases of arrest from the provision, thus making the concession largely valueless.[125]

Certainly, in the vicomté of Limousin, and probably in the comté of Périgord, Alain d'Albret administered seigneurial justice on a grand scale.[126] A series of petitions, some endorsed and some not, and all undated, illustrate its

---

118 *Ordonnances*, xvii, 576–79.

119 AM Bordeaux, II 'dons faits a la ville par sa Majesté'.

120 AM Dax, AA 2, no. 4.

121 APA, E 161, unnumbered.

122 APA, E 84 bis, no. 13 [fo 1v]. There is no evidence, however, of this actually being carried out. The article concerning *novel disseisin* is indeed lightly crossed out in the *cahier* in question.

123 APA, E 657, unnumbered *cahier* [fo 1r–v].

124 APA, E 229, unnumbered *cahier* [fo 2r].

125 *Ibid.*, [fo 4v].

126 Most of the evidence comes from the vicomté of Limousin rather than the comté of Périgord. An insight into comital justice in Périgord comes from the register of 133 folios of the comté's *juge ordinaire*, covering the years 1466–1470. Cases are not described there; but the impression is given of a large volume of judicial business. It seems likely that broadly the same

workings.[127] Indeed the surviving Albret petitions illumine the relationship between petitioner and justice in a way that the destruction of their royal counterparts prevents.

The first characteristic of the petitions to the comte-vicomte is that they are personal. Almost all are addressed 'to my lord'.[128] Only one is addressed 'to my lord, or to my lords of the council of my lord'.[129] Furthermore, the second part of the address which distinguishes this petition is in a different hand and may be a later addition.

On the other hand, the seigneur decided in practice upon his answers to petitions with his council. Fewer than half the surviving petitions are endorsed with an answer. There were probably requests which could be decided upon immediately, perhaps because those present had knowledge of the case.[130] It seems likely that when the endorsement reads 'by my lord in his council', it means just that.[131] This is almost certainly the case when, as in the endorsement of a petition from a noble claiming a village in the castellany of Excideuil in November 1480, we read the names of those present at the council, in this case 'my lord, the seigneur de La Barte, the seigneur de Saint-Macaire, the chancellor, the proctor of Bourdeilles and others'.[132] Whether Albret was himself present in other cases which are just endorsed formally by 'my lord in his council' cannot be proven. Possibly a petition from an old man of Peysac, complaining that he and twenty others had been adjourned for debt outside Albret's jurisdiction to Limoges, endorsed 'by the Council' was not in fact settled in the seigneur's presence, though even this one mentions 'my lord in his council' in the text.[133] One surviving petition, from the parishioners of Saint-Germain in 1488 who were in dispute with the seigneur de Magnac over some rents, is simply endorsed by Alain d'Albret as vicomte de Limoges and there is no mention of the council at all.[134]

The seigneur and his council probably sat for judicial purposes at the heads of the various castellanies. Surviving endorsements were made at, or mention, justice being administered at Excideuil, Thiviers, Nontron and Montignac.[135] The petitioners before the seigneur's court were not of any one type. They included clergy, nobles, townsmen and peasants.[136] The disputes related to all kinds of property and revenues, though most of the

---

kind of seigneurial justice was administered in Périgord as in Limousin, with the comte-vicomte's council at its centre.

[127] The dates of the documents are the dates of the endorsement of the petitions by Albret and his council, not of the original petitions themselves.

[128] APA, E 656, nos. 23, 25, 27, 34, 35.

[129] APA, E 656, no. 26.

[130] Un-endorsed petitions: APA, E 656, nos. 25–27, 31, 36–39. Endorsed petitions: APA, E 656, nos. 23, 34, 35, 48, 50.

[131] APA, E 867, unnumbered.

[132] APA, E 656, no. 58.

[133] Ibid., no. 50.

[134] Ibid., nos. 34, 35.

[135] APA, E 656, nos. 38, 50; E 867, unnumbered.

[136] APA, E 656, nos. 28 (clergy), 58 (nobles), 40 (merchants), 38 (peasants).

sums were small.[137] A number of petitions seem to have been brought before the seigneur on issues in which Albret's political influence was likely to be of use. For instance, there were questions concerning the encroachment of royal jurisdiction. A man of Jumilhac claimed he had been adjourned outside the vicomté against Albret's ordinances.[138] Others complained of being imprisoned by royal officers at Limoges.[139] A man of Thiviers said that he had been adjourned before the keepers of the privileges of the university of Bordeaux.[140]

Since evidence only exists showing the jurisdiction, practice, and business of the courts of the Albrets, and the bulk of this is restricted to the vicomté of Limousin, it would be unwise to assume that seigneurial justice everywhere in Guyenne operated in similar fashion. The resources from which the Albrets could draw for the administration of their domains were almost certainly unique in the region, at least by the end of the period.

It was probably the ecclesiastical courts of Guyenne which were most directly affected by the incorporation of the province into Valois France. Of the reforms introduced by the royal commissioners of 1455, those which altered the status of ecclesiastical justice probably had most impact. The king of France had always claimed to have special rights as guardian of the French church, particularly through the exercise of regalian rights and patronage. Royal involvement in diocesan affairs grew in the latter years of the fourteenth century. At this time it was argued that bishops had no right to capture clerics, execute sentences, confiscate, banish or disinherit.[141] Moreover, through the promulgation of the Pragmatic Sanction of Bourges and the institution of the procedure known as *appel comme d'abus*, of which the first clear example dates from 1448, ecclesiastical jurisdiction in France became even more subordinate to the lay power.[142] It was, therefore, into a very different judicial climate that the ecclesiastical courts of what had been English Gascony were thrust after the reduction of the province.

The churchmen of Guyenne, particularly the archbishop of Bordeaux, must have been made acutely aware of this with the publication of the commissioners' ordinances on justice. These decreed that henceforth the archbishop of Bordeaux and other ecclesiastical judges in the province were not to take cognisance of matters concerning property, inheritance, inventories of goods or the auctioning of revenues and rights.[143] The ordinances also sought to restrict ecclesiastical jurisdiction by facilitating the introduction of the *appel comme d'abus* and by sharply differentiating the royal from the clerical notariate.[144]

Predictably, these measures were vigorously opposed, especially by the

---

137 For instance, APA, E 656, nos. 31 (10 écus), 36 (80 francs), 28 (10 livres); E 867, unnumbered (3 francs).
138 APA, E 656, no. 48.
139 *Ibid.*, no. 50.
140 APA, E 867, unnumbered.
141 E. Delaruelle, E.-R Labande, P. Ourliac, *L'Eglise au temps du grand schisme et de la crise conciliaire* [Histoire de l'église, ed. J.-B. Duroselle and E. Jarry, xiv], iii (Paris, 1962), 329–33.
142 *Ibid.*, p. 363.
143 *Arch. hist. Gironde*, ix (1867), no. ii, 330–33.
144 G. Hubrecht, 'Jurisdictions', pp. 90–91.

archbishop of Bordeaux. But such resistance was doomed to failure for three reasons. First, it was politically almost impossible, and certainly imprudent, to argue against the validity of the reforms in principle. Little support could be hoped for from the pope in such a manoeuvre. The king and the papacy, even though their disputes might be bitter, understood the mutual advantages of cooperation in order to take advantage of the patronage and revenues offered by the French church.[145] Claims which directly challenged the Pragmatic Sanction were unlikely to be successful. Ecclesiastics, themselves, employed the provisions of the Pragmatic Sanction against one another in their disputes.[146]

Second, even if churchmen had tried to challenge the lay power directly, the divisions within their ranks would have precluded any chance of success. The archbishop of Bordeaux's opposition to the reforms was undermined by disputes with his own cathedral chapter of Saint-André and with other churchmen. The archbishop claimed the right to make visitations to all the churches in his archdiocese and to confirm appointments to all benefices in his diocese. The canons of Saint-André opposed this and resorted to the process of *novel disseisin* to do so.[147] In practice, it was the archbishop's claim to levy dues for the use of his seal and a procurations tax which was in dispute, rights which he said were his by 'common law' and by prescription.[148] His appeal to the *grands jours* was rejected.[149] In September 1460 he also found his right to confirm – or in this case reject – elections to the see of Saintes opposed by the canons there and by the archbishop of Bourges, who claimed to be 'primate of Aquitaine'.[150]

Third, opposition to the lay power was likely to be met with the effective use of *force majeure* by royal offices or nobles, as the archbishop of Bordeaux and other churchmen learned to their cost. In May 1455 the archbishop complained that temporal seigneurs in the Bordelais were preventing the execution of his and other ecclesiastical courts' mandates by arresting those entrusted with doing so.[151] In 1459 the archbishop's counsel complained of further victimisation. Soldiers had been billeted on him, and his other cases had been annulled.[152]

Ecclesiastical courts, even though their highest claims were effectively rejected, were not without teeth. The clergy could thoroughly humiliate their opponents when necessary. A dispute between the bishop of Agen's court and that of the town resulted, for example, in the church bells being tolled for three days, the cursing and excommunication of Agen's consuls and their wives being thrown out of church.[153] But the king and his judges could generally rely upon

---

[145] P. Ourliac, 'The Concordat of 1472: An Essay in the Relations between Louis XI and Sixtus IV', *The Recovery of France*, ed. Lewis, p. 110.

[146] *Arch. hist. Gironde*, ix (1867), no. i, 61; ADG, G 8, unnumbered *cahier* [fos 1r–4v].

[147] *Arch. hist. Gironde*, ix (1867), no. ii, 440.

[148] ADG, G 235, no. 1 [fos 1r–v].

[149] *Arch. hist. Gironde*, ix, (1867), no. ii, 442.

[150] ADG, G, 3 unnumbered. In September 1460 the archbishop obtained an *arrêt* confirming his rights of visitation in the diocese of Poitiers, in opposition to the archbishop of Bourges, AN, X^{1A} 89, fos 81v–82r.

[151] N. Valois, *Le Conseil du roi aux xive, xve, et xvie siècles* (Paris and Mâcon, 1888), p. 302.

[152] *Arch. hist. Gironde*, ix (1867) no. ii, 352.

[153] AM Agen, FF 8, unnumbered.

the traditional lay hostility to clericalism in order to reinforce their claims; while the papacy continued to be more interested in patronage than jurisdiction. In this regard there was no apparent nostalgia for the era before 1455 when, as the royal proctor put it, 'there was not much temporal justice and churchmen controlled everything'.[154]

So much for the powers of the courts: but what was the experience of litigants?

The estates general at Tours in 1484 made a number of searching criticisms of royal justice. They claimed that it was slow and expensive. Judicial officers were said to charge excessive fees: they were incompetent and they obtained their posts by purchase.[155] In response to the criticisms the regency government commissioned Odel d'Aydie, comte de Comminges, to organise a reforming commission in Guyene. He was instructed to summon three or four notable persons, such as presidents and councillors of the *parlement* of Bordeaux, to investigate whether there had been any abuses, errors or exactions in the *parlement*, sénéchaussée and other courts. If there were judges or judicial officers in the *parlement* or elsewhere who were unfit for office, Comminges was to send their names to the king.[156] There is, however, no evidence of reprimands or dismissals consequent upon this investigation. Indeed it may never have taken place.

Pressure to change the working of justice surfaced again in July 1490. The three estates of the Landes demanded improvements. It was by reference to custom, not reform, that the estates proposed the amendment of current abuses. Like Bordeaux earlier, the estates implicitly criticised the 'new' procedures used by the sénéchaux. *Procès*, written statements, commissions and orders must, it was said, conform to what was prescribed by ancient custom. Royal officers too were to behave as was 'customary'.[157] Again there is no evidence that these demands resulted in any administrative action.

There is no doubt about the volume of litigation in Valois Guyenne and the burden it imposed on those who undertook it. Archbishop Blaise de Gréelle of Bordeaux at the time of his death was fighting twenty-six cases over his jurisdictional rights at Belvès, Bigaroque, Saint-Cyprien, Millac and Couse.[158] For the young seigneur de Beauville the accumulation of law suits proved too much altogether. He was unable to sue in court for his property against the seigneur de Montpezat because he had fifteen or more cases on his hands already and his money had run out.[159] In 1477 the commander of Sallebruneau resigned his office because of the numerous cases he had with nobles trying to usurp the commandery's rights. He did so to the commander of Bordeaux who, it might be supposed, would be better able to pursue Sallebruneau's claims.[160]

Such burdens were, of course, increased when litigants found themselves

---

154 *Arch. hist. Gironde*, ix (1867), no. ii, 433.
155 Masselin, *Journal*, pp. 686–87.
156 AM Agen, AA 13, no. 10.
157 AM Dax, AA 2, no. 4.
158 ADG, G 225, unnumbered *cahier* [fos 1r–4r].
159 AM Agen, FF 141, unnumbered *cahier* [fo 17v].
160 AD Haute-Garonne, H, Fonds de Malte, Bordeaux 35 [old cataloguing: 4, no. 18].

engaged in cases before several different courts at the same time. In 1490, for example, Bergerac had fifteen cases in progress. Five of these were before the *cour des aides* at Paris. Six were before the *parlement* of Bordeaux. One was at the sénéchal of Périgord's court at Périgueux. Another was before the *juge ordinaire* of Bergerac, and the location of the last is unspecified.[161]

It was judicial delay which provoked most complaint. Delay was not just costly: it could result in the loss of cases. Even the Albrets, who knew how to use delay to good purpose, could have their interests threatened, so long were the delays which occurred in the case for the seigneurie of Ribérac, in which their opponent was the seigneur de Pons. First, their proctor died soon after the case had started and all the *sacs à procès* were handed over to Maître Nicolas d'Abbeville. He, however, went mad and the documents were passed from hand to hand until they were lost.[162] The case for the comté of Périgord went on much longer; so long indeed that it outlasted the lives of those appointed to judge it. So many councillors in the Paris *parlement* had died or become senile by May 1488 that it was seriously debated whether the court might need to begin to judge the case anew.[163]

But the same factors which disadvantaged the many advantaged the few. Some litigants gained the notoriety of being especially prone to take others to court and by influence and skill obtain favourable verdicts. One of Alain d'Albret's vassals complained to him in November 1480 that his opponent in law was a 'powerful man and a great pleader'.[164] Legal officers and lawyers were especially to be feared as litigants. The sire d'Albret had the misfortune to enter into conflict with Maître François Belcier, councillor of the Bordeaux *parlement*, over a mill at Cubzac. Belcier had the case evoked to Périgueux and won it. Albret's proctor put it down to his being 'cunning and subtle and a councillor in the *parlement*'.[165]

For the most influential litigants the personal intervention of the king was a valuable bonus. The sire d'Albret was reminded by his legal advisors that while at the royal court he should have the king send messages to the Paris *parlement* about the Albret cases pending there.[166] The great case for the comté of Périgord produced a number of letters of this sort from Louis XI.[167] They continued under Charles VIII. Most of the latter's instructions to the Paris *parlement* either ordered a speedy resolution or inquired to know what state the pleading had reached.[168] Other royal letters stated that they had been issued in favour of one of the parties.[169] Some openly told the court to favour the comte

---

161 AC Bergerac, jurade 23 (1489–1490) [fos 6r–7r].
162 APA, E 93, unnumbered.
163 BN, ms. fr. 4391, fo 27r–v.
164 APA, E 656, no. 58.
165 APA, E 657, unnumbered *cahier* [fo 1r–v].
166 APA, E 653, unnumbered *cahier* [fo 2r].
167 *Lettres de Louis XI*, ed. Vaesen, viii, no. mccccxxi, 153–54; *ibid.*, ix, no. mdcclvii, 252–53.
168 *Lettres de Charles VIII*, ed. Pélicier, i, no. cciii, 357; *ibid.*, ii, no. cccii, 125–26; *ibid.*, iii, pièce justificative xv, 399–400.
169 *Ibid.*, iii no. di, 6–8; *ibid.*, v, no. mcxii, 234–35.

d'Angoulême.[170] At other times royal messages, as in May 1488, were just sent orally via messengers.[171]

Where legitimate means of gaining an advantage over one's opponent at law were unavailable, there was always the possibility of exploiting a judge's susceptibility to bribery and influence. How many genuine cases of corruption of this sort there were it is difficult to know. Bias was on occasion admitted, even by the *parlement* of Bordeaux.[172] '*Evocation*' of a case to a higher court was the customary formal way of countering bias. For instance, in March 1472 a case concerning the sanctuary of Sainte-Croix at Bordeaux was brought before the ducal *grands jours* in the first instance because 'the lieutenant of the sénéchal is biased against the petitioner, the abbey, and is a relation of the other parties'.[173] *Evocation* to the *grand conseil* was made from the *parlement* of Bordeaux, too, where probable bias had been proven. The case between Pierre Dubois and Galeazzo della Rovere for the bishopric of Agen was evoked to the *grand conseil* in April 1478 because the Bordeaux *parlement* was alleged to be favourable to Dubois. Also noted in the *évocation* was the royal interest. It was important to the king that the affair be judged by a tribunal above suspicion since it concerned concordats made with the pope of which the magistrates were ignorant.[174] However, *évocation*, was generally an unpopular device.[175] Where possible it would be avoided. If inevitable bias was proven at one *siège* of a sénéchaussée, the case might just be transferred to another.[176]

It is impossible to know how the quality of justice in Valois Gynenne compared with that in English Gascony. Certainly some Gascon litigants seem to have considered that the standard of justice in the province in the last years of English administration had been poor. Two of them, who appeared before the Paris *parlement* in 1452, complained of the long delays which their opponent at law had managed to obtain in the court of the English 'grand seneschal'. Their case had been before the latter's court since 1445.[177]

It is undoubtedly true that the sources, with their emphasis on clashes and confusions of jurisdiction, exaggerate the difficulties which litigants faced: where possibilities for confusion did exist, they were likely to be amply exploited.[178] But, equally certainly, French justice proved costly, complicated and slow. Throughout Guyenne's judicial system, influence and wealth remained the best ways to success in litigation.

[170] *Ibid.*, ii, no. ccclxxxvi, pp. 273–74 and no. ccccxxxxv, pp. 370–72.

[171] *Ibid.*, no. cclii, pp. 55–56.

[172] ADG, B 5, fo 164r–v.

[173] ADG, H 281, unnumbered *cahier* [fo 2r].

[174] Chanoine Durengues, 'Galéas de La Rovère évêque d'Agen, 1478–1487', *R.Agenais*, lv (1928), 107.

[175] Masselin, *Journal*, p. 686.

[176] AC Périgueux, FF 18, no. 1.

[177] AN, X[1A] 81, fos 225v–26v.

[178] Guenée, *Tribunaux et gens de justice*, p. 64.

Property, possession and prescription

In Guyenne as in Normandy, there was an inevitable tension between the interests of those who hoped for revenge through dispossession and those who had recently made their peace with the victorious French. The former had to be rewarded. But the loyalty of the letter had to be secured. The province was fortunate in obtaining terms on its reduction which detailed the conditions under which property rights would be maintained and which were solemnly ratified by the king. By the terms of the reduction of Bordeaux in June 1451 those who did not wish to take the oath of loyalty to the French king had six months' safe-conduct to take away their possessions. Any remaining property would go to their heirs and successors.[179] They also had six months to collect their debts inside and outside Franch. Those who decided to remain were given a complete pardon and those who took the oath of obedience and loyalty to Charles VII were granted full possession of their property. Apart from the seigneurie of Curton, all property received by grants from the English kings was guaranteed as well.[180]

These terms were not much modified as regards property by the terms under which the second reduction of Bordeaux was achieved two years later. On 9 October 1453 the burgesses of Bordeaux received another general pardon, unless they had committed treason. Apart from certain named miscreants, they were re-instated in their property. In April 1454 it was proclaimed that those who had gone to England on business and had not committed treason could return to their property and take the oath. In practice, committing treason meant betraying the oaths taken to the French king after the first reduction.[181]

Confusion initially arose, however, about the relationship between these provisions and the terms of the edict of Compiègne.[182] The terms of the first reduction of Bordeaux, which, as has been said, still formed the basis for the agreement of 1453, had essentially sought to re-establish the social and territorial order disrupted by the last stages of the Valois invasion of Guyenne. The edict of Compiègne had a very different purpose. Issued in August 1429 and confirmed by letters of 28 October 1450, it was made in favour of those who claimed they they had lost property, benefices and money to those of the English party. The edict was both vague and sweeping. It claimed that the king had a general right through confiscation to dispose of all land held by the other party. By it, debts and arrears owed by returning members of the French party were not to be reimbursed. All property sold and exchanged by their relations in their absence was to be given back. All inheritances which would have been in their favour and had passed to others were annulled. Claims for

---

[179] Similar terms were granted to Dax and the Landes and were confirmed by Charles VII in July 1451, AM Bayonne, AA 7, no. 1.

[180] *Ordonnances*, xiv, 142–43.

[181] *Ibid.*, pp. 271–74.

[182] On similar and undoubtedly worse problems before the Paris *parlement*, see A. Bossuat, 'Le Rétablissement de la paix sociale sous le règne de Charles VII', *Le Moyen Age* (1954), 137–62. It is published in English as 'The Re-establishment of Peace in Society during the Reign of Charles VII' in the *The Recovery of France*, ed. Lewis, pp. 60–81.

compensation by those who had meanwhile improved properties were quashed. Possession was to be given to the disinherited of the French party without appeal on grounds of right. Prescription did not hold against them.[183] To apply the edict was thus effectively to overturn the terms of the pardons of Bordeaux.

The precedent from Normandy was far from encouraging for those wishing to resist an upheaval of tenure in the South-West. In Normandy the king sought to apply the terms of the edict of Compiegne with some strictness, even though, as in Guyenne, terms of reduction often contradicted them. It may be that, even after the return of the English in 1452–1453 and the harsher attitude then shown by the French monarchy, a distinction continued to be made between Normandy which had been reconquered by the French and Guyenne which was, essentially for the first time, being integrated into France.[184] At any rate, Guyenne saw no major upheaval of the kind full application of the edict of Compiègne would have required.

It was, though, for the courts in the first instance to try to reconcile the clash of principle between the edict and the terms of reduction. In 1456 Bordeaux presented articles of complaint claiming that those who had been despoiled of their property since the last reduction should be granted royal letters to reverse this. Charles VII variously told the judicial commissioners still in Guyenne and the sénéchal to deal with the matter.[185] But it was the grands jours of that year which seems to have been left to find the answer. Louis de Beaumont's counsel maintained there that Pierre de Lamothe had no right to plead by right of the edict of Compiegne, which only applied to Normandy. The royal proctor claimed, however, that it extended to the whole kingdom, including Guyenne. Lamothe's lawyer said that the edict was not intended to contradict the appointment made between the king and the Bordelais.[186] The royal proctor continued to adopt his uncompromising stance, alleging that the reduction terms did not prejudice those of the edict. In fact, Lamothe's case against Beaumont was adjourned to Paris and later lost.[187] In view of such arguments it must have seemed to many property-holders that their security of possession was less than assured.

Whatever was the case in law, however, ruthless application of the principles behind the edict of Compiègne was politically impossible. The next grands jours, three years later, was specifically told to do justice in matters of seisin in which nobles and others had been using the edict of Compiègne to take possession of the inhabitants' property.[188] Litigants took their cue. Other arguments would have to be found to challenge possession. Henceforth it would be the application rather than the principles of the settlement of 1451–1453 which would be disputed.

It was predictable that claims to property would be made after the province's

---

183 Ordonnances, xiv, 102–106.
184 C. T. Allmand, 'The Aftermath of War in Fifteenth-Century France', History, lxi (1976), 347–54.
185 Recueil des privilèges, ed. Gouron, p. 70.
186 Arch hist. Gironde ix (1867), no. i, 18–19
187 Ibid., no. i, 79, no. ii, 231.
188 Ibid., no. i, 265.

reduction by people who had been intimidated into acquiescing to *force majeure* under the English régime. For instance, Bernardon de Laborde claimed that his mother had rented out a seigneurie to Pierre de Valausun, mayor of Dax, for a limited period. But Valausun was so influential with the English that she dared not require its return.[189]

However, the central challenge to the stability of land tenure in French Guyenne centred on the issue of confiscation. Not only did the question of whether lands had been confiscated or not prompt important law-suits; the whole principle of confiscation was challenged too. Moreover, whatever the legal niceties, rights by confiscation were likely to be precarious.

Those who had taken the oath to Charles VII and then betrayed it had their property confiscated. Consequently, the crux of the matter in cases where litigants claimed property according to the terms of the Bordeaux pardon was often whether the oath of allegiance to the French had indeed been taken. For example, in a case before special commissioners in Guyenne in September 1460 the widow of Pey Makanan claimed to have succeeded to her husband's estate since her sons had left for England under the Bordeaux terms and that she was their closest relative. The royal proctor claimed, however, that they had taken the oath to Charles VII and so were rebels and their property confiscated.[190]

In practice, rights enjoyed as a result of confiscation and subsequent royal grant were fragile. What the king had given the king could – and did – all the more easily take away. Take the history of the seigneurie of Blanquefort in Médoc, for example. Confiscated from Gaillard de Durfort after his treason in 1452, it was granted to the comte de Dammartin. On Louis XI's accession it was taken from him and given to Antoine de Castelnau du Lau. Blanquefort was subsequently formally yielded by the comte de Dammartin after an exchange with the king. But the new security of its possessor did not last last long, for Castelnau de Lau in turn was convicted of treason and Blanquefort was confiscated. Louix XI now granted it and the rest of the Durfort inheritance to Louis de Laval, seigneur de Chastillon, before in 1469 handing it over to Charles of France. The new duke re-granted it and had Louis XI confirm this in April 1471 to make the gift 'sure and stable'. But it is doubtful whether anything other than prescription could make it that.[191]

Furthermore, the uncertain nature of tenure through confiscation was not just the result of the vagaries of royal policy. Local feeling was strongly against confiscation itself as even a legally valid process. It was spelt out in some local custom, as at Bayonne:

> By the custom of the town of Bayonne, for whatever crime it may be, the goods of the culprit are only forfeit to the king for a year, and that the non-moveable property only, and after the year is finished they return to the culprit's heirs.[192]

---

[189] *Arch. hist. Gironde*, ix (1867), no. ii, 335–36.
[190] *Arch. hist. Gironde*, xiii (1871–1872), no. xxvii, 61–65.
[191] AN, X^{1A} 8606, fos 247v–48v.
[192] AM Bayonne, AA 6, fo 35v.

Similarly at Sainte-Foy executed criminals could leave their property, with the exception of 10 l.t., to their heirs.[193]

It was apparently believed that royal authority had sanctioned the widespread opinion that confiscation was illegal in Guyenne. The grant to which the nobility looked back to support that contention was one of Philippe VI, to which a *vidimus* was given by Robin Petillot, sénéchal of the Landes, in August 1459. It specified that the nobles of Guyenne would not lose their lands or have their castles knocked down because of their excesses or crimes.[194] The claim was revived and developed at the three estates of the Landes in July 1490. Politics may have been at the root of the matter. In December 1490 the sire d'Albret let the French into Nantes, deserted his Breton allies and joined Charles VIII. That summer the nobles of the Landes, many of whom were more or less involved in the fortunes of the house of Albret, may have wanted to secure their own and their absent colleaues' rights against royal revenge. The estates claimed that no-one of any estate who lived in the sénéchaussee of the Landes could suffer forfeiture or confiscation, no matter what the crime. His closest heirs by testament or without it would succeed.[195]

The only case in which detailed testimony on the issue was brought forward was one of 1505 between François seigneur de Montferrand and the seigneur d'Orval, adjoined with the royal proctor, for the seigneurie of Lesparre. Montferrand's witnesses tried to prove that confiscation had never taken place in the South-West – a challenging task. Only one of them referred to the fourteenth-century royal grant to this effect. Others claimed that it was 'notorious' custom. Still other witnesses, better briefed perhaps, referred to the opinions of well-known, and perhaps conveniently defunct, legal authorities of the region. A series of instances meant to prove that confiscation of property had never occurred were adduced.[196] Inheritance and prescription remained the only respectable grounds for tenure in the eyes of many in the *pays*; even rights acquired by purchase or exchange were liable to be precarious. This is why the Valois policy of maintaining, and to some extent recreating, the broad framework of land-holding in Guyenne which had grown up under the English was a wise one. The cases where confiscation was employed demonstrate the instability in which it resulted.

Even great seigneurs who just held property through recent royal grant or purchase would find it very difficult to achieve permanent possession. Prescriptive right was understood, even if not always officially recognised, in the *pays*. The ancient rights of a family like the Foix-Graillys to the lands which constituted their inheritance would not be vulnerable to the challenges from litigants which would be faced by those whose rights were new and untested. Consequently, the most effective way for the government to ensure stability of tenure in the province was to ensure, in fact if not in theory, that the prescriptive claims to property made by the great families of Guyenne were as far as possible recognised.

193 ADG, 1B 4, fo 279r–v.
194 *Arch. hist. Gironde*, iv (1863), nos. lxvi, 802 and cxii, 152–53.
195 AM, Dax, AA 2, no. 4.
196 BN, ms. Duchesne 31, pp. 101–184 bis.

Local customs propounded differing views about the rights bestowed by prescription. Only in the Bordelais was it alleged that prescription of itself gave no right at all. The royal proctor in the *grands jours* recognised this to be the case, while condemning the custom itself.[197] In October 1505 the authority of the customs of Bordeaux was again invoked to prove that prescription did not apply. No matter how long a man possessed another's property, if he could not show his title deeds he had no right there.[198] This attitude was not shared, though, by other *coutumiers* of the province.[199]

The case of the Candale inheritance well illustrates the problems which a lack of prescriptive right to property brought with it. The inheritance was purchased by the comtes de Foix and Dunois by agreements of July 1451 for 84,000 écus. However, possession of the lands and rights of the capital de Buch and the comte de Candale, who had gone into exile, was plagued by legal disputes.[200] Foix and Dunois found their rights in Castillon and its appurtenances challenged by the Pardaillan family.[201] Their right to the seigneurie of Vautiran was contested by Louis de Beaumont.[202] As soon as one legal battle was won, another commenced. When Foix and Dunois managed to have royal letters put into effect for Castillon against the Pardaillans it was found that now the seigneur d'Orval's men had seized control of the seigneurie. The inhabitants proved equally uncooperative.[203]

Most serious of all, the comtes ran into conflict with the sire d'Albret. Charles VII heard the cases of Foix and Dunois in his great council and decided that Albret, not they, was the proper seigneur of Vayres and Vertheuil. He was granted possession in October 1451 and, in spite of the protests of the comtes' proctor, was accepted by the inhabitants as their seigneur.[204] The case was re-opened the following year. Albret apparently claimed the seigneuries in lieu of the dowry of Blanche de Foix. The comtes, however, alleged that a dower payment of 1337 had not been made by Bérard d'Albret to Pierre de Grailly's daughter and that in its place the two seigneuries had passed into the Foix-Grailly family.[205]

Moreover, the captalat de Buch had long been contested between the Albrets and the Foix-Graillys. The Albrets were claiming it in 1421.[206] The origins of the claim went back to the fourteenth century. The captalat was alleged to have been occupied by the 'English' till the fall of Bordeaux – that is by the line of the captal from whom Foix and Dunois had acquired it.[207]

The apparently endless disputes which the purchase of the inheritance had

197 *Arch. hist. Gironde*, ix (1867), no. ii, 337.
198 BN, ms. Duchesne 31, p. 101.
199 A. Moullié, 'Coutumes, privilèges et franchises de la ville d'Agen', *Rec. Trav. Soc. Agr. Sci. Arts Agen*, v (1850), 288; AM Bayonne, AA 6, fo 30v; AD Gers, E 479 unnumbered.
200 BN, ms. Doat 218, fo 202r–v.
201 *Arch. hist. Gironde*, ix (1867), no. i, 29–31.
202 *Ibid.*, pp. 13–15.
203 *Arch. hist. Gironde*, vi (1863–1864), no. xxi, 79–87.
204 AD Gers, I 28, no. 2.
205 APA, E 233, unnumbered *cahier* [fo 1r–2v].
206 Vale, *English Gascony*, p. 84.
207 APA, E 135, unnumbered.

brought with it were probably the principal cause of the agreement reached between the two comtes in July 1460. By this Dunois sold his share to Foix for 29,000 écus with another 2,000 écus for the option to choose, when groups of lands were divided, which ones he wanted. Possession of the lands and seigneuries involved was not immediately affected by the agreement, however; for Dunois was to keep control of Bénauges, Sainte-Croix-du-Mont, the captalat de La Tresne and other seigneuries and give them up only as payment was made. A sizeable loan from Jean Bureau to the comte de Foix for the purpose suggests that the royal court favoured the transaction.[208]

The sale of the Foix-Grailly inheritance to the comte de Foix meant its return into the hands of one branch of the family which had by prescription and inheritance come to be seen as its natural seigneurs. It was a step towards the re-establishment of the pattern of feudal power in Guyenne of before the Valois conquest. The next was the return in 1462 from exile of the comte de Candale and the confirmation of his lands and rights.[209] Though it would be an exaggeration to say that litigation ceased when the comte de Candale returned, it was at least possible to begin to negotiate binding settlements of the issues in question. The dispute with Jean de Pardaillan over Castillon and others lands was settled amicably. Castillon itself was eventually sold to Candale for 4000 écus d'or.[210] The long-standing conflict with the Albrets over the captalat de Buch was settled by a marriage alliance. In January 1494, the comte de Candale married Alain d'Albret's daughter, Isabelle. Alain handed over all the lands he held in the captalat, renounced all claim to it and promised never again to use the title.[211] Relations with the family of the comtes de Foix were smoothed over similarly. The comte de Foix's daughter, Catherine, married the comte de Candale's heir, the vicomte de Castillon. It was agreed that Candale would indemnify the princess of Navarre and her family for what was still owing to Dunois and Jean Bureau for the comte de Foix's re-purchase of the captalat de Buch.[212]

The involved saga of the Candale inheritance after 1451 demonstrates that inheritance and length of tenure were factors too important to be ignored either by the government or by those who sought lands and patronage in Guyenne. If, as is probable, the substantial loan which was made by Jean Bureau to the comte de Foix was made with the king's approval, the government seems to have grasped that tradition rather than executive action was the soundest basis for stable tenure in Guyenne. For it was Bureau's loan which, by uniting the Candale inheritance in the hands of the Foix family, paved the way for its transfer to the comte de Candale. With Candale's return, Louis XI not only gained a powerful and energetic servant in the royal cause, but also a guarantee against upheavals of tenure in the province.

---

208 APA, E 444, unnumbered *cahier* [fo 1r–4v].
209 *Arch. hist. Gironde*, x (1868), no. xl, 88–90.
210 AD Gers, I 2747, unnumbered.
211 APA, E 88, unnumbered *cahier* [fos 1r–3r].
212 APA, E 444, unnumbered cahier [fos 1r–3r].

PART THREE
POLITICAL CONTROL

6

The Problem of Security

The French monarchy remained acutely conscious and deeply fearful that its success in conquering what had been English Gascony might only be temporary. The fragility of Valois rule seemed to have been exposed by the events surrounding Talbot's return in 1452. The French king and his servants consequently turned their efforts and resources to fortifying, defending and provisioning the key centres of this exposed province of South-West France. Each successive crisis in relations with England renewed French fears of an English invasion and led to vigorous, sometimes frenzied, efforts to mobilise men and materials.[1] More permanently, the monarchy's preoccupation with problems of security led to a major, sustained programme of royal works to fortify the province's principal towns and defensive outposts.

The impact of royal demands for men and money and for artillery and provisions upon the urban and rural communities of Guyenne was profound. It affected the relations between central government and its agents and the towns and noble families of the province, which were conducted through lobbying and bribery in favour of pleas for exemption and privilege. It drew together some towns and *pays* in negotiating or resisting royal demands. The concern with security came effectively to dominate the attitudes of both government and governed in the province. The English never in fact returned to South-West France after 1453; but the fear they inspired lingered on with significant political results.

Castle-building and artillery

Fear of foreign intervention and doubts about the loyalties of those who lived there prompted the Valois government to embark upon a major programme of castle-building in Guyenne in the years following the reduction of the province. The most important element in the government's plans was the fortification of Bordeaux. There were apparently some who suggested after the second reduction of the town in 1453 that its walls should be entirely demolished.[2] The idea was again mooted in the time of Louis XI.[3] Not suprisingly, however, these drastic suggestions came to nothing. Instead, both to secure Bordeaux against foreign attack and to place an effective 'yoke' on the Bordelais

---

1 For relations with England, see above pp. 9–14.
2 Basin, ii, 200.
3 *Arch. hist. Gironde*, lvi (1925–1926), no. x, 37.

themselves (as Basin puts it), Charles VII decided upon the building of two castles, the Château du Hâ and the Château Trompette.[4]

The size and position of the castles equipped them well to deal effectively with both these kinds of threat. The Château Trompette was built overlooking the Gironde and was defended by three towers and a barbican. The Château du Hâ faced the hinterland of Bordeaux. Less regular in construction but no less formidable, it had five towers, the largest of these defending its eastern approaches.[5]

The work of demolition and building stretched well into the reign of Louis XI. In 1456 the Porte Saint-André was demolished in order to clear ground for the new fortifications.[6] The constable of Bordeaux was ordered in April 1463 to pay Jean de Vignes, the royal commissioner for building the Bordeaux castles, the large sum of 4000 l.t. for work done during the previous year. In all, between October 1461 and February 1464 over 2000 l.t. was spent on the Château Trompette alone.[7]

The inhabitants of Bordeaux were expected to contribute both money and labour. The demands continued during Charles VII's reign and into that of his successor. Bordeaux pressed vigorously for exemption from such levies, claiming that the maintenance of the town's traditional fortifications was burdensome enough, without adding further to the demands upon them. The townsmen seem to have had some limited success, for at a date prior to August 1468 royal letters of exemption were granted. But in practice their immunity was certainly less than complete; for in that month the town reached an agreement with the governor and sénéchal of Guyenne by which the townsmen agreed to repair and clear out the ditches of the Château Trompette.[8]

Another irritant was the demolition of buildings to make way for the new fortifications. Property owners affected pressed hard for proper compensation. In 1473 the cathedral chapter of Saint-André decided to lodge a protest with the king in person, when he was at Bordeaux, about the matter. The jurade of Bordeaux also became involved.[9]

Bordeaux argued that the burden of the castles' construction should not be confined to the town alone, but rather spread across the surrounding pays; and this was implicitly accepted by the royal government. Some towns resisted the pressure, but probably with little success. Cadillac seems to have accepted the position. In 1453, for instance, a royal sergeant arrived there demanding that the townsmen contribute to the royal works and they promptly raised a taille in order to do so. Again in 1475–1476 the town was providing pioneers for the same purpose.[10] Saint-Emilion put up more resistance, though it probably did it little good in the long run. In July 1459 the town's jurade tried to have it

---

4 Basin, ii, 200.
5 L. Drouyn, La Guyenne militaire, i (Bordeaux and Paris, 1865), 458–61.
6 Recueil des privilèges, ed. Gouron, p. 61.
7 BN, ms. fr. 20, 496, fo 7r; Arch. hist Gironde, x (1868), no. xxxix, 87.
8 Registres de la jurade, iii, 207; Recueil des privilèges, ed. Gouron, pp. 137–38.
9 Arch. hist. Gironde, x (1868), no. lxxxiii, 158; Registres de la jurade, ed. Ducaunnès, iii, 207.
10 AC Cadillac, CC 2, fos 106v–167v; CC 3, fo 117v

relieved of contributing to the royal works at Bordeaux.[11] What success this request met is unknown. In 1467 further demands were made. The captain and commissioner of works at the Château Trompette gave short shrift to the town's appeal to its alleged privilege of exemption. The townsmen's property was seized and they were locked up in the Château Trompette until they agreed either to pay 10 sous per hearth or come and work in person. A compromise was reached whereby they agreed to pay 30 francs bordelais, ostensibly as 'a free gift'. On this occasion their protests to the king resulted in his intervention on their behalf.[12] But in practice the town continued to have to send pioneers to Bordeaux.[13]

Three further centres outside Bordeaux were selected by the Valois for the sites of major fortifications. All three – Bayonne, Dax and Saint-Sever – were of considerable political and stategic significance. Bayonne, at the mouth of the Adour, was not only the second port of Guyenne and a major source of royal revenue in customs dues: it was also the base for any intervention in Spanish affairs. Though of less importance, Dax and Saint-Sever were each the centres of their own *prévôtés* and so of those areas of royal power and revenue outside the grip of the Albrets. The king's hold on the Landes depended on their defence.

The need to raise money and pioneers for the fortification of Bayonne, Dax and Saint-Sever ensured that the estates of the Landes met regularly in order to vote them. Moreover, the importance of the Albret and, to a lesser extent, the Foix families' rights within the sénéchaussée was such that royal commissioners had to pay some regard to communities' and nobles' rights there.

Work on the fortified centres of the Landes probably began at about the same time as that on the defences of Bordeaux. The demands made upon the estates from an early stage were heavy. In January 1455 the three estates of the Landes and other '*pays de Gascogne*' met at Bayonne and voted 40,000 francs and six pioneers per hearth for work on the three castles of Bayonne, Dax and Saint-Sever. A further grant of 14,600 francs was made by an assembly at Dax in June 1457 for the continuation of the works.[14] A meeting of the three estates of the Landes made a grant of 45,000 l.t. in December 1460 for the same purpose; it was to be levied over a period of three years.[15] The pressure continued under Louis XI. In December 1463 Louis instructed his commissioners to impose 15,000 l.t. on the Landes, exempting only those who had contributed to *tailles* raised for the army.[16]

Although prepared to shoulder this substantial financial burden, the estates of the Landes demanded that the levies should respect traditional rights and exemptions. They maintained that the *pays* had no obligation to pay taxes unless these were spent within the *pays* itself on its defence; and this seems to

---

11 AC Saint-Emilion, BB 1, fo 52v.
12 *Arch. hist. Gironde*, xxviii (1893), no. clxviii, 491–92; *Arch. hist. Gironde*, xxxi (1896), no. xlv, 430–33.
13 AC Saint-Emilion, CC 26, fo 1v.
14 Cadier, *Sénéchaussée des Landes*, pp. 71–72.
15 APA, E 229 [fo 7r].
16 APA, E 2191.

have been tacitly accepted by the royal government in October 1458.[17] They also insisted that nobles 'living nobly', those now serving in the royal armies or who had so served in the past but were now too old to do so should not have to contribute to any of the levies for castle-building or repairs.[18]

It was the Albrets who posed the biggest obstacle to the government. In 1456, for instance, the vicomte de Tartas submitted articles of complaint to Jean Bureau and his fellow royal commissioners. The king had ordered that for this time only Albret's subjects were to be included in that year's levy of money and pioneers. The commissioners refused to consider the vicomte de Tartas's plea for exemption, but they did offer to look into whether the Albret lands had been too heavily assessed. The sire d'Albret and the vicomte de Tartas exploited this offer to the full. They maintained that their subjects had been allotted far too many hearths in their assessment and the rest of the sénéchaussée too little. If thorough investigation of the tax-paying capacity of the royal lands of the Landes were carried out the Albret subjects would fully pay what was due.[19] The royal commissioners responded to this request with a mixture of flexibility and firmness. There was to be no new assessment of the royal lands. Those who refused to pay would be forced to do so, if necessary by garrisoning soldiers on them. But any who could show that they had already contributed to the royal works at Bordeaux would have their assessments reduced. Furthermore, there would be no new demands that year from lands contributing to the current levy.[20]

The Albrets did secure an important concession from the royal commissioners for their town of Tartas, however. The inhabitants of the town requested that they should be exempt from the *aides* levied for Bayonne, Dax and Saint-Sever, so long as they set up and maintained a cross and chapel there, instituting a yearly mass for the king, in memory of the royal relief of Tartas in 1442. The commissioners agreed to suspend payment of the *aide* there and do all in their power to have the king grant Tartas's petition. Their representations seem to have been successful. In 1461 Jean Bureau and his colleagues agreed that 600 l.t. should be paid to Albret himself, not just in order to support the religious foundation at Tartas, but also to contribute to the rebuilding of Albret's castle there, in ruins since 1442. This further concession was characteristically exploited by Albret to make new demands. In the late 1460s the vicomte de Tartas claimed that he was able to produce a grant to the sire d'Albret which freed his lands from the obligation to provide pioneers for the king and allowed him to raise them instead in order to rebuild those of his strongholds demolished by the English. He also maintained that Charles VII's commissioners had permitted Tartas's 272 l.t. share of the *aide* for the royal works for the Landes to be employed entirely on the town's defences.[21] Whether this ingenious misrepresentation of the nature of the original concession made by Charles VII was accepted is perhaps doubtful. But it serves

[17] Cadier, *Sénéchaussée des Landes*, p. 78.
[18] *Ibid.*, p. 85.
[19] APA, E 229 [fo 1r–v].
[20] *Ibid.*, [fo 1r–3r].
[21] *Ibid.*, [fo 7r–v].

to show the difficulties faced by the royal government in obtaining full payment of its demands for money and men in the Albret lands.

Perhaps the most important check exercised by the estates of the Landes was their stipulation that all of the money raised in the Landes for the royal works should in fact be spent there. The remaining fragments of accounts for the fortifications suggest that large sums of what was contributed were indeed so used. As late as September 1492, when *aides* of 13,600 l.t. were levied upon the Landes, they were still described as being specifically for the construction and repair of Dax, Bayonne and Saint-Sever and for the payment of their garrisons.[22]

The opening period of French military involvement in Italy saw a further programme of repairs and modifications to the royal fortifications of Guyenne. The castles of Bordeaux were at the centre of this. In December 1493 a new draw-bridge was made for one of the gates of the Château Trompette and alterations made to the archers' guard house. In 1497–1498 further extensive work was undertaken there, which cost 3500 l.t.[23] At La Réole, which had been fortified by new town walls to defend its spreading population, similar work was undertaken at around this time.[24] The same was true at Blaye in 1495–1496.[25] Attention was given in 1495 to the defence of Périgord and particularly to that of its most impregnable fortified town, Domme.[26] In 1498 work was in progress in Agenais at the castles of Penne and Castelculier.[27]

The burden of royal demands for contributions to the building and repair of the major fortified centres of the province fell on towns and *pays* which had similar obligations to contribute to their own defences. At Saint-Emilion, for instance, in May 1495 the jurade had to carry our orders relating to the strengthening of the town's own fortifications at the same time as meet demands for Bordeaux.[28] The fortifications of towns recognised to be of strategic importance sometimes needed such extensive and costly work that the government was prepared to grant exemption from other royal demands. In February 1469 Louis XI confirmed Libourne's exemption from royal commissioners' demands that the town should send pioneers to work on the Château Trompette. His letters stressed the importance of the town, situated where the Isle met the Dordogne, close to the sea, 'on the frontier'.[29] The burgesses put it more graphically in 1486, when they described Libourne as the 'key and bastion' of Périgord and other surrounding *pays*.[30]

In the Landes similar problems arose. A detailed report on Bayonne's defences, commissioned during Louis XI's reign, revealed their dilapidation. The importance attached by the government to the subject is illustrated by the

22 BN, mss fr. 26, 083, fo 6789r; 25, 944, fo 91r; 25, 717, fo 134r.
23 BN, mss fr. 26, 103, fo 959r; 26, 106, fos 26$^{1-2}$; 26, 105, fo 1176r.
24 BN, ms. fr. 26, 106, fo 24r.
25 BN, ms. fr. 26, 105, fo 1176r.
26 B. Soc. hist. archéol. Périgord, xxx (1903), 275–76.
27 BN, ms. fr. 26, 106, fos 3r, 8r.
28 AC Saint-Emilion, BB 1, fo 47r.
29 AC Libourne, AA 8, no. 1, fo 11r.
30 ADG, 1B 2, fos 464r – 467r.

presence among the twelve commissioners appointed for the task of three experts to give advice on ways to resist and to use artillery. The commissioners reported that a rampart should be replaced by an extension of the main ditch and that a further ditch should be dug from the Tour Normande to the river; all the ditches should be be cleared of débris.[31]

Unlike the sénéchaussées of Guyenne and Landes, that of Périgord was not usually regarded as being particularly exposed to the English. Consequently there were no royal works there on the scale of those at Bordeaux, Bayonne, Dax and Saint-Sever. This meant, however, that in Périgord the role of individual towns' fortifications in the defence of the sénéchaussée was considered all the more crucial. The town accounts of Périgueux show a regular preoccupation with the town's defences. In 1467–1468, for example, extensive work was done on the town's four draw-bridges, the Porte Taillefer and a stretch of wall between two of the town's towers.[32] Ten years later the consuls of Périgueux were concentrating on the reconstruction of the Tour Mataguerre.[33] Périgueux's accounts of 1488–1489 were burdened with work on the Porte Limogeanne. Those of 1490–1491 show that more work was also required in that year on the Porte Taillefer.[34]

At Bergerac the townsmen seem to have been more remiss than their neighbours in Périgueux in the fulfilment of the duty to maintain the town's defences. In March 1463 the sénéchal of Périgord, Pierre d'Acigné, intervened in order to command the rebuilding of the town's castle.[35] Again in March 1483 a letter was received by Bergerac, perhaps from the sénéchal, which spelt out in detail repairs which required to be done on the town's walls, bridge and bulwark. Failure to comply with this order would result in a 200 l. fine, the townsmen were told.[36]

Probably nowhere in the South-West did the burdens of building and repairing the defences of the towns bear more heavily on the local population than in Armagnac. This was the direct result of the turbulent ambitions of the house of Armagnac. The comital castles had regularly to be maintained by the surrounding *pays*: in 1458–1459 repairs on the comte d'Armagnac's castle at Manciet cost nearly 90 l. and those on his tower at Cazaubon nearly 20 l. Such sums had to be found in *tailles* and dues levied from his subjects.[37] It was, however, the needs of Lectoure which placed the heaviest and most disruptive demands upon the other towns of the *pays*. Lectoure was the strongest point of defence in Armagnac and had been very heavily fortified. On the only side from which it was vulnerable there was a double *enceinte* and a further large tower had been constructed in 1428. In 1472–1473 further work strengthening the defences of

31 BN, ms. fr. 20, 492, fo 91v.
32 AC Périgueux, CC 90, fos 15r–19r.
33 AC Périgueux, CC 91, fos 13v–22r.
34 AC Périgueux, CC 93, fos 11r–18r.
35 BN, ms. fr. 26, 088, fo 143r.
36 AC Bergerac, jurade 23 (1487–1488) [fo 42r–v].
37 AD Tarn-et-Garonne, A 285 [fo 6r].

the fortress was performed at the instructions of the 'Cadet' d'Albret.[38] The wholesale destruction which followed the death of Jean V, comte d'Armagnac placed a heavy burden on the *pays* for rebuilding Lectoure. The demands extended over the frontiers of Armagnac into Condomois. In May 1475 the consulates of the towns there decided to send a delegation to the governor of Guyenne at Bordeaux to try to have themselves discharged from contributing to the rebuilding of Lectoure. But in August a royal sergeant arrived at Montréal in order to seize property because of non-payment.[39]

Both the building of new fortifications and the requirement that towns maintain their defences led to the strengthening and enforcement of ties of obligation which bound individuals and communities to contribute. This in turn had the effect of focusing duties, and perhaps in the course of time loyalties, more closely on the leading towns of the *pays*. A co-ordinated response to royal demands was essential; otherwise problems could arise of the sort which plagued Saint-Emilion, where most of the stones from the town's barbican were seized and carried off in carts one night by men from Libourne who had been ordered by a royal commissioner to strengthen their own defences.[40] In Condomois the solution adopted seems to have been the acceptance that in the first instance obligations to contribute to the town's defence fell upon the town of Condom itself and were then distributed around the pays and its towns.[41] The primacy of Bordeaux in the Bordelais and of Bayonne, Dax and Saint-Sever in their respective *prévôtés* in the Landes must have been similarly reinforced.

The royal government was prepared to support the towns' demands that their inhabitants contribute fully to their own community's defence. When Sarlat was re-taken by the French in 1446, the king required that churchmen there should properly contribute, because of their property in the town, to guard and other duties and to the town's repairs.[42] In December 1449, Charles VII instructed the sénéchal and *juge* of Limousin to force churchmen who owned rural properties on the outskirts of Périgueux to contribute to the town's upkeep.[43] In Blaye in November 1487 the royal officers intervened in order to allot detailed responsibilities for the town's defence on each of its parishes.[44] In 1491 Bordeaux obtained royal letters in order to force the royal officers, lawyers and clergy in the city to contribute to the town watch, repairs and other charges.[45]

Towns like Agen, for example, were granted revenues to be used for the maintenance of defences. Such grants, first made in the years of warfare with the English, might be renewed in peacetime.[46] Great nobles too, were some-

[38] B. de Mandrot, 'Louis XI, Jean V d'Armagnac et le Drame de Lectoure', *R. hist.*, xxxviii (1888), 285–86.
[39] *Comptes consulaires Riscle*, pp. 71, 184; *Comptes consulaires Montréal*, pp. 137, 140.
[40] AC Saint-Emilion, BB 1, fo 49v.
[41] *Comptes consulaires Montréal*, p. 140.
[42] AD Dordogne, 4E 125/3.
[43] AC Périgueux, CC 15, no. 15.
[44] *Arch. hist. Gironde*, xii (1870), no. xiv, 36–39.
[45] *Registres de la jurade*, iii, 156.
[46] AM Agen, CC 4, CC 43, unnumbered.

times able to levy duties on their subjects on the grounds of military necessity. In 1404 Charles I, sire d'Albret, was permitted to raise a special tax in order to keep up the fortifications of Rions. This was confirmed by the sénéchal of Agenais in 1454.[47] At Vayres, the sire d'Albret called upon the inhabitants to work on his castle twice a year. Nobles and clergy were among those obliged to contribute to the town's defences.[48] In view of the Albrets' ambitions, the work required to keep up their town's defences can, of course, hardly be considered as a contribution to the security of Guyenne. Indeed, it was when Albret was in revolt that his castle of Nérac was strengthened by the addition of a new tower and other fortifications.[49] But other princes, in whom the king had greater faith, were also permitted to re-build and repair their castles, resorting to the labour of the local inhabitants. Olivier de Coëtivy, for instance, was permitted to reconstruct his castle of Dydonne in Saintonge which had been razed by the English during the previous century. He could demand that his vassals work and perform guard duty there.[50]

Just how burdensome these strengthened obligations, which Valois policy for the maintenance of security imposed on the inhabitants of Guyenne, were it is difficult to know. It was perhaps their abuse which was most resented. A royal ordinance of December 1451 was promulgated on this issue. It restricted the obligations of townsmen to perform watch duties in the castles they were bound to defend to a maximum of one day's service per month. Significantly for Guyenne, however, this did not apply to towns which were under threat from the English.[51] Abuses may well have continued. In February 1499 Blaye obtained letters from Louis XII which spoke of unfairness in the sharing out in the town of responsibilities for the watch.[52]

Towns were also expected to keep an effective arsenal which could be used in their own defence in the case of an English attack or lent to the king in furtherance of his own military enterprises. The royal artillery was often provisioned with powder and transported at the expense of the local communities too. Though not as sustained a burden as that of providing for the construction work, the strains imposed by the upkeep of the royal and urban artillery could be very disruptive. For instance, at Agen in February 1482 the demands of the comte de Comminges for saltpetre helped produce a crisis in the town's affairs, when some of the townsmen refused to pay a levy raised to supply it.[53]

The emphasis which the government placed upon having powerful, effective artillery was understandable in the light of the circumstances of the reductions of Normandy and Guyenne. The use of artillery by the French armies of 1442 to 1454 was recognised as having been a crucial element in their successes. Bourg, Castillon and Cadillac in Guyenne, for instance, had all fallen after

---

[47] APA, E 214.
[48] APA, E 233, unnumbered [fos 3v, 5r–v].
[49] APA, E 86.
[50] *Ordonnances*, xvii, 51–52.
[51] *Ordonnances*, xiv, 185–87.
[52] *Arch. hist. Gironde*, xii (1870), no. xx, 47–49.
[53] AM Agen, BB 19, fo 16r.

heavy artillery bombardment.[54] Charles VIII believed that it was the use of his artillery which had allowed him to crush the rebel forces under Odet d'Aydie, the comte de Comminges' brother.[55] The superiority of the French artillery and the importance this had as a condition of French military success was seen later in the Italian campaigns.[56]

The demands of the royal commissioners for help with the transport and provisioning of the royal artillery were resisted by towns whenever possible. Among the means of doing so was bribery: no doubt it sometimes worked. In 1450, for instance, Périgueux rewarded Gaspard Bureau, master of the royal artillery, with a present of wine and oats because he had relieved the town of its obligation to transport the royal artillery.[57] But the town was not always so successful. In April 1478 the consuls of Périgueux had to organise the transport of nine loads of saltpetre to Mareuil on the king's instructions.[58] Demands for help with transporting artillery and provisions seem to have been common throughout the province. In 1458, for example, Saint-Emilion was asked by a cannoneer to transport the royal artillery, and the jurade met to consider whether to accede to the request.[59]

Towns were also expected to lend their own artillery and provide gunpowder. The strain on their resources probably never again approached the level reached during the last years of English rule in Guyenne. Cadillac had at that period to provide gun-powder, cannon balls and cannoneers, bows, arrows and other weapons.[60] However, whenever there was a political crisis such demands would recur. In June 1484, for example, Bayonne was instructed to provide artillery, gun powder and pikes, as well as boats with sailors to man them.[61] That September the comte de Comminges wrote to Bayonne that he was going to send for four big culverins and two cannons to go to the siege of Maubourguet, held by the vicomte de Narbonne's soldiers. The Bayonnais protested that their artillery pieces had not been returned to them.[62]

As with the construction and repair of Guyenne's fortifications, the towns' own efforts complemented those of the royal government. Urban artillery was always a considerable element in the maintenance of Guyenne's security, though there is no evidence of consistent royal attempts to ensure that it was strengthened and modernised. Certainly, a town's arsenal was greatly treasured.

---

[54] M.G.A. Vale, 'New Techniques and Old Ideals: the Impact of Artillery on War and Chivalry at the End of the Hundred Years War', in War, Literature and Politics in the Late Middle Ages, ed. C.T. Allmand (Liverpool, 1976), p. 65.

[55] See below, p. 167.

[56] P. Contamine, 'L'Artillerie royale française à la veille des guerres d'Italie', A. Bretagne, lxxi, 2 (1964), 221–23.

[57] AC Périgueux, CC 84, fo 7r.

[58] AC Périgueux, CC 91, fos 5v, 7v.

[59] AC Saint-Emilion, BB 1, fo 2r.

[60] AC Cadillac, CC 2, fos 112r, 115v.

[61] Registres gascons, ed. Ducéré, i, 295.

[62] Ibid., pp. 301, 329. The siege of Maubourguet marked the opening stage of the Foix civil war, on which see C. de Vic and Dom Vaissète, Histoire génerale de Languedoc, viii (Toulouse, 1844), 184–85, 187–88, 207–209.

This was, for example, the case at Périgueux. In 1476–1477 new regulations were made there concerning the consular elections. These required that the consuls should swear not to hand over the town's crossbows, culverins, cannons and other weapons to anyone else, unless it was on the town's own business. Successful candidates for the mayoralty and consulate were henceforth to provide crossbows for the town's arsenal, in place of the dinner it had been traditional to give.[63]

Equally important was the fact that, judging from the artillery pieces in Périgueux and Bergerac, the towns modernised their arsenals in line with changing requirements. At the time of the sieges of Bayonne and of Blaye in 1451 massive bombards and 'courteaux' had been used. But increasing emphasis came to be placed on mobility and so on lighter artillery, such as culverins and 'falcons' mounted on gun carriages.[64] By 1475 Bergerac's arsenal had not only been enlarged and strengthened: it had also acquired two serpentines, nine culverins and two little hand cannons.[65] In 1484 the arsenal of Périgueux contained not only four cannons, but also four culverins, one little cannon and a serpentine.[66] The strengthening and modernisation taking place in urban artilleries, outside the royal supervision, was making its contribution to Guyenne's defence.

There is no doubt that the Valois government was highly successful in strengthening the provinces' defences. The size and strength of the fortifications of Bordeaux, Bayonne, Dax and Saint-Sever were unparalleled in the South-West. Furthermore, most of the work in on these centres took place in the years before the Bordeaux and Bayonne customs dues were making their full contribution to the royal revenue. The work was achieved after much wrangling between the royal government and local communities, but no apparent outright resistance. Yet at the same time these communities were expected to make major efforts towards the strengthening of their own defences. By the time that a further programme of alteration and repairs began at the time of the Italian campaigns, Guyenne's royal and urban fortifications and artillery were more effective than they had ever been.

Military obligations

The king traditionally summoned his noble subjects to serve him in arms by means of the 'ban et arrière-ban', the feudal levy.[67] The degree of reliance he placed upon the ban et arrière-ban varied, however, depending both upon the nature of the crisis he faced and upon the alternative military resources available. In Guyenne the feudal summons was above all the traditional response to imminent invasion by the English.[68] The ban et arrière-ban was raised on other

---

[63] AC Périgueux, BB 1, fos 5r, 8r–v.
[64] Contamine, 'Artillerie', 251–52.
[65] AC Bergerac, jurade 17 (1463–1464) [fos 5r–v, 6v].
[66] AC Périgueux, BB 14, fo 5r.
[67] Contamine, Guerre, p. 367.
[68] See above pp. 9–14.

occasions too, however, and for a variety of purposes. In Périgord the summons was made to deal with the disturbances associated with the *guerre du bien public* in 1465.[69] The duke of Guyenne employed it in January 1472 in Saintonge in order to resist the armies of Louis XI.[70] When the nobles of the sénéchaussées of the Landes and Bazadais were summoned in August 1476 it was in order to strengthen the army which the king was sending to Spain.[71] In March 1482 the *ban et arrière-ban* was raised in order to escort Charles II, comte d'Armagnac, from Casteljaloux, where he had been under the guard of the sire d'Albret, to Paris at the king's command.[72]

The obligation to serve extended in principle both to nobles and to those non-nobles who held noble fiefs.[73] In practice, however, there were many anomalies and variations. It seems likely that the degree of service demanded depended upon the seriousness of the circumstances which led to the summons. Not all summonses included poor nobles within their scope, for example. It was accepted by the seigneur de Ruffec, captain of the *ban et arrière-ban* of Périgord, in March 1480, that since the richest man at Sarlat did not posses 35 l.t. *rentes*, no-one there was bound to answer the summons.[74] At Périgueux in 1477, however, there was considerable doubt as to whether the property qualification for the summons that year applied or not. A royal herald issued a proclamation that no-one with less than 25 l.t. *rentes* a year need attend the musters; but this was swiftly contradicted by the seigneurs de Bressuire and de Mareuil who arrived in the town and demanded that all who owed service should muster at Nontron.[75]

The seriousness of the occasion for which the *ban et arrière-ban* was called also affected the measures likely to be taken against those who defaulted. At Bergerac in 1465, for example, where the town's nobles were told to muster in order to give support to the king during the disturbances of the *guerre du bien public*, refusal or delay were likely to be accounted treasonable. The town's nobles were told to be at Nontron on 31 July on pain of confiscation of their lands.[76] At Périgueux in 1480, on the other hand, the summons was known to have a different purpose. It was associated with the reorganisation of the *ban et arrière-ban* in the whole of the realm; in other words it was not a response to a real military threat.[77] The mayor and consuls had been ordered to arm and equip six archers in *brigandines* to serve in the *ban et arrière-ban* with the nobles of Périgord. The mayor and consuls protested that this was contrary to the town's privileges and that the town's revenues were only intended for repairs, the salvation of souls in purgatory and for officers' wages. Having inspected the

---

[69] See below pp. 164–65.
[70] BN, ms. fr. 20, 428, fo 51r–v.
[71] APA, E 77, no. 23.
[72] APA, E 86.
[73] Contamine, *Guerre*, p. 386. In this Chapter the term 'noble' has this dual meaning, unless otherwise stated.
[74] AD Dordogne, 4 E 125/1.
[75] AC Périgueux, CC 91, fo 27r.
[76] AC Bergerac, jurade 19 (1465–1466) [fos 27v–28r].
[77] Contamine, *Guerre*, p. 375.

town's privileges, the royal commissioners ratified Périgueux's exemption.[78] Royal demands for military service would certainly not have been so easily resisted if Guyenne was then threatened by noble revolt or foreign invasion.

The principal challenge to the effectiveness of the forces raised through the *ban et arrière-ban* came from claims to exemption made by groups, communities and individuals. Louis XI recognised the seriousness of the problem in a letter to the sénéchal of Agenais in December 1472. He wrote that many who were bound to serve in the *ban et arrière-ban* had managed to gain exemption – either through friendship with and favours from the muster commissioners, or by claiming to serve in the royal or princely *ordonnance* companies, or on other grounds. Henceforth, no town's privileges exempting its inhabitants from service were to apply. Nobles serving in the royal *ordonnances* could only be exempt if they were serving there in person; others must at least send substitutes, just as the clergy did. The sénéchal was instructed to carry out a survey of fiefs and call a general muster in order to find out the strength of the forces upon which the king could reply. Registers of the names and properties of those who were obliged to serve were to be sent to the royal council by 8 February 1473.[79]

However, strongly as the king might insist on his right to the service of his noble subjects, even more strongly and effectively did petitioners press for and gain exemptions. In January 1473 the king agreed that nobles who held royal fiefs and rear-fiefs, who lived in Bordeaux and served in the town guard, were to be exempt from the *ban et arrière-ban* which had been summoned that year.[80] In May 1479 royal letters exempted Bordeaux from the *ban et arrière-ban* altogether.[81] Charles VIII extended exemption from the summons to the presidents, councillors and officers of the Bordeaux *parlement*, their widows and children when minors. They neither had to serve in nor send substitutes to the *ban et arrière-ban*.[82]

Even in cases where royal exemptions were given, however, the king retained a recognised right to call upon all of his subjects to serve in times of dire emergency. In 1462 at Bayonne in the face of what seemed to be a threat of foreign attack, the royal summons to serve was simply addressed to all the citizens.[83] Such an obligation was often employed by Louis XI.[84] Moreover, in the Bordelais at least a duty to serve the king which stemmed from Anglo-Norman feudal obligation may have continued to be recognised. When the duke of Guyenne ordered an inquiry into the degree of service he could expect from the *pays*, his commissioners were told at Saint-Emilion that the inhabitants must serve him for forty days within the diocese of Bordeaux if any rebellion occurred.[85]

---

[78] AC Périgueux, EE 19, 1.
[79] AD Lot-et-Garonne, G 72.
[80] *Recueil des privilèges*, ed. Gouron, pp. 175–76.
[81] *Registres de la jurade*, ii, 7.
[82] *Ordonnances*, xx, 15–16.
[83] BN, ms. fr. 20, 485, fo 73r.
[84] Contamine, *Guerre*, p. 33.
[85] AC Saint-Emilion, II 1, no. 2, fo 1v.

As with other obligations in the province, influence and inducement were employed in order to maximise the exemption rights which had allegedly been granted. In July 1489, for instance, Périgueux made a present of fourteen pints of wine to the seigneur de Mareuil when he arrived in the town to hold the *ban et arrière-ban* musters.[86] On this particular occasion the results of bribery are uncertain. However, they seem clear enough on the occasion of the arrival of the seigneurs de Grignols and de Saint-Gelais in the town to hold the musters of the nobles of Périgord in September 1491. They stayed in the town for twelve days. So that they would not force any of the burgesses to go to the wars their expenses were entirely paid by the town and they were given presents of wine. It was money well spent, for no-one from the town was placed on the commissioners' rolls.[87]

In the light of such circumstances it is hardly surprising that the forces raised by these means were unimpressive. The number of town exemptions, the difficulty of checking on the activities of those nobles who were allegedly serving the king in other ways, the age and health of those who remained and the largely unquantifiable impact of personal and political influence – all contributed to undermining the effectiveness of the *ban et arrière-ban* as a means of raising soldiers for war. On all these grounds the *ban et arrière-ban* in the sénéchaussée of Guyenne was probably the weakest in the province. Its nobility was both more likely to be serving the king in some other capacity and more urban dwelling than that of other areas in the South-West. This is suggested by the musters called as a result of royal instructions to the sénéchal of Guyenne in August 1491. The nobles of the sénéchaussée were summoned to appear before the seigneur de Duras. The standard of military service required from them was much less demanding than that from the nobility of the Landes and Périgord. Never more than one man-at-arms was offered by a noble, either personally or through substitutes. Some of the more important nobles, such as the seigneur d'Anglade and the dame de Lalande, offered a man-at-arms accompanied by several archers, but these were the heaviest demands made. Most of those summoned, however, provided only one or more archers and sometimes even shared this burden among several nobles. A large proportion of those who were bound to provide men-at-arms or *brigandiniers* were for various reasons said to be unavailable. The seigneurs de Lesparre and de Génissac were at the royal court. Gaston de Monferrand was himself raising the *ban et arrière-ban* of Armagnac. Marshal Gié, the seigneur de Lansac, Lancelot de Noailles, the seigneur de Cambes and one Artus Olivier were said to be serving the king in arms already. The nobles of the Bordelais had been called upon to guard Blaye and Bordeaux, and this accounted for about eight of them. Only four men-at-arms, apart from those who may have been serving in town guards or in the regular *ordonnance* forces, were provided by the *ban et arrière-ban* of the sénéchaussée of Guyenne.[88]

In Périgord the *ban et arrière-ban* produced a more effective force, when it

---

86 AC Périgueux, CC 92, fo 7v.
87 AC Périgueux, CC 93, fo 7r.
88 Abbé Baurein, *Variétés bordeloises ou essai historique et critique sur la topographie ancienne et moderne du diocèse de Bordeaux*, ii (Bordeaux, 1784), 358–67.

was summoned by the sire d'Albret as comte de Périgord for the duke of Guyenne in August 1471. However, defaults for one reason or another were common, as was the provision of substitutes in place of service in person. The comte de Périgord was in theory able to call upon 151 nobles to serve him: but this was theory only. 21 of those summoned defaulted altogether, and, although this was rather less than the average in the realm of between 20% and 25%, it was still an important loss of strength.[89] The standard of military service provided was considerably higher than in the sénéchaussée of Guyenne: there were 11 men-at-arms and 68 brigandiniers.[90] However, illness, age and poverty were used as excuses by a number. Four of those summoned claimed to be ill, one was too old, one had just died and two were said to be too poor to serve in whatever capacity. Others were said to be involved in comital or ducal business elsewhere. Raymond de Salignac was, for instance, serving in Albret's household while the seigneur de Saint-Geniès was with the duke of Guyenne. Two nobles were serving in the companies of the seigneur de Curton and two in the royal *ordonnances*. Substitution also reduced the degree of personal service obtained from the nobility of Périgord, though substitutes were preferably chosen from one's own family. In cases of co-seigneuries substitution of at least one co-seigneur was a necessity.[91]

Of the three sénéchaussées or *pays* for which records of the musters appear to have survived, it is the musters of the nobility of the Landes at Bayonne and Dax which probably produced the most effective military forces. Elsewhere in France there is evidence that wealthy nobles were under-assessed for military service, but this does not seem to have been the case in the Landes.[92] Of those assembled at Bayonne in 1476, probably to join the expeditionary force sent to Spain, the seigneur de Cauna, the vicomte de Juliac and the seigneur de Puyôo each provided a man-at-arms and two *brigandiniers* – a costly commitment. In all at Bayonne 15 men-at-arms and 52 *brigandiniers* appeared. At Dax 4 men-at-arms and 35 *brigandiniers* were provided. At Dax, as at Bayonne, heavy demands for men-at-arms and several *brigandiniers* each were made of the wealthier and more important figures, such as the vicomte d'Orthe and the seigneur de Poylehaut. Only those deeply involved in the royal service in the province, such as the bishop of Aire and the seigneur de Talauresse, were obviously under-assessed.[93]

With the partial exception of the Landes, it is probable that the *ban et arrière-ban* forces were weak and growing weaker as grants of exemption multiplied. Once such a grant had been made it was most unlikely in the long run to be effectively over-ridden by the *ban et arrière-ban* commissioners. In October 1467, for example, the king granted Sarlat's request that those who held royal fiefs and rear-fiefs but lived in the town, contributing to royal and other taxes

---

[89] APA, E 660; Contamine, *Guerre*, p. 390.
[90] APA, E 660. For a definition of the term '*brigandinier*' see Contamine, *Guerre*, p. 302.
[91] APA, E 660.
[92] Contamine, *Guerre*, p. 393.
[93] APA, E 77, fo 19r–v.

levied there, should not have to serve in the musters. Subsequent attempts to make them serve failed.[94]

Yet just because the feudal musters were ineffective in raising a credible feudal army does not mean that the demands of the *ban arrière-ban* commissioners were other than awkward and burdensome for those who were required to serve. For the towns, demands for service continued to be a source of anxiety and expense, another element in the bargaining and bribery which characterised the relations of local communities with the agents of central government. For nobles who defaulted, the prescribed punishment was confiscation, though there is no evidence in Guyenne of noble families being permanently disinherited for this reason. Confiscation was, however, at least formally carried out. Those who defaulted at the musters of the sénéchaussée of Guyenne in August 1491 suffered confiscation. Half of the seigneurie of Puynormand and the fiefs of seven other nobles were ordered to be seized for the king.[95] Those whose default placed them in this awkward position might have to resort to the king in person to have the confiscations reversed. Six of the sire d'Albret's 'most important esquires, servants and familiars' obtained royal letters from Louis XI on such a matter in September 1480. Albret's men had accompanied him to the royal court and stayed with the king when their master returned to the South-West. In their absence they had been found in default at the musters of the nobility of Périgord and their lands had been confiscated. The king ordered that this should be reversed.[96]

The obligation to provide nobles and their substitutes was complemented by that to provide *francs-archers*. Instituted in 1448 and re-organised and doubled in numbers in 1466, the *francs-archers* were more of a burden than the *ban et arrière-ban*.[97] Like the *ban et arrière-ban*, the levy of *francs-archers* merged into a more general obligation to provide soldiers for the king in all emergencies. In July 1465, for example, orders were given for the mustering of all the nobles, *francs-archers* and cross-bowmen of Périgord.[98]

The fact that *francs-archers* were sometimes equipped with cross-bows confuses the verbal distinction between them and the other levies of archers which were made in Guyenne.[99] But it is clear that, over and above the more regularly assessed obligation to provide *francs-archers*, towns were subject to sudden heavier, though more easily negotiable, demands. At Bergerac in 1475, for instance, three *francs-archers* were grudgingly being supported by the town. But in April 1488 the comte de Candale demanded some fifty archers to guard Montcuq, though when the consuls of Bergerac protested he reduced his demand to ten.[100] The contrast between the two kinds of obligation is equally well illustrated in Condomois. Montréal was regularly obliged to provide one *franc-archer*, a duty which for some time at least was shared with the

---

94 AD Dordogne, 4 E 125/1, unnumbered.
95 Baurein, *Variétés*, ii, 358–68.
96 AD Gers, I 2630.
97 Contamine, *Guerre*, pp. 304–05.
98 *Jurades de Bergerac*, ed. Charrier, i, 270.
99 Contamine, *Guerre*, p. 305.
100 AC Bergerac, jurade 20 (1475–1476) [fo 16v]; *Jurades de Bergerac*, ed. Charrier, ii, 31.

neighbouring town of Mézin. Yet in May 1475, because of the threat of an English invasion, a further twenty cross-bowmen were ordered to be equipped. Similarly in 1491–1492 there was another emergency levy in the town of thirty archers to go to the musters of Condomois being received at Condom.[101]

Though less flexible than for the *ban et arrière-ban*, demands for the raising of *francs-archers* were also in some degree negotiable. In principle, the *francs-archers* were to be levied at the rate of one per 80 hearths.[102] In Armagnac the assessment was indeed made by hearths: but whether this was how other areas in the province were assessed is unclear.[103] Certainly Bergerac's assessment varied from year to year: in 1465 the town supported three *francs-archers* and in 1483 four.[104] In Armagnac in January 1475 one archer for every ten hearths was demanded. But no stable assessment was ever achieved. In the same month the *pays* were instructed to send 100 archers to Pavie, but this was suddenly reduced to eight.[105] The most extreme bargaining stance for towns able to adduce previous grants of privilege or useful precedents was to claim complete exemption from such levies. In Périgord, for example, the towns of Périgueux, Bergerac, Sarlat, Domme and Montignac all claimed that they were exempt. However, claims to total exemption were unlikely to succeed, as is shown by the case of one of these, Bergerac, which carried on a long and largely unsuccessful struggle with the *francs-archers* commissioners.[106]

These levies of archers were the subject of intense lobbying, frequent disagreement, but also of some cooperation in the *pays*. As in the matter of demands for the rebuilding of Lectoure, it was perhaps the *pays* of Condomois which showed most willingness to act as one in resisting and negotiating the levies of archers made upon it.[107]

The burden of providing *francs-archers* was also increased by the unruly and unreliable behaviour of the archers themselves. This was widely recognised. Charles of France, as duke of Guyenne, received a petition complaining about them.[108] When, in April 1486 Charles VIII commissioned the comte de Comminges to tell the estates of Guyenne about his new military measures, he noted that the *francs-archers* had proved themselves insolent and committed murders.[109]

The system of levying *francs-archers* and other archers was frequently corrupt and confusing. It was, for instance, far from unusual for towns to be in doubt about where their archers should go in order to be inspected at the musters. In August 1468 a commissioner from the sénéchal of Agenais arrived at Montréal

---

101 *Comptes consulaires Montréal*, pp. 142, 157, 173.
102 Contamine, *Guerre*, p. 304.
103 *Comptes consulaires Riscle*, ii, 408–17.
104 AC Bergerac, jurade 19 (1465–1466) [fos 27v–28r]; jurade 21 (1481–1482) [fo 49v].
105 *Comptes consulaires Riscle*, i, 197, 226.
106 AC Bergerac, jurade 19 (1465–1466) [fos 27v–28r,35v]; jurade 20 (1475–1476) [fo 16v]; jurade 21 (1481–1482) [fo 49r–v]; jurade 22 (1484–1485) [fo 70r].
107 *Comptes consulaires Montréal*, p. 175.
108 Stein, *Charles de France*, pièce justificative lxxxv, p. 718. The estates of Guyenne claimed that *francs archers* had no useful purpose there. All of the population knew how to use cross bows and would serve the duke with them anyway.
109 APA, E 781, fo 1r.

and ordered that the *francs-archers* of the pays should be equipped and sent to Agen under their captain. But three days later the townsmen had to send messengers to Condom in order to find exactly when they were to be there. At the last moment the archers were sent to Marmande instead, but because of time lost the archers demanded to be paid their expenses and threatened to refuse to go at all.[110] The worst examples of disruptive levies of archers and of the use of widespread extortion associated with them come, predictably enough, from Armagnac.[111]

In most cases the evidence which would allow proper quantification of the demands for archers which were made on the different sénéchaussées and *pays* of Guyenne does not exist. That which remains reinforces the impression that the demands were indeed burdensome and that the various administrative changes during the period in the way in which archers were levied did little or nothing to make the obligations more tolerable. In Périgord, for example, in May and June 1465 54 *francs-archers* were being supported by the *pays*; their and their captain's wages totalled 231 l.t. per month. There was talk of a further levy of 100 archers later in the year.[112] The abolition of the *francs-archers* in 1480 only resulted in the imposition of large sums of taxation in their stead.[113] In December 1481 an order was issued for 2,200 l.t. to be raised in the séné-chaussée of Armagnac to be used to pay the soldiers of the king's 'champ nouveau' which had replaced the *francs-archers*.[114] Agenais was expected to find 1275 l.t. in January 1483 for the same purpose.[115] In February 1487 70 men were ordered to be raised in the Landes and the estates were summoned, presumably in order to make a grant for their wages and expenses.[116]

The only sustained record of the cost to one community of the *francs-archers* and the other military levies associated with the system comes from Montignac, where it was an important and persistent element in the castellany's expendi-ture. The accounts also illustrate that the task of raising money locally for the *francs-archers* was an unpopular one which had to be shared by rote under the watchful eye of the *élus* of Périgord.[117]

Least information of all is available concerning the standard of the force raised through the *francs-archers* and other similar levies in Guyenne. It would be surprising if amid the evidence of administrative confusion which charac-terised the demands for archers an effective force was raised. The reputation of the *francs-archers* was in general poor, as has been observed. A roll of archers who arrived at a muster of *francs-archers* from the lands of sire d'Albret at Arzacq in March 1472 is suggestive of the inefficiency of the levies. 240 archers were due from the castellanies of Auberoche and Ans, yet of these no fewer than 40 failed to arrive.[118]

---

110 *Comptes consulaires Montréal*, pp. 97–98.
111 *Comptes consulaires Riscle*, i, 108–109, 117–18, 121–25, 129–30.
112 BN, ms. fr. 20, 496, fo 20v.
113 Contamine, *Guerre*, pp. 342–43.
114 AN, K 72, no. 62.
115 AN, K 72, no. 74.
116 AN, K 73, no. 48.
117 APA, E 781, fos 1r–51r.
118 APA, E 652, no. 74.

In general, the achievement of the new Valois government in castle-building and urban fortification was not matched by achievement in the sphere of raising soldiers from the province. Strong as Guyenne's fortified centres may have been, considering the quality of the province's locally raised military forces it was perhaps lucky for the Valois government that the English did not in fact come till 1475, and that when they did so it was to Normandy rather than Guyenne.

Garrisoning and provisioning

The purpose of the heavy garrisoning which characterised Valois military policy in Guyenne was, like that of castle building in the province, twofold. At least initially the king's soldiers must have been seen as an army of occupation. Subsequently, they were seen predominantly as a force for the defence of Guyenne against the English. In either case, the heavy demands which were made, particularly in times of political crisis, for the lodging of soldiers and provisioning of the garrisons and fortified centres which they occupied were highly unpopular.

The starting point for any investigation of the impact of providing for the French army in Guyenne must be an estimate of the numbers of soldiers in the province. The evidence for this is, however, patchy and incomplete, particularly in the years between the second reduction of Bordeaux and the death of Charles VII. It is clear that in 1453 there were 50 lances and 100 *morte-payes* garrisoning Bayonne.[119] There were 50 more lances stationed at Dax.[120] By the time of Charles' death the regular garrison in Bayonne seems to have been reduced to 76 soldiers, which suggests that there was some move towards reducing the level of garrisoning in the province in these years of relative tranquillity in Anglo-French relations.[121] However, the lack of any comparable figures till 1461 makes the task of finding an overall figure for garrisoning of the province before Charles VII's death impossible.

From 1461 onwards there is, though, sufficient evidence of the regular strength of most garrisons in the province's fortified centres to permit a tentative estimate of the total force based there. One such estimate has placed the over-all figure in the region of 350 soldiers.[122] By contrast, the estates general of Tours in 1484 was told that in the government's view 400 lances were required to defend the province.[123] The real figure probably lies somewhere between the two, but clearly closer to the former than to the regency government's, which was an element in special pleading for more money for the royal army. Such evidence as there is suggests that well over 500 men were involved in the

---

[119] BN, ms. fr. 24, 058, fo 1r. For the terms 'lances' and 'morte-payes' see Contamine, *Guerre*, pp. 278, 290–94.
[120] BN, ms. fr. 24, 058, fo 1r.
[121] BN, ms. n. a. fr. 8607, fo 81r.
[122] Contamine, *Guerre*, p. 292.
[123] *Ibid.*, p. 286.

regular defence of the province, although in times of crisis the figure could be substantially higher.

It seems likely that there were about 150 soldiers equally divided between the Châteaux du Hâ, Trompette and de La Lune in Bordeaux; another force served under the mayor of Bordeaux's command, which in 1475–1476, 1488, 1493 and 1494 numbered 90 men. It is, therefore, probable that about 240 men were regularly stationed at Bordeaux, defending the royal castles there and the town's own fortifications.[124] Bayonne seems to have been manned by a force of 100 morte-payes, divided between the old and new castles, the tower of Saint-Esprit and the town of Bayonne itself. Blaye usually had a garrison of 100 men in the years when information is available concerning it. To this total of 440 regular soldiers in garrison must be added the numbers of men based in Dax, Saint-Sever, and other centres – perhaps not permanently garrisoned – like Libourne, La Réole, and Bourg. It is clear also that sometimes there were important garrisons in Agenais and Périgord and, during some of the period, in Armagnac too. For these areas the shortcomings of the evidence are only too obvious. Dax may have had a garrison of 50 soldiers, perhaps more in 1467. Judging from the importance of Saint-Sever in the royal plans for the defence of Guyenne it would be surprising if a similar number of men were not stationed there. In an inquest on the privileges of Libourne, made in December 1486, Bertrand Le Piochel, proctor of Bordeaux, said that he remembered how, after Libourne had been reduced to the French obedience, Charles VII installed there a large garrison of men-at-arms.[125] Cadillac too was garrisoned in the summer of 1454.[126] In July 1454 four lances were garrisoned in Agenais.[127] Yet none of this garrisoning would be deduced from the muster rolls and orders for payment or quittances which have survived.

In later years too, there are glimpses of garrisoning at centres for which evidence is otherwise patchy or non-existent: for instance in the last quarter of 1471 43 men were in garrison at Bazas.[128] In the previous year 39 men were at Agen in garrison under the command of the sénéchal of Agenais,[129] and 30 soldiers were then stationed at Lectoure in Armagnac.[130] How permanent many of these garrisons were it is impossible to know; probably a residual presence of soldiers was maintained in most of them throughout the years, which could then be re-inforced in times of crisis. Inconclusive as the evidence is, therefore, it suggests, that, as has been observed, a considerable force of at least 500 soldiers – and perhaps much larger – was more or less permanently retained to guard the province.

What most affected the inhabitants of Guyenne, however, was less the overall numbers of soldiers whose needs directly or indirectly the province had

[124] For these estimates and the sources used to reach them, see Appendix 1 on pp. 199–203. What follows is, unless specified, based on that source.
[125] AC Libourne, AA 8, no. 2, fos 3r–4r.
[126] AC Cadillac, CC 3, no. 2, fos 3v–4r.
[127] AM Agen, CC 43.
[128] BN, ms. Clairambault 235, no. 143.
[129] BN, ms. fr. 25, 779, fo 28r.
[130] BN, ms. fr. 25, 778, fo 1905r.

to meet than the disruptive and unpredictable demands when these numbers were substantially increased in emergencies or when they were moved. In 1471, for instance, Charles of France, as duke of Guyenne, probably had more than 550 soldiers in the duchy, most of them not attached to regular garrison duties at all. In the crisis of 1475, about 1000 soldiers may well have been in the province. Other less dramatic re-inforcements of Guyenne's garrisons almost certainly made an impact too. In 1467 100 and in 1492 120 extra soldiers suddenly appear among those receiving payment for garrisoning Guyenne. Similarly, the burden of lodging and providing for the extra soldiers sent to the province in 1493, 1494 and 1495 is known to have been considerable.[131]

The level of garrisoning in Guyenne was not unreasonable. The number of soldiers in Guyenne's garrisons was probably approximately the same as that guarding France's other most exposed province, Normandy.[132] To the local population, however, the need to lodge and feed soldiers was a further source of anxiety and expense at a time when other military and fiscal demands were being made.

Bordeaux, itself, enjoyed a privileged position as regards the lodging of soldiers. The treaty for the reduction of Bordeaux in 1451 provided that soldiers who had to be lodged in the town would only be so at taverns and in other places where they could do no harm to private citizens.[133] In January 1468 it was confirmed that there was no obligation to provide beds and other things for soldiers unless they were properly paid for. Such privileges did not free Bordeaux from the duty of providing lodging for soldiers and others of the royal entourage altogether. In March 1462, for instance, the mayor and jurats of Bordeaux were instructed to lodge the king, his officers and the soldiers he brought with him.[134] But Bordeaux seems to have been able to achieve a better definition of its obligations than did other towns. The Bordeaux cathedral chapter of Saint-André managed, indeed, to obtain complete exemption from such demands. In April 1456 Charles VII noted that he had already given orders than men-at-arms should not be lodged in the canons' houses if there was anywhere else they could go.[135] In September 1461 the chapter had its privilege of not lodging soldiers renewed,[136] and this was subsequently confirmed by Charles of France.[137]

Other towns, however, were neither as powerful nor as privileged as Bordeaux, and faced greater difficulties as a result. Towns had sometimes to make provision for numbers of men which were quite beyond their resources. The sire d'Albret's period of control in Armagnac was a particularly harsh time for towns which had to lodge his soldiers.[138] Lodging just the sire d'Albret and his entourage was a massive strain for a small community. The seigneur de

131 See below, pp. 129, 145–46.
132 Contamine, *Guerre*, p. 292.
133. *Recueil des privilèges*, ed. Gouron, pp. 19–29.
134 AM Bordeaux, II 28 'Tiers Etat'.
135 *Recueil des privilèges*, ed. Gouron, p. 70.
136 *Ordonnances*, xv, 34.
137 ADG, G 285, fos 59v–60v.
138 *Comptes consulaires Riscle*, ii, 348.

Pierre-Buffière alone, one of Albret's leading henchmen, was accompanied by between fifty and sixty horsemen. When Albret himself came to Riscle in February 1493 he had over sixty horsemen with him, all of whom had to be dined at the town's expense.[139]

Even important towns could face a crushing and sudden burden. When Albret's army was preparing to go to Spain in 1476 Bayonne had somehow to provide fodder for no fewer than 248 horses; Albret and his pages alone had 23 horses with them.[140] Similarly onerous must have been the requirement for the vicomte de Narbonne's *ordonnance* forces to be lodged in Agenais, in Agen and Villeneuve, in 1495.[141]

The most usual way in which to extricate oneself from the administrative tangle associated with demands to lodge soldiers was, as in other matters, the use of bribery and influence. However, the cost and difficulty of this was increased for each local community by the fact that others too used the same methods. This was what Bergerac, for example, found in 1487 when the townsmen were lobbying those in authority to avoid having soldiers lodged there. They had heard the rumour that the soldiers who were at present in garrison at Sainte-Foy were to be sent to Bergerac. Consequently they sought from three of their most powerful local patrons – Hugues Bailly, the seigneur de La Force and the seigneur de Bellegarde – letters urging Odet d'Aydie the Younger not to station any soldiers in their town. These were taken to Odet by one of the consuls. Unfortunately, however, Sainte-Foy had also been lobbying, and apparently with greater success. The latter had persuaded the dame d'Orval to use her influence with the comte de Comminges, Odet's brother, and Comminges himself had written on their behalf to ensure that Sainte-Foy should no longer have to lodge soldiers.[142]

The misconduct of soldiers gave rise to resentment among the local inhabitants and a high level of violent crime can be closely associated with the years of heaviest garrisoning at Guyenne.[143] The economic dislocation which garrisoning caused, however, probably affected the lives of townsmen and peasants more than did individual crimes of violence. This was recognised by the royal government. At an early stage measures were taken to control and systematise the provisioning of forces lodged with civilians. In 1451, in preparation for the invasion of English Gascony, the French royal council prescribed fixed prices which were to be paid for food taken by soldiers, and issued rules of conduct which they were to observe.[144] Again, in 1492 when commissioners were appointed to lodge Marshal Gié's troops in the sénéchaussée of Saintonge and at Libourne, Saint-Emilion' and other towns, it was specified that soldiers were to pay 10 sous a month for their lodgings if they were men-at-arms and 5 sous if archers.[145] Further orders were issued by the governor of Guyenne that April as

139 *Ibid.*, pp. 380, 453.
140 APA, E 77, unnumbered *cahier*, fo 18r–v.
141 AM Agen, BB 19, fos 207r–208v.
142 AC Bergerac, jurade 23 (1487–1488) [fo 18r].
143 See below, pp. 142–46.
144 *Histoire de Charles VII*, ed. Godefroy, p. 610.
145 AC Saint-Emilion, II 1, no. 7.

to the individual centres among which the soldiers were to be distributed. The men were to retire to their allotted places quickly and not to form garrisons or remain outside the towns. The merchants there were to provide food at reasonable prices.[146] Saint-Emilion received four men-at-arms and 23 archers to lodge. Since the town did not have a big enough market, the surrounding parishes were told to bring in food and fodder for the soldiers and their horses.[147]

The government appointed special commissions to provide for the armies raised for the king's wars and for the province's strategic centres in times of crisis. Armies for Brittany, Burgundy and Spain had to be provisioned on a huge scale. Similarly, royal concern at the vulnerability of Bordeaux and Bayonne in times of political crisis prompted measures to collect provisions from all over the South-West. The network of royal commissioners used for these purposes and the problems which they faced are clearly revealed by correspondence between them and the central government in 1475 and 1476. The commissions were issued to trusted royal servants appointed to deal with a particular crisis. For instance, in 1475, when the English were believed to be about to invade, the *prévôt* of Bayonne and the bishop of Aire were placed in charge of the provisioning of Bayonne; Jean Favre and Etienne Moreau were appointed form Paris to organise the search along the coast for grain for Bayonne and Bordeaux; Jean Rousseau, another royal officer appointed from Paris rather than the South-West, was to search for corn in Poitou. There are at least two other royal commissioners mentioned as having been involved in the provisioning of Guyenne in 1475–1476.[148] The difficulties faced by those trying to find corn which could be shipped were increased considerably in 1475 by the fact that the grain-rich lands of Poitou were simultaneously being exploited to provision both Guyenne's principal centres and those of Normandy. At the same time as the Guyenne commissioners were searching for corn they were being obstructed by Jacques de Beaumont, seigneur de Bressuire, and his colleague Maître Jean Chambon who were trying to fulfil their own commission to provide for Normandy. The uncertainty as to where the English blow might fall helped to bring the bickering and complaints between the different commissioners to a head; meanwhile the areas – particularly Poitou and Saintonge – which had to bear the dual burden of demands from both sets of commissioners were becoming restive.[149]

Depending upon its location, each *pays* was faced by a different balance of obligations to provide for the royal needs. Périgord, for instance, was liable to demands for provisioning the king's armies in Burgundy, forces bound for Spain and the garrisons of the sénéchaussée of Guyenne.[150] Agenais and Condomois,

146 *Ibid.*, no. 5.
147 *Ibid.*, no. 3.
148 BN, ms. fr. 20, 488, fo 13r; 20, 487, fos 32r, 38r, 57r.
149 BN, ms. fr. 20, 487, fo 32r.
150 AC Périgueux, CC 91, fo 31r; *Jurades de Bergerac*, ed. Charrier, i, 301; AC Bergerac, jurade 21 (1481–1482) [fo 25v].

on the other hand, were principally, though not exclusively, subject to demands for the provisioning of forces for Spain and the garrison of Lectoure.[151]

Even with the supplies from Poitou, corn was at a premium when military ventures were afoot. In April 1476 the receiver of Périgord ordered the levy of corn from Bergerac, probably for Albret's army at Bayonne. The *taille* in the town was to be raised in corn rather than money.[152] But corn at such times was always difficult to obtain – partly, it was believed, because people hoarded it.[153] Consequently, money had frequently to be raised instead, in order to purchase corn where it *was* available. In May 1476, for example, the estates of Périgord were summoned to Périgueux in order to make a grant of 200 écus towards buying corn for the sire of d'Albret's army. The seigneur de Bellegarde took the money to Bayonne on the town's behalf, where it was used in order to purchase corn for Albret. The agreement was worked out in advance by consultation with Albret and his *prévôt des maréchaux*.[154]

Wine was also required for the king's armies and garrisons. In October 1481, for example, the Bergerac jurade was informed that the lieutenant of the *prévôt des maréchaux* was in town demanding large quantities of corn and wine for the soldiers at Bordeaux and Libourne.[155] Also frequent were demands to provide meat, sometimes in the form of livestock which could be driven to where it was required. Périgueux, for example, was ordered in 1478–1479 by the comte d'Angoulême to provide bacon for the king's army in Burgundy; it was to be made over to the *prévôts des maréchaux*.[156] In 1490 the seigneur de Lamothe arrived in the town in order to gather cows and pigs for the royal armies. However, five or six days later news was received that peace had been made with Maximilian and so the Périgourdins were relieved of the necessity of finding the animals.[157] Similar demands for the provisioning of the king's armies in the North were also made in Condomois. In 1491 a sergeant from Condom arrived in Montréal to gather pigs which were to go to provision the royal army in Brittany.[158] Pigs were also gathered at Bayonne for armies for Spain.[159] It is difficult to assess the over-all burden which provisioning placed on the *pays*. The impression is that it was when several conflicting and competing demands were made upon the communities simultaneously that real problems were created.

The royal commissioners appointed in order to organise provisioning in and around Guyenne never appear to have managed to impose a regular system on the province, even if they tried. There was in any case a strict limit to what they could achieve, given the strength of resistance from the *pays*. Not just on the marches of Poitou, where, as has been observed, resentment was fanned by

---

151 *Comptes consulaires Montréal*, pp. 114, 154–55; AM Agen, BB 19, fo 122v.
152 *Jurades de Bergerac*, ed. Charrier, i, 301–02.
153 BN, ms. fr. 20, 487, fo 31r.
154 AC Bergerac, jurade 20 (1475–1476) [fo 34v].
155 AC Bergerac, jurade 21 (1481–1482) [fo 25v].
156 AC Périgueux, CC 91, fo 31r.
157 *Ibid.*, fo 8r.
158 *Comptes consulaires Montréal*, pp. 175–76.
159 Bordes, *Histoires de la Gascogne*, p. 118.

demands for Normandy and for Guyenne, but also within Guyenne itself, the royal government and its agents were made aware of the danger of pressing the population too hard in times of political crisis. Louis XI was worried in 1475 that it was being said in Guyenne that the commission to have corn brought to Bordeaux and Bayonne was nothing more than an unnecessary abuse.[160] In 1476 the man delegated by the consuls of Bergerac to collect corn to be sent to Bayonne was struck and abused and the jurade decided to take the matter up in law.[161] It may also have been generally felt that if the king managed his own resources more efficiently he would not have to make such frequent calls for provisions. Bernard Gros, commander of the temple of Breuil in Agenais, believed that if the domain were better managed the people could be relieved of the need to provide corn during wars and other emergencies.[162] Wishful thinking, perhaps: but there is no doubt, either, that the monarchy's relative success in raising men, money and provisions for Guyenne's defence was only achieved at the expense of considerable popular resentment.

---

[160] BN, ms. fr. 20, 478, fo 31r.
[161] Jurades de Bergerac, ed. Charrier, i, 301–302.
[162] G. Tholin, 'Le Livre de raison de Bernard Gros, commandeur du temple de Breuil en Agenais sous Louis XI et Charles VIII', B. hist. phil. Com. Trav. hist. sci. (1839), 123.

7

Crime and Disorder

The ending of the conditions of war in Guyenne, which had themselves permitted and encouraged crime, did not lead to any serious or systematic attempt
to improve the system for detecting and apprehending criminals. Secular and
ecclesiastical seigneurs continued to feud and to terrorize the population. The
large numbers of soldiers in the province were responsible for a high proportion
of violent crime. Criminals from every background were difficult to punish
because of the unreformed rights of sanctuary and the difficulty of pursuing
criminals from one jurisdiction to another. Professional thieves, forgers and
sometimes murderers could lead long and profitable careers over a large geographical area. If caught, criminals frequently escaped from poorly maintained
or badly administered goals. Ferocious punishment was no effective substitute
for detection and apprehension. The central government, however, was much
more concerned with maintaining security than peace: only 'political' disorder
was likely to evoke a prompt governmental response.

The *lettres de rémission*

The information which is available concerning the causes, location and incidence of crime in French Guyenne comes almost exclusively from the *registres
du trésor des chartes*, JJ 180 to JJ 229. The *registres* give valuable details of crimes
committed during the period. But the evidence they provide must be treated
with some caution for a number of reasons.

First, the contents of pardons registered were to a large degree influenced by
the nature of the *lettre de rémission* as it had grown up by the mid-fifteenth
century. The *lettres de rémission* appear in abundance from about 1350. From
soon after that they were given only for homicides where there were extenuating circumstances. Henceforth other crimes were pardoned by means of *lettres
d'abolition*. Homicide was understood in law to have as its automatic punishment the death penalty; so the *lettres de rémission* were in theory all that
prevented the culprit from being executed.[1] The great majority of pardons for
Guyenne registered in the *trésor des chartes* are *lettres de rémission*. It would,
therefore, be unwise to assume that the apparently overwhelming preponderance of murders or killings recorded implies that a similar preponderance of *all*
crimes committed involved homicide. Nor, needless to say, can any conclusions
be drawn, other than impressionistic, of the *total* volume of crime.

It would similarly be wrong to take too seriously all of the extenuating

---

[1] G. Tessier, *Diplomatique royale française* (Paris, 1962), pp. 261–63

circumstances which the *lettres de rémission* record. The *lettre de rémission* is not just an act of royal grace, it is also intended to exculpate.[2] The *lettre* probably followed very closely the text of the request which had been submitted.[3] Some petitioners for pardon claimed that the death which had ensued from their actions was not their fault at all. For example, a carpenter of Doazit alleged that a surgeon had failed to stop the bleeding of a man whom the carpenter had stabbed and that this had resulted in his victim's death.[4] Nearly all the *lettres de rémission* add that the death in question took place through 'lack of proper care or otherwise'.

For those who actually admitted responsibility for the crime they were held to have committed it was necessary to prove both a lack of premeditation and, if possible, good character. Sometimes the petitioners' accounts given to deny premeditation were distinctly far-fetched. For example, a man who killed a long-standing enemy after the latter and others had set on him in a tavern brawl claimed that he had been blinded by blood flowing from a head wound.[5]

Loyalty to the French crown was the virtue most likely to be emphasised when petitioners sought to exculpate themselves. Some petitioners, indeed, spent far more time detailing their valuable services than recounting the crimes they wanted pardoned. A petitioner who had killed a dishonest tax-collector noted that the petitioner's father was a noble and had always fought against the English. He himself had served in the *ban et arrière-ban* of Saintonge, had been wounded at Blaye, and had served at the battle of Castillon.[6] Others just slipped in a detail which, it was clearly hoped, would warm the royal heart. In 1462 a man of Saint-Martin-de-Peyrac in Agenais noted in his request for pardon that the relevant events had occurred on his return from Louis XI's coronation.[7]

Second, it is worth bearing in mind when examining the contents of a *lettre de rémission* that neither were all the facts alleged in it verified by the king or his servants when the document was granted, nor were they accepted automatically by those in Guyenne or elsewhere who were summoned to put them into effect. Petitions for pardon in general have received relatively little detailed examination.[8] The only clue to the process from Guyenne is provided by part of a confession by a man living in the sanctuary at Saint-Macaire which was probably drawn up for insertion into the form of a petition for pardon. It was prepared by a notary in August 1483 and was presumably intended, in its finished form, to be sent to wherever the king was at that time.[9]

It seems likely that petitions of this sort were drawn up and presented at the

---

2 C. Gauvard, 'L'Image du roi justicier en France à la fin du moyen âge, d'après les lettres de rémission', in *La Faute, la répression et le pardon* [Actes du 107e congrès national des Sociétés savantes, Brest, 1982. Section de philologie et d'histoire jusqu'à 1610.], i (Paris, 1984), p. 165.
3 P. Braun, 'La Valeur documentaire des lettres de rémission', in *idem*, p. 216.
4 AN, JJ 198, no. 554.
5 AN, JJ 205, no. 357.
6 AN, JJ 185, no. 265.
7 AN, JJ 198, no. 322.
8 Tessier, *Diplomatique royale*, p. 261.
9 ADG, 3E 7131, fo 4r.

royal court like other '*requêtes*'. Those which survive suggest that the process of preparing and presenting petitions was still fairly informal; they are poorly written, on poor quality paper and differ in format. Although they were supposed to be examined and sorted by the royal *maîtres de requêtes* a good contact could ensure that they went straight to the king in person wherever he was.[10] In these circumstances the main burden of verifying and making effective *lettres de rémission* fell to the courts and officers of the *pays* to which they were directed; the process of registration in the *trésor des chartes* gave the grants no special authority and was a matter of record not adjudication.[11] Not all of the *lettres de rémission* which supplicants presented for *entérinement* were accepted by the inferior courts. Letters pardoning one Jean du Casso for a murder were rejected in the Bordeaux *parlement* in September 1474, though the precise grounds are not stated.[12] Similarly, *lettres de rémission* obtained by a convicted forger were disallowed and he was banished in 1483.[13]

The third consideration which prompts caution in using the registered *lettres de rémission* as a guide to crime in Guyenne relates to the difficulties which might be faced by those seeking the royal pardon in gaining access to the king. Some petitioners, admittedly, managed to gain pardon from prison with apparently little or no outside help.[14] Those in prison at Louis XI's accession were particularly fortunate in this regard. But even their release was not always automatic. The councillors of the duc d'Alençon in March 1464 demanded the release of prisoners in the Ombrière palace at Bordeaux on these grounds, but it was opposed by the royal proctor.[15] Others, though, had to rely on those who remained at liberty to help them. Louis de Fayolles, for example, was incarcerated in the castellany of Carlux in the vicomte de Turenne's gaol, when he was pardoned in August 1475 at the instance of his friends and relations. This was also necessarily the case with those who had fled the *pays*; and this group, because of the ineffective methods of arrest and detention, was a large one.[16]

Pardons were certainly much easier to obtain, as were other favours, when the king was in the vicinity. This is borne out by the large numbers of *lettres de rémission* granted by Louis XI and, rather less so, by Charles VIII when they came to the South-West. The flow of royal grace depended also, however, on political circumstances, as can be illustrated by a brief summary of the trends in the numbers of *lettres de rémission* and *lettres d'abolition* granted to supplicants from Guyenne during the period 1451 to 1498.

The circumstances of Charles VII's visit to the South-West in the summer of 1451 were unpropitious for the granting of many individual *lettres de rémission*. The background to the king's return with his armies in 1453 was even less so.

---

10 Tessier, *Diplomatique royale*, pp. 269–72.

11 *Ibid.*, pp. 288–91. From the fourteenth century, *lettres de rémission* were not of themselves 'exécutoires' but had to be verified and accepted by the judicial officers mentioned in the '*formule exécutoire*'.

12 ADG, B 5, fos 45v–46r.

13 ADG, B 6, fo 31v.

14 AN, JJ 198, no. 105.

15 AN, JJ 187, no. 297.

16 *Ibid.*, nos. 252, 289, 305; JJ 222, no. 47.

Some pardons were granted, however. They often related to crimes committed many years before.[17] In August 1451, for example, a man from Agen was pardoned for a murder he had committed in the late 1430s.[18] More typical of the period of 1451 to 1453 were the blanket grants of pardon to towns and other communities for their wartime misdeeds by *lettres d'abolition*, though these had sometimes to be reinforced by *lettres de rémission* granted subsequently to people who were sufficiently anxious about the enormity of their crimes or the machinations of their enemies.[19] Only 9% of the pardons (*lettres de rémission* and *lettres d'abolition*) granted between 1450 and 1494 at the instance of petitioners, or their families and friends, living in Guyenne are dated between 1450 and 1454.[20]

There were many more pardons granted between 1455 and 1459; indeed 20% of all the Guyenne pardons in the period before 1494 went to supplicants during these years. Some of this increase was undoubtedly the result of grants of pardon for crimes committed in war by those who felt that they had little chance of avoiding prosecution or revenge now that peace had returned to the province. But the number of pardons also to some extent reflects the number of crimes committed by soldiers in this period of semi-occupation in Guyenne.

Louis XI's arrival in the province shortly after his accession was responsible for the sudden upsurge of grants of pardon between 1460 and 1464; 30% of all grants recorded for Guyenne up to 1494 were made in this short period. In 1462–1463 royal grants of pardon were probably easier to obtain than they had been before or were likely to be again. The accessibility of the king at this time is testified by grants to peasants and townsmen who could hardly have been able to employ the services of influential people in the royal entourage to have their *requêtes* received favourably.[21] The rest of Louis XI's reign, in contrast to these early years, saw very few pardons granted to petitioners from Guyenne – even though crime may have persisted at a high level.

The period of Charles of France's control in Guyenne, between 1469 and 1472, saw a virtual cessation of royal pardons issued to people in the South-West. But this did not mean that the prerogative of grace fell into disuse, only that it was the duke of Guyenne who exercised it. Pardons may indeed have been thought too easy to come by from the duke. In January 1471 ducal ordinances were issued stating that no letters of pardon could be sealed without the consent of the ducal council.[22] The attitude adopted by the duke of Guyenne's *grand jours* during these years may have discouraged suitors from applying for *lettres de rémission* and *lettres d'abolition* from the king. According to a noble who petitioned the king in 1483, the ducal *grands jours* had refused to accept the full pardon which he had been granted twenty years previously, probably on Louis XI's visit to Guyenne. His victim's widow had opposed the

---

[17] AN, JJ 185, nos. 147, 150, 161, 166, 195.

[18] *Ibid.*, no. 166.

[19] AN, JJ 181, no. 26.

[20] See Appendix 2 for this and for all the statistical generalisations which are to be found in this chapter.

[21] AN, JJ 198, nos. 288, 293, 300, 322, 382, 517, 519, 521, 525, 540, 554.

[22] Stein, *Charles de France*, pièce justificative cv, p. 748.

ratification of the noble's *lettres de rémission* by the Paris *parlement* and the case was subsequently evoked to the ducal *grands jours*. The *grands jours* would only accept his pardon in a severely modified form.[23]

Charles VIII's brief stay in the South-West resulted, like his father's, in the granting of a number of pardons to local petitioners in March 1487.[24] These again went to suitors who cannot have been able to wield much influence in the king's entourage.[25] But Charles was only in Guyenne for a short time and soon set off North again. Furthermore, he had come to suppress rebellion, not principally to pardon miscreants. The period 1485 to 1489 does not, therefore, seem to have been one in which pardon in Guyenne was particularly easy to obtain. For the rest of the reign the rate of pardons settled at a lower level, which, though hardly significant of prodigality, at least shows that the fount of royal grace had not dried up entirely.

However, although they are unreliable *ex parte* statements, although they did not always result in executive action in the province itself, and although the number of pardons is not in itself a sufficient guide to the number of crimes, the *lettres de rémission* are extremely valuable. First, the often lengthy confession which comprises the body of the document reveals most of the circumstances of the crime committed, even if they are deliberately placed in a favourable light. Second, even though the date of the pardon may largely depend upon factors unconnected with the level or nature of crimes being committed at any particular time, in most cases the approximate date of the crime itself is given in the document; consequently periods of considerable crime and disorder are still recorded, though this may be some or many years after they have occurred. Third, the *lettres de rémission* are in most cases clear about where the crimes took place and the status or occupation of the petitioner. It is, therefore, possible tentatively to plot the relative incidence of criminal violence, the areas in which it occurred and the kind of persons responsible for it.

Crime and the seigneurs

Of the crimes committed between 1450 and 1494 in Guyenne as a whole for which *lettres de rémission* were received, 21% were perpetrated by nobles. The proportion though was much higher in areas like the Landes and Armagnac, which were away from the centre of the royal authority at Bordeaux. It is likely that nobles, particularly members of families which had contacts at the royal court, were more likely than other less influential people to obtain pardon for their crimes. For example, the nature of a *lettre de rémisssion* granted to the bastard of Orval suggests that he himself may have dictated its terms informally and that these were accepted word for word.[26] Yet, while many nobles may have had contacts – through those at court, royal officers and the connections to

23 AN, JJ 209, no. 179.
24 AN, JJ 217, nos. 154, 191, 194, 196, 197, 199, 208.
25 *Ibid.*, nos. 199, 209; these are pardons for 'poor men' of Entre-Deux-Mers dated March 1487.
26 AN, JJ 205, no. 71.

which they belonged – which could ease access to the king's mercy, the importance of the criminal violence for which nobles were responsible in Guyenne is
probably not exaggerated in the *lettres de rémission*. Feuds between nobles were
difficult to resolve and involved many more individuals than the two original
participants. The size of a noble's entourage, the extent of his landed rights, the
breadth of his family connections and his and their martial traditions – all were
likely to ensure that criminal violence among the nobility would affect more
individuals and interests than that among other groups.

In English Gascony noble jealousy and ambition had been intricately involved in the war between the Lancastrians and the Valois for its future.[27] The
disorder of these years had allowed noble connections in some areas to engage
in private war. For instance, a seigneur of the comté of Comminges in April
1451 obtained pardon for himself and his '*societas*' for crimes committed in a
feud between two other noble families of the region.[28]

With the return of peace and greater order after the final reduction of
Guyenne the opportunities for full-scale private war diminished. But even if
disputes which might previously have led to violence were now more likely to
be taken to court in order to resolve outstanding differences, court cases themselves could spark off further violence. In August 1489, for example, festivities
presided over by Arnaud de La Fayolle at the parish of Notre-Dame-de-Pardus
were broken up by Guiot de Bourdeilles accompanied by fifteen or twenty
servants armed with bows, javelins, daggers and swords. Guiot's father, Arnaud
de Bourdeilles, was apparently the Fayolles' mortal enemy because of a case
before the *parlement* of Bordeaux.[29] Guiot de Bourdeilles and one of Fayolles
were killed.[30]

The most long-standing and disruptive feud was that between the families of
Gramont and Luxe. The great feud was liable to burst forth in the most trivial
of circumstances, so deeply had it been ingrained into each side's supporters.[31]
The importance of maintaining order in the Pyrenean area of the South-West
was increased by the requirements of French policy towards Spain and Navarre
under Louis XI and Charles VIII. Consequently the government could not
afford to stand back from the Gramont-Luxe feud. In March 1476 a royal
herald told the seigneur de Luxe that he and his adherents were not to attack
the seigneur de Gramont and his party for the duration of the war against
Spain. Gramont had received similar instructions.[32] In August 1476 the sire
d'Albret and the seigneur du Puy-du-Fou, the two most important commanders
in the army assembling at Bayonne, were instructed to arbitrate between the
two noble houses. Their sentence was to be accepted as definitive on pain of
payment of 10,000 écus. The influence of the seigneur de Gramont, who was
actually with the Bayonne army, however, may have allowed him to escape
censure for his servants' attacks on the Luxe faction. According to Luxe, only

27 Vale, *English Gascony*, pp. 154–215.
28 AN, JJ 180, no. 192.
29 B. *Soc. hist. archéol. Périgord*, xvii (1890), 206-207.
30 *Ibid.*, p. 208.
31 AN, JJ 220, no. 268; JJ 217, no. 168.
32 APA, E 76, unnumbered.

days after Albret, who was said to be biased in the Gramonts' favour, had sent commissioners renewing earlier orders not to continue feuding in Navarre, Gramont's men had begun pillaging more than ever.[33] The Gramonts used their great political influence in negotiations with the Luxes. In November 1490 Roger de Gramont appointed representatives to witness and swear on his behalf to uphold the peace treaty between the two houses' partisans. Among his representatives figured such important people as the lieutenant of the sénéchal – Gramont held the latter office – of the Landes, and Etienne Makanan, mayor of Bayonne.[34]

In practice, the French crown proved incapable of establishing control over the subjects of the Luxes and Gramonts who lived on the periphery of or outside the kingdom. In August 1495, in order to stop the disorders caused by the feud, the governor of Guyenne, himself, was sent to the vicomté of Soule to talk to the seigneur de Gramont. Predictably, however, the latter contented himself with swearing that the disorders were not his fault and submitting himself and all his property to the king – as long as the Luxes did the same.[35]

Once such deep-rooted hostility between nobles and their subjects had been generated, the ordinary processes of law were unlikely to be sufficient to settle disputed issues. A conference was the means chosen to resolve differences between the subjects of the sire d'Albret and the comte de Foix in the Landes in June 1454. Representatives were to be appointed by both sides in order to work out compensation for the losses which had been suffered in previous fighting.[36]

The only sure way to avoid the generation of a feud and the violence and destruction of property which it would entail was, however, to have the injured party publicly renounce his 'right' of revenge. This was the course of action adopted by the entourage of the bastard of Lustrac in March 1498. Even though Lustrac had been almost beaten to death by the seigneur de Rigolères and others, he accepted the advice of the master of his household and pardoned Rigolères in a written statement; in the event of Lustrac's death no-one was to do Rigolères or his men any harm.[37]

The feud was essentially a conflict between social equals; but it often involved those who were unfortunate enough to be associated with a noble's enemy and who were not necessarily of noble birth. A noble's tenants could prove easy victims.[38]

Insolent behaviour from social inferiors was always likely to be a sufficient motive for noble violence. When a serf who claimed that he was owed some wine asked for it from a noble of Agenais, he was killed because his manner was deemed insulting.[39] The great families of Bordeaux showed equal arrogance.

---

[33] APA, E 543 unnumbered *cahier* [fos 2v, 4r].

[34] J. de Jaurgain and R. Ritter, *La Maison de Gramont, 1040–1967*, i (Lourdes, 1968), 111.

[35] AD Gers, I 1600, unnumbered.

[36] APA, E 68, unnumbered.

[37] AD Lot-et-Garonne, *Registre de notaire déposé aux archives en 1947 par Y. de Scorailles à Sangruère; minutes de notaire J. Cassolle*, fo 186r.

[38] AN, JJ 198, no. 144.

[39] AN, JJ 187, no. 324.

Lettres de rémission issued to Jean de Rostaing, jurat of Bordeaux, in 1482 tell how Rostaing, describing himself as being from a 'very old noble family of Bordeaux', and his victims as 'mere rustics', trapped them in a back street of Bordeaux and with his entourage beat them, killing one. Though he had to flee the city it was only a month before he received the royal pardon. Even the punishment of a man like Rostaing reflected his social position: he had to give 25 l. to the sénéchal which was to be distributed to the city poor.[40]

Towns faced major problems from noble violence. Agen, for example, engaged in a dispute with Etienne de Durfort, seigneur de Bajamont, concerning land on the outskirts of town. When the town officers entered the disputed area they were attacked by Bajamont, accompanied by other members of his family and his household. Two of the town officers were severely wounded. The town court issued a warrant for his arrest; but Bajamont apparently maintained that 'a king of England once gave Agen to a seigneur de Bajamont and he cannot be arrested'.[41]

More prolonged and still more violent were Agen's disputes with the seigneur de Montpezat. In the early 1460s, when the royal proctor and Agen were preparing their case against him, Montpezat apparently sent 27 armed men on horseback into Agen's jurisdiction and seized all the crops belonging to the royal proctor.[42] He also ambushed the royal officers and consuls because he heard they were going to try to impound his livestock, grazing on royal pasture.[43]

When a seigneur or group of nobles were seriously determined to terrorise a small town there was little which could stand against them. In May 1486, for instance, the seigneur de Longa ordered his servants to patrol the streets of Mussidan seeking out his enemy and defying the orders of the town council.[44] At Domme in 1486 the royal officers were faced with a formidable attempt by local nobles to break one of their number out of prison. The attack was only driven off when the captain of the castle cried 'for the king!', rang the tocsin, and the citizens of Domme forced the nobles to flee.[45]

The Albrets' treatment of the town of Fleurance in Gaure stands out in its ruthless use of violence. Between 1452 and 1506 possession of Gaure was disputed between the Albrets and the crown.[46] Benefiting from the government's paralysis resulting from the *guerre du bien public*, the vicomte de Tartas sent 300 or more archers to Fleurance to take it by storm. The citizens were gaoled and robbed; some were hanged and others drowned.[47] Nor was this the last time such methods were employed there.[48]

---

[40] AN, JJ 207, no. 184.

[41] AM Agen, FF 138, unnumbered.

[42] AM Agen, FF 141, unnumbered *cahier* [fo 15v].

[43] *Ibid.*, [fos 17v–18r].

[44] AN, JJ 218, no.10.

[45] *Ibid.*, nos. 9, 77.

[46] Luchaire, *Alain le Grand*, pp. 139–52. Gaure was re-taken by force by the royal officers in 1506; see Viala, *Parlement de Toulouse*, ii, 78.

[47] APA, E 162, unnumbered *cahier* [fos 1v–3r].

[48] Luchaire, *Alain le Grand*, pp. 145–78.

Large and ill-disciplined noble entourages were a source of disorder wherever they went. The three estates of Armagnac found it necessary to ask their comte, Charles, on his accession to keep proper order in his household.[49] Moreover, the noble entourage could easily degenerate into the noble gang, available for hire by unscrupulous men. The archbishop of Bordeaux seems to have appointed the seigneur de Grignols, Jean de Talleyrand, as his *baile* in May 1467 for just this purpose. The archbishop was at that time in dispute with the commander of Cours, Argenton and Romestaing over a prisoner in the *commanderie* goal. Accompanied by more than twenty armed men, Grignols broke open the prison, beat a priest almost to death and promised to do the same to the commander if he found him.[50]

Of the groups of criminals between 1450 and 1494, the clergy as a whole appear as one of the least important. Less than 3% of those pardoned were clerics. It may be that the proximity of sanctuary for clerical criminals or the latent hostility of ecclesiastical judges to lay justice provided opportunities for the culprits to avoid the threat of capital punishment and so the need for pardon. But the behaviour of ecclesiastical *seigneurs* was quite a different matter. Like their secular counterparts, they employed violence on a large scale to serve their ends. The bishop of Cahors, for example, apparently had a force of eighty to a hundred mounted and armed men, who patrolled his lands and intimidated his enemies.[51]

Sometimes it was sees or benefices which were in dispute. The see of Agen was the subject of a long and violent struggle between Galeazzo della Rovere, the royal and papal nominee to the bishopric, and Pierre Dubois. Armed men were employed to gain control of the temporality of the see in 1477. When the sénéchal of Agenais imposed Galeazzo della Rovere by force, Dubois responded by sending in his men to attack Rovere's officers.[52] Possession of important benefices was also something worth employing soldiers in order to obtain. Before the *grands jours* of 1459 Geoffroi de Pompadour claimed that he had been dispossessed of the priory of Saint-Cibian by the archbishop of Bordeaux, accompanied by eighty men-at-arms.[53]

But other incidents of violence between ecclesiastical – just as between lay – seigneurs resulted from clashes of jurisdiction. For example, a dispute over the limits of the jurisdictions of the commander of Condat and the abbot of Terrasson in 1494 led to violent scenes. About thirty armed men, three of them priests, attacked the commander's house by night, hurled stones through his windows, burnt the gates and threatened to throw him in the river.[54]

It is clear, then, that nobles and ecclesiastical seigneurs continued to use violence ruthlessly and with relative inpunity to achieve their ends. Such

[49] AD Tarn-et-Garonne, A 46, unnumbered.

[50] AD Haute-Garonne, H, Fonds de Malte, Argenteins 30 [old cataloguing: Cours 2, no. 32], fos 1r–2r.

[51] AN, JJ 208, no. 141.

[52] Chanoine Durengues, 'Galéas de La Rovère, évêque d'Agen, 1478–1487', R. *Agenais*, 1v (1928), 103–105.

[53] *Arch. hist. Gironde*, ix (1867), no. ii, 311–12.

[54] AD Haute-Garonne, H, Fonds de Malte, Condat 9 [old cataloguing: 9, no. 16], fos 5r–6r.

violence was not generally a political threat to the government – though it could be to the royal officers – so it prompted little government action to repress it. But it seems to have been sufficiently widespread to mean that the ending of war cannot in Guyenne be said to have amounted to the arrival of peace.

Crime and soldiers

Violent crimes committed by soldiers in Guyenne are very fully represented in the *trésor des chartes* registers. Even allowing for the number of violent crimes in the years after 1450 which were but the working out of wartime animosities, it seems likely that the years after the French reductions of Bordeaux were ones of considerable disorder. Both the high level of crimes committed during Charles VII's last years and the large number of grants of pardon by Louis XI on his accession suggest this. The principal cause was undoubtedly the very heavy garrisoning of the major centres of the province during these years. Between 1450 and 1464 over 30% of all pardoned crimes were committed by soldiers. That compares with an average of about 20% over the whole period. In the sénéchaussées of Guyenne and Bazadais, which included the most important centre for garrisoning, Bordeaux, the problem was, not surprisingly, at its worst. Between 1450 and 1464, 46% of all the crimes mentioned in the *trésor des chartes* registers as committed there were the the the work of soldiers. The evidence points to the fact, then, that heavy garrisoning brought crime and disorder with it.

Guyenne had suffered in the early 1450s from the pillaging and unruly behaviour of the English and French armies sent to the province. By March 1453 the army with which Talbot had restored part of Guyenne to English rule had been increased by the arrival of a relief force to over 7,300 men.[55] Talbot tried to regulate the activities of his soldiers in Bordeaux, but not perhaps with great success. The English seem to have behaved just as badly as the French who succeeded them. In January 1453 English soldiers lodging with a man at Bordeaux pillaged his house and drove him into sanctuary.[56]

It is, however, the French armies for whose crimes most evidence exists. The main French armies of 1453 consisted of 200 lances under the command of the comte de Foix, 150 lances under the comte d'Armagnac, and 100 lances under the sire d'Albret. Special care was taken to ensure that each lance consisted of the proper number of soldiers.[57] These armies were not only large; they were also undisciplined. In July 1453, for example, at the taking of Castillon, when rumours circulated that an English relief force had arrived, the army seems to have lost all sense of discipline. The soldiers of all companies ran among the English defenders taking prisoner those who could later be profitably ransomed.[58] The invading French force was riven by tension, and sometimes

---

[55] Vale, 'Last Years', p. 132.
[56] ADG, H 735, fo 55v.

[57] APA, E 68 unnumbered.
[58] BN, ms. Duchesne 10, fos 35r–42r.

violence on a large scale, between the different nationalities of which it was composed.[59]

When peace had returned to the province and the last English forces had left Bordeaux, the misdeeds of soldiers continued to be a source of fear and resentment among the inhabitants. The principal threats to peace and order seem to have come from the activities of four groups – the *francs-archers*, foreigners, soldiers on the move from one centre to another, and soldiers who were lodged or who tried to settle down in the *pays*.

The *francs-archers* in Guyenne seem to have lived down to their low reputation. Those who commanded them must be ready to defend their lives. In 1458 the captain of those of Saintonge was insulted and attacked by the archers of his charge and had to fight for his life after an argument.[60] Two archers fought at Bordeaux in 1455 after each had alleged that the other had committed the worst pillaging.[61] There appears to have been a steady stream of archers deserting their companies for fear of punishment for their crimes.[62] Lingering resentment felt by *francs-archers* against their social superiors, the men-at-arms, might be fanned into disorder by a trivial incident. In 1451 Saintes was the scene of one such affair as a result of which a band of *francs-archers* attacked the men-at-arms in their lodgings. The riot was only suppressed with the help of Théaude de Valpergue and of the local captain.[63]

Perhaps the most unpopular soldiers in Guyenne were the Scottish and Spanish troops who played a major part in the conquest of the province. Bayonne was the scene of armed clashes between Scots under Robert Conyngham and Spaniards under Martin Garcie in 1453. The participants were still committing murderous acts of revenge in Armagnac four years later.[64] Large numbers of Scottish soldiers had to seek *lettres de rémission*.[65] The Spaniards were probably no less violent. Spanish soldiers serving under the command of Martin Henriquez, sénéchal of Saintonge, were said to have terrorised the inhabitants of one village there so much that they left their homes and hid in the marshes and woods, while their land lay untended and untilled.[66]

The inhabitants of Guyenne drew little distinction between the 'foreigners' who came from outside France and those who originated from distant provinces. Bergerac blamed the ills the town suffered on its garrison of Bretons.[67] The violence and pillaging committed by soldiers in Libourne from 1488 to 1493 was blamed on 'foreigners' from Picardy, Brittany and elsewhere.[68]

Soldiers who were moving from one centre to another across the *pays* were probably more difficult to subject to effective discipline and control than those in permanent garrison. Little could be done, it seems, to reduce the ills they wrought. Périgueux paid 7 sous to the captain of the *francs-archers* of Agenais,

---

59 BN, JJ 187, no. 289.
60 AN, JJ 187, no. 322.
61 AN, JJ 191, no. 165.
62 *Ibid.*, JJ 198, no. 541.
63 AN, JJ 181, no. 9.
64 AN, JJ 187, no. 289.

65 *Ibid.*, nos. 287, 289; JJ 191, no. 239; JJ 199, nos. 334, 489.
66 AN, JJ 190, no. 58.
67 *Jurades de Bergerac*, ed. Charrier, i, 245.
68 AC Libourne, AA 9, no. 1, fo 19r.

Quercy and Rouergue in 1467–1468; but when 300 archers passed through the *pays* they still left a trail of destruction behind them.[69]

Every attempt would be made to keep the soldiers away altogether. But when such efforts proved in vain all that could be stolen or destroyed was moved into the towns and locked in the safest place possible. In May 1471 the Bordeaux chapters of Saint-Seurin and Saint-André buried their long-standing differences when they learned that the soldiers of the duke of Guyenne and of the king were at large in the *pays*. The treasures and relics of Saint-Seurin were locked up in the cathedral treasury.[70] Similarly, in March 1483 the townsmen of Bayonne agreed that thirty pipes of wine could be brought into the town for fear that it might be seized by the soldiers in Bearn.[71]

Finally, acts of violence were perpetrated too by those who came to acquire roots in the province into which they had come as soldiers. This process could sometimes lead to tension in the garrisons. Property disputes arose which provoked violence.[72] The more social contact which soldiers had with the indigenous population, the more opportunities there were for jealousy and resentment. Competition between soldiers and local townsmen for the favours of women, for example, led to bitterness and violence.[73] Those soldiers who were lodged with families easily caused friction from which bloodshed could follow.[74]

Soldiers who retired to farm the country which they had recovered from the English may never have lost their taste for violence. After being insulted, such a man at Vendoire in Périgord lay in wait for his neighbour and killed him.[75] When soldiers tried to establish themselves in the country by marrying into important local families, they might run up against hostility. Few were those who, like Robin Petillot, managed to marry into a great family like the Gramonts.[76] More typical were probably the attempts of Pierre Karlaguen, a Breton archer, to marry the daughter of the seigneur de Roquetaillade. He and other soldiers tried to kidnap her and when this failed sought to intimidate her intended husband, who was a local noble. Foiled on this score, they planned instead to kidnap her sister.[77]

The attitude of the authorities to the criminal activities of the soldiers in Guyenne seems to have been one of slightly ambiguous disapproval. It was laid down that in criminal matters of minor importance, like the seizure of provisions, as long as no blood had been shed, the complainant should approach the duc de Bourbon, the lieutenant general of Guyenne, or Poton de Xaintrailles, the marshal, or in their absence, the soldier's captain. These would deal out summary justice as long as both sides agreed. If they did not, the case went before the sénéchal of Guyenne. If the crime were a serious one, the matter appertained in the first instance to the sénéchal, and should an arrest be

[69] AC Périgueux, CC 90, fo 10r.

[70] ADG, G 285, fo 77r.

[71] *Registres gascons*, ed. Ducéré, i, 211–12.

[72] AN, JJ 191, no. 239.

[73] AN, JJ 185, no. 281; JJ 199, no. 334.

[74] AN, JJ 181, no. 28; JJ 211, no. 373.

[75] AN, JJ 187, no. 242.

[76] AD Gers, I 1600, unnumbered *cahier* [fos 1r–4r].

[77] AN, JJ 211, no. 318.

needed the civil and military authorities would cooperate to bring it about. If the malefactor was of noble birth the marshal must be present at the trial.[78]

But the royal government's attitude to military misbehaviour was more ambiguous than this would suggest. It is possible that the wave of crime associated with the very heavy garrisoning of the province in the years after the second reduction of Guyenne was viewed in some circles as having at least the merit of punishing the province. The threat of pillaging soldiers certainly had its uses for the government or indeed anyone else who was in a position to make it. The prospect of the misdeeds which would be committed by the royal soldiers if they were not paid was used by Charles VIII's government to justify the levy of taxation[79] – though the authorities in Guyenne also had good reason to know that the disorder created by the soldiers' pillaging could result in a loss of taxable income. In June 1487, for instance, the élus of Périgord granted the inhabitants of the castellany of Veragne a 20 l. t. reduction in their taille assessment because the royal army had stayed there for some days before going on to besiege the sire d'Albret and his men in Nontron.[80] The looting and intimidation which followed the murder of Jean V, comte d'Armagnac, in 1473 were probably in part the result of royal determination to terrorise the population into obedience.[81] The king's army seized the occasion to plunder what was left of Lectoure after the castle had been demolished and burnt. They then moved off to pillage Auch, which had been unlucky enough to have an Armagnac as its archbishop.[82] It is doubtful either whether the royal government would have been particularly disturbed at the fate of Libourne which had refused to accept royal troops into the town and was duly persecuted by soldiers from nearby Fronsac.[83] Nobles also well understood the value of pillaging as an instrument of politics. For example, the vicomte de Castillon decided to make an illegal levy on his subjects in Lomagne but could not ensure that they paid it. Consequently, he asked Odet d'Aydie the Younger to provide royal soldiers from Bourg and Blaye in order to intimidate his reluctant subjects into obedience. This Odet did and the soldiers' crimes and pillaging had the desired effect.[84]

A detailed account of the depredations of soldiers over three years at the expense of a local community is provided by the articles of complaint presented by Libourne and the inquest made upon them in 1494. Shortly before the events took place, Marshal Gié had, after a protracted struggle, at last obtained control over the castle and seigneurie of Fronsac. He placed a strong garrison there in order to hold it from the vicomte de Lautrec who refused to drop his claim to Fronsac and who, it was feared, might try to seize it. Gié possibly exploited his commission to lodge soldiers in the pays in order to strengthen his garrison. Some of the soldiers were ordered to be lodged in neighbouring

---

78 Recueil des privilèges, ed. Gouron, pp. 189–90.
79 AM Agen, CC 4, unnumbered.
80 AN, K 73, no. 51.
81 Samaran, Maison d'Armagnac, pp. 193–94.
82 AD Tarn-et-Garonne, A 45, no. 3 [fos 8v–9v].
83 AC Libourne, AA 9, no. 1, fo 7r.
84 BN, ms. Duchesne 117, fos 125v–26v.

Libourne, but the town refused them entry, probably fearing that they would indulge in the same disorderly activity as Gié's own garrison at Fronsac. Gié's troops seem at an early stage to have decided to terrorise Libourne. With their artillery the garrison fired into Libourne in July 1488, July 1489 and during the summer of 1493, demolishing houses and killing people. Fronsac was also well positioned to serve as a base from which to prey on those using the river. The soldiers intercepted and robbed fishermen and merchants. Jewels and money were stolen from those unfortunate enough to be caught. They beat a jurat and attacked two of Libourne's sergeants. They held the citizens to ransom whenever they could succeed in capturing them. Armed bands of soldiers marauded through the *pays*, robbing and rustling. The town's articles of complaint mention that the soldiers ill-treated them 'as if they had been enemies of the king.'[85] Even though it is only Libourne's point of view which is preserved, there can be no doubt that for several years the *pays* was the scene of considerable disorder. Violence was apparently widespread and indiscriminate. Forty years on, the association between heavy garrisoning and violent crime still applied, as it had in the years after the second reduction of Guyenne.

Tackling crime and disorder

As has been observed, the *lettres de rémission* do no more than suggest the relative incidence of the worst violent crime, point to those groups responsible for it and indicate the years when the problem was most acute. It was the violence of the seigneurs and of the soldiers which were most likely to have political importance; though the great majority of these crimes too, even if they might unsettle political conditions, had no direct political purpose. The crimes of humbler people were still less likely to be noticed or, of course, to be pardoned. Yet even in the *lettres de rémission* over half of the crimes mentioned were committed by townsmen or peasants. The number of crimes committed in each sénéchaussée by each of these two groups probably depended more upon the proportion of town to country dwellers than upon relative inclinations towards crime. Most of these people's crimes could, of course, have been committed by anyone at any time. In the towns they covered disputes about goods and payments.[86] In the *plat pays* land, livestock, crops and tithes were the focus of strife.[87] In both, crime was frequently associated with drinking, gambling and vice.[88]

Though probably under-represented in the *lettres de rémission*, we can also glimpse a world of professional criminals, ranging from paid assassins to forgers of documents and money, from rustlers to robbers.[89] Of these it is worth noting the continuation, even after the final suppression of rebellion in 1453, of mention of bands of robbers lying in wait for the unwary. Some robbers enjoyed

---

85 AC Libourne, AA 9, no. 1, fos 2v–10r; II 1, nos. 3–7.
86 AN, JJ 190, no. 155; JJ 198, no. 288.
87 AN, JJ 198, no. 288; JJ 217, no. 168; JJ 218, no. 208; JJ 181, no. 103.
88 AN, JJ 199, no. 505; JJ 208, no.149; JJ 199, no. 544; JJ 198, no. 554; JJ 186, no. 50.
89 AN, JJ 204, no. 45; JJ 221, no. 248; APA, E 806 [fos 1r–5v].

profitable and long careers, perpetrating their crimes in one jurisdiction before fleeing to the next. Among the prisoners freed by Louis XI on his entry into Bordeaux was an archer whose robberies extended over fourteen years, from Toulouse to Bordeaux.[90] Ten years' crime by Bernard Carle, in the Ombrière prison on Louis' accession, brought him 536 écus of money and plate.[91]

Woods were the robbers' most frequent haunt. Bernard Georges lived with other robbers in the woods in Entre-Deux-Mers.[92] He claimed under interrogation in February 1454 that there were 20 or 30 'brigands' there and that their principal retreats were at Curton and Saint-Quentin where there was plenty of wine to steal.[93] In 1477 a man of Podensac complained that a bridge over the Cyron in the *prévôté* of Barsac was in ruins and the area around it overgrown with bushes and undergrowth. In it 'numerous thieves, brigands and highwaymen' assembled.[94] Similarly, a wood near the town at Sarlat was described as a very dangerous place because of the robbers there.[95]

The task of repressing crime and violence in Guyenne was one with which the authorities were poorly equipped to deal. No special commissions for the repression of criminal violence in the South-West were issued by the king. General commissions, such as that to Geoffroi du Puy-du-Fou in 1492, might indeed mention the need to suppress criminal disorder; but they were essentially given for military and political reasons.[96] It was left to the governor or the sénéchaux of the province to issue specific commissions for the capture of known criminals. Although all such written commissions for Guyenne seem to have perished, fragments of accounts show their existence. For instance, at the governor of Guyenne's orders Bernard d'Abzac and ten archers were sent in 1486 to arrest and try four thieves at Sainte-Foy, who were subsequently executed.[97] That such operations were fairly regular is clear from payments made in November 1490 to two registrars who had been making inquests into six such incidents in the *prévôté* of Saint-Sever over the previous year.[98]

It would normally fall to royal or town sergeants or the first *huissier* of the *parlement* to make arrests, though a particularly heinous crime might provoke both civic dignitaries and inhabitants to search out the culprit. They did so in July 1493 at Périgueux and discovered him in a local brothel.[99] Some arrests, however, were made by private individuals just on grounds of suspicion. Jean de Podaings, for instance, seeing a page on horseback with no master, arrested him on the spot and took him back for questioning.[100]

The government did nothing to reform the right of ecclesiastical sanctuary, though resort to sanctuary was certainly a major cause of crime. At Bordeaux the sanctuaries of Saint-André, Saint-Michel, Sainte-Croix and Saint-Seurin all harboured criminals. Criminals who once gained sanctuary might slip away from the *pays* altogether. Such was the case of a murderer from Bordeaux in 1485.[101] Sanctuary also served a more sinister purpose. A man of Bordeaux who

90 AN, JJ 198, no. 400.
91 *Ibid.*, no. 195.
92 BN, ms. fr. 6963, fo 27v.
93 *Ibid.*, fo 27v.
94 ADG, 3E 2, fos 71r–73r.
95 AN, JJ 227, no. 241.

96 AC Saint-Emilion, II 1, no. 6.
97 BN, PO 2900, 'Tustal', fo 2r.
98 BN, PO 2843, 'du Tilh', fo 5r.
99 AC Périgueux, CC 94, fo 5v.
100 AN, JJ 198, no. 25.
101 AN, JJ 218, no. 194.

had fled there crept out and tried to murder his enemy.[102] Though the right of sanctuary was jealously guarded by the chapter of Saint-André, it proved a mixed blessing to the canons personally. By the cathedral were situated the archbishop's and the canons' houses and the sanctuary land. Because there were no gates around it robbers and murderers congregated there and frequently attacked and stole from them.[103]

The sanctuary of Sainte-Croix seems often to have been used by perpetrators of violent crimes and by those who had escaped from prison. In November 1455, for instance, sanctuary was granted to an escaped prisoner from the Ombrière and a cobbler who had committed an assault.[104] Sometimes it was just a commercial quarrel which sent men into sanctuary.[105] But usually it was more serious. In July 1459, for instance, eight men entered Sainte-Croix after a brawl in which a man had been killed.[106]

Sometimes the church would be prepared to forgo its sanctuary rights.[107] Sometimes too sanctuary rights were ignored by the authorities. Nobles at Domme who had gone into sanctuary were dragged out and put in irons.[108] The claim that one had entered sanctuary and then been arrested there was a common one.[109] Royal officers must frequently have become exasperated at the way in which they were so often thwarted by sanctuary rights. The abbot of Sainte-Croix alleged, for example, that the lieutenant of the sénéchal of Guyenne and the royal proctor were determined to reduce the abbey's franchise.[110]

When criminals were successfully apprehended the authorities faced major problems in keeping such men secure until they could be tried and punished. Prisons were often insecure, gaolers often incompetent and corrupt. Gaolbreaks were frequent. Inside and outside help were sometimes available.[111] In 1485 a group of prisoners managed to climb over the wall of the *conciergerie* prison at Bordeaux using a rope.[112]

Some prisons were known to be so unsafe that dangerous criminals would be sent to more secure ones in the vicinity. In 1451 a criminal sent back from Toulouse was first taken to Condom, and then, because its gaol was so unsafe, transferred to Lectoure.[113] At Condom the new French administration found this intolerable and work was promptly ordered to begin rebuilding the town prison.[114] Improvements were also made to Agen's prison.[115]

The practice of farming out gaol profits to the highest bidder must have been a further obstacle in the way of attempts to improve the system's effectiveness. In 1490, for example, the town prison at Bazas was farmed out to two inhabitants for 34 l. t.[116] The Commission of 1455 laid down detailed regulations for

102 AN, JJ 198, no. 522.
103 AN, JJ 218, no. 198.
104 ADG, H 532, no. 10, fo 18r.
105 *Ibid.*, fo 18v.
106 *Ibid.*, fo 19r.
107 AN, JJ 209, no. 37.
108 AN, JJ 218, no. 77.
109 AN, JJ 187, no. 303; JJ 218, no. 196.
110 ADG, H 281, no. 1 [fos 1r–2r].
111 AN, JJ 218, no. 77; JJ 226 bis, no. 396.
112 AN, JJ 218, no. 196.
113 BN, ms. fr. 25,080, fo 6332r.
114 *Ibid.*, fo 6441r.
115 BN, ms. fr. 26,093, fo 947r.
116 ADG, 3E 653, unnumbered.

the administration of Bordeaux's Ombrière prison.[117] In the Bordeaux *conciergerie* prison, however, where most of the important prisoners were kept, favouritism and inefficiency continued to characterise its administration. Jacques Rabat was made keeper there by royal letters of gift when he was just nineteen years old.[118] Incompetent gaolers were sometimes punished by the Bordeaux *parlement*. Two were imprisoned in January 1468 for having allowed a forger to escape.[119]

The shortcomings of the methods employed to apprehend and secure criminals in Guyenne had two notable consequences. First, order was, as a result, likely to be enforced outside the formal judicial processes, with the emphasis on avoiding out-breaks of crime rather than retrospectively trying to punish those responsible. Second, the deterrent aspect of punishment was particularly pronounced, since the chances of detection were so poor.

The emphasis on prevention rather than cure can be perceived both in the use of injunctions against committing offences and in the use of techniques of arbitration. Sometimes a local cleric might be called in to arbitrate.[120] More frequently the arbitrator would be a leading local noble – especially when the feuding parties were nobles too.[121]

The *parlement* also intervened in disputes between great seigneurs with injunctions to avoid violence. In December 1488, for example, the seigneurs de Pardaillan and de Montferrand were ordered not to do any harm to each other on pain of the payment of a fine of 1000 gold marks.[122] Such injunctions were by no means always successful. Nor were those issued by the sub-mayor of Bordeaux.[123]

As has been noted, the deterrent provided by harsh punishments was most important when detection and capture were so difficult. Prison was not generally used by the secular authorities as a punishment; though the chapter of Saint-André sentenced a clerical miscreant to two years on bread and water in gaol in 1471.[124] But prison was still, not least for its cost and unsavoury conditions, a deterrent.[125] Unfortunately the deterrent value of prison only resulted in an increased urge to break out of it.

Local customs imposed fierce penalties for those whose crimes were deemed most to threaten moral, social and political order. At Auch in 1489 those leading immoral lives were to leave the town in three days.[126] Local customs prescribed harsh and humiliating treatment for those who committed adultery.[127] Blasphemy in the South-West would be punished by being fastened in

---

117 *Livre des coutumes*, ed. Barckhausen, no. xxiii, 676–78.
118 AN, JJ 215, no. 82.
119 ADG, B2, fo 60r.
120 AN, JJ 198, no. 25.
121 AN, JJ 221, no. 324.
122 ADG, B5, fo 107v.
123 AN, JJ 218, no. 191.
124 ADG, G 285, fo 64v.
125 ADG, G 1713, fo 326r; 3E 4809, fos 1r–v, 2r–3r.
126 P. Lafforgue, *Histoire de la ville d'Auch*, i (Auch, 1851), 377.
127 AM Bayonne, AA 6, fo 33r–v; AC Périgueux, CC 93, fo 39v; ADG, G 184, fo 287V.

an iron collar or having one's tongue pierced, or indeed both.[128] Those whose blasphemy was deemed heretical would be fined too.[129] Crimes committed by night were in general more harshly punished than by day.[130] At Auch a curfew was imposed on all the citizens unless they carried a torch; at Bordeaux it was just imposed on the English.[131]

Political order was maintained by humiliating punishment exacted against those who transgressed it. Insults to royal or town officers were publicly dealt with.[132] The fate of Charlot d'Anglade, whose head was placed on the town gate at Sarlat and whose truncated corpse was hung from the Sainte-Croix tower at Bordeaux, was meant to serve as a lesson to more humble persons who flouted the royal authority.[133]

Social order was deemed in judicial codes to be based on the fundamental relationships between husband and wife, parents and children, master and servant. Dereliction of such duties was treated with special ferocity. In 1475, for example, a mother who allowed her child to die through negligence was whipped and banished.[134] Theft of one's master's belongings was viewed similarly.[135]

The problem of restoring order to the province which had been re-conquered from the English in 1453 was, therefore, never fully or systematically tackled by the government or its agents. Clashes of jurisdiction between courts and the immunities offered by sanctuary would in any case have ensured that the difficulties faced by the government in bringing wrong-doers to justice were considerable. The problems of Valois Guyenne were by no means unique. In Lancastrian England a weak government was probably even less effective; and at least the Valois, once the exigencies of the war years were over, rarely granted the general pardons to criminals which have been seen as proof of the English government's inability to govern effectively.[136] Yet it remains true that except in times of political or military crisis the French government and its agents were unwilling to issue commissions which might have made more effective the pursuit and trial of criminals. The burden of enforcing order all too frequently rested on local courts or *ad hoc* local commissions which lacked the resources or the motivation to apprehend criminals once they had ceased to

---

[128] Iron collars were used at Cadillac and Montréal-du-Gers (AC Cadillac, CC4, fo 22r; *Comptes consulaires Montréal*, p. 172). Tongues were pierced at Bayonne (*Registres gascons*, ed. Ducéré, i, 29). Both collars and tongue-piercing were employed at Auch (Lafforgue, *Histoire de la ville d'Auch*, i, 373–74).

[129] BN, ms. fr. 26, 099, fo 51v.

[130] A. Moullié, 'Coutumes, privilèges et franchises de la ville d'Agen', *Rec. Trav. Soc. Agric. Sci. Arts Agen*, v (1850), 280; *Ordonnances*, xv, 24–25; *Livres des coutumes*, ed. Barckhausen, no. iii, 24–25, 40–41, 79–80.

[131] Lafforgue, *Histoire de la ville d'Auch*, i, 375; AN, JJ 208, no. 149.

[132] AC Saint-Emilion, BB 1, fo 40v; *Registres gascons*, ed. Ducéré, i, 237, 302.

[133] ADG, B 7, fo 83v.

[134] AD Haute-Garonne, H, Fonds de Malte, Argenteins 30, unnumbered [old cataloguing: 2, no. 16].

[135] AD Haute-Garonne, H, Fonds de Malte, Argenteins 36, unnumbered [old cataloguing: 6, nos. 178, 181].

[136] R.L.Storey, *The End of the House of Lancaster* (London, 1966), pp. 210–12.

plague the local community currently affected. For all the ferocity of punishments and the misery of imprisonment, the means of detection and detention were so inadequate that criminals could have long careers before being caught – when they were caught at all. Perhaps political upheavals increased the level of disorder; even more tenuously there may be a connection between poverty and crime, after some of the lucrative opportunities of war had dwindled. But to those of the *pays* political crisis or economic problems alike must only have seemed mildly to worsen a continuing and chronic state of criminal disorder in the province.

8

Rebellions and Conspiracies

In the forty years which followed the French reduction of Guyenne, the government faced both noble rebellions and upheavals in the towns. It crushed revolt with ease and brought order to the urban communities without heavy-handed intervention. This was partly because of the sheer military power which the government had at its disposal in the wake of its victory against the English. It was partly because political upheavals in England prevented an English return until 1475, and then not to Guyenne. No doubt it was partly also because the habit of obedience grew as the conquerors developed closer interests in the region and as the benefits of stability and economic revival became more evident. But it is also explained by the limited purpose of rebellion itself. Whether it was noble revolt or urban discontent, the fundamental purpose of disobedience was generally to win pensions, offices, privileges and exemptions rather than to topple the régime. There were, of course, exemptions. The fall of Jean V, comte d'Armagnac showed what happened to those unprepared to play the game within its unwritten rules. There clearly were also treasonable contacts with the English during the *'guerre folle'* – though how firm or serious these were it is hard to tell. The ambitions of the sire d'Albret in Brittany may also have, on occasion, encouraged him to envisage for himself a future more or less independent of the favour of the king of France, though his experience must have quickly disillusioned him. But, in general, rebellion was an often successful pursuit of advancement by other means: and ultimately such advancement could only come from the king.

If the objectives of rebellion and disobedience were, by and large, limited, so were the effects of their repression by the royal government. Neither urban nor noble rebellion in Guyenne – nor their suppression – achieved any fundamental political change. The towns were by 1494 no less obligarchic, in spite of some hesitant and ephemeral attempts to reform their ruling bodies: indeed the overall tendency was towards oligarchy. The power of the Albret connection emerged unscathed and ultimately consolidated from the upheavals of the early years of Charles VIII's reign.

In fact, the principal significance of the threat of internal upheaval was its impact on the attitudes and actions of government. First, it ensured that the Valois monarchs and their servants continued to rule through rather than against the interests of those individuals and groups most able to threaten armed rebellion, above all through the great seigneurs. Second, it ensured that even more attention and resources were applied to problems of security, and so even less to changes and possible improvements in the administration of justice.

Guyenne, 1452–1454

The political paranoia which lay at the root of Valois military policy in Guyenne owed not a little to the circumstances of Talbot's return in October 1452 and the subsequent French re-conquest. To go back on an oath of allegiance already taken was to incur the king's vengeance. Those who had sworn to be 'French' and were captured by the advancing Valois armies had already been singled out for specially harsh treatment before the fall of Bordeaux in 1451.[1] The same attitude was shown by the pardon terms granted after the second reduction. It was also, as has been observed, believed that the population remained secretly anglophil in sympathies.

The background to Talbot's return to Guyenne at the head of an English army is not entirely clear. Thomas Basin, Jean Chartier and Guillaume Leseur describe a mission sent by Gascon supporters of the English cause to urge the launching of a new campaign.[2] These accounts would be detailed and consistent enough to be convincing, were it not for the fact that those said to have been members of the party which was sent to England could not in fact have been so. This has understandably led to the mission's being dismissed as a piece of fanciful historical fiction.[3]

On the other hand, it is possible that such a mission as that described by the French chroniclers arrived in England only to find that a new invasion fleet was already on the sea. Chartier places the Gascon mission in September 1452; Talbot was in Bordeaux the following month.[4] The lack of any trace of a Gascon mission in English records might be satisfactorily explained by the fact that the members of it re-embarked for Bordeaux very soon after their arrival in England.

The Gascon rebels appear to have been a small but powerful and determined clique who were able to exploit genuine and general resentment against the French now administering the city. The resentment was understandable. Although Basin's account of 'tailles and some other taxes' levied by the French after the first reduction is almost certainly unfounded, the burden of feeding and lodging frequently disorderly soldiers must have been unpopular enough.[5] Only the text of the lettre d'abolition granted to Bordeaux in 1453 suggests that the English met with other than a general welcome.[6] Basin noted that Talbot's entry was greeted with joy by all the citizens.[7] Even after the news of the English defeat at Castillon which spelt the end of any real chance of restoring English rule to the duchy, the three estates of the Bordelais apparently cried that they would rather die than come under the French obedience.[8]

---

[1] Histoire de Charles VII, ed. Godefroy, pp. 223, 225.
[2] Ibid., pp. 260–61; G. Leseur, Histoire de Gaston IV, comte de Foix, ed. H. Courteault [Soc. de l'Histoire de France], ii (Paris, 1896), 3–4; Basin, ii, p. 184.
[3] Vale, 'Last Years', 126–27.
[4] Histoire de Charles VII, ed. Godefroy, p. 260.
[5] Basin, ii, 176.
[6] Ordonnances, xiv, 270.
[7] Basin, ii, 186.
[8] BN, ms. fr. 6963, fo 27r.

The soudic de La Trau, Pierre de Montferrand, was the key figure among the conspirators. He was in a more powerful position to help the English than has sometimes been imagined, for although his principal seigneurie, that of Lesparre, had in theory been confiscated by the French king, in fact he seems to have continued to enjoy its revenues.[9] The soudic's ties of marriage and of interest with the English were strong.[10]

The members of the clique which actually let the English into Bordeaux all lived in close proximity to each other in the parish of Saint-Michel.[11] The meeting at which their final plans were laid was only attended by a few key figures, not by the jurade.[12] According to Guillaume Leseur, the weapons and armour of the French were seized by stealth while they slept, which, if true, again argues a high degree of coordination by a few conspirators.[13] The soudic de La Trau and the sub-mayor of Bordeaux, who were both deeply involved in the plot, may have been responsible.[14]

More difficult to unravel is the evidence suggesting that others outside Bordeaux were informed and involved. On balance, it seems likely that the seigneur de Gramont and his associates were prepared to try and seize Bayonne for the English, but that lack of cooperation from citizens in the town foiled their attempt to do so. In 1454 the commissioners for justice in Guyenne sent from Dax a list of fourteen accusations against François de Gramont for him to answer. According to these his treason stretched back to 1452. It was alleged that when in October of that year the English made their descent upon the duchy, Gramont had agreed to let them into Hastingues and had arranged to be pardoned for his previous desertion of the English king. He was said to have made an alliance with the vicomte d'Orthe and to have promised to join the English forces, both of these alleged conspirators having received prior notice of the invasion in letters from Talbot. The articles mention that Gramont had arranged the marriage of his daughter with Robin Petillot, captain of Bayonne and sénéchal of the Landes, with the sole aim of having him let into the town the English troops which were expected. When the English finally arrived at Bordeaux, Gramont had decided to act, and the soudic and others had been given a small force of 120 archers to enter Bayonne. It looks as if it was planned to enact a repeat of the events which led to the fall of Bordeaux to Talbot.[15]

Many too, however, must have been those presented with a political *fait accompli* and who responded accordingly. Jean de Lalande, claimed his son, was only three leagues from Bordeaux when Talbot arrived and so joined the English because of the impossibility of resistance.[16] Jean d'Anglade gave a more elaborate account of how he had been compelled by force of circumstances to break his oath. He had been sent out to spy on the English movements in 1452, but when he tried to report back his findings he found that the French had all fled. He grudgingly agreed to join the English after he could hold out no longer,

---

[9] BN, ms. Duchesne 31, pp. 166–70.
[10] Peyrègne, 'Les Emigrés gascons', 114, n. 5.
[11] BN, ms. fr. 6963, fo 27r.
[12] BN, ms. Duchesne 31, pp. 166–70.

[13] Leseur, *Histoire de Gason IV*, ii, 4–5.
[14] BN, ms. fr. 6963, fo 27r.
[15] AD Gers, I 1600, fos 1r–3r.
[16] AN, JJ 199, no. 170.

but then had the misfortune to be captured by the victorious French at Castillon.[17]

In February 1454 the soudic de La Trau made a last attempt to secure an English return to the province. He was arrested, given a preliminary interrogation, then led to Poitiers and forced in a further interrogation to confess his plans. He was condemned to death, executed, and his body was cut into six pieces and placed on show as a deterrent to other would-be conspirators. Very few details survive of the plot. The soudic was apparently banished in 1453.[18] Yet it is not at all clear that he actually left Guyenne. Mystery, and perhaps deliberately contrived confusion, surround his activity at this time. Even his leading lieutenants claimed to have been left unaware of the soudic's involvement in the English return of 1452; for after the battle of Castillon two of them, the brothers Jean 'Pochin' and Jean d'Abzac, tried to hold out for him at Lesparre against the routed English force.[19]

A certain Bernard Georges was arrested by the vigilant French authorities at Bordeaux just at the time of the soudic's plot in February 1454.[20] His own return to the city had been prompted by the soudic's desire for news about an expected English army.[21] Georges described the soudic as at that moment having 4000 or 5000 soldiers with him and residing at the castle of Gramont. The conspirators were still planning to seize Bayonne and Georges would have joined them had he not been arrested.[22] From allegations made about the involvement of the seigneur de Gramont in the soudic's conspiracy, it appears that the latter was still in France under cover of a safe-conduct which he and his fellow exiles had received by the terms granted at the fall of Bordeaux.[23] The soudic was arrested after his safe conduct had expired, or so it was claimed, while trying to get back to England.[24]

The seigneur de Gramont and the soudic de La Trau seem, therefore, to have continued to plot for an English return undaunted by the débacle of Castillon and the departure of the lord of Camoys and the English soldiers from Bordeaux. Gramont subsequently denied all knowledge of the plot, protesting his loyalty and past services. He pointed out that considering his bad relations with the vicomte d'Orthe, of the Luxe faction, he was unlikely to have plotted with them. Witnesses, however, claimed that the seigneur de Gramont had indeed continued to shelter the soudic de La Trau, Thomas de Lalande and others adhering to the English cause in his castle of Bidache for as long as possible. It was also alleged that Gramont and his wife had remained in treasonable contact with the soudic even after his arrest.[25]

It seems likely, then, that the Landes remained largely out of control long after the fall of Bordeaux. The ambiguous position of the soudic and of his fellow conspirators, enjoying a royal safe-conduct, combined with the influence of Gramont, appear to have permitted them to raise a substantial force. Just

17 AN, JJ 198, no. 292.

18 Histoire de Charles VII, ed. Godefroy, pp. 284–85.

19 BN, ms. Duchesne 31, pp. 166–70.

20 BN, ms. fr. 6963, fo 26r.

21 Ibid., fo 26r–v.

22 Ibid., fo 27r.

23 AD Gers, I 1600, fo 27r–v.

24 Ibid., fos 1r–3v.

25 Ibid., fos 1v–3v.

how the soudic was captured remains unclear. But his supporters must have quickly melted away again afterwards.

The royal government was evidently (and probably rightly) suspicious of Gramont. He lost his seigneurie of Mussidan until his wife had this decision reversed. It was not till 1458 that Charles VII intervened to stop further court proceedings on the matter of the seigneur de Gramont's 'pretended intelligence' with the English.[26] As for the vicomte d'Orthe, he had certainly earlier been involved and admitted it. He had held out in his vicomté with bands of 'brigands' till Talbot's death. He was banished and his property confiscated; he only returned to France in November 1461.[27]

The contrast between the failure of the plot of 1454 and the brief success of that of 1452–1453 is suggestive of political circumstances in Valois Guyenne in the years following the reductions of the province. The plot of 1452–1453 succeeded for three reasons. First, a substantial English expedition was ready to take control once more. Second, resentment against the new French administration may have been wide-spread. Third, a small, influential group of conspirators with contacts inside Bordeaux was determined to reverse the defeat of 1451. In 1454, however, neither outside military aid nor collaborators in Bordeaux seem to have been available. If the French government could eliminate or at least suppress disaffection in Bordeaux and Bayonne and defend the province against the English, security could be maintained. This was the programme which the Valois government now proceeded to put into practice.

Urban revolt and repression

Not the least of the difficulties with which the French government had to contend were the problems posed by the fragility of political order in the urban communities. The towns' financial and strategic importance never permitted the government to ignore urban politics entirely, although in general the authorities showed little desire to interfere with or reform the institutions which had grown up. It was the possibility of a connection between urban disorder and any wider and more pervasive political crisis which was most likely to prompt firm action from the royal officers. It is, however, worth noting that for the most part town oligarchies were remarkably successful, both at retaining power and at playing the wider political system in their own interests.[28]

Although there were exceptions, the broad trend was probably towards oligarchy in the towns of Guyenne during the fifteenth century. At Bordeaux, the jurade continued to use cooption to select its members.[29] At Périgueux, membership of the 'council of thirty' prud'hommes had fallen to six by the end

---

[26] J. de Jaurgain and R. Ritter, La Maison de Gramont, 1040–1967, i (Lourdes, 1968), 77.

[27] AN, JJ 198, no. 293.

[28] P.S. Lewis, 'The Centre, the Periphery, and the Problem of Power Distribution in Later Medieval France', in The Crown and Local Communities in England and France in the Fifteenth Century (Gloucester, 1981), ed. J.R.L. Highfield and R. Jeffs, pp. 46–47.

[29] Histoire de Bordeaux, iv, 79.

of the century.[30] At Montréal the number of consuls was reduced from six to four in 1490: they were chosen from 20 jurats, themselves drawn from the noble families of the town.[31] The motivation to reduce the numbers involved in the town's government may have been as much financial as social and political. The same impulse could, though, lead in a different direction, allegedly for the same reason of economy: Bergerac decided to abolish the office of mayor in 1475, against resistance from the royal officers.[32] In Bordeaux and Bayonne, where the mayor was appointed by the king 'from among his most trusted officers' such moves would, of course, have been impossible.[33]

The troubles at Périgueux in 1464–1465 occurred against the back-cloth of the disturbances of the *guerre du bien public*. The evidence of any conspiratorial connection between events in the town and noble rebellion outside it is, however, slight. It may be that a few malcontents believed that the government's problems gave them increased opportunities; but essentially the urban crisis in Périgueux was of a kind with those recurring in other towns where 'popular' movements were aimed at redressing alleged maladministration by an incompetent ruling clique.[34]

The troubles which occurred at Périgueux can be fairly accurately chronicled. They were over by 10 February 1465 when payment was made to a notary for documents sent by the mayor and consuls to the Bordeaux *parlement*, containing the evidence against those who had fomented the disorder.[35] The lack of any surviving town accounts for 1462 to 1464 makes it difficult to gauge how far back lay the origins of the crisis. However, some light is shed by the *livre jaune* chronicle which for 1464 shows that the mayor, Fortanier de Saint-Astier, died in mid-term and that it was on his death that problems commenced.[36] The mayor had been a guarantee of stability. It was the third time he had served and as seigneur des Bories he had brought to his office the resources and prestige of a great figure and house of the surrounding *pays*.

The mayoral inter-regnum which now followed was exploited by one of the previous year's consuls to call the people together and to try to prevent the newly elected consuls from taking office, while demanding to be made mayor himself.[37] This attempted *coup* failed, however. With only one dissenter, the assembly approved the consuls' taking up their offices. That this signalled the beginning of the disorder is shown by the fact that the dissenting voice was that of one who would play a leading role in the ensuing disturbances.[38]

The continuing dispute about the validity of the consular election and approval provided a motive or an excuse for disobeying the consuls' orders. The list of offences for which fines were levied upon the disobedient shows that this

---

30 Higounet-Nadal, *Périgueux*, p. 9.
31 *Comptes consulaires Montréal*, pp. 24–25.
32 AC Bergerac, jurade 20, 1475–1476 [fo 4v].
33 *Histoire de Bordeaux*, iv, 542; AM Bayonne, AA 3, fo 309r–v.
34 Cf. E. Delcambre, *Le Consulat du Puy-en-Velay, des origines à 1610* (Le Puy, 1933), pp. 69–70.
35 AC Périgueux, BB 14, fo 3v.
36 *Ibid.*, fos 14r, 19r.
37 *Ibid.*, fos 14r, 16r.
38 AC Périgueux, CC 88, fos 6r, 23v.

was the case. It was claimed that the consuls were not properly appointed officers. One of the town sergeants refused to raise a tax which they imposed. Héliot Cluzel, the previous year's receiver, refused to render his accounts because he claimed that the consuls had no authority to judge him.[39] Cluzel was among those who entered the consular chamber with a list of accusations, which the consuls called the 'libel diffamatori'. This indictment of consular misgovernment and corruption was sent to the Bordeaux parlement. Cluzel's fine of 50 l. compared with 10 l. or less for most of the others suggests that the consuls regarded this action as more dangerous than the riots for which they pretended to consider 'simple people' to be responsible.[40] The consuls evidently feared the royal government more than they did the town's rebels.

The riots themselves consisted more of words than actions. The town proctor was threatened. A trouble-maker rushed into the consular chamber swearing at the consuls and was arrested, but then jumped out of the window crying 'kill, kill.'[41] One of the town officers, who had been condemned to heavy penalties because he refused to take the customary oath to the consuls, also tried to excite the populace by similar means.[42] According to the consuls, matters would have become much worse were it not for the presence at the height of the crisis of the Bordeaux parlement in Périgueux, there because of the plague in Bordeaux.[43]

The deeper problem facing the town's administration was that of finance. This, rather than external interference or propaganda, seems to have been the principal cause of the crisis in the town's affairs. The accounts of 1464–1465 showed that expenses exceeded receipts by 164 l.17s.9d. The sums left owing were for the salaries of the mayor, consul and other town officers.[44] The town had to pay for extensive repairs to walls, bridges and gateways, and a new tower was being constructed.[45]

The most serious aspect of the situation revealed by the accounts was the non-payment of taxes. The general trend in Périgueux during the century was of increasing numbers enjoying tax exemption.[46] But administrative incompetence seems to have worsened the problem. Non-payment of taxes certainly constituted the crux of the opposition faction's complaints, since two auditors were appointed to go over the past years' accounts, because there was a great demand to know who the debtors were and what they owed.[47] Part of the results of this inquiry survive.[48] Some of the names of those who owed back taxes had been lost altogether. Other cases of non-payment stretched over several generations in the same family. The heirs of one man, the names of whom were apparently lost, owed for the years between 1430 and 1464.[49]

Even though the problems faced by the town were essentially internal ones of administration and order, other circumstances combined to increase the possibility of events becoming out of hand. By an unhappy coincidence the

[39] Ibid., fos 22r–24r.
[40] Ibid., fos 5r, 23r–v.
[41] Ibid., fo 5r–v.
[42] Ibid., fo 23r.
[43] Ibid., fos 4v, 12v, 23v.
[44] Ibid., fo 34v.
[45] Ibid., fos 5r–18v.
[46] Higounet-Nadal, Périgueux, pp. 131–32.
[47] AC Périgueux, CC 88, fo 4r.
[48] AC Périgueux, CC 89.
[49] Ibid., fos 4r, 5r, 18v.

disturbances coincided with the arrival in the town of crowds of pilgrims who had come to take advantage of the indulgence which Hélie de Bourdeilles, bishop of Périgueux, had obtained from the pope. The consuls ordered that torches should be purchased to illumine the town where so many possible malefactors might be at work and the Porte Limogeanne was shut in order to control the flow of people.[50]

More important still must have been the awareness of events taking place in the kingdom of France at the time. The townsmen knew of the disorders of the *bien public*. A rider arrived in the late summer of 1465 to tell the townsmen that the king's enemies were assembling against him and that the clergy should pray for the conservation of the realm.[51] But how much of this was known in earlier months when the threat of riots was more acute is unclear.

The consuls may have hoped that by stressing a connection between the outbreak of internal disorder at Périgueux and civil war in the realm they would be assured of unconditional support by the royal government. If so they were disappointed. Letters from the Bordeaux *parlement* had been obtained for the case to be tried before it.[52] Suitable measures of bribery were employed upon the councillors of the court to influence them in the consular interests. Each councillor received wine, candles and money and the president was especially favoured. The consuls complained that at the *parlement* money fell like rain.[53] But it was all to no avail. The fines levied upon the miscreants were pardoned. Royal commissioners were appointed to settle the dispute. The clerk who wrote the accounts complained that this was bad policy because such a pardon would encourage others to rebel against legitimate authority in the same way.[54]

The lenient attitude taken by the royal officers towards those who had caused the disturbances is probably explained above all by their wish to see order restored as soon and as amicably as possible. There had, after all, clearly been financial misgovernment by the ruling clique of the town. Although such procedures were not altogether uncommon, it is likely that realisation of this lay behind the demand made by the sénéchal's brother, acting as his lieutenant, that the consuls should hand over their accounts for inspection, threatening heavy penalties if they failed to do so.[55]

The consuls tried to pretend that it was the lower orders who were responsible for the disturbances, but this was clearly not in fact entirely true. A number of the ringleaders of the revolt were officers and one was a former consul. For example, Jean Le Veyrier, one of the leading opponents of the ruling group, had in 1461 been charged with the delicate task of raising credit in Limoges.[56] Such a man had important connections. According to the consuls, one of the sénéchal's lieutenants, who had advised that the town's accounts should be scrutinised, was Le Veyrier's uncle and biased in his favour. Le Veyrier certainly emerged unscathed from the crisis. In 1477–1478 he was still opposing the town council's edicts, refusing to pay *taille* imposed by the town,

50 AC Périgueux, CC 88, fos 7r, 15v.
51 *Ibid.*, fo 11v.
52 *Ibid.*, fo 4v.
53 *Ibid.*, fos 12v, 11v.

54 *Ibid.*, fo 22r.
55 *Ibid.*, fo 7v.
56 AC Périgueux, CC 87, fo 7v; CC 88, fo 3r–v.

and had even appealed against them to the Bordeaux *parlement*.[57] His immunity is significant of his influence and status. In fact, the dispute was essentially one within the ruling group, one section of which exploited the discontent of the lower orders in its own interests. It was not a revolution; and it was not prompted by sympathy with the aristocratic opponents of the royal government.

But the central motive behind the royal decision to patch up the local dispute by means of judical commissioners rather than allow it to take its course in proceedings before the Bordeaux *parlement* was to restore peace and order in tense and volatile political conditions. The king seems to have decided that the need for security was more important than the rigours of strict justice. Certainly, the monarchy had no intention of embarking on major reforms of the town's constitution. Périgueux continued to be governed by a consulate of twelve members, usually presided over by a mayor, with the assistance of the 'council of thirty'.[58]

The case of Périgeux was exceptional in that the troubles there coincided with a broader based political crisis. This was not so at Agen in 1481, though outside pressures were by no means unimportant. As at Périgueux, taxation and the membership of the governing body of the town were the principal focus of dissension.

The inhabitants of Agen alleged in letters of commission issued on 6 July 1481 that the richest and most powerful citizens had been imposing taxes on the poor without justification.[59] Royal letters obtained by the consuls and jurats of Agen claimed, however, that some of the common people had caused a riot and rebelled against those who had always governed the town and spread lies and scandals about them.[60] The town register itself put the blame on a certain Nautrec, who, with '*plusieurs populars*' of the town had made a great assembly and drawn up articles against the town burgesses.[61] How violent the disturbances were is hard to say. But they were clearly not as significant as those at Périgueux.

The background was different too. At Agen the butchers initially played the principal role. On 19 July it was the butchers' representative who appeared before Pierre Champeaux, the commissioner sent by the Bordeaux *parlement* to execute the populace's letters to oppose the consuls.[62] The articles containing the demands of the *populars* concerned, among other matters, the payment of dues by the butchers. When the consulate decided in September to try to reach an accommodation as quickly as possible, they drew up a document with the

[57] AC Périgueux, CC 88, fo 7v; CC 91, fo 5r.
[58] Higounet-Nadal, *Périgueux*, p. 9.
[59] The affair is described by Adolphe Magen in 'Un Essai d'organisation démocratique dans la ville d'Agen en 1481', *Rec. Trav. Soc. Agr. Sci. Arts Agen*, 2e série, v (1877), 114–30. Magen publishes the letters of commission of 6 July 1481, *ibid.*, pp. 131–32.
[60] *Ibid.*, pp. 146–47.
[61] AM Agen, BB 19, fo 6v.
[62] Magen, 'Essai d'organisation démocratique', p. 144.

butchers settling the question of their payment of dues, remitting half of them, and resolved to have it confirmed by the Bordeaux *parlement*.[63]

The wider and more fundamental issues involved, however, were the constitution of the town's governing body and the levy of taxation. It was a combination of factors which seems to have brought Agen's financial problems to a crisis. The town had been subject to heavy demands from the comte de Comminges to provide saltpetre for his artillery, for which a tax was levied upon Agen's citizens. Comminges' soldiers were billetted in the town, which added to Agen's problems. The town's coffers had also been drained because of the need to build another bridge across the Garonne, for which those who had contracted to build it demanded the substantial sum of 6000 francs. That finance was the root of the matter is shown by the fact that in February 1482 the town council was informed that the *populars* were still refusing to pay their assessments.[64] Moreover, at the only council meeting on 13 February at which the popular scheme of government seems ever to have been put into practice, the popular elements were very concerned with tax collection. At that meeting were twenty-four *populars*, who, from their names, included a ploughmen, an archer, a butcher and a tailor. They were told that the comte de Comminges was coming to hold the three estates of Guyenne in the town. The *populars* agreed to confirm the council's earlier decision to give generous gifts to him. But they specified that when the levy to pay for them was made it should be done correctly and honestly, with the proper people present.[65]

The dispute was also fought out, as at Périgueux, over control of the town's governing body. The *populars* were sufficiently politically sophisticated to know that the abuses of which they complained could only be remedied in the longer term by close scrutiny of the town's administration. This was the point over which compromise proved most difficult. By August 1481 the consuls could report that it was the only point of difference still outstanding. The popular elements wanted the consulate to include four *prud'hommes* from the commune, two being chosen from the guilds and two from the labouring classes. The ruling group resolved to resist these demands, though with varying degrees of intransigence. Twelve members of the town's governing councils said that the popular leader should be told that the town was very prosperous and well-governed, as indeed was the sénéchaussée of Agenais. The town should be properly administered, especially since it was the chief town of the *pays*, and the consuls needed to be wise and experienced. But to avoid more trouble, and excepting the king's wishes to the contrary, they would place two members of the lower orders who were of a prudent and proper disposition among their number. The view was not unanimous. One consul wanted eight plebeians appointed; another believed that to accept any at all would just cause confusion. In fact it was decided to appoint three of the most respectable of the lower orders to the consulate and also to appoint a treasurer who would raise the town's money, whom the populace would elect. Nautrec, however, rejected the scheme entirely; it was all or nothing.[66] Though 24 *populars* attended a council

---

63 AM Agen, BB 19, fos 10r–11v.
64 *Ibid.*, fo 16r–v.
65 *Ibid.*, fo 17v.
66 *Ibid.*, fo 9r–v.

meeting in February 1482 the new scheme of government was never put fully into effect; popular intransigence lost the day.[67]

As at Périgueux, the royal government's reaction to the disturbances of Agen in 1481-1482 was conciliatory. As at Périgueux, also, popular resentment had not been levelled at the royal government or its agents but at the town's ruling body, even though the demands made by the comte de Comminges for the royal armies were in part at least responsible for the financial crisis in which Agen fell. Indeed, the popular faction of Agen had appealed to royal justice at an early stage against the consular opponents.[68]

The consuls of Agen, like those of Périgueux, employed arguments concerning the need for firm rule and security, in order to influence the commissioners and parlement in their interest. They claimed that their rule had restored Agen from ruins at the end of the war fought by the French to recover Guyenne, and then noted that Agen must, as the key town of the pays, avoid dissension which could spread to her urban neighbours.[69] Whether this attempt to imply a wave of popular commotions ready to ripple across Agenais was seriously considered by the royal government is doubtful. The lack of severe or urgent methods used to restore order suggests that it was not.

The third urban disturbance with which the Valois government had to deal in Guyenne provides an instructive comparison with the other two. Unlike the events which had occurred at Agen, the upheavals at Bayonne coincided with a worsening political crisis because of deteriorating relations with England.[70] Unlike the troubles at both Périgueux and Agen, those which occurred at Bayonne threatened security at a centre of major strategic and economic significance. Consequently, the royal government's response, though still measured, was swifter, firmer and more far-reaching.

The disturbances at Bayonne began in 1488. They were closely connected with a dispute between the town's guilds and a section of the populace. It centred on the powers claimed by the receivers of the guilds, which a number of Bayonne's townsmen had challenged. A royal commission of investigation was established.[71] Bayonne's ruling council initially showed some reluctance to become involved in this quarrel. In due course, however, the town council agreed to take up the guild receivers' claims and entered into litigation with a section of the townsmen. The case was heard before the Bordeaux parlement.[72]

What provoked the riots of Corpus Christi 1489 was probably a combination of bitterness at the continuing court case which was dividing the town and the strains of the preparations being made at the king's orders to defend and provision Bayonne against possible English attack.[73] From now on there seems to have been a continuing state of tension. The royal government moved swiftly to restore order. The governor of Guyenne was instructed to send an

[67] Ibid., fo 17v.
[68] Magen, 'Essai d'organisation démocratique', pp. 131-32, 149-50.
[69] Ibid., p. 146.
[70] See above p. 13.
[71] Registres gascons, ed. Ducéré, i, 240.
[72] Lettres de Charles VIII, ed. Pélicier, ii, no. ccccli, 378-79.
[73] Ibid., ii, no. cccci, 294-96; Registres gascons, ed. Ducéré, i, 319-320.

agent to Bayonne whose powers would virtually supersede those of the mayor and councillors of the town in matters of justice and finance. No conspiracies or assemblies would be permitted and no threats or abuse uttered.[74]

A further commission was sent to Bayonne in July to make a thorough investigation and institute whatever changes were required.[75] Initially, it consisted of Jean Chambon and other councillors of the Bordeaux *parlement*, accompanied by Marshal Gié. On the following day, however, the composition of the commission was changed to exclude the Bordeaux councillors because of the possible bias arising from their involvement in the proceedings between the populace and the governing body of Bayonne.[76]

Gié issued a series of ordinances to reform the internal affairs of Bayonne and prevent further disturbances. These specified that the electors were not to choose their relations and allies. There was to be no re-election of jurats or échevins for three years from the time of their first election. The town's debtors were not to be elected. Échevins were not allowed to be officers. The twenty-four councillors were to be paid for their services, in order to encourage them to attend to the town's business. These moves against oligarchy were balanced by others designed to repress disturbance among the lower orders. The syndic of the people was publicly to ask pardon of God, the king and the mayor. No-one was ever again to take arms against other citizens on pain of death and confiscation.[77]

In the short run at least, royal intervention seems to have produced some change in the town government's membership. In August jurats and échevins were elected according to the ordinances. The same applied in the consular elections in September.[78] But there is no evidence of any lasting alteration in the town council's social complexion. It is significant, however, that the only time when the king is known to have taken a personal interest in such events, the only time when a great military figure led a reforming commission, and the only time when changes were instituted in a town's government after a crisis was at Bayonne. The different response of the royal government to urban upheaval depended above all upon one consideration, the risk to security.

Noble rebellion

In practice, the royal government was able without too much effort to retain firm control over the towns of Guyenne after 1453. To control the nobility was more difficult, although a mixture of terror and patronage allowed the king to counter the manoeuvres on most occasions of even his most turbulent subjects.

In this the fortunes of the house of Armagnac, which have been described earlier, set it apart from those of the other great noble houses of the South-

---

[74] *Lettres de Charles VIII*, ed. Pélicier, ii, no. ccccxxx, 342–43.

[75] *Registres gascons*, ed. Ducéré, i, 319–20.

[76] *Lettres de Charles VIII*, ed. Pélicier, ii no. ccccli, 378–79.

[77] AM Bayonne, AA 6, fos 48v–51r.

[78] *Registres gascons*, ed. Ducéré, i, 243, 245.

West.[79] From the time of the invasion of the Armagnac domains in May 1455 until the death of Jean V comte d'Armagnac, the comte was a continual source of upheaval, involved in every major political disturbance.[80] The incompetence of Jean V's successor and the contested succession to the Armagnac inheritance allowed Armagnac to be brought firmly within the framework of the royal administration.[81] But it was essentially because the Armagnacs, unlike the Albrets, Foix and others, had repeatedly shown that it was impossible for the royal government to work through rather than against them that the house of Armagnac had to be destroyed as a political force.

As a general rule, noble conspiracy and revolt in Guyenne was aimed at ensuring that noble power and influence in the *pays* were fully recognised by the government through pensions and offices rather than at the overthrow of the royal power. For upon that power many of the advantages which those in rebellion sought ultimately depended.

This was, for example, the case of the conspiracy which led to the *guerre du bien public*. It was initially hatched at the Burgundian court in November 1464 during a visit of the duc de Bourbon.[82] In order to nip Bourbon's preparations in the bud the king led an army into Bourbonnais where he seized a number of strongholds. There the royal forces were faced with armies recruited in the South-West, some as deserters from the royal *ordonnance* companies, under the command of the duc de Nemours, the comte d'Armagnac and the sire d'Albret. The comte d'Armagnac was playing a characteristically devious game. In March 1465 Jean V had pledged his support to the king and promised to join him with his army.[83] In April Louis XI was still maintaining publicly that the comtes de Foix and d'Armagnac had promised him their aid.[84] More reliable proved the support pledged by Bordeaux for the king at this time. The townsmen offered Louis 200 archers to be maintained for a month at their expense.[85]

After some inconclusive campaigning the king agreed a truce with the rebel princes by which the comte d'Armagnac promised to follow Louis XI in arms.[86] Instead, however, Armagnac, Nemours and Albret seem to have moved slowly North towards Paris, where they eventually joined the other rebel armies. Their troops were unpaid, undisciplined and pillaged as they went.[87] In October, by the treaty of Conflans, Louis XI yielded to most of the princes' demands.[88] The loyalty of the rebel princes from the South-West was dearly purchased. The comte d'Armagnac probably had clearly defined aims; he received a 16,000 l.t. pension and the return of his lands which had been

---

[79] See above, p. 000. For a much fuller account, see Samaran, *Maison d'Armagnac*, pp. 106–327.

[80] *Ibid.*, pp. 121–94.

[81] *Ibid.*, pp. 281–320.

[82] Commynes, *Mémoires*, ed. Calmette, i, 9–10.

[83] Samaran, *Maison d'Armagnac*, p. 147.

[84] *Documents historiques inédits*, ed. Champollion-Figeac, ii. 2 (Paris, 1843), no. xiii, 211–12.

[85] *Ibid.*, no. xi, 204–205.

[86] Samaran, *Maison d'Armagnac*, p. 151.

[87] Commynes, *Mémoires*, ed. Calmette, i, 18, 59–60.

[88] See above, p. 17.

confiscated. Armagnac's soldiers pillaged Brie and Champagne on their way home, so they too may have been well satisfied.[89] Although the sire d'Albret's aims are far from clear, he at least seems to have received from now until the time of his death the regular payment of his ordinary pension, which he had been granted since 1448, of 3,500 or 4,000 l.t.[90] The comte de Foix was rewarded for his loyalty during the disturbances and for maintaining control of Guyenne for the king by the grant of an increased pension and a gift of 10,000 écus secured on Mauléon-en-Soule.[91] The king was still apprehensive about the continued plotting of Nemours, Armagnac and Albret in the summer of 1466.[92] But in practice the worst noble disorders of the reign were over. The king had paid the price required to end them.

Guyenne itself does not seem to have suffered from the effects of the *guerre du bien public* in any great degree. Under the over-all authority of the comte de Foix, who had been appointed governor and lieutenant general of Guyenne and Languedoc, the *pays* had remained calm.[93] The towns had been ordered to take appropriate measures to ensure their security.[94] At Bergerac the jurade was warned of the prospect of the comte d'Armagnac passing through and spreading destruction as he went.[95] But whether Périgord in fact suffered this fate is unclear.

The political crises which marked the early years of the reign of Charles VIII had more direct impact upon Guyenne than had the fortunes of the house of Armagnac or the *guerre du bien public*. This was partly the result of the key role played by the sire d'Albret in the disturbances under Charles VIII and the extent of both his resources and his ambitions. It was also due to the position of the comte de Comminges, who was made governor by Louis XI and put in charge of the most important strategic centres of Guyenne. Jaligny notes that Comminges had such authority that 'he was feared and obeyed as if he had been its duke'.[96] Because of his control over these strongholds, the Beaujeux left him unmolested long after he was known to be in conspiracy with the duc d'Orléans and the comte de Dunois for fear that he would call in foreign assistance.[97]

The towns of the South-West were exhorted by the government to resist the rebels when the storm broke at the end of 1484. On 18th January 1485 Charles VIII wrote to Agen enclosing a copy of the duc d'Orléans' letter to him of four days previously which accused the government of not keeping the agreements made at the estates general held at Tours and alleged that Anne of Beaujeu and others had usurped the young king's authority and were holding him in

89 Samaran, *Maison d'Armagnac*, p. 153.
90 BN, PO 25, 'Albret', nos. 174, 179–82, 184, 187–89.
91 APA, E 353, unnumbered; Courteault, *Gaston IV*, pp. 288–89.
92 *Lettres de Louis XI*, ed. Vaesen, ii, no. cclvi, 62–63.
93 Leseur, *Histoire de Gaston IV*, ii, pièce justificative xxix, 363–65.
94 AC Périgueux, CC 88, fo 4r.
95 AC Bergerac, jurade 19 (1465–1466) [fo 7r].
96 *Histoire de Charles VIII*, ed. Godefroy, p. 17.
97 *Ibid.*, p. 18.

subjection.[98] Charles also enclosed his reply to Orléans in which he rejected all the allegations and offered to consider the duc's demand for an estates general to be held in Paris.[99] The king told Agen that Orléans had no justification for his attitude. The Agenais were to inform the king if they received any letters from the duc and to send a worthy representative to bear witness that the king's servants at court were obeying his orders.[100] Further royal letters of 23 January repeated the government's rejection of the rebels' accusations.[101] The stream of royal propaganda kept flowing.[102]

Because of the power and influence of the Albret and Aydie connections in Guyenne, it was difficult to know who could be trusted and who not.[103] On several occasions during the following months Agen had to seek advice on whether to accept ostensibly 'royal' garrisons.[104] The townsmen of Agen were kept well informed of and involved in the next phase of the princes' rebellion too. In February 1487 the duc d'Orléans wrote to the town explaining what had prompted him once more to take up arms in the public good.[105] In the same month royal letters were sent to Agen in order to counteract the possible effects of this rebel propaganda. The townsmen were ordered by the king not to receive any communication from the rebels.[106]

In fact, by the time that the royal government had sent its instructions to keep out rebel propaganda, the decision had already been made to launch a campaign against the rebels in the South-West where they were most vulnerable. In response to the king's march towards Guyenne, the comte de Comminges at last fled to join the other rebel princes at Nantes, leaving his younger brother, Odet, at Saintes with 100 lances, most of them recruited from Béarn and so less likely to be loyal to the king.[107]

On hearing that the Beaujeux had sent a large army against him, and having lost control of the bridge at Saintes, Odet withdrew to Pons and fortified it with the intention of holding it against the royal forces. On further consideration, however, he fell back on the already heavily fortified centre of Blaye.[108] Between Pons and Blaye, most of his men left him and joined the advancing royal army. The king secured their loyalties by having them paid immediately. The rebel cause in the South-West was crumbling fast; even Odet's father-in-law now opened negotiations.[109]

Odet and what was left of his supporters had, however, no intention of yielding without a fight. According to Gaston de Montferrand, in command of

98 AM Agen, BB 19, fo 53r–v.
99 Ibid., fos 53v–54v.
100 Ibid., fo 52v.
101 Ibid., fos 51r–52r. These letters were received by other towns too and are printed in Lettres de Charles VIII, ed. Pélicier, i, no. xxxvi, 62–65.
102 AM Agen, BB 19, fo 46r.
103 On the extent of these connections, see below pp. 187–90.
104 AM Agen, BB 19, fos 46v, 66r, 74v, 75r, 76r, 93v.
105 Ibid., fos 100r–101v.
106 Ibid., fos 103r–104r.
107 Histoire de Charles VIII, ed. Godefroy, pp. 19–20.
108 Lettres de Charles VIII, ed. Pélicier, i, no. xcv, 161.
109 Histoire de Charles VIII, ed. Godefroy, p. 21.

the royal garrison at Bourg, Odet still had 20 or 30 lances with him at Blaye. They pressed Montferrand hard.[110] The king first of all sent the marshal of his lodgings to Blaye, but he was refused entry. Shortly afterwards Marshal Gié and others arrived. They were met with a hail of missiles from the rebel artillery which killed a number of the royal force. It was like the English all over again, the king remarked in a letter to Imbert de Batarnay on 9 March.[111] The day after the besieging army had been lodged in Blaye abbey and around the town, the royal artillery arrived and started to batter down the walls of Blaye. When the royal army prepared for an assault, some of the rebel troops decided to leave while they could and so save their lives.[112] For two days the artillery battle continued; and according to Charles VIII the royal artillery's strength was decisive in forcing Blaye to yield. Odet surrendered, his life and property having been promised him by Gié, and was then taken around by the royal force to induce the other places held by the two brothers to yield. By the time Charles wrote to Batarnay the government had once more complete control of Guyenne.[113]

Charles VIII stayed at Bourg about a week.[114] On 7 March he entered Bordeaux and stayed there a week too. Changes were made in the distribution of power in Guyenne. Beaujeu, himself, received the governorship and the comte de Candale was made his lieutenant. The comte de Comminges also lost the admiralty of Guyenne which went to the seigneur de Graville.[115] The sénéchaussée of Bazadais was given to Gaston de Montferrand who had proved his loyalty at Bourg. Etienne Makanan replaced Guillaume de Soupplainville, one of Albret's and the Aydies' leading henchmen, as mayor of Bayonne. In February Roger de Gramont had been appointed to guard Bayonne and raise soldiers there and the following month he was made sénéchal of the Landes.[116]

When Albret did at last march in May it was towards Angoulême to go and join the rebels at Nantes where the comte de Comminges was pursuing the project of Albret's marriage with Anne of Brittany. With him, Albret took an army of Navarrese and Spanish soldiers.[117] Albret's army was intercepted and besieged at Nontron. The surrounding country seems to have suffered severely from the presence of the royal troops.[118] On 1 June the king told the comte de Candale, the seigneur de Bressuire, Gaston du Lyon and Robert de Balsac, who were negotiating with Albret in Nontron, that he had already had sufficient experience of Alain's bad faith. Eight hostages were to be given and Albret was sent to Casteljaloux or his other lands in Gascony to await the royal pleasure.[119]

---

110 BN, ms. fr. 20,486, fo 15r.

111 *Lettres de Charles VIII*, ed. Pélicier, i, no. xcv, 162.

112 For the dangers of allowing a defended stronghold to be taken by assault see M. H. Keen, *The Laws of War in the Middle Ages* (London and Toronto, 1965), pp. 119–22.

113 *Lettres de Charles VIII*, ed. Pélicier., i, no. xcv, 162–63.

114 *Arch. hist. Gironde*, xii (1870), no. viii, 18.

115 *Histoire de Charles VIII*, ed. Godefroy, p. 22.

116 Jaurgain and Ritter, *Maison de Gramont*, p. 107.

117 AD Dordogne, 2E 1851/68, no. 5.

118 AN, K 73, no. 15.

119 *Lettres de Charles VIII*, ed. Pélicier, i, no. cxiv, 190–91.

Charles VIII was persuaded reluctantly to pardon him.[120] All grants made of Albret's and his servants' lands were to be annulled and all confiscations revoked.[121]

Charles VIII had reacted to news of Albret's long-expected moves by putting the towns of Guyenne on the alert. On 15 May the king informed Périgueux that he had heard that Albret intended, if he could, to come with his men into Brittany. In passing through the *pays* he might try to surprise towns like theirs. The bishop of Périgueux and the seigneur de La Douze were to cooperate with the town for its defence.[122] A fortnight later the king wrote to Lectoure and other towns telling them to ensure that those spreading dissension and revolt were arrested and handed over to the royal officers.[123] The lessening of tension in the South-West after Albret's pardon was reflected in the decision taken in June by the town authorities at Agen that he should be allowed to enter the town in state as elsewhere in Agenais.[124]

Albret's machinations (and so the disturbances in the South-West) did not stop after Nontron. In letters of August the king reminded Lectoure of how Albret had received the king's pardon after Nontron and since then had tried again to march to Nantes and had been stopped by the royal army. He was now back in Guyenne, according to the king, and was raising troops, even though his own and the seigneur de Saint-Cricq's lands had been taken into the king's hand. This action had been taken because the king had observed that it was from these lands during the last year that Albret had drawn his recruits. The king called on Lectoure to lend all possible help, and to dispel the mischievous mis-information that Albret was busy spreading. He had apparently pretended that he was raising his forces to defend the king.[125] However, in February 1488, having been promised Anne of Brittany's hand in marriage, Albret went by sea to Brittany and induced royal soldiers there to mutiny and join him.[126] The battle of Saint-Aubin-du-Cormier decided the following Breton campaign in July. The comte de Comminges and the sire d'Albret fled. Alain d'Albret, the comtes de Comminges and de Dunois and their servants were pardoned once more in September.[127]

But all this was only after six months of vigorous activity to seek out and repress conspiracy in Guyenne. For example, in February at Bergerac Jean d'Abzac, as lieutenant of the sénéchal of Périgord, came into the jurade and conducted a long and detailed investigation of one Jonannet de Bonneraze, who had loaded two ships with corn which he said he wanted to take to Libourne and sell there or at Bordeaux. He was suspected of wishing to transport it in fact to the comte de Comminges' men who were at Fronsac and who

---

[120] *Histoire de Charles VIII*, ed. Godefroy, p. 37.

[121] APA, E 163, unnumbered.

[122] AC Périgueux, FF 185. Also printed in *Lettres de Charles VIII*, ed. Pélicier, i, no. cx, 183–84.

[123] *Documents*, ed. Champollion-Figeac, iii. 2, no. xxxii (12), 510.

[124] AM Agen, BB 19, fo 106v.

[125] *Documents*, ed. Champollion-Figeac, iii. 2, no. xxxii, pp. 502–505.

[126] *Histoire de Charles VIII*, ed. Godefroy, pp. 45–46; AD Dordogne, 2E 1851/68, no. 5.

[127] AN, JJ 219, nos. 197, 202, 203.

anyway would let nothing pass along the river. He was asked how long ago he had been in Fronsac, why he had been there, how heavily manned with soldiers it was. The jurade decided to send a letter to the mayor of Libourne to find out whether he was telling the truth. Two of the consuls thought that since he knew quite well that the comte de Comminges and Fronsac were in rebellion against the king, he and his cargo should be locked up securely.[128]

In the same month the jurade decided that because of the divisions in the realm between the great seigneurs and the king, they should keep especially good guard of the town. Various dispositions were taken; holes in the walls were blocked up; the town militia was arrayed by *quartiers*; a pallisade was erected on top of the walls; guards and gate-keepers were appointed. No-one was allowed to enter the town without permission. A general oath of loyalty to the king was taken from the citizens. The military equipment possessed by each of the inhabitants was inspected and a roll drawn up placing them under captains in groups of ten.[129] In early March the jurade promised their full support to the king. They ordered that all provisions, except wine, should be taken inside the town. Jean d'Abzac commanded that all boats were to be hidden away and the same orders went through the bailliage and elsewhere to stop Albret, who was recruiting a new army, getting across the river. At this time of crisis the jurade of 4 March was expanded to include the seigneur de Beauregard, the lieutenant of the *prévot des maréchaux*, the lieutenant of the captain of Bergerac's castle and the *juge ordinaire* of the town. Provisions were levied for the royal army stationed at Blaye.[130]

At Agen too Albret was now regarded with the deepest suspicion. At the end of January 1488 the town decided to reply to Albret's letters only by word of mouth, clearly conscious of the dangers of entering into possibly treasonable correspondence.[131] Next month the council was told how Albret was making a great gathering of men-at-arms. It was decided to keep watch every day at the two gate-ways.[132]

A document, probably of 1488, evidences the way in which the agents of royal government were at this time following up allegations of treason resting only on hearsay.[133] It suggests too that the position built up by the comte de Comminges and his brother in Guyenne and their subsequent disloyalty had seriously threatened royal control over the Gascon nobility. A notary of Sainte-Foy alleged that three weeks before he had been at Lauzun and had spoken with one Bernard de Lusières. The latter had told him that eight days earlier Odet d'Aydie, the comte de Comminges' younger brother, had arrived at Lusières' home and lodged there. Lusières had told Odet that he had learned that a great force of men-at-arms was being sent by the king to lay hold of the main strongholds in the South-West. Odet had replied that Charles could send all

---

128 AC Bergerac, jurade 23 (1487–1488) [fo 37r–v].
129 *Jurades de Bergerac*, ed. Charrier, ii, 15–16.
130 *Ibid.*, pp. 16–19.
131 AM Agen, BB 19, fo 113v.
132 *Ibid.*, fo 114r.
133 APA, E 84 bis, no. 31.

the men he wished but they would never enter the places in question without his or his brother's permission.[134]

The notary also claimed that a gentleman of the household of the seigneur d'Estissac had said that as soon as it was learnt that the English had seized some territory in Guyenne or Normandy, the seigneur d'Estissac and others had decided to lay hold of the castle of Biron and drive the seigneur out of it.[135] The Sainte-Foy notary's is not the only testimony to the involvement of Comminges and others with the English at this time. According to Jaligny, Orléans and his fellow rebels had been in negotiation with the English and Spanish but dared transact nothing for fear of the French king.[136] In fact there was no major English intervention in France proper till 1492. But clearly the presence of the English again on French soil would have allowed the re-opening of old feuds.

A meeting at Cahuzac between the seigneurs d'Estissac, de Lauzun and de Caumont had apparently then taken place in a private chamber of the castle where a servant who had entered to place logs on the fire was able to hear their conversation. The prospect of an English invasion of Guyenne was not, it seems, sufficient to restore the confidence of all the conspirators. Lauzun wished he had never become involved. But Estissac was in treasonable correspondence with the comte de Comminges about an English intervention already.

On balance, the notary of Sainte-Foy's account seems credible. It was supported in some points by the testimony of Estissac's servant. Albret and Odet had both been visiting Cahuzac too. Again local ambitions and aims were involved. The comte de Comminges and his brother had their eyes on Mussidan which they hoped to seize for themselves.[137] Local and individual interests were being tied up, it seems, into a far-flung political conspiracy based on the Albret-Comminges connection.

The suppression of revolt in the South-West, the departure of Albret to Brittany and the installation of new commanders at the strategic centres of the province meant the end of Guyenne's direct involvement in the political crises of these years. As has been noted, in December 1490 Albret agreed to let the French into Nantes and, upon very advantageous terms, was welcomed permanently back to the royalist camp. In March 1491 a general pardon and restoration of goods and lands was granted by the king to Alain d'Albret, the comte de Comminges, Raymond de Cardeilhac, seigneur de Saint-Cricq, Regnault de Saint-Chamant and Raymond de Saint-Maurice, their allies and servants – in other words to the whole Albret-Comminges connection.[138] The allegiance of the group was dearly purchased. Moreover, though a few faint-hearts had sought individual pardons from the king earlier, it was as a powerful connection that the rebels were treated and bought off.[139] Albret demanded territorial or financial recompense for what he had lost to the French king and the king of the Romans in Brittany and Avesnes, the payment of debts to him of 110,000

[134] *Ibid.*, p. 4.
[135] *Ibid.*, p. 1.
[136] *Histoire de Charles VIII*, ed. Godefroy, p. 27.

[137] APA, E 84 bis, no. 31, pp. 1–8.
[138] AD Dordogne, 2E 1851/68, no. 5.
[139] AN, JJ 221, no. 155.

écus, 18,000 l.t. in pension and the command of 100 lances. His son, the king of Navarre, was to have a pension of the same value, the duc de Nemours one of 6,000 l.t.[140]

Albret's and his servants' control was to be secured once more over the South-West. The captaincy of Bayonne and offices of the seigneur de Gramont there were to go to Alain himself. Saint-Cricq and Saint-Maurice were each to have 6,000 l.t. in cash and pensions. Saint-Cricq was to be made sénéchal of the Landes and have charge of 50 lances, while Saint-Maurice should have control of the Bordeaux royal seal. Even such minor figures as Maître François Faure, juge d'Albret, were to be recompensed by provision to the first councillorship vacant in any of the parlements.[141]

Not all of these terms were carried out. They were subject to continuing adjustment. Thus in August 1494 Albret was recompensed for renouncing 25,000 l.t. rentes, granted when he gave up his Breton claim, and accepting only 6,000 l.t. instead, by the dropping of royal pretensions to Gaure and Fleurance.[142]

The overall basis for the settlement of the Breton question is clear, however. Charles VIII had yielded a pre-eminent position in terms of wealth, prestige and political influence in Guyennne to the sire d'Albret and his connection. Moreover, with the death of the comte de Comminges, the royal government had lost its one hope of attracting back into the royal camp and away from Albret any of the latter's support. It was perhaps the only policy which could give stability to the province – rule through rather than against the local potentates, and particularly the house of Albret.

The question which must arise from such a study of political upheavals in Valois Guyenne is, why were there rebellions at all? Only Talbot's presence in 1452 allowed resentment at the Valois régime to effect a temporary change in government. For all the propaganda of the princes in the guerre du bien public the towns stood firm behind the king. Only when financial and social problems prompted an internal crisis did urban politics threaten the security of the pays. Even the Albret-Comminges faction's control of the South-West was shattered when the king moved in person to suppress revolt. The military power at the king's disposal and his control over the important strategic centres were adequate in normal times to make a prospect of successful rebellion remote. Moreover, the growth of vested interests in the new order at all levels encouraged a preference for working through rather than against the royal administration and judiciary. The alternative, as the seigneur de Lauzun realised, was to risk the penalty for treason, only too easily suspected in this exposed and allegedly anglophil province.

Political realists responded to the new conditions. Though, like the sire d'Albret, they did not necessarily renounce the opportunities for revolt in a time of royal weakness, it was revolt which allowed a return into the royalist fold on generous terms rather than revolt which aimed at permanently

---

[140] AD Dordogne, 2E 1851/68, no. 4, fo 1r–v.
[141] Ibid., fos 2r–3v.
[142] APA, E 163, unnumbered.

overthrowing the king's authority. Those, like Jean V, comte d'Armagnac, who failed to observe and abide by that fine distinction suffered for it.

Riots in the towns too may have been regarded by the more sophisticated elements involved as being the means of gaining a betterment of conditions rather than of challenging the royal authority. Indeed, it was to royal justice that the dissidents turned; though the conservative aims of the government when it was induced to intervene made it unlikely that any radical change in the complexion of the town councils would be achieved. A few may have in the early days of the French rule thought, like a man at the siege of Blaye, that Charles was just 'the king of cards', but experience of the conditions under the Valois régime must soon have convinced them otherwise.[143] Only the powerful could defy the king, and with skilful management their power could increase rather than diminish his.

[143] AN, JJ 198, no. 293.

9

Controlling the Nobility

The loyalty of the nobility of South-West France had been expensively purchased in time of war. From 1453 a policy was required by the monarchy to
sustain its support in time of peace. Although the direct relationship between a
seigneur's military resources and his importance to the king was less evident
once English soldiers had left Gascon soil, the military demands upon leading
nobles were still likely to be important. Moreover, the more delicate functions
which noble families were expected to perform in lending to Valois rule an
authority in the *pays* accorded by tradition to the great seigneurs were no less
important. The counterpart to this, which even the Valois could not afford to
forget, was the ability of nobles to cause disorder and division in Guyenne.
However much fear and intimidation were used, and however many soldiers
were employed in holding down the province, the French monarchy was ultimately compelled by circumstances to work through rather than against the
local nobility.

Moreover, it would be wrong to exaggerate the problems which the nobility
of Guyenne faced in its dealings with the monarchy. It may well be that noble
incomes rose with economic and, particularly, agricultural revival towards the
end of the century.[1] Although the nobility of Guyenne, with the exception of
the temporary involvement of the sire d'Albret in the affairs of Brittany, did
not have an opportunity after the province's reduction to play off rival conten-
ders for sovereignty,[2] they possessed the status and expertise to hold key commands and other offices. The Gascon nobility, unlike for example its
counterparts in the duchy of Burgundy had,[3] moreover, sought to ensure that
noble inheritances and incomes were not dispersed among junior lines. In
particular, since the fourteenth century the Albrets had, by circumventing
custom in Guyenne, prevented their inheritance being divided among
daughters.[4] In the early fifteenth century others followed the Albret example.[5]
Both Charles II and Alain d'Albret pursued the same policy in marriage settlements.[6] By keeping their patrimonies together, the Albrets laid the future basis
for its extension.

---

1   P. Contamine, 'La France de la Fin du xve siècle: pour un état des questions', in *La France de
la Fin du xve siècle. Renouveau et apogée*, pp. 4–5.
2   Cf. M. Jones, 'The Breton Nobility and their Masters from the Civil War of 1341–64 to the
late Fifteenth Century' in *The Crown and Local Communities*, ed. Highfield and Jeffs, pp. 64–65.
3   M.-T. Caron, *La Noblesse dans le duché de Bourgogne 1315–1477* (Lille, [1988]), p. 538.
4   Poumarède, *Recherches sur les successions*, pp. 253–56.
5   *Ibid.*, p. 264.
6   APA, E 62, unnumbered; E 88, unnumbered.

Commands, pensions and ecclesiastical preferment

The classic means employed in order to secure the support of the seigneurs was through grants of important military commands and of pensions and gifts of cash. Military commands were evidently highly prized by the three princely houses of Albret, Foix and Armagnac. Charles II d'Albret's long military career of service to the French crown was probably effectively terminated after he relinquished command of the army which he and his sons had led during the campaign to reduce Guyenne. His grandson and successor as sire d'Albret, Alain, continued, however, to exploit the opportunities which the king of France's ambitions offered for profitable military commands. He served Louis XI against the duke of Burgundy and received 2,000 l.t. for 'part of his expenses'.[7] In 1475 Albret was placed in command of the royal armies being sent to intervene in Spain.[8] From the time of his return to the royal allegiance, after yielding Nantes to Charles VIII, Albret claimed and seems to have been granted command of 100 lances, receiving 1,200 l.t. as his wages.[9]

The Foix family, through the long and successful military career of Gaston IV, comte de Foix, was similarly favoured by grants of military commands. The martial exploits of Gaston IV were chronicled by Guillaume Leseur; and, for all Leseur's exaggeration, the comte de Foix provided valuable military service in the wars against the English and the reduction of Guyenne. It was upon the comte de Foix that Louis XI relied to hold the South-West for the government during the *guerre du bien public*. The comte was permitted by the king in the last years of his life to employ his military resources in order to further his family's interests in Navarre.[10]

The house of Armagnac is in some degree the exception which proves the rule. Jean V had been, in all senses, profitably employed in the royal service in the war to reduce Guyenne. For example, in 1451–1452 he received not only his wages as a commander but also generous cash gifts for military services rendered, one of which alone amounted to over 4,000 l.t.[11] But the comte d'Armagnac, either through personal taste or lack of royal favour, never afterwards managed to continue his military career. His soldiers from then on were employed in rebellion and pillage, rather than war in the French king's service. Jean V had amply proved by the time of his death at Lectoure that he was not willing or able to fulfil the constructive role which was envisaged for great seigneurs once French control in Guyenne had been achieved.

Most importantly, the loyalties of the nobility would be cemented by pension and other payments. Again this is most obviously true of the houses of Albret, Foix and Armagnac. Charles II d'Albret continued to receive a modest and probably regular pension until the time of his death.[12] His grandson, Alain, was from an early age more generously provided for by the king. Albret's return

---

7   BN, PO 25, 'Albret', no. 191.
8   Luchaire, *Alain le Grand*, p. 20.
9   BN, PO 25, 'Albret', nos. 218, 219.
10 Leseur, *Histoire de Gaston IV*, i, 20.
11 BN, PO 93, 'Armagnac, comtes de', no. 139.
12 BN, PO 25, 'Albret', nos. 174, 179–82, 184, 187–89.

from serving Charles of France, on the latter's death, was marked by a substantial increase in pension to 5,000 l.t.[13] Towards the end of Louis XI's reign Alain was receiving a pension of 8,000 l.t.[14] In 1491 as a result of the terms agreed for his and his followers' submission the sire d'Albret was in receipt not only of a pension of 18,000 l.t. but also a cash grant of 30,000 l.t., allegedly for losses which he had incurred during the years of civil war.[15]

Understandably, with the financial stakes as high as this, seigneurs like Alain d'Albret and their servants were ever anxious about their pension payments. Visits to the royal court were seen as useful opportunities to press for prompt payment of one's pension, as Albret's lawyers reminded him.[16] Similarly, bribery and negotiation at a local level might be required in order to ensure that pension payments were duly made. The royal receiver of Limousin, for example, was given 50 l.t. by Albret in order to induce him to pay what Alain was owed.[17]

Though never reaching quite the level of payments made to the sire d'Albret, Gaston IV and his family demanded and received large pensions. From 1450 till Charles VII's death the comte de Foix received a regular pension of 6,000 l.t. a year.[18] Shortly after Louis XI's accession the sum was increased to 10,000 l.t.[19] When Foix was ordered to come to court he received, and indeed expected, a special payment to cover the cost involved. He was, for example, paid 2,000 l.t. on these grounds in 1468.[20] The value which Foix, himself, and others placed upon his loyalty was high, and consequently the cost to the monarchy in pension payments was expected to be correspondingly high too. Imbert de Batarnay wrote to the king that Foix expected a pension of 20,000 francs if he were expected to be at court and 12,000 francs if he were not. Batarnay noted, 'If you treat him well, he will do you great service, more than anyone else in your kingdom could do for you'.[21] But such service was dear.

Pension payments to the comte d'Armagnac were, because of his mercurial political loyalties, much less regular, but on occasion they could be large. Between 1465 and 1468 the comte was in favour and the price which he had received as a result of his actions during the *guerre du bien public* was increased by other grants.[22] In 1467–1468, for example, Jean V received a pension of 6,000 l.t. which was soon supplemented by a grant of 10,000 l.t. required to pay the soldiers which he still had with him.[23] Even when Jean V was in disgrace this did not mean that other members of his family need be excluded from royal consideration. His brother Charles was granted a 2,000 l.t pension to be raised

13 *Ibid.*, no. 201.
14 BN, ms fr. 2900, fo 14v.
15 BN, PO 25, 'Albret', nos. 211, 212.
16 APA, E 653, no. 22.
17 APA, E 550 [fo 18r].
18 BN, PO 1173, 'Foix', nos. 104–108, 112–17.
19 BN, ms. fr. 26,089, fo 209r.
20 BN, ms. fr. 22,293, fo 145r.
21 BN, ms. fr. 2909, fo 7r–v.
22 For the *guerre du bien public*, see pp. 16–17.
23 BN, PO 94, 'Armagnac, comtes de', nos. 321, 322.

form the Armagnac lands in the royal hand in 1461.[24] In 1465–1466 Charles d'Armagnac was still in receipt of a modest pension of 1,200 l.t.[25]

Office, command and pensions were, therefore, the principal means by which the royal government controlled its noble subjects. A suspension or cut in pension payments, as in 1480–1481, was consequently a severe blow to many important and some humbler figures upon whom the king had to depend for support.[26] Pensions were unpopular with those unlucky enough not to receive them. They were undoubtedly a heavy burden on public finances. It has been estimated that some 35% of royal revenues in February 1470 were being paid out in pensions.[27] The estates general at Tours in 1484 considered them excessive.[28] But inducements and rewards were the means by which government could be made to operate; and if inducements and rewards were not offered in sufficient number by the royal government the royal interests would not be served.

One further source of rewards should, however, be mentioned before examining how different groups of noble families exploited the king's favour: that is ecclesiastical patronage. The king had his own interests and intentions in the award of sees and other important benefices. He was, for example, determined to maintain the archbishopric of Bordeaux vacated, probably under pressure, by the anglophil Pey Berland, in the hands of trusted, useful and well connected royal servants: and he succeeded in doing so.[29] Similarly, in the turbulent *pays* d'Armagnac, the king had every reason for insisting that his own candidates for the sees of Auch and Lectoure were successful.[30] In Bordeaux, as has been described, royal officers competed for vacant benefices. Finally, the king's relations with the pope, on which the smooth running of the machine of ecclesiastical patronage depended, might mean, as at Agen, that an unpopular foreign candidate might have to be imposed.[31]

Yet the nobility of Guyenne also had a claim to preferment and, although the evidence of such pressure is lacking, there is little doubt that, particularly away from Bordeaux where other claims might prove too strong, they were successful. Sometimes, as with the appointment of Pons de Salignac, both of an

[24] *Ibid.*, no. 252.

[25] *Ibid.*, no. 308.

[26] BN, ms. fr. 2906, fos 8r–9v.

[27] P.S. Lewis, 'Les Pensionnaires de Louis XI', in *La France de la Fin du xve siècle. Renouveau et apogée*, p. 169.

[28] Masselin, *Journal*, p. 676.

[29] *Histoire de Bordeaux*, iii, 538–39; D. Sammarthan, *Gallia Christiana*, ii (Paris, 1720), cols 834–45.

[30] Samaran, *Maison d'Armagnac*, pp. 115–17; *Lettres de Charles VIII*, ed. Pélicier, iii, no. dcxcviii, 309–310; *ibid.*, v, no. dccxcvii, 85–86.

[31] Chanoine Durengues, 'Galéas de la Rovère, évêque d'Agen, 1478–1487', *R.Agenais*, lv (1928) 92, 94; Chanoine Durengues, 'Léonard de La Rovère, cardinal et évêque d'Agen, (1487–1519)', *R. Agenais*, lvi (1929), 111–13. For the relations between the king and pope as regards nomination to benefices, see P. Ourliac, 'Le Concordat de 1472. Etudes sur les rapports de Louis XI et de Sixte IV', *R. hist Droit français et étranger*, 4e série, xxi (1942), 174–223; xxii (1943), 117–54, re-printed in translation as 'The Concordat of 1472: An Essay on the Relations between Louis XI and Sixtus IV', *The Recovery of France in the Fifteenth Century*, ed. P.S. Lewis (London, 1971), p. 184.

important Périgord family and a councillor in the *parlement*, to benefices in Agenais and Périgord, it is impossible to know how much royal or seigneurial influence was at work.[32] There is, though, no doubt that through whatever balance of pressures both the great and the less great noble families received a large share of ecclesiastical patronage.

As in secular affairs, the two families whose claim upon royal ecclesiastical patronage was most difficult to deny were the houses of Foix and Albret. The Foix family was the more influential of the two, largely for reasons of personality rather than politics. Both the cardinals Pierre de Foix were great ecclesiastical statesmen. The elder Pierre, who was son of the captal de Buch, Archambaud de Grailly, and uncle of Gaston IV, comte de Foix, was appointed to the sees of Lescar, Comminges and Arles, and briefly made administrator of the archbishopric of Bordeaux, before his death in 1464.[33] The king allowed him to prepare the way for the succession of his great-nephew, Pierre the younger, Gaston IV's son, within the archdiocese. For example, Pierre the elder was appointed abbot *in commendam* of the important abbey of Sainte-Croix at Bordeaux in 1455.[34] In October 1461 when Pierre II was only 13 years of age the pope agreed to grant him Sainte-Croix to be administered by his great-uncle until he reached the age of 24.[35] In fact Pierre II never even visited the abbey before his death in 1490 and it passed to the new archbishop, André d'Espinay.[36] By then Pierre II had been well rewarded by pensions and benefices for a career of diplomacy.[37] His nephew at the age of 18 was made archbishop of Bordeaux.[38]

The Albret family claimed two cardinals also, though neither was as influential as those of the house of Foix. Louis d'Albret, son of Charles II sire d'Albret, was appointed cardinal by Pius II in 1461; he enjoyed the bishopric of Aire till his death four years later.[39] Alain d'Albret's son, Amanieu, unlike Louis d'Albret, barely seems to have behaved as a churchman at all, spending most of his life at Montignac or his abbey at Brantôme. He was appointed to no fewer than eight sees during his life-time, including those of Bazas and Condom within Guyenne, and died in 1520.[40]

With the exception of the very great such as the cardinals de Foix and d'Albret, however, the rich benefices occupied by members of noble families were largely just a recognition of their influence and power in the *pays*. Nowhere is this clearer than in Périgord. There the families of Bourdeilles, Pompadour and Salignac were dominant in the assertion of claims to ecclesiastical preferment. Hélie de Bourdeilles became bishop of Périgueux in 1447 and

---

32 R. de La Batut, 'Notice sur les prélats issus de familles périgourdines avant 1789'; *B. Soc. hist. archéol. Périgord*, x (1883), 490.
33 Sammarthan, *Gallia Christiana*, i, col. 1064; Anselme de Sainte-Marie, *Histoire généalogique*, iii, 372–73.
34 A. Chauliac, *Histoire de l'abbaye de Sainte-Croix de Bordeaux* (Paris, 1910), pp. 190–91.
35 *Ibid.*, p. 191.
36 *Ibid.*, pp. 193–95
37 Anselme de Sainte-Marie *Histoire généalogique*, iii. 374.
38 Sammarthan, *Gallia Christiana*, ii, col. 846.
39 *Ibid.*, i, col. 1162.
40 Luchaire, *Alain le Grand*, pp. 33–36.

remained so for more than twenty years before being appointed archbishop of Tours.[41] Geoffroi de Pompadour succeeded to the bishopric of Périgueux by exchange with Raoul du Fou in July 1470.[42] As the brother and son of seigneurs de Pompadour, the bishop was well placed to gain promotion to rich benefices in Périgord.[43] He subsequently indulged in an active, if not always successful, political career at the royal court.[44]

Though the family never produced an ecclesiastical statesman of such importance as the Bourdeilles and Pompadours, the Salignacs were also rich and influential clerics. Raymond seigneur de Magnac's brother, Louis de Salignac, was appointed abbot of the important abbey of Saint-Astier.[45] Raymond seigneur de Salignac's brother, Pons, became abbot of Clairac in Agenais in 1462, and bishop of Sarlat in 1485, by which time he had also become a councillor in the Bordeaux *parlement*.[46]

The attitude of the nobility towards the church was doubtless not entirely cynical or self-interested. Great seigneurs cared about religious matters. Charles II d'Albret chose to express his devotion by ordering that he be buried in a Franciscan habit.[47] Others spent beyond their means on pious donations to foundations of their choosing.[48] But there is no doubt that ecclesiastical preferment was of great importance to the noble families of Guyenne, and to the extent that the king could secure his control over it he increased his control over them.[49]

Rewarding loyalty

The Valois monarchs were by no means free agents in bestowing patronage upon the nobility of Guyenne. A number of the greatest noble families of the South-West, especially those of Limousin and Périgord, had a long record of service to the French monarchy. Such families needed to be rewarded and this meant an effective limitation upon the ability of the government to buy support from those who had previously served the kings of England. Six families stand out within this category of Valois loyalists; they are the Beynacs, the Bourdeilles, the Pompadours, the La Rochefoucaulds, the Salignacs and the Talleyrands.

Pons de Beynac had been made sénéchal of Périgord as far back as 1420. Much of the military service he gave seems to have been unrewarded, for in

[41] Sammarthan, *Gallia Christiana*, ii, cols 1480–81.

[42] W. Mallat, 'Notes biographiques sur Raoul du Fou, évêque de Périgueux (1468–1470)', *B. Soc. hist. archéol. Périgord*, ix (1882), 63–64.

[43] *Ibid.*, p. 185.

[44] Pélicier, *Gouvernement de la dame de Beaujeu*, p. 60; Sammarthan, ii, col. 1482.

[45] BN, ms. Périgord 165, 'Salignac', fo 192r.

[46] La Batut, 'Notice sur les prélats', 490.

[47] BN, ms. Périgord 10, p. 5.

[48] R. Boutruche, 'Aux Origines d'une crise nobiliaire: donations pieuses et privilèges successorales en Bordelais du xiiie au xve siècle', *A. Hist. soc.* (1939), 162–77.

[49] For noble families' enjoyment of benefices in Languedoc, see J. L. Gazzaniga, *L'Eglise du midi à la Fin du règne de Charles VII (1444–1461)* (Paris, 1976).

1437 he was said to have been unpaid for twelve years. Beynac, like many others in the South-West in these years, seems to have become the man of Jean de Bretagne, with whom he made an *alliance* and from whom he received a pension.[50] The Beynacs came to regard the office of sénéchal of Périgord as almost an hereditary one, even after the expulsion of the English. Pons de Beynac's daughter married the seigneur de Barlaimont, to whom in September 1452 Pons resigned the sénéchaussée.[51] The pride of the family of Beynac was something with which any government in Guyenne would have to contend. The Beynacs claimed to be first barons of Périgord from the days of Charlemagne.[52] For such a family the fruits of royal patronage were regarded as a right not a privilege.

No less traditionally loyal to the French monarchy were the Bourdeilles. Like Pons de Beynac, Arnaud II de Bourdeilles was for some years in receipt of payments from Jean de Bretagne, comte de Périgord. Indeed between 1441 and 1453 he was receiving wages as the comte's captain of Bourdeilles itself, whose castle Arnaud had had re-built in 1453.[53] The noble connections in which the Bourdeilles became entwined in Périgord varied from time to time. In July 1475 Arnaud II, for example, was referred to as councillor and chamberlain of the comte d'Angoulême.[54] What was constant, however, was the family's devotion to the royal service. It had been a tradition since Arnaud II's grand-father had served in the wars of Charles V a century earlier. It was continued in the military service of Arnaud's son, Archambaud.[55] With such a record, and enjoying the prestige of one of the four leading noble houses of Périgord, the family of Bourdeilles' interests and ambitions could not be ignored.[56]

Although the military exploits of the Pompadours in the campaigns to reduce Guyenne are obscure, members of the family were serving the French monarchy in other capacities from the early fifteenth century, when the son of Raoul seigneur de Pompadour was a councillor in the Paris *parlement*.[57] Jean seigneur de Pompadour served as a royal councillor and chamberlain and man-at-arms under Louis XI and in 1485 was engaged in the campaign of that year against Brittany.[58] At court, Pompadour was an ally of the sire d'Albret and was probably involved with his influential and ambitious younger brother, the bishop of Périgueux.[59] Here again was a family whose call upon lay and eccle-siastical patronage could not easily be over-ridden.

A history of service to the crown in war to recover the South-West also characterised the family of La Rochefoucauld. Foucaud III seigneur de La Rochefoucauld was knighted by Charles VII before the castle of Fronsac in

---

50 J. Maubourguet, *Sarlat et le Périgord méridional*, iii (Paris, 1930), 62; BN, ms. Périgord 121, 'Beynac', fo 2r.

51 BN, ms. Périgord 121, 'Beynac', fo 2r; Dupont-Ferrier, *Gallia regia*, iv, 416.

52 BN, ms. Périgord 121, 'Beynac', fo 2r.

53 APA, E 643, unnumbered; BN, ms. n. a. fr. 23,793, fo 9v.

54 APA, E 643, unnumbered.

55 BN, ms. n. a. fr. 23,793, fo 9v.

56 BN, ms. Périgord 121, 'Beynac', fo 2r.

57 BN, ms. Périgord 155, 'de Pompadour', fo 5v.

58 *Ibid.*, fo 7v.

59 *Arch. hist. Gironde*, vi (1864), no. iii, 3–4.

1451 in the company of the comte de Vendôme and noble members of the royal army.[60] His son and heir, Jean, quickly moved from a military career during the last stages of the Guyenne campaigns to high office in the province. In 1453 he was in command of 50 lances at Bayonne.[61] He subsequently became sénéchal of Périgord and a royal councillor and chamberlain under Charles VII and Louis XI.[62] Jean de La Rochefoucauld's son continued to serve as a councillor to three monarchs and was made a comte by François I.[63]

Though not to be numbered among the greatest noble families of Périgord, the Salignacs managed to obtain appointments to a large number of important military and governmental posts. As with the other families mentioned here, the Salignacs had proved their worth in the wars against the English. Raymond seigneur de Salignac had fought the English in the armies of Charles VI and the dauphin, the future Charles VII. He had been rewarded with the offices of sénéchal both of Quercy and of Périgord and the captaincy of Montcuq.[64] The offspring of the seigneur de Salignac continued to enjoy favour and office. His son and principal heir, Antoine seigneur de Salignac, was a royal councillor and chamberlain, entrusted as a great figure in Périgord with such tasks as the raising of the *ban et arrière-ban* of the *pays*.[65] One of Antoine's brothers, Pons, became abbot of Clairac in Agenais, bishop of Sarlat in 1485 and was a councillor in the Bordeaux *parlement*.[66] The other, Jean seigneur de Fénélon, commenced a new line of Salignacs, which, no less than the heirs of the seigneur de Salignac, continued to give service and acquire offices and pensions.[67] Raymond de Salignac, of the line of seigneurs de Chapdeuil and Magnac, served as sénéchal of Périgord in 1468–1469.[68] Not least because of their numbers of active male offspring, the Salignac families continued to dominate much of the political life of the *pays*.

Finally, among the traditionally loyal and well rewarded noble houses of Périgord must be numbered the Talleyrands. François de Talleyrand, seigneur de Grignols, was present with the French forces at the fall of Bordeaux in 1453.[69] Jean de Talleyrand, who succeeded to the family inheritance after the early deaths of François's immediate heirs, had a long and distinguished military and political career, serving in Roussillon and Cerdagne, and was subsequently appointed by the king mayor of Bordeaux.[70]

Yet although it was necessary to reward the loyal service of families such as these who had provided the resources for the reduction of Guyenne, even more

---

[60] Anselme de Sainte-Marie, *Histoire généalogique*, iv (Paris, 1728), 425.

[61] BN, ms. Clairambault 194. no. 42.

[62] *Ibid.*, nos. 42, 45, 46; Anselme de Sainte-Marie, *Histoire généalogique*, iv, 425.

[63] Anselme de Sainte-Marie, *Histoire généalogique*, iv, 426.

[64] BN, ms. Périgord 164, 'Salignac', fos 21r–22r.

[65] *Ibid.*, fo 23r–v; AN, K 73, nos. 2, 43.

[66] BN, ms. fr. 22,252, fo 62r; La Batut, 'Notice sur les prélats', p. 490; *Les Chroniques de Jean Tarde*, ed. G. de Gérard (Paris, 1887), p. 201 n. 1.

[67] BN, mss. fr. 22,252, fo 92r; 2900, fo 14v; ms. Périgord 164, 'Salignac', fo 191v.

[68] Dupont-Ferrier, *Gallia regia*, iv, 416; BN, ms. Périgord 165, 'Salignac', fo 26r.

[69] BN, ms. Duchesne 103, fos 41v–42r.

[70] *Lettres de Charles VIII*, ed. Pélicier, iii, no. dxii, 21–22; *Arch. hist. Gironde*, vi (1864), no. xxii, 87–88.

important was the task of inducing other families to defect from the English and then securing their continuing allegiance and obedience. Many of the initial defections from the English party had, of course, been prompted by French military success. But rewards and inducements were necessary to consolidate such switches of allegiance. Above all, the integrity of a family's landed inheritance had ultimately to be respected. Lands confiscated from one branch of a family would be restored to another so that the overall pattern of tenure remained broadly unchanged. These two imperatives were in some degree mutually contradictory; for the ability to secure loyalties by means of grants of lands and rights was limited by the need to keep properties within the same family. The extent to which this problem was solved by the French government can be examined by the treatment of two groups of defectors; first, those who joined the Valois before the reduction of Guyenne, and, second, those who joined them after the reduction, some of whom returned from exile many years later.

In the first category the most important family was probably the Gramonts. François seigneur de Gramont was one of a number of important noble figures to join Charles VII in 1442.[71] He was rewarded with grants of lands and money.[72] Gramont's continued plotting after the reduction of Bordeaux in 1451 put him at the mercy of the king at least until 1458, so there was no great inducement to bestow patronage upon him in these years. However, in October 1459 Gramont's extensive claims to revenues in Guyenne were recognised and in lieu of them he was granted Blaye; the following year this was exchanged for other sources of income in less politically sensitive areas.[73] In spite of his uneasy relationship with the French government Gramont succeeded in turning the French king's promises of 1442 into a profitable reality.

The royal government might try with some success to escape from its obligations to pay war-time pensions in later years. But as has been noted above in the case of the Foix, the tradition whereby a seigneurial inheritance, even if confiscated, should not perpetually be taken from a noble family was much less easily broken.[74] The cases of the Caumonts, the Gontauds and the Abzacs illustrate this point.

Although the junior line of the Caumont family, who were seigneurs de Lauzun, had joined the French allegiance as far back as 1404, the seigneur de Caumont himself continued to serve the English.[75] Nompar II de Caumont seigneur de Caumont's lands were confiscated by Charles VII and given to Nompar's younger brother, Brandelis.[76] Brandelis had secured himself firmly to the interests of the French party in Guyenne by his marriage in 1444 to Marguerite de Bretagne, daughter of Olivier de Bretagne, comte de

---

71 Vale, *English Gascony*, p. 208.
72 BN, ms. fr. 25,711, fo 180r; Vale, *English Gascony*, pp. 209–10; Jaurgain and Ritter, *Maison de Gramont*, i, 73.
73 Jaurgain and Ritter, *Maison de Gramont*, i, 77–79.
74 See above, pp. 104–105.
75 Vale, *English Gascony*, pp. 207–208.
76 BN, ms. Périgord 126, 'de Caumont', fo 7v.

Penthièvre.[77] Under Brandelis, the house of Caumont's fortunes were restored. The restoration of the seigneurie of Caumont to him was definitively granted in 1453.[78] Ten years later Brandelis was granted permission to re-build the castle of Caumont, which was in ruins.[79] Both lines of the Caumonts were soon linked firmly once more to the traditionally French noble houses of Périgord by marriage.[80]

The family of Gontaud similarly benefited from a policy of transferring lands from disloyal to loyal members of the same family. The senior line of Gontauds, the seigneurs de Biron, who disputed that they and not the Beynacs were first barons of Périgord, had joined the French allegiance twice. The first time was in 1432 when Gaston V de Biron left the English in order to have Biron itself restored to him – though with little success.[81] The second time, and definitively, was as a result of the French invasion of 1442.[82] It was, however, in the junior line of the seigneurs de Badefols that the device of transferring an inheritance between brothers was practised. Richard de Gontaud, bastard son of Pierre de Gontaud, seigneur de Badefols, unlike his father who served the English cause, seems to have spent his career in the Valois army of re-conquest. He was present at the coronation of Charles VII at Rheims. For his loyalty he was rewarded with the grant of the confiscated seigneurie of Badefols, was legitimised and then confirmed in his rights by the *parlement* of Toulouse after the conquest of Guyenne.[83]

The third, and most illuminating, case is that of the Abzacs, who, in spite of the varying fortunes and dubious loyalties of one branch of the family, emerged as one of the most influential noble houses in Périgord. The Abzac seigneurs of Bellegarde and Montastruc had been deeply involved with the English in Guyenne. Jean d'Abzac seigneur de Bellegarde was certainly thoroughly mistrusted by the French royal officers in 1453; they described him as 'one of the principal leaders of the said rebellion'.[84] That perhaps was an exaggeration. But the roles of Jean's father and brothers were important in sustaining the English cause, all the same. Bertrand d'Abzac, seigneur de Bellegarde, had been the leading 'English' captain in Périgord. In 1438 Bellegarde was forced to yield Domme to the French. Although his wife and children were spared, the seigneur de Bellegarde himself was taken to Limoges and executed for treason in the following year.[85] However, Bertrand d'Abzac's children were permitted to inherit his lands and rights.[86] This was in spite of the continued disloyal behaviour which they exhibited; for none seems to have been fully converted to service of the French monarchy until the final English defeat in 1453, and in

---

77 *Ibid.*, fo 8r.
78 AD Gers, I supplément 134, unnumbered; APA, E 643, unnumbered.
79 AN, JJ 193, no. 153.
80 AD Gers, I supplément 134, unnumbered; BN, ms. Périgord 126, 'de Caumont', fo 13r; APA, E 34 bis, no. 31, p. 1.
81 Maubourguet, *Sarlat*, iii, 84.
82 Vale, *English Gascony*, p. 208.
83 BN, ms. Périgord 1242, 'Gontaut', fos 38r–39v.
84 BN, ms. fr. 26,082, fo 627r.
85 BN, ms. Duchesne 31, pp. 183–84 bis; BN, ms. Périgord 115, 'd'Abzac', fo 14r.
86 BN, ms. Duchesne 31, pp. 183–84 bis.

some cases later than this or not at all. One son Jean was still holding out against the French in 1450.[87] He subsequently joined the soudic de La Trau and then departed finally for England leaving his property to his brother, Jean 'Pochin' d'Abzac.[88] Jean 'Pochin' had also been in the soudic's service.[89] Although Jean seigneur de Bellegarde now realised that conditions in Guyenne had changed permanently, and that it was necessary to work with the new regime, as did his brother 'Pochin', seigneur de Montastruc, a third brother Bernard did not. Bernard d'Abzac only returned very late on in his life, receiving a pardon from Louis XII in 1500.[90] In fact, only one member of the Bellegarde line of Abzacs appears to have accepted the French allegiance earlier than was absolutely necessary; this was Bertrand d'Abzac's brother, Archambaud, who was persuaded to join the French with a 300 l.t. pension from the duc d'Orléans and the grant of Auberoche for life.[91]

It was, therefore, with a record of treachery and shifting loyalties that the Bellegarde line of Abzacs finally and definitively entered the service of the king of France. Yet both lines of Abzacs flourished under the Valois régime. The position of the second line, the La Douzes, was reinforced by marriage and by promotion. Of Guinot d'Abzac de La Douze's sons, one became a soldier and two became clerics of no great importance; but the third, Pierre de La Douze, was to become a councillor of the Bordeaux *parlement*, a distinguished diplomat in the service of Louis XI employed in Burgundy, Provence and Italy, and finally archbishop of Narbonne.[92] Pierre de La Douze renounced the archbishopric in favour of his nephew Andouin.[93] Pierre's other nephew, Guillaume, was also a councillor of the Bordeaux *parlement* and a recipient of valuable benefices.[94] Guinot d'Abzac's successor, Jean I seigneur de La Douze, married into the influential local noble family of Saint-Astier and then into the Talleyrands; while Guinot's grand-son, who was also to succeed as seigneur de La Douze, married one of the daughters of the seigneur de Salignac. The seigneurs de La Douze remained great figures in Périgord living the conventional life which was expected of them. Jean II de La Douze was described by one who knew him as a man of honour, a soldier and a great hunter.[95]

The Bellegardes were perhaps even more influential and important in the life of the *pays*. They were entrusted by the king with tasks relating to the defence of Périgord and the levying of men and provisions.[96] They were great

---

87 Maubourguet, *Sarlat*, iii, 47.

88 BN, ms. Duchesne 31, pp. 183–84 bis.

89 See above p. 155.

90 BN, ms. Périgord 115, 'd'Abzac', fo 88r–v.

91 *Ibid.*, p. 25.

92 BN, ms. Périgord 115, 'd'Abzac', fos 56v, 57r, 61v, 62r.

93 *Ibid.*, fo 61v.

94 AC Périgueux, CC 94, fo 16v; AD Dordogne, 2E 1851/74, no. 2; 'Lettres d'investiture de Gabriel évêque de Périgueux, conférant à Guillaume d'Abzac la cure de Saint-Victor de La Force (11 mai 1492)', ed. Marquis d'Abzac de La Douze, in B. *Soc. hist. archéol. Périgord*, xvi (1889), 192–93.

95 BN, ms. Périgord 115, 'd'Abzac', fo 65v.

96 AC Bergerac, jurade 21, 1481–1482 [fo 51r–v], jurade 22, 1484–1485 [fos 34v–35r].

property owners, especially in and around Bergerac.[97] Like their cousins of La Douze, they were anxious to increase their land-holding when the price was deemed right.[98] In short, the Abzacs had become a powerful and wealthy noble house, as influential in the *pays*, in the towns, and perhaps with the provincial government too, as any in Périgord. From being branded with treachery they had quickly become indispensable to the secure government of the sénéchaussée of Périgord.

We have investigated the fortunes of those noble families who had a long tradition of loyalty to the Valois and of those who, while continuing for as long as possible to serve the English, eventually rejoined the French allegiance. It is now necessary to examine a third group – those who by conviction or miscalculation went into exile.

Gascon merchants who went into exile in England were probably more likely to put down firm roots and acquire permanent incomes and interests there than nobles who had fled the duchy; certainly fewer of the merchants ever returned to France.[99] However, the way in which even long-serving agents of the old English régime were able to escape victimisation after the second reduction of Bordeaux must have given the lie to the fears of some who had fled. Bernard Angevin, seigneur de Rauzan, for example, had been a registrar of the supreme court of appeal at Bordeaux, a royal councillor, judge and chancellor of the great seal there. He had been richly rewarded in lands by his English masters and was ennobled in 1445. One of the negotiators of the terms of the reduction of Bordeaux in 1451, he had joined in the soudic's conspiracies in 1452–1454. Yet he escaped reprisals in 1453.[100] Angevin's grand-daughter, sole heiress of his son Jacques, married the son of another exile, Jean de Durfort, in 1487.[101] Angevin's family seems to have flourished and enjoyed the royal favour. In 1463 his son, Bernard, was given permission to rebuild his castle of Civrac which had been demolished during the English wars.[102] In 1475 Bernard II was a litigant in the court of the sénéchal of Guyenne.[103]

Not all of those who had served the English and remained behind in 1453 were so well treated. Jean d'Anglade who had been captured at the battle of Castillon and who had broken his earlier oath of allegiance to Charles VII was, for example, imprisoned. But he was released on the accession of Louis XI and his lands restored.[104] The king went on to entrust him with the captaincy of Monflanquin and Villeréal in Agenais.[105] He was another example of royal

97   AD Dordogne, 2E 1806/22. Known as the *'livre noir'*, this register contains only recognisances to the seigneurs de Bellegarde – with the exception of fos 1r–7r and 69r–76v; AD Haute-Garonne, H, Fonds de Malte, Condat 26 (old cataloguing: Saint-Nexans 2, no. 14).
98   BN, ms. Périgord 115, 'd'Abzac', fo 64r.
99   Peyrègne, 'Les Emigrés gascons', 113–28.
100 R. Boutruche, *La Crise d'une société. Seigneurs et paysans du Bordelais pendant la guerre de cent ans* (Paris, 1947) p. 374.
101 Anselme de Sainte-Marie, *Histoire généalogique*, v, 734.
102 AN, JJ 199, no. 330.
103 ADG, H 242, unnumbered.
104 AN, JJ 191, no. 5.
105 BN, PO 64, 'Anglade', no. 14.

leniency, whose significance may not have been missed by others contemplating an early return.

The accession of Louis XI provided an opportunity for those who feared Charles VII's and his officers' retribution to take advantage of the clemency associated with the beginning of a new reign. The most distinguished figure to do so was undoubtedly the comte de Candale. Every effort was made by the royal government to ensure his swift and easy return to the position of a great seigneur. He was pardoned in May 1462 and allowed to succeed to the lands of his late father, the captal de Buch. In the meantime, while he was trying to obtain possession of them, Candale was to be recompensed with other lands and revenues; he was to receive a pension and be acquitted of all his debts. In fact he received a pension of 6,000 l.t.[106]

The king was similarly helpful towards the Lalandes. Jean de Lalande had broken his oath to Charles VII and joined the English under Talbot; he and his family had then fled to England. The seigneurie of Lalande was given by Charles VII to Louis de Beaumont, seigneur de La Forêt. In 1463 Jean de Lalande's son, also called Jean, returned to France and was pardoned. Louis XI apparently went so far as to recompense Beaumont with 10,000 écus d'or so that he would return the seigneurie to Lalande.[107] Thomas de Lalande, who probably returned at the same time, was favoured by the king too. In 1476 for unspecified services he was granted 5,000 écus d'or for his marriage, which sum he was to take from the revenues of Marmande and La Réole.[108]

The last of the most important Gascon nobles to return was Gaillard de Durfort, seigneur de Duras. Durfort had served the English from 1434 as sénéchal of the Landes.[109] In 1453 he was perpetually banished.[110] He was said in 1455 to have been very strongly influenced by the soudic of La Trau and was probably involved closely in the latter's plans for an English return.[111] Honoured and promoted by both the king of England and the duke of Burgundy, it was not until the settlement of Picquigny that Durfort was prepared to return to France.[112] Gaillard de Durfort and his family were well received by Louis XI. He was pardoned in 1477. He and his three children, Jean, Georges and Marguerite, were to enjoy and succeed to their lands and rights.[113] In 1477–1478 Durfort was receiving 6,400 l.t. in pension and wages.[114] Even his legitimate children and his bastard were provided with pensions.[115] Durfort's eldest son, Jean seigneur de Duras, proved a paragon of

---

106 *Ordonnances*, xv, 482; BN, ms. fr. 26,096, fo 1555r.

107 AN, X[1A] 8607, fos 228v–230r.

108 ADG, 1 B1, fos 1r–2r.

109 Vale, *English Gascony*, p. 248.

110 *Recueil des privilèges*, ed. Gouron, pp. 46–47.

111 AD Gers, E 19, unnumbered.

112 Anselme de Sainte-Marie, *Histoire généalogique*, v, 733.

113 AN, X[1A] 8607, fo 67r–v.

114 *Comptes du trésor, 1296–1477*, ed. R. Fawtier and C. V. Langlois [Recueils des historiens de France. Documents financiers, ii] (Paris, 1930), p. 197.

115 BN, ms. fr. 26,099, fo 23r.

loyalty to the French crown, serving the king in his Italian wars.[116] The wisdom of Louis XI's treatment of the late seigneur de Duras and his family was thus amply demonstrated.

The most remarkable example of a noble house whose members had been deeply implicated in the English interest in the duchy becoming favoured and loyal adherents of the Valois monarchy is, however, that of the Montferrands. The family had to work their way back into the royal favour; but this was swiftly accomplished. Even the line of La Trau, the descendants of Pierre de Montferrand, regarded by the French chroniclers and others as the most hardened and anglophil conspirator, soon lived down their treasonable past. In 1452 the soudic de La Trau, the vicomte d'Uza and Bertrand de Montferrand all joined the English, the last two at least leaving the duchy for exile.[117] Bertrand de Montferrand was pardoned for treason in May 1454 and was partially restored to his former seigneuries.[118] He was in receipt of a pension of 600 l.t. from Charles VII and this was subsequently increased by Charles of France, as duke of Guyenne, to 1,200 l.t.[119] In 1474 Bertrand was succeeded by his son Gaston who was granted by the king the seigneurie of Langoiran, previously held by his father in the days before the reduction of Guyenne.[120] Gaston de Montferrand enjoyed a successful military career and was well rewarded for his service to the crown. From Louis XI he received 1,200 l.t. a year in pension and also the seigneurie of Sauveterre.[121] He fought for the regency government of Charles VIII in Brittany and against the rebels in Guyenne in 1487.[122] Appointed sénéchal of Périgord, he was relied upon by the monarchy as its most trusted lieutenant in the South-West until the end of his life.[123] In these years when the power of the sire d'Albret and his connection was so great in Guyenne, that cannot have been an entirely comfortable position for one who had thwarted Albret's and his allies' earlier plans for revolt.

The vicomte d'Uza never returned to France and died in England. His son, Bernard, seigneur de Belin, had, however, never joined him there. Indeed he subsequently claimed he had always taken the side of the French. In 1460 he was given permission to rebuild the castle of Belin, which the French had pulled down.[124]

Most remarkable of all, however, was the fate of the soudic de La Trau's son and heir, François. The latter was taken into the royal household after his father's execution and brought up with Louis XI and Charles of France.[125]

---

116 Anselme de Sainte-Marie, *Histoire généalogique*, v, 734.
117 Communay, *Essai généalogique sur les Montferrand de Guienne* (Bordeaux, 1889), p. xxviii.
118 *Arch. hist. Gironde*, xxvi (1888–1889), no. xcii, 366–68.
119 *Ibid.*, no. xciv, 372–73; BN, PO 2019, 'Montferrand', no. 339.
120 AN, JJ 207, no. 339.
121 *Comptes du trésor*, ed. Fawtier and Langlois, pp. 174–75, 196; BN, PO 2019, 'Montferrand', no. 53.
122 *Lettres de Charles VIII*, ed. Pélicier, i, pièce justificative xii, 381–383; BN, ms. fr. 20,486, fo 40r–v.
123 BN, ms. fr. 26,099, fo 5r; PO 2019, 'Montferrand', nos. 57, 58; AD Gers, I 2378, unnumbered.
124 AN, JJ 190, no. 140.
125 BN, ms. Duchesne 31, p. 171.

François de Montferrand subsequently served the king of France in Italy.[126] Each of the three lines had thus been restored to wealth and favour by their former enemy, the Valois monarchy.

The problem which the French government ultimately faced in controlling the nobility of Guyenne was the result of its own partial success. Important noble families naturally became immersed in the life of the *pays*; the local seigneurs upon whom the king had to depend were viewed, and viewed themselves, as the representatives of the *pays* and the communities which constituted it in their dealings with the royal officers and the king. In Périgord this role was most frequently attributed to the Talleyrands and the Abzacs, who expected to be properly rewarded for fulfilling it. In 1477–1478, for example, the seigneur de Grignols was employed to remonstrate with Louis XI at court concerning the taxation of Périgueux.[127] Périgueux agreed to pay the seigneur de Grignols' expenses when he came to the town in 1492–1493, as the town accounts put it, 'because he is a great friend to us at court and elsewhere.'[128]

The seigneurs de Bellegarde and their family were more closely involved with Bergerac, where they were looked upon as spokesmen and patrons of the town. It was entirely natural that the seigneur de Bellegarde, who had experience of such matters, should be sent by Bergerac to the estates of Périgord in order to negotiate their contribution to the requirements of the sire d'Albret's army of 1476.[129]

Both Bergerac, until the mayoralty was abolished, and Périgueux ensured that their relationship with the local nobility was formalised through the appointment of members of noble families as mayor. The list of mayors of Périgueux reads like a local *nobiliaire*, with seigneurial figures interspersed with royal officers. There was one seigneur de La Douze appointed as mayor in 1458; two Saint-Astiers between them enjoyed the office six times until 1490.[130] Political and propertied interests bound such families closely to the localities in which their power lay. With any loosening of the bonds between seigneurs and the royal government, it was easy for such influence to be used in order to inhibit rather than advance the government's control of the province.

Noble connections

What posed a real threat to the royal power, however, was the growth of noble 'connections', constituting more or less loose networks of clientage, having at their centre a great seigneur with political ambitions. The sire d'Albret's connection was by far the most sophisticated, important and well exploited of such connections in Guyenne.

The device of the formal *alliance* between nobles had by the time of the final

126 Communay, *Essai généalogique*, p. lxix.
127 AC Périgueux, CC 91, fo 26r.
128 AC Périgueux, CC 94, fo 15r.
129 AC Bergerac, jurade 20, 1475–1476 [fo 34v].
130 AC Périgueux, BB 14, fos 7r 14r, 15r, 16r, 42r, 52r.

reduction of Guyenne become much less common.[131] Written undertakings to serve in arms could still sometimes be given, of the sort agreed between Louis XI and Gaston IV comte de Foix in 1467. This was intended to assure the king of Foix's willingness to oppose the enterprises of Charles of France, the comte de Charolais, the duke of Brittany and other conspirators.[132] More specific was the written undertaking given by Alain d'Albret to the comte de Comminges and his brother, Odet, in 1488 that he would guard, defend, favour and protect their estates and persons, make no agreement to which they were not party and help them recover their lands.[133]

Much more often, however, the links between families and individuals through clientage were informal and are not always easy to deduce. For example, the seigneurs d'Estissac seem to have acted as patrons to the Bideran family. In 1455 Malrigon de Bideran was given a noble house at Bergerac by Estissac.[134] The Biderans were regarded as proctors of the seigneur d'Estissac for the purposes of homage.[135] Malrigon and Jean de Bideran were appointed as captains of the Estissac castles of Estissac itself and Cahuzac.[136] Yet the Estissacs, themselves, were not independent of such ties of clientage, for they were members of the wider connection of the sire d'Albret. Bertrand seigneur d'Estissac was present, probably in that capacity, at the marriage of Jean d'Albret and Catherine of Navarre in 1484 and was, as has been observed, involved in the plot to raise the South-West in 1487 for Albret and the rebels.[137]

The Albret connection was probably in part so difficult to break or oppose because it was so nebulous. It extended everywhere. Albret's and the Aydies' influence was so great that it is probably only possible to say with any degree of certainty what prominent figures were *not* subject to it. The most important of those who seemed to have escaped the Albret web entirely were the comtes de Foix and de Candale, Gaston de Montferrand, Gaston du Lyon and Robert de Balsac.[138] Beyond them, however, it is hard to tell.

The influence of the sire d'Albret resulted from the combination in Alain d'Albret of the inheritances of the Albrets themselves and of the Bretagne comtes de Périgord.[139] Families who had served Charles II d'Albret, his off-spring and successors also joined his grandson. For instance, in 1456 Louis de Noailhan was described by Charles II as his 'beloved and loyal *compère*'.[140] By 1480 Jean de Noailhan had become one of the 'squires, servants and familiars' of Alain d'Albret.[141] A similar case is that of the Montpezats. In December

---

[131] P.S. Lewis, 'Decayed and Non-Feudalism in Later Medieval France', B. *Inst. hist. Research*, xxxvi (1963), 178.
[132] BN, ms. fr. 2811, fo 70r.
[133] BN, ms. Doat 224, fos 12r–14v.
[134] BN, ms. Périgord 122, 'de Bideran', fo 2v.
[135] *Ibid.*, fo 3r.
[136] *Ibid.*, fos 8r, 21r.
[137] APA, 84 bis, no. 3. See above, p. 170.
[138] AD Gers, I 2630, unnumbered.
[139] See above, pp. 93–95, 98–99.
[140] AD Gers, I 28, no. 2.
[141] AD Gers, 2630, unnumbered.

1457 Charles II d'Albret was to be found in a low room, in front of the fire, surrounded by the nobles of the *pays* at Aiguillon as the guest of Charles de Montpezat.[142] In 1483 Montpezat was still regarded as one of Alain d'Albret's servants when he was at the royal court.[143] One of the key figures of the Albret household was Bertrand du Barry. In 1469 he was able to claim that he had already served the Albrets for thirty years.[144] This was the kind of continuity from which abiding loyalties could be forged.

Just as important, however, were the power and influence which Albret acquired through his marriage to Françoise de Bretagne. The respect owed to the memory of Jean de Bretagne was a potent source of influence among those who had known him and now joined the service of the new comte de Périgord. The late comte had apparently epitomised the aristocratic virtues which could inspire respect and loyalty in noble society. He was described as having been a 'man of good faith who got on with all estates of people and who tried to please them, who was generous and free from constraint'.[145] Most of Jean de Bretagne's old servants and the guardians of his daughter, Françoise, seem to have accepted it as natural to follow the new comte, whose background, and probably personality, was so different.[146] Lurs, Pierre-Buffières, Talleyrands, Pérusses, Salignacs and Pompadours all became trusted servants of the sire d'Albret.[147] It applied over more than one generation. For example, Bertrand de Lur was Alain d'Albret's councillor in 1476; both his sons, Jean and Bardin, became sénéchaux of Albret.[148] In fact, of those who had served Jean de Bretagne probably only two families failed to become entwined in the Albret connection, the Bourdeilles and the Beaupoils. In both cases this seems to have been the result of bitter property disputes.[149]

The dangerous potential of such political strength does not seem to have been fully grasped by the royal government. The marriage of Alain's son and heir, Jean, to the queen of Navarre was pressed vigorously by the court, ostensibly in order to keep the South-West firm its loyalty to the king.[150] The sire d'Albret's connection with the comte de Comminges and his supporters brought within the Albret network many who had previously remained outside it. In December 1490 it was as an expanded and well rewarded connection that the rebels were received back into the royal allegiance.[151] The death of the comte de Comminges had consolidated Albret's own hold over those who had followed him to Brittany. Odet d'Aydie, the Younger, was probably the most important adherent acquired by Albret during these years. Odet had had dealings with Albret as comte de Périgord. He had married the daughter of Guy

---

142 APA, E 70, unnumbered.
143 *Arch. hist. Gironde*, xxxv (1900), no. vii, 42.
144 APA, E 850, unnumbered.
145 APA, E 710, unnumbered, fo 5v.
146 Luchaire, *Alain le Grand*, p. 14.
147 BN, ms. Périgord 150, 'de Lur-Saluces', fos 8r–9r.
148 APA, E 70, unnumbered; E 80, unnumbered; AD Dordogne, J 1384, unnumbered *cahier* [fos 1r–20r].
149 APA, E 643, unnumbered; E 710, unnumbered.
150 APA, E 353, unnumbered; BN, ms. Doat 223, fos 333r–36v.
151 See above, pp. 170–71.

seigneur de Pons in February 1484.[152] But he badly needed Albret's support to secure his position as a new-comer to the *pays*. Alain d'Albret and his son, Jean, granted Odet all their rights to Ribérac, Larche, Terrasson and Espeluche in exchange for Odet's services to them during the Foix civil war.[153] Even with Albret's aid it was not until June 1493 that Odet's vassals would recognise him as seigneur.[154] It was probably a combination of these circumstances in Périgord and the manoeuvres of his elder brother which linked Odet firmly to Albret. Odet d'Aydie was already referred to as Albret's 'servant' at the time of the yielding of Nantes.[155]

The fact, therefore, that the Valois monarchy was so successful in wooing the Gascon nobility away from the English and then, with two brief interludes, keeping them firmly under the royal authority should not be allowed to disguise the deficiencies of the means which were employed to exert control in these years. The need to reward both those who had proved loyal and those whose loyalty had to be bought placed a strain on the resources of the government; this was all the more true because of the need to rule through local noble families whose claims to lands, office and pension could not easily be over-ridden. The last opportunity to create strong bonds of gratitude and service came with the return of the exiles from England; for with such families a little generosity was at a premium when there was a past of treasonable disloyalty to be lived down. However, the steady growth of vested interests and local ties, both among the royal officers and the seigneurs upon whom the king depended for the operation of his government, eroded the royal ability to control events and personnel in the province as it had succeeded in doing in the years after the reduction of Guyenne. The development of the Albret connection, at the head of which was a seigneur whose ambitions rivalled those of the monarchy, at a time of weak government during a minority, took this process to its logical conclusion. By the time of the outbreak of the Italian wars in 1494 the nobility of Guyenne, especially that part of it which was enmeshed in the service of Alain d'Albret, was freer of royal political control than at any time since 1453.

[152] AD Dordogne, 2E 1851/72, no. 1.
[153] AD Dordogne, 2E 1851/90, no. 10.
[154] AD Dordogne, 2E 1851/91, no. 1.
[155] Ad Dordogne, 2E 1851/68, no. 4.

Conclusion

The Valois government's aims in Guyenne were limited. It may be that in the first few years after the fall of English Gascony there were some who sought consciously to reform the duchy's institutions; but even in the spheres of administration and justice English precedent and custom were never forgotten.

At no stage, moreover, was there any deliberate attempt to transform the cultural or social identity of Guyenne. Take language, for example. The trend, particularly from the time of the installation of the *parlement* of Bordeaux, was certainly towards greater use of French in the notarial registers, which are perhaps the best guide to the language in which commercial and judicial business was conducted. But throughout the period French, Gascon, and, very much in third place, Latin are still to be found side by side.[1] Of course, 'gallicisation' was occurring, but only slowly and through adaption to new political and social realities. In the *comptes consulaires* of Montréal, for instance, there is an increase in the number of gallicisms, but the *comptes* continue throughout the period to be written in Gascon.[2] In 1501–1502 the accounts of the *trésorier* of Bordeaux were also still in Gascon; but this was about to change. The customs of Bordeaux would shortly for the first time be written in French and the first surviving registers of the jurade, in 1520, were by now in French too.[3] Similarly, and not surprisingly, the architectural style of Bordeaux after 1453 shows clear continuity from before the reduction by the French.[4] It was only at the turn of the the century, and then as a result of Italian influence, that the style of public buildings and noble châteaux shows any marked change.[5]

The *pays* which constituted Guyenne and Gascogne had, as has been observed earlier, little in common except their common experience of English rule. The French government did not seek to apply one 'system', whether of law, administration, representative institutions or taxation, in order to change that. The impact of the Bordeaux *parlement*, at least once its *ressort* had been properly fixed, may increasingly have had such an effect; but there is no reason to believe that this was an act of policy. The most important condition uniting the South-West by the end of the period was rather perhaps – and paradoxically – the prevalent influence of the Albrets and their connection.

Similarly, the way in which the administrative and judicial institutions of English Gascony were adapted rather than uprooted has already been noted.[6]

---

1 *Histoire de Bordeaux*, iv, 87.
2 *Comptes consulaires Montréal*, p. 14.
3 *Histoire de Bordeaux*, iv, 282–83.
4 *Ibid.*, pp. 257, 260.
5 J. Secret, *Le Périgord: châteaux, manoirs et gentilhommières* (n.p., 1966), pp. 10–11.
6 See above, p. 23.

Such a policy mirrored that adopted by the monarchy in other areas integrated or reintegrated into France. Local institutions were respected, modified and sometimes strengthened where they proved of service. The Norman *échiquier* was retained by Charles VII to form the basis of a *parlement* under Louis XII.[7] In Brittany, the financial institutions of the duchy continued to be used by the French monarchy after the duchy's return to the French crown and, although the chancery of Brittany was suppressed in December 1493, the Breton *parlement* effectively continued in the form of annual *grands jours*.[8] It is, therefore, not surprising to see the administrative framework of English Gascony reflected in that of Valois Guyenne.

Moreover, the French monarchy continued to show a prudent and practical sensitivity in its treatment of local sentiment. This was, for example, shown in the monarchy's attitude to the immensely popular cult of Pey Berland. Louis XI motivated, no doubt, by both politics and piety, pressed vigorously for the canonisation of Berland, the last 'English' archbishop of Bordeaux. On the face of it this was surprising: for Berland had played a major role in the affairs of the city under English rule, rallying the citizens to the English cause. Perhaps under pressure, he resigned his archbishopric and retired to his college of Saint-Raphaël in 1456, dying there in January 1458.[9] Berland was immediately recognised by the populace as a saint. Large sums were collected by the cathedral chapter of Saint-André from those who came to pray at his tomb. In 1466, for example, 317 l. t. was collected there.[10] Louis XI took a particular interest in gathering accounts of the late archbishop's miracles for his canonisation.[11] In 1475 a special procession, unfortunately marred by brawls between the prelates of Bordeaux, was held to intercede for Pey Berland's cause.[12] By this time the chapter was keeping its revenues from Berland's tomb in a separate account, so important had they become.[13] Although the bid to have him canonised eventually failed, it was not through a lack of effort on the part of monarch, estates and chapter.[14] Louis XI also protected and confirmed the privileges of the university of Bordeaux, founded under the English rule at Pey Berland's inspiration.[15] This too has a parallel elsewhere: under French rule in Normandy, the university of Caen was enlarged.[16]

The government's main objective, therefore, was not fundamentally to reform, let alone re-create, Guyenne in its own image. It was, above all, simply to

---

[7] C.T. Allmand, 'Local Reaction to the French Reconquest of Normandy: the Case of Rouen', in *The Crown and Local Communities*, ed. Highfield and Jeffs, pp. 154–55.

[8] Kerhervé 'L'Etat breton, ii, 950–51; Pocquet, *Histoire de Bretagne*, iv, 588.

[9] *Histoire de Bordeaux*, iii, 508, 538–39.

[10] ADG, G 311, fo 128v.

[11] *Ibid.*, fo 83r–v.

[12] *Ibid.*, fos 116r–117r.

[13] ADG, G 241, fos 264r–271r.

[14] *Histoire de Bordeaux*, iii, 539–60.

[15] *Statuts et réglements de l'ancienne université de Bordeaux (1441–1793)*, ed. H. Barckhausen (Libourne and Bordeaux, 1886), pp. 5–8, 19–22.

[16] Allmand, 'Local Reaction', p. 154.

govern, using all the means at its disposal to do so; to keep this allegedly anglophil and certainly exposed province under royal control. This can be seen in the heavy emphasis given to the building of castles, maintenance of artillery and munitioning of garrisons and armies. The king's and the nobility of Guyenne's ambitions in Spain reinforced the priority given to military matters. Preoccupation with security undoubtedly limited the government's capacity to concentrate resources on improving justice or repressing criminal disorder; but then there is no evidence that either featured largely in its aims.

Considerations of security also affected the government's financial policy. The increase in taxation in Louis XI's last years and under Charles VIII was permitted by more general economic revival and by financial and political concessions to the influential – to nobles, royal officers and town oligarchies. It did not, however, result in the period as a whole in any increase in the importance of the estates: on the contrary. This was partly because of the disparateness of what constituted Guyenne; partly because of the importance of the Bordeaux and Bayonne customs as a source of royal income; and partly, after 1484, because of the trend throughout France to levy taxes on the supposed authority of the grant by the estates general of that year.

There can be no doubt that in keeping the province in submission and in drawing upon its resources for this purpose the government was largely successful. Imposing fortifications at Bordeaux, Bayonne, Dax and Saint-Sever soon testified to the government's achievement. Towns had to maintain and often to strengthen their own defences and artillery. They and the rest of the *pays* were expected to contribute men and money for the royal works and to lend their artillery and provided gun-powder when necessary. The levies of soldiers for the defence of the province and for the king's campaigns elsewhere were, however, less successfully organised. So was the lodging of the royal soldiers in the province. So in all probability was the provisioning of royal garrisons, of the key centres for Guyenne's defence, and of the king's armies.

It was doubtless of considerable advantage to the French government that it was not faced by a determined English campaign in France until 1475 and that this, when it came, was not launched at the South-West. The political upheavals in England after the fall of English Gascony ensured that the French government's system of defence in this newly conquered province was not put to the test. However, assisted as they were by these circumstances, the French kings' ability to mobilise the province's resources so frequently and, in the case of fortifications at least so effectively, is impressive. Similarly, the swift success of royal campaigns against the comte d'Armagnac and of the royal armies against rebels in Guyenne in 1487 provide eloquent testimony to the military superiority of the monarchy over its potential opponents. At least in part, the relative freedom from political upheaval enjoyed by Guyenne after 1453 resulted directly from the royal government's financial and military resources and from the system of provincial defence in which they were employed.

But there was more to political control than force of arms; fear, which military strength admittedly symbolised and increased, was undoubtedly important too. The fate of Jean V, comte d'Armagnac, demonstrated to all the consequences of taking royal power lightly; so had that of other rebels, like the soudic de La Trau. Louis XI seems to have instilled little short of terror among some of the French nobility.[17] It was fear of the results of royal vengeance which caused the seigneur de Lauzun to cry tearfully to his fellow conspirator, the seigneur d'Estissac, 'Would to God that you had never been involved in this venture and that you never knew of it. We are lost and dishonoured for ever.'[18]

At the heart of the royal government, unless during a minority, was inevitably the king's own personality. Indirect contact with him was possible to a wide range of petitioners in Guyenne, at least on his journeys to the South-West.[19] The great seigneurs, of course, had direct access to the court; a few of the nobility like François de Montferrand actually grew up there.[20] Some petitioners and representatives obtained sight of the king in person and of the other princes of the blood when visiting the royal court or estates. The Périgueux *livre jaune* chronicle, for example, describes the entry of the young Charles VIII at the estates general of Tours in terms which show conclusively that the author was present.[21] Others may have gained their impression of the king through his likeness.[22] To celebrate Charles VIII's victory at the battle of Fornova in 1495, the jurade of Bordeaux constructed an impressive effigy of the king on the Porte Caillau, facing the river.[23]

Pageantry and processions helped reinforce royal authority at every level. The submission of Bordeaux in 1451 was clearly used by the king's servants as an opportunity to impress the inhabitants with the power and wealth of France. At the solemn entry of the French into the city the procession included trumpeters, heralds, pursuivants of the king and other seigneurs bearing their coat of arms. Before the chancellor of France rode a white palfrey, upon which was a blue velvet-covered box, bejewelled with fleur-de-lys, containing the royal seals. The army's commanders were resplendent. Poton de Xaintrailles sat astride a great war-horse hung with silk cloth. Dunois's armour was white, his horse hung with blue velvet and gold.[24] The procession made its way to the cathedral of Saint-André where it was joined by the archbishop of Bordeaux and all the clergy singing the *Te Deum*.[25] Dunois was led by the hand by the archbishop up to the high altar where he swore on his own and the king's behalf to honour the treaty of submission. Then the clergy, nobles and some burgesses took their oath to the king amid cries of 'Noël!'.[26]

At the yielding of Bayonne, it was given out that God's approval of the

---

[17] W. Paravicini, 'Peur, pratiques, intelligences. Formes de l'opposition aristocratique à Louis XI d'après les interrogations du connétable de Saint-Pol', in *La France de la Fin du xve siècle. Renouveau et apogée*, pp. 186–88.

[18] APA, E 84 bis, no. 31.

[19] See above, pp. 135–57.

[20] BN, PO 2019, 'de Montferrand', no. 47.

[21] AC Périgueux, CC 88, fo 11v.

[22] Vale, *Charles VII*, pp. 197–98.

[23] *Histoire de Bordeaux*, iv, 270.

[24] *Histoire de Charles VII*, ed. Godefroy, p. 249.

[25] *Histoire de Charles VIII*, ed. Godefroy, p. 22.

[26] Escouchy, i, p. 358.

French success was shown by the appearance in the sky of a white cross.[27] For ostentatious dress on this occasion pride of place probably went to the comte de Foix, who entered Bayonne seated upon a richly dressed war horse, bearing steel armour set with gold and precious stones, and again to the comte de Dunois whose horse was covered with cloth of gold. Dunois descended to kiss the church of Bayonne's relics and gave his horse's cloth of gold to be made into ecclesiastical copes.[28]

Circumstances never seem to have proved propitious for a solemn royal entry into Bordeaux – though elsewhere under Charles VII and his successors these became ever more splendid.[29] Charles VII and Charles VIII only came to Guyenne to repress rebellion: and Louis XI's personal idiosyncratic dislike of excessive formality may explain the apparent lack of one when he was in the South-West.

The use of pageantry and the invocation of sacred authority, however, continued. On the entry of the duke of Guyenne to Bordeaux in April 1470, the streets were hung with cloth of gold, although the occasion was marred by rain. When Charles of France arrived by boat from Lormont he was met by the archbishop and clergy of Bordeaux. The semi-spiritual origins of his authority were symbolically emphasised. The duke was dressed in the habit of a canon and bread and wine were given to him when he entered the cathedral, where he was to take and to receive the appropriate oaths.[30]

Even the appointment of a new lieutenant general to the province was the occasion for a solemn entry. He would be met by a procession of Bordeaux clergy who escorted him to the Ombrière palace and then to the cathedral where oaths would be taken and received in the chapel of Saint-Martial.[31]

In some cases the archaic symbolism of such occasions must have proved somewhat embarrassing to the government. When Pierre de Bourbon received the oaths of the consuls of Nogaro in their church of Saint-Nicolas, for example, he had to receive their homage and fealty in the manner of the late Jean V, referred to as 'comte d'Armagnac *dei gratia*', a phrase strictly forbidden by the king.[32] But, in general, such occasions served their purpose in the government's eyes well enough and were not discontinued.

Display in furnishings and in dress was used also to increase the authority of more humble bodies, upon which the effectiveness of royal government depended. In March 1491, for example, the assessor of the sénéchal of Guyenne, paid 31l. 12s. 6d. t. for Flemish cloth used to decorate the sénéchaussée court.[33] The consuls of a town were naturally expected to appear clad in suitably impressive robes when they were summoned to court. In 1487 the royal

---

[27] *Ibid.*, p. 359.

[28] *Histoire de Charles VII*, ed. Godefroy, pp. 256–57.

[29] B. Guenée and F. Lehoux, *Les Entrées royales françaises de 1328 à 1515* (Paris, 1968), pp. 25–29.

[30] ADG, G 285, fo 54r.

[31] *Ibid.*, fo 27v.

[32] J.-F. Bladé, *Coutumes municipales du département du Gers* (Paris, 1864), p. 181. For the use by the comtes d'Armagnac of 'dei gratia', see Samaran, *Maison d'Armagnac*, pp. 96–97.

[33] BN, ms. fr. 26, 106, fo 636r.

proctor in the court of the *juge ordinaire* at Bergerac required its consuls to wear their robes, in order to show that they were consuls 'chosen by the king or his officers and in order to honour the court'.[34] By the end of the period towns were vying with one another for permission to attire their consuls with dignity. Penne and Tournon sought and obtained the right for their consuls to wear hoods and robes like those of Villeneuve and elsewhere in Agenais.[35]

The clergy had a crucial role to play in ensuring the loyalties of the province in times of crisis. At Périgueux, for example, prayers, masses and processions were expected from the canons of Saint-Front. In 1487 the town consuls ordered that masses should be said at Saint-Front for the king and for victory over his enemies. On 1 May the arm of the saint himself was carried in procession and prayers were said for peace, for the safety of church and king and that God should defend the town from plague.[36] In 1488 special masses were said when Charles VIII's army faced the Bretons and other rebels. God, Our Lady and Saint-Front were all invoked to intercede for the king's success. One of the purposes of occasions such as these was nicely summed up by the chronicler of the chapter of Saint-André at Bordeaux as being 'to set others an example'.[37]

Fear, pomp and a regard for provincial sensibilities undoubtedly all had a major part to play in effective political control: but in fifteenth century France, in Guyenne as elsewhere, it was the ability to reward and retain loyalties, through patronage and promotion, which was the abiding condition for success. It was in this that, in spite of the growth of tax revenues and offices, the Valois monarchy had by the end of the period suffered its most serious reverse.

This was in part the result of political miscalculation. The element of miscalculation lay in the royal government's treatment of the house of Albret. The linking of the Albret domains with the comté of Périgord and the vicomté of Limousin through the marriage of Alain d'Albret and Françoise de Bretagne, which the king did nothing to prevent, allowed the sire d'Albret to create a connection and entertain ambitions which could only ultimately threaten the king's and his officers' political control over Guyenne. The marriage of Alain's son and heir, Jean, to the queen of Navarre, which the French government actively encouraged, consolidated the house of Albret's influence in the South-West. The power of the Albrets had become so great that the king could only rule Guyenne effectively with their cooperation and through their connection.

What no amount of calculation could avoid, however, was the erosion of the government's control which followed from years of political stability. Stability meant that politically a lower price was put upon the preferment and patronage which the king had to offer. There were no exiles whose loyalty and gratitude could cheaply be bought. There were fewer opportunities for the granting of confiscated lands, for the appointment to offices and to commands, for major changes in the allocation of pensions and other grants. The royal domain was already largely alienated and resumptions were too politically sensitive to prove effective. Unless the king was to challenge the integrity of a noble inheritance,

---

[34] AC Bergerac, jurade 23, 1487 [fo 14r–v].

[35] AN, JJ 227, nos. 9, 404.

[36] AC Périgueux, CC 92, fo 4r.

[37] ADG, G 285, fo 119r.

which was socially and politically unthinkable, his ability to implant his own trusted servants in the *pays* was severely limited. The greater resources which increased taxation gave to the monarchy, although these could be and were used for pensions and for other favours, had also to be employed in satisfying the ever greater demands of those for whom the king was already providing. The great seigneurial families of the province and those of the most important officers claimed almost as of right the advantages which royal patronage could offer. The more that they enjoyed through office, commands, pensions and benefices, the more costly it was to provide for their future requirements. Conseqently the Valois government experienced the inescapably unfortunate results of its own success. The more vested interests which were built up by the operation of government in the new régime among officers, nobles, clergy and towns, the less effective was the control over affairs in the province which the government could exert.

The events of the minority of Charles VIII must have permitted the implications of these developments to be grasped. Although Charles VIII's government could crush rebels it was forced to encourage the very trends which had allowed the monarchy's control to be eroded. The government would still exercise the other elements of political control skilfully enough – through propaganda, pageantry and fear of the king's displeasure. But it required the launching of the great Italian venture, with all the opportunities for patronage, promotion and prestige which that offered, to secure political control by the monarchy over French society of the kind once exercised by Charles VII and Louis XI.

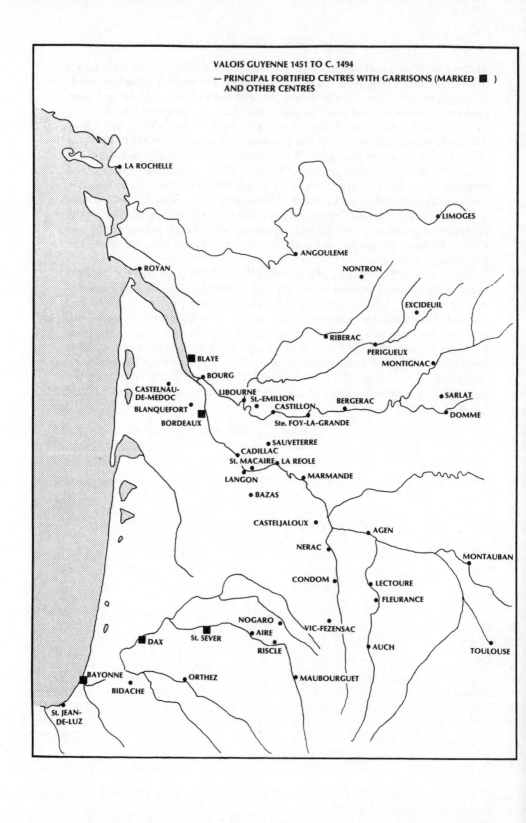

VALOIS GUYENNE 1451 TO C. 1494
— PRINCIPAL FORTIFIED CENTRES WITH GARRISONS (MARKED ■)
AND OTHER CENTRES

LA ROCHELLE

LIMOGES

ROYAN

NONTRON

EXCIDEUIL

RIBERAC

BLAYE

PERIGUEUX

MONTIGNAC

BOURG

LIBOURNE

SARLAT

CASTELNAU-
DE-MEDOC

St.-EMILION

BLANQUEFORT

CASTILLON

BERGERAC

DOMME

BORDEAUX

Ste. FOY-LA-GRANDE

SAUVETERRE

CADILLAC

St. MACAIRE   LA REOLE

LANGON

MARMANDE

BAZAS

CASTELJALOUX

AGEN

NERAC

MONTAUBAN

CONDOM

LECTOURE

FLEURANCE

NOGARO

VIC-FEZENSAC

DAX   St. SEVER   AIRE

RISCLE

AUCH

TOULOUSE

BAYONNE   ORTHEZ

MAUBOURGUET

BIDACHE

St. JEAN-
DE-LUZ

APPENDIX 1

Soldiers in Guyenne

(For sources, see page 203)

Date	Place	Numbers
10 April 1453, for Jan–March 1453	Bayonne	100 foot soldiers
10 April 1453, for Jan–March 1453	Bayonne	50 lances
10 April 1453, for 15 Feb–30 April 1453	Dax(?)	50 lances
1 August 1453	Bayonne	50 lances
13 July 1460, for April–June 1460	Bayonne	20 men at arms of *ordonnances*, 4 men-at-arms of *morte-payes*, 52 archers = 76 men
18 Dec 1460, for Oct–Dec 1460	Bayonne	10 men-at-arms and 4 archers of *ordonnances*, 3 men-at-arms and 18 archers of *morte-paye* = 35 men
28 Sept 1461, for July–Sept 1461	Bayonne	20 men-at-arms of *ordonnances*, 4 men-at-arms of *morte-paye*, 52 archers = 76 men
2 Sept 1467, about to enter garrison for 2 months	Bordeaux (Château du Hâ)	40 extra soldiers
2 Sept 1467, about to enter garrison for 2 months	Dax	20 extra soldiers
2 Sept 1467, about to enter garrison for 2 months	Bordeaux (Château Trompette)	40 extra soldiers
3 and 4 Feb 1471, for Oct–Dec 1470	Bazas(?)	14 men-at-arms and 29 archers = 43 men
13 June 1470	Lectoure	10 men-at-arms and 20 archers = 30 men
7 Feb 1471	Agen	13 men-at-arms and 26 archers = 39 men
2 Feb 1471 for Oct–Dec 1470	–	30 men-at-arms and 82 archers of *ordonnances* of duke of Guyenne = 112 men

199

6 Feb 1471 for Oct–Dec 1470	–	20 men-at-arms and 40 archers of *ordonnances* of duke of Guyenne = 60 men
28 May 1471 for Oct–Dec 1470	–	11 men-at-arms and 37 archers
18 April 1471 for Jan–March 1471	–	20 men-at-arms and 40 archers of duke of Guyenne's *ordonnances* = 60 men
27 Oct 1471	Dax	20 men-at-arms and 40 archers = 60 men
28 Sept 1471, for April–June 1471	Bordeaux	30 archers
11 Oct 1471, for July–Sept 1471	Blaye	13 men-at-arms and 74 archers = 87 men
2 Oct 1471, for July–Sept 1471	Bordeaux (Château du Hâ)	14 men-at-arms and 13 archers = 27 men
28 Nov 1471, for July–Sept 1471	Agen	10 men-at-arms and 20 archers of *ordonnances* of duke of Guyenne = 30 men
30 Dec 1471, for Oct–Dec 1471	Bordeaux (Château du Hâ)	14 men-at-arms and 13 archers = 27 men
13 Feb 1494, for Oct–Dec 1471	Bayonne (old and new castles)	100 *morte-payes*
19 Jan 1472, for Oct–Dec 1471	Pons	22 *men-at-arms* and 55 archers of *ordonnances* of duke of Guyenne = 77 men
28 March 1472, for Jan–March 1472	Blaye	13 men-at-arms, 13 *coustillers*, 74 archers = 100 men
7 Jan 1473, for July–Sept 1472	Bordeaux (Château de La Lune)	5 archers
7 Jan 1473, for July–Sept 1472	Bordeaux (Château du Hâ)	10 men-at-arms and 25 archers = 35 men
5 Jan 1473 for Oct–Dec 1472	Bordeaux (Château du Hâ)	50 archers
14 Jan 1474, for Oct–Dec 1473	Bordeaux (Château du Hâ)	36 *morte-payes*
27 June 1474 for Oct–Dec 1473	Bordeaux	10 men-at-arms, 2 *coustillers*, and 70 archers of *morte-payes* = 82 men
18 June 1474, for April–June 1474	Bayonne	100 *morte-payes*
27 Sept 1474, for April–June 1474	Bordeaux (Château Trompette)	50 *morte-payes*

4 Oct 1474, for April–June 1474	Blaye	100 *morte-payes*
15 Dec 1474, for July–Sept 1474	Bordeaux (Château de La Lune)	50 *morte-payes*
4 Oct 1474, for July–Sept 1474	Blaye	100 *morte-payes*
22 April 1475, for July–Dec 1474	Bayonne	100 *morte-payes*
5 April 1475, for Oct–Dec 1474	Bordeaux (Château du Hâ)	50 *morte-payes*
5 April 1475, for Oct–Dec 1474	Bordeaux (Château Trompette)	50 *morte-payes*
16 Jan 1475, for Oct–Dec 1474	Blaye	100 *morte-payes*
18 May 1475, for Oct–Dec 1474	Bayonne	100 *morte -payes*
22 May 1475, for April–June 1475	Labatut, near Dux	100 men-at-arms and 200 archers of *ordonnances* = 300 men
21 Sept 1475, for April–June 1475	Bayonne	96 men-at-arms and 190 archers of *ordonnances* = 286 men
30 Nov 1475, for July–Sept 1475	Blaye	100 *morte-payes*
1476, for 1475–6	Bordeaux (Château Trompette)	50 foot soldiers
1476, for 1475-6	Bordeaux	10 men-at-arms, 10 *coustillers* and 70 archers = 90 men
1476, for 1475–6	Bordeaux Château du Hâ	50 foot soldiers
1476, for 1475–6	Blaye	100 foot soldiers
1476, for 1475–6	Bayonne	100 foot soldiers
3 August 1487, for April–June 1487	Bordeaux (Château Trompette)	50 *morte-payes*
24 Oct 1487,	Bordeaux (Château Trompette)	50 *morte-payes*
30 Oct 1487, for July–Sept 1487	Bayonne	100 *morte-payes*
20 April 1488, for Jan–March 1488	Bordeaux (Château Trompette)	50 *morte-payes*
23 April 1488, for Jan–March 1488	Bordeaux	10 men-at-arms and 80 *morte-payes* = 90 men

20 April 1488, for Jan–March 1488	Bordeaux (Château du Hâ)	50 *morte-payes*
6 May 1488, for Jan–March 1488	Bayonne (town and castles)	100 *morte-payes*
25 July 1488, for April–June 1488	Blaye	100 *morte-payes*
16 Nov 1488, for July–Sept 1488	Blaye	100 *morte-payes*
19 Nov 1488, for July–Sept 1488	Bordeaux (Château Trompette)	50 *morte-payes*
21 Feb 1489, for Oct–Dec 1488	Bayonne	100 *morte-payes*
21 May 1489, for Jan–March 1489	Bayonne	100 *morte-payes*
3 May 1489, for Jan–March 1489	Bordeaux (Château du Hâ)	50 *morte-payes*
7 March 1490, for Oct–Dec 1489	Blaye	100 *morte-payes*
27 July 1490, for April–June 1490	Bordeaux (Château du Hâ)	50 *morte-payes*
3 Nov 1490, for July–Sept 1490	Blaye	100 *morte-payes*
10 Feb 1491 for Oct–Dec 1490	Bayonne	100 *morte-payes*
20 April 1491, for Jan–March 1491	Bordeaux (Château Trompette)	50 *morte-payes*
8 May 1491, for Feb–March 1491	Bayonne	100 *morte-payes*
22 Nov 1491, for July–Sept 1491	Bordeaux (Château Trompette)	50 *morte-payes*
5 Nov 1491, for July–Sept 1491	Bayonne	100 *morte-payes*
2 Feb 1492, for Oct–Dec 1491	Blaye	100 *morte-payes*
4 May 1492, for Jan–March 1492	Bordeaux (Château Trompette)	50 *morte-payes*
30 June 1492, for Jan–March 1492	Bordeaux	40 men-at-arms and 80 archers on horse-back of *morte-payes* = 120 men
2 Nov 1492, for July–Sept 1492	Bordeaux (Château Trompette)	50 *morte-payes*
7 Nov 1492, for July–Sept 1492	Blaye	100 *morte-payes*

20 Jan 1493, for Oct–Dec 1492	Bordeaux (Château du Hâ)	50 *morte-payes*
29 Jan 1493, for Oct–Dec 1492	Bayonne (old and new castles)	100 *morte-payes*
1 May 1493, for Jan–March 1493	Bordeaux	10 men-at-arms and 80 *morte-payes* = 90 men
23 Sept 1493, for April–June 1493	Bordeaux	10 men-at-arms and 80 *morte-payes* = 90 men
12 Dec 1493, for April–Sept 1493	Bayonne (old castle)	48 *morte-payes*
25 May 1494, for Oct–Dec 1493	Bayonne (new castle)	50 *morte-payes*
10 May 1494, for Oct–Dec 1493	Bordeaux	10 men-at-arms and 80 *morte-payes* = 90 men
7 May 1494, for Oct–Dec 1493	Bordeaux (Château du Hâ)	50 *morte-payes*
15 July 1494	Bayonne (town and castles)	100 *morte-payes*

Sources

BN, mss fr.
2906, fo 50v
8607, fos 81r, 87r
8608, fos 43r, 44r, 45r, 46r, 47r, 58r, 80r,
8609, fos 4r–5r, 6r–v.
8610, fo 46r, 48r
8611, fo 1r, 2r, 9r, 10r, 19r, 21r, 25r, 26r, 27r,
    28r, 29r, 32r

20, 496, fo 74r

24, 058, fos 1r, 5r
25, 778 fos 1905r, 1910r
25, 779, fos 36r, 37r, 38r 49r, 52r, 128r

25, 780, fos 55r, 56r, 61r, 66r,
25, 781, fo 26r, 30r, 41r, 44r

25, 782, fo 130r
25, 786, fo 62r

BN, n.a. fr
8608, fos 62r–63v, 80r
8610, fos 45r, 46r, 53r

BN, ms Clairambault
223, nos. 17, 18, 48, 52
235, nos. 141, 143, 145, 151, 155, 161
236, nos. 185, 211, 243
237, nos. 277, 279, 289, 297, 307
238, nos. 285, 353

AD Gers, 28, no. 7.

Crime in Guyenne

Note

Apart from the important limitations upon their usefulness outlined above (pp. 133–37), the figures for the incidence of criminal disorder in *lettres de rémission* on which charts 1–3 are based are also to be treated with caution on several grounds.

First, they do not necessarily represent the number of criminals pardoned, for some pardons applied to several people. Nor do they necessarily represent the number of crimes committed, since several crimes might be pardoned within one *lettre de rémission*.

Secondly, there are problems presented by the social and professional categorisation of criminals. Frequently, social status has to be inferred from incomplete evidence; sometimes it is impossible to judge it at all. In the latter case a pardoned crime will, therefore, be omitted from the number of socially categorised crimes altogether; and this results in differences, within the same table and between tables, in 'totals' of criminal incidents recorded.

Of those criminal incidents which yield to social and professional categorisation according to the background and occupation of those responsible for them, the following criteria have been used:

(i) 'Nobles': those referred to in the *lettre* as 'noble', those belonging to known noble families, those described as 'escuier' or 'seigneur'.

(ii) 'Clergy': only where the description of 'cleric' is employed is clerical status imputed.

(iii) 'Townsmen': those described as burgesses, merchants, tradesmen, those living in places where *sénéchaussée sièges* are known to have functioned.

(iv) 'Peasants': those described as '*pouvre laboureur*' or a similar variant, and those of the third estate not able to be classed as 'townsmen'.

(v) 'Foreigners': those who are not subjects of the king of France or of his vassals.

(vi) 'Soldiers': crimes are listed as committed by 'soldiers' when a person, of whatever social status, committed them while acting *as* a soldier.

(vii) 'Officers': similarly those crimes committed by royal or ducal officers *acting as such*, whatever their family background, are denoted within this category.

It should be noted that when the status or function of a criminal has changed between the time of the crime being committed and its being pardoned, the crime may now appear under more than one heading.

Finally, it is not always possible to specify the date when a crime was committed, though internal evidence usually allows this.

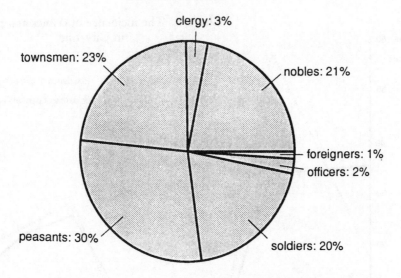

**Chart 1. Crimes within Guyenne (province)
by category of criminal**

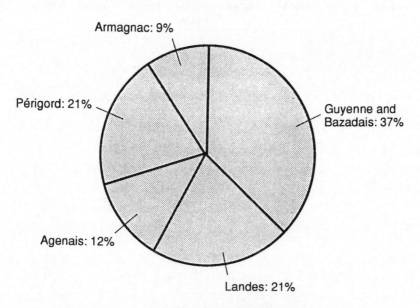

**Chart 2. Crimes within Guyenne (province)
by sénéchaussées**

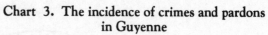

Chart 3. The incidence of crimes and pardons in Guyenne

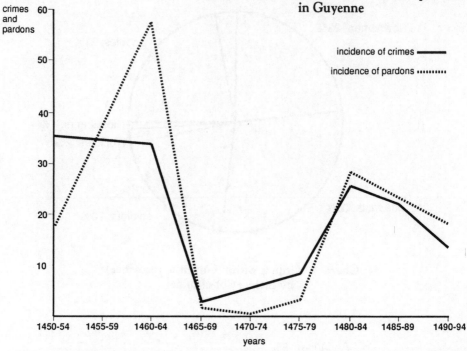

incidence of crimes ——

incidence of pardons ··········

206

Sources for charts 1–3

Archives nationales:

JJ 180, Nos. 63, 92, 140
JJ 181, Nos. 2, 24, 28, 32, 103, 143
JJ 185, Nos. 150, 161, 166, 190, 192, 195,
257, 281, 288, 289
JJ 187, Nos. 9, 19, 20, 28, 44, 51, 110, 119,
122, 125, 126, 164, 167, 212, 252, 259,
287, 289, 297, 303, 322, 336, 338
JJ 188, Nos. 18, 28, 42, 58, 146, 155, 180,
192, 197, 207
JJ 189, No. 238
JJ 190, Nos. 11, 28, 29, 30, 34, 57, 108, 116,
122, 137, 140, 155, 160
JJ 191, Nos. 26, 36, 64, 82, 89, 165
JJ 198, Nos. 1, 7, 25, 38, 84, 90, 195, 246,
288, 293, 300, 322, 337, 382, 400, 434,
447, 450, 487, 517, 519, 521, 522, 525,
534, 540, 544, 546, 549, 554
JJ 199, Nos. 144, 148, 150, 170, 172, 279,
280, 303, 308, 333, 334, 343, 479, 505
JJ 204, No. 133
JJ 205, Nos. 86, 161, 181, 357, 362, 363

JJ 207, Nos. 21, 87, 155, 184, 223, 289, 294,
321
JJ 208, Nos. 72, 149, 196, 214
JJ 209, Nos. 37, 70, 108, 179
JJ 210, Nos. 55, 96, 157
JJ 211, Nos. 98, 123, 310
JJ 213, Nos. 11, 87
JJ 215, Nos. 71, 82
JJ 217, Nos. 168
JJ 218, Nos. 9, 10, 21, 154, 191, 194, 196,
197, 199, 208
JJ 219, Nos. 12, 40, 52, 113, 151, 184
JJ 220, Nos. 70, 115, 220, 268, 333
JJ 221, Nos. 1, 98, 114, 158, 194, 248, 293,
304, 324
JJ 222, Nos. 36, 47, 83
JJ 223, Nos. 187, 240
JJ 226 b, Nos. 29, 84, 388, 396, 787
JJ 227, No. 11
JJ 229, Nos. 53, 90, 92

Bibliography

Manuscript sources

British Library
Additional Manuscripts
18,790

Public Record Office
Gascon Rolls
C/61/ 129–144

Constable of Bordeaux's Accounts
E 101/193–195

Archives Nationales
Trésor des Chartes
JJ 180–229
K 66–77
P 550^2, 552^2, 2229, 2300, 2533

Paris Parlement
X^{1A}81–92, 8324, 8605–8610

Cour des Aides
Z^{1A}19–32, 67–69

Bibliothèque Nationale
Manuscrits français
2811, 2893, 2895, 2897, 2899, 2900,
2902, 2905–6, 2909, 2911, 4390–2,
4421, 5909, 6963–4, 11,219–20,
20,083, 20,427–8, 20,483, 20,485–6,
20,488, 20,490–1, 20,492–3,
20,495–8, 20,855, 22,252, 22,293,
22,368, 22,379, 22,422, 24,058,
25,711–7, 25,778–81, 25,944
   26,079–26,106: (*Quittances et
   Pièces diverses*)

Nouvelles acquisitions françaises
2840, 3657, 8607–11, 23,793

Fonds latin
17,131

Collection Clairambault
138–238, 473, 1060

Collection Doat
117, 218–26, 246

Collection Duchesne
31, 103, 117

Pièces originales
4:    Abzac
15:   Aidie
25:   Albret
94:   Armagnac
104: Arpajon
155: Avril, Aydie
178: Balsac

1667: Lauzières
1682: Lehet
1701: Lestrange
1735: Lomagne
1777: Lustrac
1781: du Lyon
1810: Makanan
2019: Montferrand
2267: Picot
2356: Poton de Saintrailles

2404: Puy-du-Fou
2715: Sorbier
2721: Soupplainville
2843: du Tilh
2900: Tustal
2924: Valpergue, Valsac

Collection de Périgord
9, 84, 114

Genealogical information is provided for the following families in the
following volumes of the *Collection de Périgord*:

115: Abzac
117: *Idem*
120: Baume, Bailly, Beaupoil
121: Belcier, Beynac
122: Bideran
123: La Borie
124: Bourdeilles
125: Carbonnières
126: Caumont
130: La Cropte
132: Estissac
137: Flamenc, Ferrand
142: Gontaut
150: Lur
151: Mareuil, La Martonie

154: Noaillan
155: Pérusse, Berre-Buffière,
Pompadour
157: Pons
159: Roffignac
160: Saint-Astier
161: *Idem*
162: *Idem*
163: Saint-Chamans
164: Salignac
165: *Idem*
169: Talleyrand

Carrés d'Hozier
32: Arnal

Archives départementales de la Dordogne

Family dossiers
2E 35: Arnal
2E 203: Bourdeilles
2E 205: *Idem*
2E 1795: Salignac
2E 1796: *Idem*
2E 1806: Abzac
2E 1836: Carbonnières
2E 1841: Castelnau
2E 1851: Albret, Foix, Aydie
J 1384: Albret
J 2773: Bourdeilles

Town records
Archives communales de Périgueux:
AA 7–14, BB 1, BB 14, CC 15, CC
84–94, EE 19, FF 18, FF 90, FF 98,
FF 100, FF 101, FF 185
Archives communales de Bergerac:
Registers 15–23: Jurades 1456–1490
Archives communales de Domme
(These are deposited at Périgueux):
4E 42, 46
Archives communales de Sarlat
(These are deposited at Périgueux):
4E 125–126

Archives départementales du Gers

Family dossiers
The following *dossiers* in series I:

I 28:   Albret, Foix, Gramont
I 111:   Armagnac
I 228:   Aydie
I 229:   *Idem*
I 1193:   du Lyon
I 1408:   Lomagne
I 1598:   Gramont
I 1599:   *Idem*
I 1600:   *Idem*
I 2378:   Montferrand
I 2497:   Montaut
I 2498:   *Idem*
I 2629:   Noaillan.
I 2630:   *Idem*
I 2746:   Pardaillan
I 2747:   *Idem*
I 2748:   *Idem*

The following *dossiers* in series I *supplément*:

I suppl. 130:   Castelnau
I suppl. 134:   Caumont
I suppl. 135:   Cauna
I suppl. 231:   Faudoas
I suppl. 275:   Gramont

Town records
Archives communales d'Auch: AA 1, AA 4, EE 1
Archives communales de Nogaro (These records are at Auch): AA1
Archives communales de Montréal: Now published, see p. 212.

Archives departementales de la Gironde

Bordeaux parlement
1 B, 1, 2, 4, B 1–6

Family dossiers
2E 2723

Notarial registers
3E 81–87, 1145, 2517, 4808–4811, 5634, 6501, 6532, 7131, 7132, 10,010, 11,012, 12,415

Ecclesiastical records
Secular clergy: G 3, 33, 84, 105–106, 139, 181, 225, 235, 241, 271, 274, 285, 308, 311, 312, 338, 1132, 1160–1161, 1256, 1299, 1300, 1347, 1455, 1456, 1458, 1713–1714, 2031
Religious: H 15, 33, 43, 46, 159, 161, 193, 194, 235, 240, 242, 248, 281, 504, 532, 735, 736, 738, 766, 817, 1183–88

Town records
Archives municipales de Bordeaux: MSS 207, 208, AA 9, AA 13, II 17–29
Archives communales de Cadillac: CC 2–4
Archives communales de Réole: AA 3–4
Archives communales de Libourne: AA 4, AA 8–9
Archives communales de Saint-Emilion: BB 1, 2, 43, 46, 48, CC 26, II 1
Archives communales de Saint-Macaire: FF 1

Archives départementales de Haute-Garonne

Toulouse parlement
B1, 3–4, 6–9

Religious
The *Fonds de Malte* is deposited at Toulouse. Most useful are:
Argenteins 30, 31, 36, 48
Bordeaux 35
Breuil 7
La Cavalerie 30
Condat 3, 5–6, 9–10, 13, 26

Archives départementales de l'Hérault
Chambre des comptes de Langudoc
B 13

Archives départementales des Landes
Religious
H 4, 6, 7

Town records
Archives municipales de Dax (These archives are deposited at Mont-de-Marsan): AA 1–2, CC 1, CC 3, DD 1–2, FF 2
Archives communales de Saint-Sever: AA 1, CC 1, DD 1, EE 1
E 57: (Now deposited at Mont-de-Marsan). Customs of Saint-Sever. FF 1

Archives départementales de Lot-et-Garonne
Notarial registers
Registre de notaire déposé aux Archives en 1974 par Y. de Scorrailles à Sangruère; Minutes du notaire Jan Cussolle
E Suppl. 1681 and 1682

Secular clergy
G 20, 72

Archives municipales d'Agen
AA 12–15, 18, BB 19–21 *Livre des jurades* (1481–1501), CC 42–45, EE 18, FF 7, 8–9, 132, 134, 138, 141, 148, 197, 217, 218

Archives départementales des Pyrénées-Atlantiques
Family dossiers (Albret and Foix)
E11, 65–66, 68–80, 84, 84 bis, 88–9, 93, 131, 135, 161–66, 169, 186, 203–204, 214, 219, 229, 233, 246–8, 280, 323, 350, 355, 379, 444–45, 543, 643, 647–61, 693, 697, 704, 710, 711–29, 737, 771, 780–1, 791, 798–99, 806, 807, 842–43, 843, 850, 853, 867, 873, 983, 2191

Secular clergy
G 84

Religious
H 70

Town records
Archives municipales de Bayonne: AA 3, 6, 7, 10, 15, BB 1, CC 1, DD 1, EE 1, 17

Archives départementales de Tarn-et-Garonne
A 45–50, A 283–90

Printed primary sources

Chronicles

Basin, T., *Histoire de Charles VII*, ed. C. Samaran [Classiques de l'Histoire de France au Moyen âge, xv, xxi], 2 vols. (Paris, 1933, 1944)

Chronique de Mathieu d'Escouchy, ed. G. du Fresne de Beaucourt [Soc. de l'Histoire de France], i (Paris, 1863)

Commynes, P. de, *Mémoires*, ed. J. Calmette [Classiques de l'histoire de France au Moyen âge, iii, iv], i, ii (Paris, 1925)

Histoire de Charles VII, roy de France, ed. D. Godefroy (Paris, 1661)

Histoire de Charles VIII, roy de France, ed. D. Godefroy (Paris, 1684)

Les Chroniques de Jean Tarde, ed. G. de Gérard (Paris, 1887)

Leseur, G., *Histoire de Gaston IV, comte de Foix*, ed. H. Courteault [Soc. de l'Histoire de France] 2 vols. (Paris, 1893, 1907)

Oeuvres de Georges Chastellain, ed. Kervyn de Lettenhove, ii (Brussels, 1863)

Town records

Agen

'Coutumes, privilèges et franchises de la ville d'Agen', ed. A. Mouillé, *Rec. Trav. Soc. Agr. Sci. Arts Agen*, v (1850), 235 ff

Bayonne

Registres gascons, ed. E. Ducéré [Arch. municipales Bayonne], i (Bayonne, 1892)

Bergerac

Les Jurades de la ville de Bergerac, ed. G. Charrrier, 2 vols. (Bergerac, 1892)

Bordeaux

Inventaire sommaire des registres de la jurade (1520–1783), ed. D. le Vacher de Boisville *et al.* [Arch. municipales Bordeaux, vi–xiii], 8 vols. (Bordeaux, 1896–1947)

Livre des bouillons, ed. H. Barckhausen [Arch. municipales Bordeaux, i] (Bordeaux, 1867)

Livre des coutumes, ed. H. Barckhausen [Arch. municipales Bordeaux, v] (Bordeaux, 1890)

Livre des privilèges, ed. H. Barckhausen [Arch. municipales Bordeaux, ii] (Bordeaux, 1878)

Recueil des privilèges accordés à la ville de Bordeaux par Charles VII et Louis XI, ed. M. Gouron (Bordeaux, 1937)

Lectoure

Archives de la ville de Lectoure: coutumes, statuts et records du xiiie au xvie siècle, ed. P. Druilhet [Arch. hist. Gascogne, ix] (Paris and Auch, 1885)

Montréal-du-Gers

Comptes consulaires de Montréal en Condomois (1458–1498), ed. C. Samaran and G. Loubès [Collection de Documents inédits sur l'histoire de la France, section de philologie et d'histoire jusqu'à 1610, xiii] (Paris, 1979)

Riscle
Comptes consulaires de la ville de Riscle, 1441–1507, ed. P. Parfouru and J. de Carsalade du Pont [Arch. hist. Gascogne, xii–xiii], 2 vols. (Paris and Auch, 1886, 1892)

Other printed primary sources
Arch. hist. Gironde: the following volumes contain useful material: iv (1863), v (1863), ix (1867), x (1868), xii (1870), xiii (1872), xxv (1887), xxvi (1888–1889), xxviii (1893), xxxi (1896), xxxv (1900), xxxvii (1902).
B. Soc. hist. archéol. Périgord, xii (1885) [*Ordonnance* concerning justice at Carlux], 290–93
B. Soc. hist. archéol. Périgord, xvii (1890) [*Lettres de rémission* for Arnaud de Fayolles], 204–11
Comptes du trésor, 1296–1477, ed. R. Fawtier and C.-V. Langlois [*Recueils des historiens de France. Documents financiers*, ii]. (Paris, 1930)
Documents historiques inédits, ed. Champollion-Figeac, i–iii (Paris, 1841–1847)
Lettres de Charles VIII, roi de France, ed. P. Pélicier [Soc. de l'Histoire de France], 5 vols. (Paris, 1898–1905)
Lettres de Louis XI, roi de France, ed. J. Vaesen [Soc. de l'Histoire de France], 10 vols. (Paris, 1883–1908)
Messelin, J. *Journal des états généraux de France tenus à Tours en 1484 sous la régence de Charles VIII*, ed. A. Bernier (Paris, 1835)
Métivier, J. de, *Chronique du parlement de Bordeaux*, ed. A. de Brezetz and J. Delpit, 2 vols. (Bordeaux, 1886, 1887)
Ordonnances des rois de France de la Troisième race, ed. Bréquigny et al., xiv–xxi (Paris, 1790–1849)
Statuts et règlements de l'ancienne université de Bordeaux (1441–1793), ed. H. Barckhausen (Libourne and Bordeaux, 1886)

Secondary sources

Actes du 104e congrès national des Sociètes savantes, Bordeaux 1979, Section de philologie et d'histoire jusqu'à 1610 (Paris 1981), *La Reconstruction après la guerre de cent ans*
Actes du 107e congrès national des Sociétés savantes, Brest 1982. Section de philologie et d'histoire jusqu' à 1610, i (Paris, 1984), *La Faute, la répression et le pardon*
Allmand, C.T. 'The Lancastrian land Settlement in Normandy 1417–1450,' *Econ. H.R.* 2nd series, xxi (1968), 461–79
Allmand, C.T. 'The Aftermath of War in Fifteenth-Century France', *History*, lxi (1976), 344–57
Anselme de Sainte-Marie, *Histoire généalogique et chronologique de la maison royale de France*, 9 vols. (Paris, 1726–1803)
Autrand, F., *Naissance d'un grand corps de l'état. Les gens du parlement de Paris, 1345–1454* (Paris, 1981)
Balsac, R. de, *Le Chemin de l'ospital*, ed. P. Tamizey de Larroque (Montpellier, 1887)

Baurein, abbé, *Variétés bordeloises, ou essai historique et critique sur la topographie ancienne et moderne du diocèse de Bordeaux*, 4 vols. (Bordeaux 1784–1786)

Beaucourt, G. du Fresne de, *Histoire de Charles VII*, 6 vols. (Paris, 1881–1891)

Bladé, J.-F., *Coutumes municipales du département du Gers* (Paris, 1864)

Bordes, M. et al., *Histoire de Gascogne des origines à nos jours* (Roanne, n.d)

Boutaric, E., *La France sous Philippe le Bel* (Paris, 1861).

Boutruche, R., 'Aux Origines d'une crise nobiliaire: donations pieuses et privilèges successorales en Bordelais du xiiie au xve siècle', A. Hist. soc. (1939), 161–77, 256–77

Boutruche, R., *Bordeaux de 1453 à 1715* [*Histoire de Bordeaux*, iv] (Bordeaux, 1966)

Boutruche, R., *La Crise d'une société. Seigneurs et paysans du Bordelais pendant la guerre de cent ans* (Paris, 1947)

Boutruche, R., *Une Société en lutte contre le régime féodal. L'Alleu en Bordelais et en Bazadais du xie au xviiie siècle* (Rodez, 1943)

Burne, A.H., 'La Bataille de Castillon, 1453: la fin de la guerre de cent ans', R. hist. Bordeaux, nouvelle serie, ii (1953), 293–305

Cadier, L., *La Sénéchaussée des Landes sous Charles VII, administration royale et états provinciaux* (Paris, 1885)

Calmette, J., *Louis XI, Jean II et la Révolution catalane* (Toulouse, 1903)

Calmette, J., *La Question des Pyrénées et la marche d'Espagne au Moyen âge* (n.p., 1947)

Calmette, J. and Périnelle, G., *Louis XI et l'Angleterre* (Paris, 1930)

Caron, M.-T., *La Noblesse dans le duché de Bourgogne 1315–1477* (Lille, [1988])

Chabannes, H. de, *Histoire de la maison de Chabannes*, 10 vols. (Dijon, 1892–1901)

Chabannes, H. de, *Preuves*, 4 vols. (Dijon, 1892–1897)

Chaplais, P., *Essays in Medieval Diplomacy and Administration* (London, 1981)

Chauliac, A., *Histoire de l'Abbaye de Sainte-Croix de Bordeaux* (Paris, 1910)

Chrimes, S.B., *English Constitutional Ideas in the Fifteenth Century* (Cambridge, 1936)

Chrimes, S.B., *Henry VII* (London, 1972)

Colloque international du centre national de la recherche scientifique. La France de la Fin du xve siècle, Renouveau et apogée (Paris, 1985)

Communay, A., *Essai généalogique sur les Montferrand de Guienne* (Bordeaux, 1889)

Contamine, P., *Guerre, état et société à la fin du Moyen âge* (Paris and The Hague, 1972)

Contamine, P., 'L'Artillerie royale française à la veille des guerres d'Italie', A. Bretagne, 1xxi. 2 (1964), 221–61

Courteault, H., *Gaston IV, comte de Foix, vicomte souverain de Béarn, prince de Navarre, 1423–1472* (Toulouse, 1895)

Declareuil, *Histoire générale du droit français des origines à 1789* (Paris, 1925)

Delaruelle, E., Labande, E.-R., Ourliac, P., *L'Eglise au temps du grand schisme et de la crise conciliaire* [*Histoire de l'église*, ed. J.-B Duroselle and E. Jarry, xiv], iii (Belgium, 1962)

Delcambre, E., *Le Consulat du Puy-en-Velay, des origines à 1610* (Le Puy, 1933)

Dienne, comte de, 'Robert de Balsac', R. Agenais, xxxvi (1909), 20–29

Doucet, R., *Les Institutions de la France au xvie siècle*, i (Paris, 1948)

Drouyn, L., *La Guienne militaire*, 2 vols. (Bordeaux and Paris, 1865)

Dupont-Ferrier, G., *Etudes sur les institutions financières de la France à la fin du Moyen âge*, 2 vols. (Paris, 1930, 1932)

Dupont-Ferrier, G., *Gallia regia, ou état des officiers royaux des bailliages et des sénéchaussées de 1328 à 1515*, 7 vols. (Paris, 1942–1965)

Dupont-Ferrier, G., *Les Officiers royaux des bailliages et des sénéchaussées et les institutions monarchiques locales en France à la fin du Moyen âge* [Bibl. Ec. Hautes Etudes, cvl] (Paris, 1902)

Dupont-Ferrier, G., *Les Origines et le premier siècle de la cour du trésor* [Bibl. Ec. Hautes Etudes, cclxvi] (Paris, 1936)

Durengues, Chanoine, 'Galéas de La Rovère, évêque d'Agen, 1478–1487', *R. Agenais*, 1v (1928), 92–122

Durengues, Chanoine, 'Léonard de La Rovère, Cardinal et évêque d'Agen, 1487–1519', *R. Agenais*, 1vi (1929), 111–26, 155–75

Durengues, Chanoine, 'Piérre Bérard, évêque d'Agen, 1461–1477', *R. Agenais*, 1iv (1927), 293–95

Gandilhon, R., *Politique économique de Louis XI* (Paris, 1941)

Gazzaniga, J. -L., *L'Eglise du midi à la fin du règne de Charles VII (1444–1461)* (Paris, 1976)

Gilles, H., *Les Etats de Languedoc au xve siècle* (Toulouse, 1965)

Gouron, M., *L'Amirauté de Guienne* (Paris, 1938)

Guenée, B., *Tribunaux et Gens de Justice dans le bailliage de Senlis à la fin du Moyen âge* (Paris, 1963)

Guenée, B, and Lehoux, F., *Les Entrées royales françaises de 1328 à 1515* (Paris, 1968)

Highfield, J. R. L. and Jeffs, R. ed., *The Crown and Local Communities in England and France in the Fifteenth Century* (Gloucester, 1981)

Higounet, C., *Le Comté de Comminges de ses origines à son annexion à la couronne*, 2 vols. (Toulouse and Paris, 1949)

Higounet-Nadal, A., *Périgueux aux xive et xve siècles. Etude de démographie historique* (Bordeaux, 1978)

James, M. K., *Studies in the Medieval Wine Trade*, ed. E.M. Veale (Oxford, 1971)

Jaurgain, J. de, 'Deux Comtes de Comminges béarnais au xve siècle', *B. Soc. archéol. Gers*, xv (1914), 13–25, 117–129, 198–209; *ibid.*, xvi (1915), 74–89, 230–40, *ibid.*, xvii (1916), 127–39; *ibid.*, xviii (1917), 13–33, 197–211; *ibid.*, xix (1918), 43–57, 149–160

Jaurgain, J. de, and Ritter, R., *La Maison de Gramont, 1040–1967*, 2 vols. (Lourdes, 1968)

Jones, M. ' "Bons Bretons et Bon Francoys": The Language and Meaning of Treason in Later Medieval France', *Trans. Roy. hist. Soc.*, 5th series, xxxii (1982), 91–112.

Jouet, R., *La Résistance à l'occupation anglaise en Basse-Normandie 1418–1450* (Caen, 1969)

Keen, M. H., *England in the Later Middle Ages* (London, 1973)

Keen, M. H., *The Laws of War in the Late Middle Ages* (London and Toronto, 1965)

Kerhervé, J., *L'Etat breton aux 14e et 15e siècles. Les ducs, l'argent et les hommes*, 2 vols. (Paris, 1987)

Labande-Mailfert, Y., *Charles VIII et son milieu* (Paris, 1975)

La Batut, R. de, 'Notice sur les prélats issus de familles périgourdines avant 1789', *B. Soc. hist. archéol. Périgord*, x (1883), 488–98

La Douze, Marquis d'Abzac de, 'Lettres d'investiture de Gabriel, évêque de Périgueux, conférant à Gillaume d'Abzac la cure de Saint-Victor de La Force (11 mai 1492)', *B. Soc. hist. archéol. Périgord*, xvi (1889), 192–93

Lafforgue, P., *Histoire de la ville d'Auch*, 2 vols. (Auch, 1851)

Lapouyade, M. Meaudre de, and Saint-Saud, A. Arlot de, *Les Makanam, les Ayquem de Montaigne. Recherches historiques* (Bordeaux, 1943)

La Roncière, C. de, *La Guerre de cent ans* [Histoire de la marine française, ii] (Paris, 1900)

Lartigaut, J., *Les Campagnes du Quercy après la guerre de cent ans* (Toulouse, 1978)

Lewis, P. S., 'Decayed and Non-Feudalism in Later Medieval France', *B. Inst. hist. Research*, xxxvi (1963), 157–84

Lewis, P.S. ed., *The Recovery of France in the Fifteenth Century* (London, 1971)

Luchaire, A., *Alain le Grand, sire d'Albret* (Paris, 1877)

Magen, A., 'Un Essai d'organisation démocratique dans la ville d'Agen en 1481', *Rec. Trav. Soc. Agr. Sci. Arts Agen*, 2e série (1877), 114–132

Major, J.R., *Representative Government in Early Modern France* (Newham and London, 1980)

Mallat, W. 'Notes biographiques sur Raoul du Fou, évêque de Périgueux (1468–1470)', *B. Soc. hist. archéol. Périgord*, ix (1882), 62–64

Mandrot, B. de, 'Louis XI, Jean V d'Armagnac and le Drame de Lectoure', *R. hist.*, xxxviii (1888), 241–304

Marchegay, P., 'La Rançon d'Olivier de Coëtivy', *Bibl. Ec. Chartes*, xxxviii (1877), 5–48

Maubourguet, J., 'Le Suaire de Cadouin', *B. Soc. hist. archéol. Périgord*, lxiii (1936), 348–63

Maubourguet, J., *Sarlat et le Périgord méridional*, iii (Paris, 1930)

Pélicier, P., *Essai sur le gouvernement de la dame de Beaujeu, 1483–1491* (Paris, 1882)

Perroy, E., *La Guerre de cent ans* (Paris, 1945)

Peyrègne, 'Les Emigrés gascons en Angleterre (1453–1485)', *A. Midi, nouvelle série*, lxvi (1954). 113–28

Pocquet, B., and Le Moyne de La Borderie, A, *Histoire de Bretagne*, iv (Rennes, 1906)

Poumarède, J., *Recherches sur les successions dans le sud-ouest de la France au Moyen âge* [Thèse de doctorat en droit] (Toulouse, 1968)

Powicke, M., *The Thirteenth Century* (Oxford, 1953)

Powis, J. K., 'The Magistrates of the Parlement of Bordeaux c.1500–1563' [Unpublished Oxford D.Phil. Thesis, 1975; Bodleian Shelf-mark: MS. D.Phil. c.1699]

Renouard, Y., 'Les Conséquences de la conquête de la Guienne par le roi de France pour le commerce des vins de Gascogne', *A. Midi, nouvelle série*, lxi (1948), 14–31

Renouard, Y., *Bordeaux sous les Rois d'Angleterre* [*Histoire de Bordeaux*, iii] (Bordeaux, 1965)

Rey, M., *Le Domaine du roi et les finances extraordinaires sous Charles VI, 1388–1413* (Paris, 1965)

Ross, C., *Edward IV* (London, 1974)

Rowe, B. H. 'John Duke of Bedford and the Norman "Brigands",' *Engl. hist. R.*, xxxxvii (1932), 583–600

Samaran, C., *La Maison d'Armagnac au xve siècle* (Paris, 1907)

Sammarthan, D., *Gallia Christiana*, 16 vols. (Paris, 1715–1865)

Secret, J., *Le Périgord: châteaux, manoirs et gentilhommières* (n.p., 1966)

Sée, H., *Louis XI et les Villes* (Paris, 1891)

Spont, H., 'La Tailles en Languedoc de 1450 à 1515', *A. Midi*, ii (1890), 365–84, 478–513; ii (1891), 482–94

Stein, H., *Charles de France, Frère de Louis XI* (Paris, 1919)

Storey, R. L., *The End of the House of Lancaster* (London, 1966)

Sutherland, D., *The Assize of Novel Disseisin* (Oxford, 1973)

Tessier, G., *Diplomatique royale Française* (Paris, 1962)

Tholin, G., 'Le Livre de raison de Bernard Gros, commandeur du temple de Breuil en Agenais sous Louis XI et Charles VIII', *B. hist. phil. Com. Trav. hist. sci.* (1889)

Thomas, A., *Les Etats provinciaux de la France centrale sous Charles VII*, 2 vols. (Paris, 1877, 1879)

Vale, M. G. A., *English Gascony, 1399–1453* (London, 1970)

Vale, M. G. A., 'New Techniques and Old Ideals: the Impact of Artillery on War and Chivalry at the End of the Hundred Years War', in *War, Literature and Politics in the Late Middle Ages*, ed. C. T. Allmand (Liverpool, 1976), pp. 57–72

Vale, M. G. A., 'The Last Years of English Gascony', *Trans. Roy. hist. Soc.*, 5th series, xix (1969), 119–38

Valois, N., *Le Conseil du roi aux xive, xve et xvie siècles* (Paris and Macon, 1888)

Valois, N., 'Le Conseil du roi et le grand conseil pendant la première année du règne de Charles VIII', *Bibl. Ec. Chartes*, xliii (1882), 594–625; xliv (1883), 594–625; xliv (1883), 419–44

Vaughan, R., *Philip the Good, the Apogee of Burgundy* (London, 1970)

Viala, A., *Le parlement de Toulouse et l'administration royale laïque. 1420–1525 environ*, 2 vols. (Albi, 1953)

Vic, C. de and Dom Vaissète, *Histoire générale de Languedoc*, viii (Toulouse, 1844)

Vigier, M. A., 'Extraits du cartulaire de Philipparie', *B. Soc. hist. archéol. Périgord*, xxxvi (1909), 99–119

Vigier, M. A., *Histore de la châtellenie de Belvès* (Périgueux, 1902)

Index

economic recovery of 47–49
see also estates

Hastingues (Landes) 154
Henriquez, Martin 143
Henry V 3
Henry VI 9
Henry VII 13, 14, 18
Huntingdon, John Holland earl of (later
duke of Exeter) 3–4

Isle-Jourdain (Gers) 52
Italy 14, 31–32, 35, 70, 117, 186, 197

Jaligny 165
Jaubert, Jean 39
Juliac, vicomte de 122
justice *see coutumiers*, customs (local),
law, parlement, seigneurial justice

Karlaguen, Pierre 144

La Baume:
Aymond de 65
Raymond de 65
Laborde, Bernardon de 102
Labourt, *pays de* 5
see also estates
La Fayolle, Arnaud de 138
La Force, seigneur de 129
La Haye, Guillaume de 43
Lalande:
Dame de 121
Jean I de 154
Jean II de 185
Thomas de 155, 185
La Martonie, family of 43
Lambard, Jean 40
Lamothe:
Madeleine de 41
Pierre de 101
Lancaster, House of 3, 11, 138
Landais, Pierre 18
Landes:
fortification of 111–113
nobility of 103
profits of justice in 52
revenues from 56
see also Bayonne, Dax and Saint Sever,
estates
Langoiran (Gironde) 29, 50, 186
Langon (Gironde) 6

Languedoc 23
Lansac:
Guillaume de 59
Seigneur de 121
Larche (Corrèze) 190
La Réole (Gironde) 52, 82, 85, 113,
127, 185
La Rochefoucauld:
Foucauld III, seigneur de La
Rochefoucauld 179–80
Jean, seigneur de La Rouchefoucauld
55, 180
La Rochelle (Charente-Maritime) 11
La Tresne (Gironde) 105
Lauzun (Lot-et-Garonne) 169
Seigneur de 169, 171, 194
Laval, André de, seigneur de Lohéac 17
Laval, Louis de 102
Lavedan, seigneurie of 30
law:
customary (*droit coutumier*) 78–85
written (*droit écrit*) 78–85
see also customs
Lectoure (Gers) 16, 28, 55, 69, 88, 114,
115, 124, 127, 131, 145, 176
Lefils, Jean 89
Le Piochel:
Artus 39
Bertrand 39, 42, 43, 127
Lescun, Jean de, 'bastard of Armagnac'
29, 33, 36
see also Aydie *and* Comminges
Leseur, Guillaume 153, 154, 176
Lesparre (Gironde):
Seigneur de 121
Seigneurie of 9, 103, 155
Le Veyrier, Jean 159
lèse-majesté 86
Libourne (Gironde) 6, 47, 52, 54, 73,
113, 127, 129, 131, 143, 145–46,
168–69
Limoges (Haute-Vienne) 94, 159
Limousin 48, 55, 84
lieutenancy-general *see* governorship
lieutenant of sénéchal *see* sénéchaussée
loans 71–72
Lohéac *see* Laval
Lomagne 15
Longa, seigneur de 140
Louis XI:
and economic recovery 48–49
appointments in Guyenne 29–35